WOMEN IN NINETEENTH-CENTURY RUSSIA

Wendy Rosslyn is Emeritus Professor of Russian Literature at the University of Nottingham, UK. Her research on Russian women includes *Anna Bunina (1774-1829) and the Origins of Women's Poetry in Russia* (1997), *Feats of Agreeable Usefulness: Translations by Russian Women Writers 1763-1825* (2000) and *Deeds not Words: The Origins of Female Philantropy in the Russian Empire* (2007).

Alessandra Tosi is a Fellow at Clare Hall, Cambridge. Her publications include *Waiting for Pushkin: Russian Fiction in the Reign of Alexander I (1801-1825)* (2006), *A. M. Belozel'skii-Belozerskii i ego filosofskoe nasledie* (with T. V. Artem'eva et al.) and *Women in Russian Culture and Society, 1700-1825* (2007), edited with Wendy Rosslyn.

Women in Nineteenth-Century Russia: Lives and Culture

Edited by
Wendy Rosslyn and Alessandra Tosi

http://www.openbookpublishers.com

© 2012 Wendy Rosslyn and Alessandra Tosi

Some rights are reserved. The text of this book is licensed under a Creative Commons Attribution-NonCommercial-NoDerivatives 2.0 UK (CC BY-NC-ND 2.0). This license allows you to share, copy, distribute and transmit the work providing attribution is made to the authors (but not in any way that suggests that they endorse you or your use of the work). However, you may not use it for commercial purposes nor alter, transform, or build upon this work. Attribution should include the following information:

Rosslyn, Wendy and Tosi, Alessandra (eds). *Women in Nineteenth-Century Russia: Lives and Culture*. Cambridge, UK: Open Book Publishers, 2012, http://dx.doi.org/10.11647/OBP.0018

Further details about this license are available at: http://creativecommons.org/licenses/by-nc-nd/2.0/

Digital material and resources associated with this volume are available from our website at: http://www.openbookpublishers.com/isbn/9781906924652

ISBN Hardback: 978-1-906924-66-9
ISBN Paperback: 978-1-906924-65-2
ISBN Digital (pdf): 978-1-906924-67-6
ISBN Digital ebook (epub version): 978-1-906924-68-3
ISBN Digital ebook (mobi version): 978-1-906924-69-0
DOI: 10.11647/OBP.0018

Please see the list of illustrations for attribution and copyright information relating to individual images. Acknowledgment is made to the State Russian Museum (St Petersburg), the State Hermitage Museum (St Petersburg) and Sotheby's (London) for permission to reproduce artwork in their possession.

Every effort has been made to identify and contact copyright holders; any omissions or errors will be corrected if notification is made to the publisher.

Cover: Ekaterina Khilkova, *The Interior of the Women's Department of the St Petersburg Drawing School for Auditors*, 1855. © State Russian Museum, St Petersburg, all rights reserved.

All paper used by Open Book Publishers is SFI (Sustainable Forestry Initiative), PEFC (Programme for the Endorsement of Forest Certification Schemes) and Forest Stewardship Council (FSC) certified.

Printed in the United Kingdom and United States by Lightning Source by Lightning Source for Open Book Publishers

Contents

	Page
Illustrations	vi
Contributors	vii
1. Introduction: Framing the View: Russian Women in the Long Nineteenth Century *Sibelan Forrester*	1
2. Women and Urban Culture *Barbara Alpern Engel*	19
3. Russian Peasant Women's Culture: Three Voices *Christine D. Worobec*	41
4. Mary and Women in Late Imperial Russian Orthodoxy *Vera Shevzov*	63
5. Women and the Visual Arts *Rosalind P. Blakesley*	91
6. Women and Music *Philip Ross Bullock*	119
7. The Rise of the Actress in Early Nineteenth-Century Russia *Julie A. Cassiday*	137
8. 'How Women Should Write': Russian Women's Writing in the Nineteenth Century *Arja Rosenholm and Irina Savkina*	161
9. Between Law and Morality: Violence against Women in Nineteenth-Century Russia *Marianna G. Muravyeva*	209
10. Index	239

Illustrations

		Page
1.	Marie Louise Elisabeth Vigée-Lebrun, *Self-portrait*, 1800. Oil on canvas, 78.5 x 68 cm. Inv. no. GE-7586. © The State Hermitage Museum, St Petersburg, all rights reserved. Photo by Vladimir Terebenin, Leonard Kheifets, Yuri Molodkovets.	92
2.	Grand Duchess Maria Fedorovna, three Imperial buttons comprised of drawings in graphite on vellum of architectural features in the gardens of Pavlovsk Palace and Tsarskoe Selo, mounted in gold frames with rims chased in a laurel leaf design. Part of a set of twenty-two buttons placed in a gilded wooden frame with a hand-written dedicatory inscription and presented to Catherine the Great, 1790. Lot no. 424, The Russian Sale, Sotheby's, London, 1 December 2004. © Sotheby's, all rights reserved.	95
3.	Grand Duchess Maria Fedorovna, three Imperial buttons, 1790 (detail of fig. 2). © Sotheby's, all rights reserved.	96
4.	Ekaterina Khilkova, *The Interior of the Women's Department of the St Petersburg Drawing School for Auditors*, 1855. Oil on canvas, 73 x 89 cm. © 2011, State Russian Museum, St Petersburg, all rights reserved.	99
5.	Christina Robertson, *Portrait of Grand Duchess Maria Nikolaevna*, 1841. Oil on canvas, 249 x 151 cm. Inv. no. GE-4784. © The State Hermitage Museum, St Petersburg, all rights reserved. Photo by Vladimir Terebenin, Leonard Kheifets, Yuri Molodkovets.	100
6.	The dynamics of rape, 1834–1893. Graph by the author.	212

Contributors

Rosalind P. Blakesley is Senior Lecturer in the History of Art and a Fellow of Pembroke College at the University of Cambridge. Her publications include *Russian Art and the West* (co-editor, 2007); *The Arts and Crafts Movement* (2006); *An Imperial Collection: Women Artists from the State Hermitage Museum* (co-editor, 2003); and *Russian Genre Painting in the Nineteenth Century* (under her maiden name of Rosalind P. Gray, 2000). She has curated exhibitions in London, Moscow and Washington DC, and is now working on a new book on Russian painting from 1757 to 1873.

Philip Ross Bullock is University Lecturer in Russian at the University of Oxford and Fellow in Russian at Wadham College. He has published widely in the fields of modern Russian literature and music and has a particular interest in the theory and practice of gender studies. He is the author of *The Feminine in the Prose of Andrey Platonov* (2005) and *Rosa Newmarch and Russian Music in Late Nineteenth and Early Twentieth-Century England* (2009), and the editor and translator of *The Correspondence of Jean Sibelius and Rosa Newmarch, 1906-1939* (2011).

Julie A. Cassiday is Professor of Russian and Chair of the Department of German and Russian at Williams College in Williamstown, Massachusetts. Her book, *The Enemy on Trial: Early Soviet Courts on Stage and Screen* (2000), examines the theatricality of show trials in the 1920s and 1930s, as well as their roots in avant-garde theatre and cinema. She has published several scholarly articles on Russian theatre of the early nineteenth and twentieth centuries and Stalinist film. She is currently writing a monograph on early nineteenth-century theatre and theatricality, which investigates the role of gender performance in the construction of Russian national identity, and completing an article on the personality cult surrounding Vladimir Putin.

Barbara Engel is Distinguished Professor and member of the history department of the University of Colorado, Boulder. A recipient of support from the National Endowment for the Humanities and the John Simon Guggenheim Foundation, among others, she is the author of *Mothers and Daughters: Women of the Intelligentsia in Nineteenth Century Russia* (1983); *Between the Fields and the City: Women, Work and Family in Russia, 1861–1914* (1995) and *Women in Russia: 1700–2000* (2004), and most recently, *Breaking the Ties that Bound: The Politics of Marital Strife in Late Imperial Russia* (2011), as well as of numerous articles. She has made more than a dozen trips to Russia and the former Soviet Union.

Sibelan E. S. Forrester is Professor of Russian and Chair of the Department of Modern Languages and Literatures at Swarthmore College in Swarthmore, Pennsylvania. She is co-editor of two volumes, *Engendering Slavic Literatures* (1996) and *Over the Wall/After the Fall: Post-Communist Cultures through an East-West Gaze* (2004). She has published translations of a number of Russian women poets, including Anna Bunina and Evdokiia Rostopchina.

Marianna Muravyeva is Associate Professor of Law at Herzen State Pedagogical University of Russia. She teaches courses in human rights of women, gender and law and history of crime and political and legal theories in Russia and Europe. She is a member of several editorial boards and treasurer of Russian Association of Women's and Gender Historians. She has published extensively in the fields of the history of women, gender, family and crime in Russia and Europe between 1600 and 1900. Her recent publications include: *Vina i pozor v kontekste stanovleniia evropeiskikh gosudarstv novogo vremeni* (2011); *Cultural History of Sexuality* (2010).

Arja Rosenholm is Professor in Russian Literature and Culture and Director of the Russian Studies programme in the School of Language, Translation and Literary Studies at the University of Tampere, Finland. Her expertise encompasses various aspects of Russian and Soviet literature and culture, especially women's writing, popular culture and media and ecocritical reading of Russian literature. Her publications include *Gendering Awakening. Femininity and the Russian Woman Question of the 1860s* (1999); and a number of co-edited works including: with S. Autio-Sarasmo, *Understanding Russian Nature: Representations, Values and Concepts* (2005); with A. Litovskaia, I. Savkina and E. Trubina, *Obraz dostoinoi zhizni v sovremennikh rossiiskikh SMI*

(2008); with A. Nordenstreng, and K. and E. Trubina, *Russian Mass Media and Changing Values* (2010).

Irina Savkina is Lecturer in Russian Literature at the Department of Russian Language and Culture, University of Tampere, Finland. Her fields of interest include Russian literary history, gender studies and popular culture. She is author of *Provintsialki russkoi literatury (zhenskaia proza 30–40-kh godov XIX veka)* (1998) and *Razgovory s zerkalom i Zazerkal'em: Avtodokumental'nye zhenskie teksty v russkoi literature pervoi poloviny XIX veka* (2007).

Vera Shevzov is Professor of Religion at Smith College. She received her B.A. and Ph.D. from Yale University. Supported at various stages by the National Council for Eurasian and East European Research, the National Endowment of the Humanities, and the Social Science Research Council, her research has focused on Orthodox Christianity in Russia and has explored issues related to the notions of sacred community and collective religious identity, lived religion, women and religion, religion and visual culture and historical memory and national identity. Her book *Russian Orthodoxy on the Eve of Revolution* (2004) was awarded the Frank S. and Elizabeth D. Brewer Prize of the American Society of Church History. Currently, she is writing a book on the image of Mary in modern and contemporary Russia. Recent publications include contributions to volume six of *A People's History of Christianity* (2007); *Sacred Stories: Religion and Spirituality in Modern Russia* (2007) and *Letters from Heaven: Popular Religion in Russia and the Ukraine* (2006).

Christine D. Worobec, a Board of Trustee Professor and Distinguished Research Professor at Northern Illinois University, is the author of *Peasant Russia: Family and Community in the Post-Emancipation Period* (1991) and *Possessed: Women, Witches, and Demons in Imperial Russia* (2001). She is also co-editor with B. Evans Clements and B. Alpern Engel of *Russia's Women: Accommodation, Resistance, Transformation* (1991) and co-editor with M. Zirin, I. Livezeanu, and J. Pachuta Farris of *Women and Gender in Central and Eastern Europe, Russia, and Eurasia: A Comprehensive Bibliography* (2007). Worobec is currently working on a history of Orthodox pilgrimages to holy sites in Russia and Ukraine as well as to shrines in the Holy Land and Mt. Athos from 1700 to the present.

1. Introduction: Framing the View: Russian Women in the Long Nineteenth Century

Sibelan Forrester

Thinking of nineteenth-century Russia, we may find ourselves thinking of a woman's image, perhaps one of the memorable heroines in the great Russian novels written by men: Sonia Marmeladova from Dostoevskii's *Crime and Punishment* (*Prestuplenie i nakazanie*), Natasha Rostova from Tolstoi's *War and Peace* (*Voina i mir*), or any of the Turgenev heroines so exemplary that a special adjective was created for the type. These characters have deeply influenced our perceptions of Russian life, to the point where one Western scholar could entitle his cultural history of Russia *Natasha's Dance*, and the publisher did not dissuade him.[1] But what of the non-fictional women who lived in that time, who left traces of their lives and concerns in written records and artistic production? Women were a vital part of the cultural process of their times and scholars in recent decades have worked to recover and interpret the records that inform us about their experiences. The present collection, edited by Wendy Rosslyn and Alessandra Tosi, contributes to this effort, examining Russian women's history and creative activity during the long nineteenth century, 1800–1917.

---

1. Orlando Figes, *Natasha's Dance: A Cultural History of Russia* (London: Macmillan, 2002; New York: Picador, 2002).

http://dx.doi.org/10.11647/OBP.0018.01

By the end of the Imperial period, women's creativity was attracting more attention and admiration in Russia than ever before; the articles about female cultural figures in the Brokgaus-Èfron *Encyclopedic Dictionary* (*Entsiklopedicheskii slovar'*) produced in St Petersburg in 1890–1907 are respectful and often quite detailed, even if most of the articles were authored by men. For a variety of reasons, the topic of women's creativity and self-perception fell out of favour in the Soviet period and was neglected for decades.[2] As late as 1985, a Western encyclopedia of Russian literature could provide an article, 'Women in Russian Literature', that treated women primarily as characters in works created by men, artefacts rather than artists.[3] In histories of Russia, any tendency to focus on rulers meant that the eighteenth-century empresses (often themselves born in Western Europe) were de facto representatives of Russian women.

Over the past three decades, however, ground-breaking publications in Russian women's studies have broadened our view of women's experiences and creative activity, recovering sources of information and framing them in suggestive new ways. Here is just a brief listing of some of the most important Western authors of monographs, editors of collections, and translators of primary sources. Rather than weigh down this introduction with a long list of works that should be easy to find, we offer this abbreviated series of names to inspire searching or recognize intellectual debts. In history, our work is shaped by Barbara Clements, Barbara Engel, Eve Levin, Barbara Norton, Christine Worobec; important presentations of women's lives and influence may also appear in biographies of individual women like the politician Aleksandra Kollontai, or in studies of pre-revolutionary philanthropy, or the Russian fashion industry.[4] In literature, vital scholars

---

2. The treatment of feminism under Soviet rule has been discussed in detail by scholars. Primarily, Bolshevik discourse assumed that socialism had solved 'the woman question' and that continuing attention to feminist issues revealed a bourgeois attitude. Indeed, as Amy Bug has shown, data on the number of female scientists in socialist Eastern Europe (based on her own field, physics) suggests that planned economies did relatively well at getting women into the professional 'pipeline' and keeping them there: Amy Bug, 'Has Feminism Changed Physics?', *Signs*, 28.3 (2003), 881–99.
3. Xenia Gasiorowska, 'Women and Russian Literature', in Victor Terras, *Handbook of Russian Literature* (New Haven and London: Yale University Press, 1985), pp. 519–22. The length of this article shows recognition of the importance of the topic, but where it discusses women writers its tone is generally dismissive.
4. Kollontai is best known for her activities during the Revolution and the early Soviet period, but her birth in 1872 gives her biography resonance for the nineteenth-century as well. See Beatrice Farnsworth, *Aleksandra Kollontai: Socialism, Feminism, and the Bolshevik Revolution* (Stanford, CA: Stanford University Press, 1980); Cathy Porter, *Alexandra Kollontai: The Lonely Struggle of the Woman who Defied Lenin* (New York: Dial Press, 1980).

and editors include Joe Andrew, Pamela Chester, Jehanne Gheith, Frank Göpfert, Diana Greene, Barbara Heldt, Catriona Kelly, Marina Ledkovsky, Charlotte Rosenthal, Christine Tomei, and Mary Zirin. Monographs and articles on individual authors from the period (Akhmatova, Gippius, Tsvetaeva) offer insight to readers of women's writing. Issues that concern women, gender and sexuality frequently arise in interdisciplinary or cultural studies works by Lynne Attwood, Adele Barker, Toby Clyman, Jane Costlow, Helena Goscilo, Diana Greene, Beth Holmgren, Catriona Kelly, Andrea Lanoux, Rosalind Marsh, Wendy Rosslyn, Christine Ruane, Judith Vowles, and Faith Wigzell. Treatments of actresses and celebrities enrich the field as well, by Goscilo, Holmgren, and Catherine Schuler. Work by Russian scholars obviously offers essential information and perspectives: just one example, available in English, is Natalia Pushkareva's monumental history of women in Russia.[5] Recent volumes in Russian cultural studies that do not concentrate on women's issues *per se* include articles or sections on women's experience and issues of gender and sexuality.[6]

This collection differs from many (though not all) of the works mentioned above in bringing together articles from a variety of disciplinary positions in the framework of women's lives and culture in the long nineteenth century. The contributors are international, hailing from Britain, Canada, Finland, Russia, and the United States. While the overall result is largely historical, the different approach of each author allows the articles to strike sparks off one another. All are grounded in concrete detail and richly contextualized but also theoretically informed. Some topics have been relatively neglected until now, and establishing the presence of female artists, musicians or composers, and victims of gendered violence through institutional records and primary sources is a large part of the authors' task. Some of the articles present exciting archival discoveries, situated in a rich context and usefully interpreted. Other articles treat parts of the field that are relatively well-explored, allowing a

---

See also Adele Lindenmeyr, *Poverty Is Not a Vice: Charity, Society and the State in Imperial Russia* (Princeton, NJ: Princeton University Press, 1996) and Christine Ruane, *The Emperor's New Clothes: A History of the Russian Fashion Industry* (New Haven: Yale University Press, 2009).

5. Natalia L. Pushkareva, *Women in Russian History: From the Tenth to the Twentieth Century*, ed. and trans. by Eve Levin (Armonk, NY: M.E. Sharpe, 1997).

6. These include *Russian Cultural Studies: An Introduction*, ed. by Catriona Kelly and David Shepherd (Oxford: Oxford University Press, 1998); Catriona Kelly and David Shepherd, *Constructing Russian Culture in the Age of Revolution: 1881–1940* (Oxford: Oxford University Press, 1998) and *The Human Tradition in Imperial Russia*, ed. by Christine Worobec (Lanham, MD: Rowman and Littlefield, 2009).

general overview of Russian women writers or a more detailed examination of the nature of the lives and memoirs of nineteenth-century Russian actresses. At the same time, some of the more historical presentations give subtle close readings of textual evidence. The result is a collection of essays that may with profit be read severally or as a whole.

As Victoria E. Bonnell and Lynn Hunt note, 'If culture is more than a predetermined representation of a prior social reality, then it must depend on a continuing process of deconstruction and reconstruction of public and private narratives. Narrative is an arena in which meaning takes form, in which individuals connect to the public and social world, and in which change therefore becomes possible'.[7] Combining approaches drawn from history and from the humanities, this volume enriches the reader's knowledge and suggests promising avenues for future research and reading. Several threads run through more than one of the articles: the importance of religion in women's experience, both in what they received from the culture and what they (re-)produced in their own lives and experiences; and the vexed position of women with creative ambitions that tempted them to move beyond the realm of family life or domestic social gatherings. Most of all, the articles devote attention to the narratives with which women worked, which they created, and which they (sometimes) changed or exploited to suit their own purposes.

What distinguished the nineteenth century from the earlier Imperial period, and from the Soviet era that followed? In one review (1835),[8] the critic Vissarion Belinskii included the following passages concerning women authors:

> For her [woman] – the representative on the earth of beauty and grace, priestess of love and self-sacrifice – it is a thousandfold more praiseworthy to inspire *Jerusalem Liberated* than to write it herself, just as it is a thousandfold more praiseworthy to hand her chosen one a shield with the device 'With it or upon it!' than to throw herself into the heat of battle with weapon in hand (30).

> The mind of woman knows only a few aspects of being or, to say it better, her feeling has access only to the world of devoted love and submissive suffering; omniscience is horrible in her, repulsive, while for a poet the whole boundless world of thought and feeling, passions and deeds must be open (31).

---

7. *Beyond the Cultural Turn: New Directions in the Study of Society and Culture*, ed. by Victoria E. Bonnell and Lynn Hunt (Berkeley: University of California Press, 1999), p. 17.
8. I cite from my translation of his review of a French author's work in Russian translation: V. G. Belinskii, 'Review of *A Victim*', in *Russian Women, 1698–1917: Experience and Expression*, ed. by Robin Bisha, Jehanne M. Gheith, Christine Holden, and William G. Wagner (Bloomington: Indiana University Press, 2002), pp. 28–32.

Une femme emancipée – this word might be very accurately translated with a single Russian word, but unfortunately its use is permitted only in dictionaries, and not in all of them at that, but only in the most extensive. I will add only that a woman writer is, in a certain sense, *la femme emancipée* (32).

Although this represents just parts of one review by one critic, Belinskii acquired such prestige as a literary and social critic, especially with left-leaning readers and creators who might otherwise have tended to favour equal creative rights for women, that his comments are gravely suggestive and reminiscent of some of the comments Barbara Engel finds in judicial archives about women who strayed to physically different places rather than into artistic pretensions. It is no wonder that some creative women in Russia preferred to publish music only under their initials, or to write novels and stories under pseudonyms. Comments like these by Belinskii could serve to keep creative women in their place (perhaps only until marriage, as in the case of Evdokiia Sushkova, who published as Rostopchina), or endow the woman who dared to transgress gender boundaries with the energy of resistance and narratives of punishment (as for example in the writing of Marina Tsvetaeva). Julie Cassiday notes the success of Vera Komissarzhevskaia, whose career suggested that she was blending art and life by playing wounded, sexually fallen women in transgressive roles (p. 182). At the same time, the nineteenth century witnessed the development of scholars' and bibliographers' interest precisely in women as writers, autobiographers, and creators. Women who produced elite kinds of art were sometimes kept or written out by gate-keeping male critics or competitors, but sometimes they were cited with approval and respect as examples of Russia's rising level of culture and education, listed in reference sources or awarded prestigious prizes for their paintings and poetry. By the early twentieth century women had emerged as important creators or actors and canny manipulators of the emerging popular culture of the Russian empire.

Thus, this collection offers thought-provoking snapshots and outlines of the stages women in Russia moved through over time, from the still largely traditional society of the late eighteenth century to the greater cultural prominence, growing economic importance, and (on the whole) vastly improved educational and professional situation that many Russian women enjoyed on the eve of the Revolution. As the reader will observe in the overview below, the articles cover a wide range of topics and disciplinary angles, yet all will appeal to one another's readers: the very visible figure of the actress would clearly shape the self-understanding (and much societal criticism) of women writers, visual artists and composers, while some actresses took on the role of author in writing their memoirs, continuing to shape their images. The status and depiction of Mary in writing by both clerical and lay figures could not help but impact the religious experience of Russian women and their descriptions of that experience. Violence against women or societal control of women's behaviour (by way of legal definition, literary depiction or journalistic reportage) would lurk at the edges of every woman's experience, no matter her level of safety and privilege (or not). In its breadth, the book aims to serve both students and experts in Russian culture, specialists in its various fields, as well as general readers from a variety of intellectual positions and backgrounds.

Barbara Engel's 'Women and Urban Culture' presents discoveries from legal archives about the lives of urban women from various 'middle' classes. As Engel points out, until recently (as indeed in the nineteenth century) most scholarly information about women treated either the women of the upper class — relatively powerful and culturally dominant in artistic, dramatic and literary depictions as well as in urban society — or of the peasantry, members of a mysterious and yet idealized group, though familiar to the aristocracy and merchant class as nannies and servants.[9] Engel usefully cites information on these women's lives from two distinct perspectives: their own words in the petitions they filed, which occasioned the preservation of those words, and the opinions of police and court officials about the women's reputations, recorded in other parts of the files. Engel teases out the implications of the contrast or clash between the women's self-images and society's image of them, and she notes the impact of these differences on the women's own subsequent lives and liberty. Drawn from different geographical areas, the three cases show changing mores over time as public discourse on the woman question percolated through popular literature, women's journals, and other entertainments to influence women's expectations and behaviour. The commercial culture women encountered when they moved to the city could inspire new ambitions, or fuel new discontent. As Christine Worobec notes

---

9. Ol'ga Semenova Tian-Shanskaia made the hero of her ethnography a generalized, composite peasant Ivan, but her *Village Life in Late Tsarist Russia* (published in Russian in 1914, six years after her death, as *Zhizn' Ivana*) also includes copious information about peasant women and girls. See her *Village Life in Late Tsarist Russia*, ed. by David Ransel, trans. by David Ransel and Michael Levine (Bloomington and Indianapolis: Indiana University Press, 1993).

elsewhere, even superficial changes such as new hairstyles and choices in clothing could significantly transform a woman's self-image, as well as the impression she might make on others.[10] Engel shows how much that impression could shape a woman's life as mores evolved and women were read by powerful men as either loose or respectable.

Worobec's 'Russian Peasant Women's Culture: Three Voices' likewise draws connections between individual records and larger social and historical patterns. Scholars of peasant women's culture have had to penetrate through layers of censorship (as Worobec puts it, archives come to contain 'sanitized versions of the originals'); moreover, she lists the many factors that might have limited the information provided by peasant women even before it reached the archive. (It is worth noting in this connection that when masses of peasant women became literate, in the 1920s or 1930s, they began making written records of the most precious things they held in memory, including their own repertoires of folk magic, especially medicinal and prophylactic charms, and fragments of liturgy, material that would similarly have languished in archives in the Soviet period, if scholars had dared to collect it at all.) This contrasts with the details left by women from the upper classes, such as Anna Labzina, Elizaveta Vodovozova, and Nadezhda Sokhanskaia, and underlines the importance of literacy in our access to women's understanding of their own lives and control of their representation.[11]

Even after emancipation ended serfdom, the Russian peasantry continued to exist in public discourse almost as a fantasy property of the educated classes, a repository of traditional culture that ethnographers (many of them with limited understanding of the nature of oral culture) feared would be

---

10. Christine Worobec, 'Introduction', in *The Human Tradition in Imperial Russia*, p. xv.
11. See Anna Labzina, *Days of a Russian Noblewoman: The Memories of Anna Labzina, 1758–1821*, ed. and trans. by Gary Marker and Rachel May (Evanston, IL: Northwestern University Press, 2001); Elizaveta Vodovozova, 'The Challenged Gentry', trans. by Sibelan Forrester, in *The Russia Reader*, ed. by Adele Barker and Bruce Grant (Durham and London: Duke University Press, 2010), pp. 134–39 and Sokhanskaia (1825–1884), 'An Autobiography', in *Russia Through Women's Eyes: Autobiographies from Tsarist Russia*, ed. by Toby Clyman and Judith Vowles (New Haven, CT: Yale University Press, 1999), pp. 47–59. Barbara Heldt, in her *Terrible Perfection* (Bloomington and Indianapolis: Indiana University Press, 1987), points out Russian women's success as authors of poetry and autobiography; the memoir, like lyric poetry, is at once personal and individual and thus free from the hubris of daring to depict larger society, as novelistic prose did. Authors like Nadezhda Khvoshchinskaia proved that Russian women could be both artistically impressive and successful authors of prose fiction, but they did not become part of the nineteenth-century canon and are only relatively recently being rediscovered in Russia and the West.

lost in contact with modernity. Worobec notes that one and the same source might decry the backwardness of the peasants, especially the women, and then complain that they were acquiring 'corrupt' modern habits. She thoughtfully describes how collectors' attitudes towards 'authenticity' and the role of official and folk Orthodoxy impacted what was recorded from or about Russian peasant women in the nineteenth and early twentieth centuries. She also warns against overestimation of the extent of *dvoeverie*, the coexistence of pagan and Christian religious symbols and beliefs, in the Russian peasantry; as her citations show, women historians and scholars of women's history have played a major role in this corrective re-evaluation. The article points to the many cultural and economic connections between urban and rural Russia. After richly establishing this context, Worobec examines a group of letters written by three Russian peasant women in the nineteenth century. Orthodox language and practices are central in their communication, and in the lives their letters describe. The details remind us that many Orthodox practices (from purchasing candles to supporting oneself on a religious pilgrimage) required money and so were closely bound to the economic life of the family and of the country. Worobec's careful reading of these sources demonstrates that religious practice was largely a constant for Russian women across class boundaries. For some Russian women before the Revolution, the role of a religious pilgrim might be an unexpected alternative to other versions of a female life.

Vera Shevzov's 'Mary and Women in Late Imperial Russian Orthodoxy' examines nineteenth-century narratives about a central figure in Russian culture: Mary the Mother of God.[12] Authors of nineteenth-century *Lives of Mary* included men from the clerical hierarchy and monks as well as laymen, plus at least two women; Shevzov notes that copies of the two *Lives* which we know were authored by (noble) women eventually found their way into peasants' homes as well as libraries. She describes the ways the *Lives* could reveal opinions by Orthodox clergymen and church authorities about the equality of the sexes – or not – in reaction to discussions of women's emancipation. Over time, these *Lives* began to include reproductions of well-known icons of Mary, bringing together narrative and visual images in the era of mechanical reproduction and laying the groundwork for both scholars and believers to understand icons in new ways, though

---

12. Mary's image and prestige in Russian Orthodoxy are more strongly linked to her giving birth to Christ than to her virginity and she is described as Mother of God (*Bogoroditsa*, from the Greek *Theotokos*) more often than as the Virgin.

the illustrations accompanying the *Lives* were doubtless meant to serve as additional resources for readers' devotional practice. The *Lives* offer both exempla of ideal behaviour and illustrations of episodes from a human biography that might inspire or impact women's everyday choices. Narratives about Mary could be mined for spiritual insight, emulated by women in pursuit of a life agreeable to God, or interpreted as empowering women to do what they most needed to do in their own lives, as Shevzov notes: '[W]omen, and mothers in particular, might […] have also identified with, and been emboldened by, her fierce sense of vocation and the fervent way she pursued it, despite the social precepts and political pressures of her times' (p. 89). The vocabulary of the Russian titles listed in Shevzov's abundant bibliography, *Tsaritsa nebesnaia* (heavenly tsarina) and *vladychitsa* (ruler, female), do indeed suggest why women might have felt entitled to read Mary as a source of authority, be it spiritual, moral, or even potentially political. This reader would love to hear more about the feminist theologian E. Liuleva: here, as elsewhere, the article points readers towards new topics of interest.

Rosalind Blakesley's 'Women and the Visual Arts' begins with a sensitive and thought-provoking reading of Marie Louise Elisabeth Vigée-Lebrun's portrait of Empress Maria Fedorovna (1800). This presentation is only possible because the picture survived in the collection of the Russian Academy: 'the occasional acclaimed foreigner' (p. 92) is the exception to the rule. Although women's faces and bodies were all over the canvases of elite male painters, Russian women who made art were practically invisible in the early nineteenth century, confined to the domestic sphere rather than active in the public one, and their work has rarely survived to be studied. Blakesley discusses the importance in women's lives of handicrafts or the applied arts, as distinct from elite work in the fine arts. Women's private production of artistic images in early nineteenth-century Russia was as widespread in the educated classes as in the peasantry: many women and men practiced drawing or painting in watercolors, much as we take photographs today as mementos or travel records.[13] We know Aleksandr Pushkin's doodles and

---

13. This was true not only in Russia. In the mid-1980s in Bloomington, Indiana, I discovered a detailed, beautifully rendered portrait of a young woman in Victorian dress, drawn in pencil on a blank page in the back of a novel by George Sand (perhaps the 1832 *Indiana*), a French edition published in the nineteenth-century. This anonymous example of skill in portraiture had survived at least a century because it was bound inside a library book in a university library, a book in French that had never attracted enough readers to damage it. This portrait is one exception to the disappearance of works of art by women,

Mikhail Lermontov's drawings and paintings because their fame as writers preserved every scrap of paper they used, not because they were unusual in creating visual art of this kind. The Countess's portrait in Pushkin's 'Queen of Spades' ('Pikovaia dama') reminds us that women of means had themselves painted all the time, and such a painting could serve variously as a mirror, a signifier of female vanity, and a time machine.

Blakesley describes the kinds of artistic education that were available to girls, at first only to noble girls, then as time passed to girls from broader segments of society. Readers of fiction from the era might recall Lelenka, heroine of Nadezhda Khvoshchinskaia's novel *The Boarding School Girl* (*Pansionerka*, 1861),[14] who at the novel's end makes a comfortable living by painting and selling copies of famous pictures in the Hermitage gallery. (One thing she enjoys in her liberated urban lifestyle is treating herself to regular tickets to the theatre: she participates in that realm of art as a spectator). Khvoshchinskaia does not intend to create an image of female genius – Lelenka is a talented copyist, not an original artist – but the idea that a woman could support herself in any way as a visual artist did not disrupt the realism of the novel. Indeed, Khvoshchinskaia's sister Sof'ia (1824–65) was a reasonably successful painter as well as being a writer. Women who had ability eventually acquired training and the right to make the kinds of high-status art for which male artists were recognized – paintings to hang on walls, not tapestries or purses knitted for charity balls. The chapter provides an important outline of the institutional history of women's access to artistic education and production, be it through the Academy or in more private spaces such as the workshops of Abramtsevo. At the same time, making works of art with expensive media, be they oil paints or cameos turned on a lathe, would have been prohibitively expensive for most men in Russia, as well as for most women. Blakesley describes the repeated petitions of Mariia Kurt to the Academy for financial assistance; these may reflect the cost of the materials she favoured as much as her own lack of commercial success. However, by the early twentieth century many women had access to excellent artistic training, and Blakesley's study leads up to the famous names of the time.

---

pointing up the importance of institutional recognition. A work kept in a museum (or library) is preserved, whereas one kept at home is liable to be damaged, lost in a fire, used to wrap pastries, or simply discarded by unappreciative heirs.

14. See Nadezhda Khvoshchinskaia, *The Boarding School Girl*, trans. Karen Rosneck (Evanston, IL: Northwestern University Press, 2000).

Like other authors in this collection, Blakesley zooms in on instructive little-studied examples, such as the buttons made for Catherine the Great by her daughter-in-law, eventually Empress Maria Fedorovna (the same one painted by Vigée-Lebrun); she reads these with attention to the ways they defer to the male architect and male miniaturist who had created the buildings and their images, respectively. The buttons are at once practical and ornamental, associated with women's work in handicrafts but still placed behind glass in a frame, bringing all those associations together in a new medium. Feminist art historians have argued that the decorative arts should be valued in assessing women's creative careers, and the first generation of world-famous Russian women artists, tellingly, were engaged in scene painting and fabric design as well as elite easel painting. Blakesley's work is deeply informed by scholarship on female artists in Britain and France, as well as the literature on Russian women's culture. She cites cheering evidence of recent exhibitions (in Russia and abroad) and of serious scholarly attention to the work of Russian women artists, including some of those from the nineteenth century whose work has been preserved and recovered.

Philip Ross Bullock's chapter, 'Women and Music', broaches a topic that scholars have barely begun to study, as he himself points out. As in the visual arts, nineteenth-century women's access to music was determined largely by class, with folk songs (despite their tremendous importance in the development of a Russian school of classical music) analogous to handicrafts in their handmaid relationship to the fine arts and lack of authorial attribution. Bullock briefly outlines what is known about women's participation in music before 1800, then traces the institutional history forward until the twentieth century. Eighteenth-century empresses played a major role in the introduction of Western music to Russia, especially opera; unlike artists and writers, however, aspiring female musicians and especially composers had no Western European role models. Nevertheless, Bullock cites evidence of Russian women composing music as early as the end of the eighteenth century. Aside from unusually prominent serf performers like Praskov'ia Kovaleva, whose life is treated in Douglas Smith's *The Pearl* and briefly outlined here by Bullock,[15] at that time only upper-class women had much chance of taking memorable steps in music, even if after modestly publishing their work with only initials they were left anonymous, gendered but not named.

---

15. Douglas Smith, *The Pearl: A True Tale of Forbidden Love in Catherine the Great's Russia* (New Haven: Yale University Press, 2008).

Bullock addresses women's role in secular and society music-making, in composition as well as performance. The state theatres featured many foreign performers along with Russians, at first from the lower classes. The performances of dilettantes in upper-class salons have left traces in literature, supplementing the information on performances from memoirs and theatre archives. As Bullock suggests, citing some titles from 1820 collections of music aimed at women (p. 125), in the sentimental period music seems to have been considered particularly interesting and satisfying for women. Later, the lines between public performance and private amusement might have become blurred in a salon where the best minds in town were in attendance, but women understood the difference. Karolina Pavlova's *Double Life* (*Dvoinaia zhizn'*, 1848) describes the heroine and her best friend singing a duet together in the way marriageable young women were supposed to sing, demonstrating their talents and culture without being too talented or off-puttingly ambitious.[16] The male guests applaud even more enthusiastically than they do for genuine professionals: their interest is piqued by a performance where the marriage market is at stake. Bullock cites comments from men of the time suggesting that they meant to exclude women composers to keep the real estate values high in the most elite precincts of music, such as composition. At the same time, male composers relied on a largely female substrate of performers, copyists, and patrons (matrons?).

The mothers of modernist poets Boris Pasternak and Marina Tsvetaeva were both marvellous pianists with outstanding musical training, but performing careers were precluded by their roles as mothers and wives. They turned, instead, to teaching music to their own children. The place of women in Russian music impacts our understanding of other spheres as well, and Bullock's survey of the topic suggests a number of promising figures to investigate. One can hope that graduate students, the next generation of scholars, are taking notes and making plans as they read.

Julie Cassiday's article, 'The Rise of the Actress in Early Nineteenth-Century Russia', examines the position of women in Russian theatre as it first took shape, connecting it with the careers and memoirs of the first female theatrical superstars in the early twentieth century. The development of the theatre in Russia, where for many decades the state

---

16. Karolina Pavlova, *A Double Life*, trans. by Barbara Heldt (Oakland, CA: Barbary Coast Books, 1990), p. 57.

directed its growth and content almost without reference to the public, had particular consequences for the lives of actresses, though in other ways they led lives not dissimilar to those in Western Europe. Quoting Jean-Jacques Rousseau on the questionable virtue of actresses as 'public women', Cassiday underlines the societal assumption that actresses were more or less synonymous with prostitutes. Again, this equation dogged not only actresses but women who performed in any way, even those who published writing in what would seem to be a bodiless self-exposure. Concern with propriety kept many women from taking their art before an audience, sometimes only until marriage, like Rostopchina, but others for their whole lives. Women like Roza Kaufman Pasternak and Mariia Aleksandrovna Tsvetaeva found the outlet for their passionate artistic energy and ambitions in their children, female or male.

Cassiday points out the divide into private and public realms for women with dramatic talents: women were welcome (and eager) to take part in amateur theatricals in domestic spaces for audiences of friends and family, but professional actresses drew suspicion, perhaps, in part, because when the modern Russian theatre was born in the eighteenth century many were serfs, *devki*, a word used to refer to prostitutes as well as peasant girls. Evidently a peasant girl's virtue was already questionable, since she would have trouble fighting off unwelcome attentions from men of a higher class. Some of the scholars quoted in the article refer to the famous serf actress Praskov'ia Zhemchugova ('The Pearl') as 'Parasha', an intimacy that might suggest condescension or a peculiar, perhaps sympathetic, intimacy, but which in any case takes liberties with the respect Zhemchugova commanded as a brilliant actress. (Ekaterina Semenova, whose reputation for sublime tragic gifts was attenuated for some of her fans by her chillier public persona, as Cassiday notes, apparently does not inspire scholars to refer to her as 'Katia'.)

Alexandrine actresses not only moved audiences with the words of male playwrights; they also took up the pen to initiate 'the sentimental narrative of the Russian actress' in memoirs that both explained their lives and fed their celebrity. Cassiday studies the way actresses began to write their own lives, building on publicity information to convey more of the sense of personal contact audiences wanted and supporting the sense that an actress was projecting her *self* to her audience. At the same time, Semenova insisted on her own artistic vocation. Cassiday also examines the way subsequent historians of the theatre have described and justified the lives and careers of these actresses, probably the best-known and most prestigious female artists of their day despite their questionable propriety and use (intentional or forced) of liaisons with powerful men to advance their careers.

Cassiday cites spectators' memoirs to describe the actress's function of bringing the audience to a climax of tears, and uniting the community of the audience in the shared experience of that emotional catharsis. The affective community thus created in the secular space of the National Theatre shares traits with the *sobornost'* (religious shared experience) advanced by the Slavophiles as a special trait of Russia. Though the status of actresses had improved tremendously by the end of the century, Vera Komissarzhevskaia (who had her own theatre) built her reputation playing wounded or fallen women like Nina Zarechnaia in Chekhov's *The Seagull* (*Chaika*). Though her professional success was even greater than that of the Alexandrine actresses, Komissarzhevskaia still played with the intersection of life and dramatic role that audiences had learned to expect, one that, as Cassiday points out, came to define other realms of art in Silver Age life-creation (*zhiznetvorchestvo*).

Arja Rosenholm's and Irina Savkina's article '"How Women Should Write": Russian Women's Writing in the Nineteenth Century' treats the realm of discourse that is perhaps best represented and most analysed among those covered in the collection. Literary activity has the advantage of producing results that take up relatively little space and can be mechanically multiplied in publication, and even forgotten authors may be retrieved from archives and libraries. In the early nineteenth century, Russian women wrote in French as often as in Russian, and the self-deprecatory strategies Rosenholm and Savkina connect to women associated with Karamzin's movement are more broadly typical of European women at the time and the 'anxiety of authorship' in Sandra Gilbert's and Susan Gubar's famous formulation.[17] As Rosenholm and Savkina note, Karamzin's discursive project does allow room for women, but only on his terms. It is intriguing that literary women seemed to get a better reception from the *Colloquium of Admirers of the Russian Word* (*Beseda liubitelei russkogo slova*) than from the horny young men of the *Arzamas* circle; the outstanding poet Anna Bunina (1774–1829), an honourary member of the *Beseda*, is probably most familiar, if at all, to readers in the West because Dostoevskii cited Konstantin

---

17. See Sandra M. Gilbert and Susan Gubar, *The Madwoman in the Attic: The Woman Writer and the Nineteenth-Century Literary Imagination* (New Haven: Yale University Press, 1980), especially the Introduction and Chapter 1.

Batiushkov's sexist epigram (probably) about her in *The Brothers Karamazov* (*Brat'ia Karamazovy*); that novel's canonical status, rather than Bunina's importance and delightful poetry, means that the quote is glossed in critical editions.

Barbara Heldt in *Terrible Perfection* notes the greater prominence of Russian women who wrote poetry and autobiography, two genres that foreground and privilege personal experience, rather than prose fiction that aimed to depict and critique Russian society.[18] As Catriona Kelly and David Shepherd note, Russian literature was used in particular ways in the nineteenth century: 'The identification between literature and document was enhanced by the fact that social criticism rendered as fiction or literary criticism could more easily pass through the censorship than works of publicistic and journalistic enquiry'.[19] This high-stakes use of writing surely put special pressure on women who wished to compose prose fiction, the kind of work that typically involved social criticism, and it may in part explain the lack of attention to women like Khvoshchinskaia (who wrote under the masculine pseudonym V. Krestovskii), or later on Ol'ga Shapir and Valentina Dmitrieva, who were not involved in symbolist or modernist stylistic experimentation. The disruptive effect of the Revolution, on the other hand, may have 'frozen' and thus assured the status of the most important female figures in Russian symbolism and modernism: just as syllabotonic poetry remained the dominant form through the Soviet period, the women who had written important poetry in the Silver Age (no matter how the Soviet literary establishment tried to suppress it) could not be 'written out' of the narrative, as had happened with successful women writers in earlier generations. This too would tend to privilege poetry over prose genres in women's writing of the canon Heldt described in the late 1980s.

Rosenholm and Savkina point out the pernicious side of putatively feminist male writers such as Chernyshevskii, who so coddled his female characters that the male characters did everything for them. The authors rightly note that repeated revisions of feminine ideals, followed by the demand for a 'new woman', continued to require women to remake themselves according to male advice and preferences. Where female writers were cut off from their predecessors by changes in literary fashion (for who would want to learn from a writer who was mocked by Pushkin's

---

18. Heldt, *Terrible Perfection*, p. 7.
19. *Constructing Russian Culture in the Age of Revolution: 1881–1940*, p. 1.

friend?), they were thrown back for guidance on what men wrote and said, if they sought guidance for their own conduct in literature.

In the nineteenth century, Russia produced such a wealth of women writers that it is impossible to discuss more than a few in detail. By the end of the period, women enjoyed great success in many genres, from elite poetry or realistic muck-raking to pot-boiling best-sellers. The serious attention given to women in the Silver Age – and the fact that in the Silver Age women writers firmly entered the canon of Russian literature for the first time – runs parallel to that period's increased openness to otherness of many kinds, as peasants, Jews, gays and lesbians, and other ethnic and religious minorities joined the literary scene. Readers who picked up works by women as examples of some theoretical 'feminine' creative principle may have taken a condescending or essentialist approach, but it was certainly better for women than not being read at all. The Silver Age also moved to recover women authors from earlier decades: Rostopchina remained in print until the 1910s, and her lyrics were frequently set to music as romances, while Pavlova's work was reissued in 1915 in a collection edited by symbolist *maître* Valerii Briusov. As mentioned above, the literary production of women was considered part of the country's heritage and a mark of its advancement. This sense of a growing tradition, even if neglected or tendentiously shaped by some male critics,[20] surely contributed to the atmosphere for women writers in the early twentieth century. Many of the less familiar names Rosenholm and Savkina mention deserve to be more widely known: translated, read, taught, and studied.

The book's final chapter, Marianna Muravyeva's 'Between Law and Morality: Violence against Women in Nineteenth-Century Russia', turns from the production of culture back to the status of women in society. Here too, however, the issue of violence emerges in discourse, like the journalistic depictions of the kind that Dostoevskii would collect and weave into his fiction. The ingrained violence of proverbs that assert that a man beats his woman because he loves her contrasts with journalistic and literary depictions that deplored this treatment and the barbarity it suggested, viewing treatment of Russian women as an index of the country's level of civilization. Contemporary examples of violence set a benchmark and

---

20. The Silver Age also saw the emergence of a number of female literary critics. See Catriona Kelly, 'Missing Links: Russian Women Writers as Critics of Women Writers', in *Russian Writers on Russian Writers*, ed. by Faith Wigzell (Oxford and Providence: Berg, 1994), pp. 67–80.

occasioned soul-searching; violence against women, especially sexual violence, continued to be an important topic of legal and journalistic discourse in the early Soviet period.[21]

Muravyeva poses urgent questions: '…why [did] relatively powerful and well-protected Russian women suddenly [turn] into the powerless and abused serfs of their families? What happened in the first half of the nineteenth century that demoted Russian women to the lowest level ever? How come that protection from rape, allegedly high in the seventeenth century, suddenly ceased in the nineteenth century and left women alone to prove their right to bodily integrity?' (p. 211). She examines the legal status of rape and statistics on its prosecution in thought-provoking detail.

Russian Women in the Nineteenth Century examines both women's actual lives and the narratives they tell about their lives, often interwoven in the same piece, as in those by Engel, Worobec, Shevzov, and Cassiday. Blakesley, Bullock and Muravyeva helpfully outline the institutional history in parts of the field that have until recently been neglected; Engel and Worobec bring rich new information from the archives. Rosenholm and Savkina offer alternatives to the literary narratives that have come to define Russian women and their literary production for readers. All this adds to and continues the work of research in the field of Russian women's and gender studies and it represents a significant contribution to scholarship in nineteenth-century Russian history and culture, where awareness of the roles and experiences of women are essential in good scholarship. Rosslyn and Tosi, this volume's editors, have done a service for each individual discipline: for courses in women's studies and for our overall understanding of Russia in the nineteenth century.

---

21. See Eric Naiman on the case of Chubarov Alley, in his *Sex in Public: The Incarnation of Early Soviet Ideology* (Princeton, NJ: Princeton University Press, 1997) and Dan Healey's *Bolshevik Sexual Forensics: Diagnosing Disorder in the Clinic and the Courtroom, 1917–1939* (DeKalb, IL: Northern Illinois University Press, 2009).

2. Women and Urban Culture

Barbara Alpern Engel

In the final decades of the nineteenth century, Russia underwent the social and economic transformations that, centuries earlier, had given rise to urban culture in much of Western Europe. In the West, the commercial revolution and rise of a market economy had resulted in a critical mass of urban population that did not depend on the land. The development of urban-rural differences in lifestyle and mentality; the existence of forms of commercial activity that affected the 'physical fabric' of their setting; and the growth of regular non-familial, non-domestic forms of sociability that occurred in comparatively public and/or commercialized settings[1] – these circumstances, the preconditions of urban culture, did not really exist in Russia until the Reform Era (1855–81). Even then Russia's commercial revolution accompanied industrialization and the spread of modern transport, rather than preceding them, as had been the case in the West. Still, when economic changes gathered momentum in the 1880s and accelerated in the 1890s, they affected even Russia's provincial towns. Many evolved from 'tsarist outposts' into genuine urban centres following the expansion of railway networks, which enhanced personal mobility and reduced cultural isolation. Even relatively remote peasant communities were affected, as Christine Worobec notes in her contribution to this volume.[2]

---

1. 'Introduction', in *The City in Central Europe: Culture and Society from 1800 to the Present*, ed. by Malcolm Gee, Tim Kirk and Jill Steward (Brookfield, VT: Ashgate, 1999), p. 4 and Klaus Tenfelde, 'Urbanization and the Spread of an Urban Culture in Germany in the Nineteenth and Twentieth Century', in *Towards an Urban Nation: Germany since 1780*, ed. by Friedrich Lenger (New York: Berg, 2002), pp. 26–34.
2. Daniel R. Brower, *The Russian City Between Tradition and Modernity, 1850–1900* (Berkeley, CA: University of California Press, 1990), pp. 30–51 (37).

http://dx.doi.org/10.11647/OBP.0018.02

One result of these developments was what historian Daniel Brower has called the 'migrant city'.[3] Hundreds of thousands of people, a substantial minority of them female, most of them peasants released from serfdom only after 1861, inundated Russia's major cities seeking jobs in the burgeoning industrial, construction and, especially in the case of women, service sectors of the economy, swelling the ranks of the urban poor. Another result was a sizeable increase in the number of 'middling' people, as townspeople (*meshchanstvo*) and merchants, as well as entrepreneurial peasants and nobles, took advantage of new opportunities to make money. Unlike peasants and nobles, townspeople and merchants were already classified as urban, according to Russia's system of *sosloviia*, legally constituted categories that established an individual's rights and responsibilities in relation to the state.[4] The number of white-collar workers, professionals and semi-professionals also grew dramatically, the result of expanding opportunities for education and professional employment that attracted young women and men from the provinces as well as urban residents. The women might find work as physicians, midwives, telegraph workers, or most commonly of all, teachers.

In his groundbreaking study of Russia's urban development, Daniel Brower noted the ways that Russia's urban culture differed from as well as resembled that of the West. Differences included not only the comparative tardiness of Russian developments, but also the depth of the social divide that separated wealthy 'municipal elites' from the urban poor, a divide characteristic of urban life throughout Europe, but which in Russia was widened by the Westernized culture of the elites and the folk culture of the migrant poor, and by the propensity of tsarist officials to favour education according to rank. The outcome, in his words, was a 'contested' urban cultural dynamic, with elites and folk vying for hegemony and little to no middle ground.[5] More recent work has qualified this stark picture suggesting that, by the second half of the century, a middling, if not middle, class had come to occupy some of this contested terrain, however small and powerless the group remained by Western European standards and however fragmented by differences of social, geographic and ethnic origin. Emerging as early as

---

3. Brower, *The Russian City*, pp. 75–91.
4. See Gregory Freeze, 'The *Soslovie* (Estate) Paradigm and Russian Society History', *American Historical Review*, 91 (1986), 11–36.
5. Brower, *The Russian City*, pp. 137, 153, 149, 160.

mid-century, it grew rapidly thereafter.⁶ Encouraged by the new commercial, educational and professional opportunities, some people began to imagine or adopt ways of living substantially unlike those of their parents. For beneficiaries of opportunities for social mobility, Russia's *soslovie* order became less meaningful as a way of conceiving the self and its possibilities.

Cultural developments associated with urban life reflected and reinforced the social flux. The new and more individualistic values of the capitalist marketplace and commercial culture challenged older ways of being in the world and contributed to the crafting of new social identities. Books and magazines aimed at the upwardly mobile dispensed advice on how to dress, maintain and furnish the home, and behave with refinement. Advertising enticed women to consume the items displayed in department store windows and on the pages of popular magazines and to employ beauty aides to decorate the self.⁷ Encouraging the pursuit of pleasure, the new consumer culture, which reached well beyond the cities, as Worobec's essay in this volume shows, was particularly unsettling for a people long accustomed to subordinating individual needs to family and community.

Historians differ in their assessment of how industrialization, urbanization and associated cultural changes affected women. They draw primarily on the experience of Great Britain, where the Industrial Revolution and then Victorianism rendered public space off limits to 'respectable' women, developments mirrored elsewhere in Europe as well. Some emphasize the ways that cultural changes associated with urbanization increased women's sexual vulnerability. Urban space, they argue, was male space and women who ventured into it risked their sexual reputation if not worse. For women, writes Richard Sennett, the public life of the city was 'where one risked losing virtue, dirtying oneself, being swept into "a disorderly and heady swirl"'. Elizabeth Wilson puts the issue

---

6. Aleksandr I. Kupriianov, *Gorodskaia kul'tura russkoi provintsii: konets XVIII-pervaia polovina XIX veka* (Moscow: Novyi khronograf, 2007). On fragmentation, see Alfred J. Rieber, 'The Sedimentary Society', in *Between Tsar and People: Educated Society and the Quest for Public Identity in Late Imperial Russia*, ed. by Edith W. Clowes, Samuel D. Kassow, and James L. West (Princeton, NJ: Princeton University Press, 1991), pp. 343–66.
7. Sally West, 'The Material Promised Land: Advertising's Modern Agenda in Late Imperial Russia', *Russian Review*, 57. 3 (1998), 345–63; Steve Smith and Catriona Kelly, 'Commercial Culture and Consumerism', in *Constructing Russian Culture in the Age of Revolution: 1881–1940*, ed. by Catriona Kelly and David Shepherd (New York: Oxford University Press, 1998), pp. 106–55; Catriona Kelly, *Refining Russia: Advice Literature, Polite Culture and Gender from Catherine to Yeltsin* (New York: Oxford University Press, 2001).

still more starkly: 'The problem in nineteenth-century urban life', she notes, 'was whether every woman in the new, disordered world of the city [...] was not a public woman and thus a prostitute. The very presence of unattended – unowned – women constituted a threat both to male power and a temptation to male frailty'.[8] Some studies of Russia's popular urban culture appear to corroborate such observations. They suggest that lower-class men were profoundly hostile to women's presence in public and regarded such women as fair game. Jeffrey Brooks, for example, observes that the violence commonly directed against women in popular bandit novels might have 'appealed to readers uncomfortable with the loosening of traditional family ties and with the novelty and confusion that increasing geographic and social mobility brought to relations between the sexes'. As Joan Neuberger has shown, women who ventured into urban public space at the turn of the century risked harassment, if not worse.[9]

Others, however, argue for the positive impact of urban culture on women. In their view, it enhanced women's personal freedom and ability to shape their own lives. This was to some extent the case for a relative handful of noblewomen in the late eighteenth and early nineteenth centuries, a period when Russia's urban culture, an extension of noble culture, involved primarily a thin layer of noble elites. In this period, noblewomen might preside over, or attend as guests, salons held in private homes, just as elite women were doing all over Europe. Promoting culture and the unimpeded exchange of ideas, Russia's female-led salons influenced the development of

---

8. Richard Sennett, *The Fall of Public Man: On the Social Psychology of Capitalism* (New York: Vintage, 1974), p. 23; Elizabeth Wilson, *The Contradictions of Culture: Cities, Culture, Women* (London: Sage, 2001), p. 74. See also Deborah Epstein Nord, *Walking the Victorian Streets: Women, Representation and the City* (Ithaca, NY: Cornell University Press, 1995), pp. 3–4 and Elizabeth Munson, 'Walking on the Periphery: Gender and the Discourse of Modernization', *Journal of Social History*, 36 (2002), 63–75.

9. Jeffrey Brooks, *When Russia Learned to Read: Literacy and Popular Literature, 1861–1917* (Princeton, NJ: Princeton University Press, 1985), p. 188; Joan Neuberger, *Hooliganism: Crime, Culture and Power in St Petersburg, 1900–1914* (Berkeley, CA: University of California Press, 1993), pp. 29, 31–32, 37, 80, 104, 114, 124–25, 228. See also Catriona Kelly, 'A Stick with Two Ends, or, Misogyny in Popular Culture: A Case Study of the Puppet Text "Petrushka"', in *Sexuality and the Body in Russian Culture*, ed. by Jane Costlow and Judith Vowles (Stanford, CA: Stanford University Press, 1993), pp. 73–96 and '"Better Halves"? Representations of Women in Russian Urban Popular Entertainments, 1870–1900', in *Women and Society in Russia and the Soviet Union*, ed. by Linda Harriet Edmondson, (New York: Cambridge University Press, 1992), pp. 5–31; Brower, *The Russian City*, p. 144 and Roshanna Sylvester, 'Cultural Transgressions, Bourgeois Fears: Violent Crime in Odessa's Central Entertainment District', *Jahrbücher für Geschichte Osteuropas*, 44 (1996), 503–21.

intellectual life and the nascent public sphere.¹⁰ By the end of the nineteenth century, opportunities to earn their own living, to interact with others of their sex on the shop floor, in the classroom and in the dormitory and through charitable works, to contribute to the common good, had drawn a far more numerous and socially diverse range of Russia's women from the home.¹¹

There, some found the freedom from the constraints of custom and community that provided women, even lower-class women, unprecedented opportunities for redefining and expressing the self, according to some historians of urban culture. 'The city should be understood as offering a set of spaces for the everyday negotiation of self and identity', as Lynda Nead has put it.¹² The democratizing effects of consumerism contributed to the process. Even in the second quarter of the nineteenth century, merchant and wealthy townswomen living in Russia's provincial towns had adopted Western modes of dress in order to 'express their social identity' and distinguish themselves from the common people, despite official efforts to enforce *soslovie*-based standards of dress. By the century's end, working class women, too, had begun to dress and present themselves in the fashion of their social betters (and not, as in New York City, in 'hot-looking dresses' or the 'disorderly' shop floor fashion of their German counterparts), further blurring the social boundaries that separated elites from the masses and reducing the importance of social origins.¹³ New opportunities to express the self included sexual self-expression in Russia, where the cult of domesticity appears to have been less hegemonic than elsewhere in Europe. While some forms of Russia's mass urban entertainments might foster misogyny, other forms, including pulp fiction, music halls, pleasure gardens and theatre, encouraged women's emotional self-expression by exploring romantic love and sexual passion 'with an exuberance that

---

10. Lina Bernstein, 'Women on the Verge of a New Language: Russian Salon Hostesses in the First Half of the Nineteenth Century', in *Russia. Women. Culture*, ed. by Helena Goscilo and Beth Holmgren (Bloomington, IN: Indiana University Press, 1996), pp. 209–24.
11. Louise McReynolds and Cathy Popkin, 'The Objective Eye and the Common Good', in *Constructing Russian Culture*, pp. 57–99 (65–66).
12. Lynda Nead, 'Gender, Space and Modernity', in *Rewriting the Self: Histories from the Renaissance to the Present*, ed. by Roy Porter (New York: Routledge, 1997), pp. 167–85 (185).
13. Kuprianov, *Gorodskaia kul'tura*, pp. 330, 339, 349; Christine Ruane, 'Clothes Make the Comrade: A History of the Russian Fashion Industry', *Russian History/Histoire Russe*, 23 (1996), 311–43. For the comparison, see Barbara Alpern Engel, *Between the Fields and the City: Women, Work and Family in Russia, 1861–1914* (New York: Cambridge University Press, 1995), p. 155.

was historically unprecedented', in the words of Steve Smith.¹⁴ Among historians of Russia, Louise McReynolds has been particularly emphatic in her emphasis on the growth of the new 'middle' and on the liberating effects for women of modernization. Considering the pursuit of pleasure as one of modernization's key features, and incorporating into her definition of modernization forms of play such as theatre, dance halls, and other mass entertainments, she contends that these venues offered pleasure-seekers new ways of conceiving the self. For McReynolds, popular female figures, whether actresses such as Mariia Savina or singers like Anastasiia Vial'tseva, both personified and expanded the new possibilities. Thus, Vial'tseva, born a peasant in 1871, at the turn of the century sang bitter-sweet romances about sexual desire. She attracted hordes of worshipping fans and earned fabulous sums of money, which she spent lavishly and conspicuously on herself.¹⁵

Far less attention has been paid to how ordinary women actually experienced urban culture in its many forms or how urban culture might have affected their lives. Most of what we know focuses on the female population of Brower's 'migrant cities', and historians' observations, my own among them, are primarily negative. Historians have emphasized the hardships and sexual dangers that faced peasant women who left their villages, not unlike those faced by lower-class women elsewhere in Europe, too.¹⁶ We have drawn attention to the isolation from kin and community that, rather than liberating women, left them vulnerable to sexual predation and the shame of an out-of-wedlock pregnancy, and we have described a job market that provided only a limited range of poorly-paid and exploitative choices to women lacking skills. While acknowledging that an independent wage, however modest, might expand women's options and provide access to new ways of presenting, imagining and enjoying the self, we have stressed limitations, not opportunities.¹⁷ Studies of women

---

14. S. A. Smith, 'Masculinity in Transition: Peasant Migrants to Late-Imperial St Petersburg', in *Russian Masculinities in History and Culture*, ed. by Barbara Evans Clements, Rebecca Friedman and Dan Healey (New York: Palgrave, 2002), pp. 94–112 (105).
15. Louise McReynolds, *Russia at Play: Leisure Activities at the End of the Tsarist Era* (Ithaca, NY: Cornell University Press, 2003), pp. 5–6, 113–31; Louise McReynolds, 'The "Incomparable" Vial'tseva and the Culture of Personality', in *Russia. Women. Culture*, pp. 273–91.
16. Rachel Fuchs and Leslie Page Moch, 'Pregnant, Single, and Far from Home: Migrant Women in Nineteenth-Century Paris', *American Historical Review*, 95. 4 (1990), 1009–31.
17. Rose Glickman, *The Russian Factory Woman: Workplace and Society, 1880–1914* (Berkeley, CA: University of California Press, 1984); David Ransel, *Mothers of Misery: Child Abandonment in Russia* (Princeton, NJ: Princeton University Press, 1988); Engel, *Between the Fields and the City*.

of Russia's educated and cultured elites offer a more positive assessment of the impact of urban culture. To be sure, few such studies, whether of women students, professionals or participants in the women's movement, address the issue of urban culture as such. Nevertheless, there seems little question that the new and sometimes unconventional forms of female behaviour increasingly visible in cities served to expand the options of educated women and their opportunities for self-expression.[18]

In this article, I explore the question of the impact of urban culture by looking at the experience of women who belonged to a very different milieu, that of townspeople. These women occupied a social position below that of the educated elites but above that of peasants as exemplified by Evdokiia Kulikova, whose experience of urban freedom and its limitations I have examined elsewhere and who, as a seamstress earning her own living in the city, remained a member of Russia's labouring classes.[19] Urban born and bred, the women featured in this essay were candidates for membership in Russia's nascent and still tiny middle class. They represented a substantial segment of Russia's urban population: 21.2 per cent of the population of St Petersburg around the turn of the century, 19.4 per cent of the population of Moscow. Constituting 10.6 per cent of the population of the Russian empire overall, townspeople were the second largest social group in Russia after the peasantry. Townspeople were far the better educated. In St Petersburg, townswomen were roughly twice as likely as peasant women to be able to read and write, and thus better positioned to take advantage of urban opportunities and enjoy urban pleasures.[20]

Townswomen are a group to which historians have paid very little attention and historians of women, almost none.[21] The neglect is at

---

18. Bianka Pietrow-Ennker, *Russlands "neue Menschen": Die Entwicklung der Frauenbewegung von den Anfängen bis zur Oktoberrevolution* (Frankfurt: Campus, 1999); Irina Iukina, *Russkii feminizm kak vyzov sovremennosti* (St Petersburg: Aleteiia, 2008).
19. Barbara Alpern Engel, 'Freedom and its Limitations: A Peasant Wife Seeks to Escape her Abusive Husband', in *The Human Tradition in Imperial Russia*, ed. by Christine Worobec (Lanham, MD: Rowman and Littlefield, 2009), pp. 115–27.
20. Daniel Orlovsky, 'The Lower Middle Strata in Revolutionary Russia', in *Between Tsar and People*, pp. 248–68 (249–50). On comparative literacy, see *S.-Peterburg po perepisi 15 dekabria 1890*, 4 vols (St Petersburg: Gorodskaia uprava, 1891–92), ch. 1, vyp. 1, pp. 82, 84; *Petrograd po perepisi naseleniia 15 dekabria 1910 goda*, ed. by V. V. Stepanova (Petrograd: Gorodskaia uprava, 1914-), pp. 138–39. No end date is given. Publication remained incomplete.
21. In English, see Elise Kimerling Wirtschafter, *Social Identity in Imperial Russia* (DeKalb, IL: Northern Illinois University Press, 1997), pp. 134–36. In Russian, see Iurii M. Goncharov and Vadim S. Chutchev, *Meshchanskoe soslovie zapadnoi Sibiri vtoroi poloviny XIX-nachala XX v.* (Barnaul: Az Buka, 2004); A. N. Zorin et al., *Ocherki gorodskogo*

least partially the result of townspeople's complicated social profile: the group is a vivid example of the anachronistic character of Russia's system of ascribed social status. Those who belonged to the category of townspeople occupied a wide range of occupational niches. They might earn their living as merchants, tradespeople, and shopkeepers or as carpenters and other manual labourers, including factory workers and domestic servants. Although they were 'urban' by definition, at the close of the nineteenth century perhaps ten per cent of townspeople actually supported themselves by farming.

These significant economic and social differences notwithstanding, historians who have examined this group concur that its members shared a deep-seated conservatism, expressed in family practices as well as attitudes towards social and political change. Indeed, in many respects townspeople appear indistinguishable from the peasantry from which most of them, or their forebears, derived. Among townspeople, family patterns remained patriarchal in the traditional sense of the word, that is, they rested on the authority of the old over the young, as well as of men over women. Subject to the will of their parents, sons as well as daughters married according to parental wishes. Male heads of households controlled all household resources. Wife-beating was commonplace, tolerated by members of the community. Religious values shaped people's worldview, while sexual conduct, and especially the conduct of women, remained subject to stringent community scrutiny and control.[22] This milieu was likely to be especially inhospitable to female pleasure seeking, and strongly to resist female efforts to redefine and re-imagine the self.

Yet, as this essay will also show, attitudes towards female pleasure seeking appear to have grown more tolerant over time in this milieu, with urban culture and the more individualistic values of the marketplace having a discernible impact on some women. How typical the women were remains a question that a preliminary exploration such as this one cannot answer; nevertheless, their experience suggests at the very least that much more research is needed about

---

byta dorevoliutsionnogo Povolzh'ia (Ul'ianovsk: Izdatel'stvo Srednevolzhskogo nauchnogo tsentra, 2000); and Boris N. Mironov, *Sotsial'naia istoriia Rossii perioda imperii (XVIII-nachalo XX v.) Genezis lichnosti, demokraticheskoi sem'i, grazhdanskogo obshchestva i pravovogo gosudarstva*, 3rd edn, 2 vols (St Petersburg: Dmitrii Bulanin, 2003) I, 110–22; 332–45.

22. Goncharov, *Meshchanskoe soslovie*, pp. 126–36; Zorin et al., *Ocherki gorodskogo byta*, pp. 93–106; 291–92.

the culture of this group and the impact upon it of economic and related changes. At the same time, the anxieties such women aroused bear witness to the disturbing aspects of the economic and cultural changes underway, while the social and institutional strictures they encountered, which derived largely from the authoritarianism of the tsarist state, demonstrate the difficulties that might confront women who transgressed gendered norms of conduct.

Rather than undertaking a broad survey, this essay will examine the impact of urban culture through three case studies of townswomen who sought to redefine their lives and escape the constraints of their milieu. The first is set in the 1880s, the second in the 1890s, and the third in the aftermath of the revolution of 1905. The women who serve as my examples are very far from typical. As wives who sought to escape unsatisfactory marriages, they were by definition unusual in a society where divorce, adjudicated by religious rather than civil courts, carried a severe social stigma and remained highly restricted. The Orthodox Church, to which the women belonged, permitted divorce only for adultery, abandonment, sexual incapacity and penal exile, and even then only reluctantly. This prompted a substantial number of unhappily married women to appeal to a different venue. The three women's stories are drawn from the archive of the Imperial Chancellery for Receipt of Petitions (henceforward, the chancellery), which served as a kind of final court of appeals for unhappy wives unwilling or unable to satisfy the narrow grounds for divorce, but seeking release from the strictures of marital and passport law. Under Russian law, a wife owed her husband 'unlimited obedience' and required his permission before she could take a job, enrol in an educational institution or acquire the internal passport she needed to reside more than about fifteen miles from the husband's official place of residence. The law strictly forbade any action leading to the separation of spouses. Acting in the name of the tsar, the chancellery held the power to supersede the law forbidding spousal separation and, if investigation upheld her allegations, to allow a woman an internal passport of her own. Of the 30–40,000 unhappily married women who petitioned the tsar requesting separation between 1884 and 1914, roughly twenty-eight per cent were townswomen.[23]

---

23. On the chancellery and its officials, see Barbara Alpern Engel, 'In the Name of the Tsar: Competing Legalities and Marital Conflict in Late Imperial Russia', *Journal of Social History*, 77 (2005), 70–96.

The women who figure in this essay were atypical even of these, however. The vast majority of petitioners complained, with reason, of drunken, brutal and neglectful husbands, allegations upheld by members of their community. Couched in the language of submission, using 'the humble terms of the supplicant who trusts in the tsar's benevolence', women's petitions invariably presented the petitioner as a helpless victim of (male) abuse.[24] The petitions of the three women whose stories will be told below did, too. However, in their cases investigation revealed a more complicated story. These three women were not only – perhaps not even – victims, but in fact, nourished a taste for pleasure and desire for more from life, indeed a different life, than that of their parents or grandparents. The character of that 'more' and of the women's efforts to refashion their lives accordingly reflected the possibilities available to them in their urban settings, even as the institutional, social and cultural constraints that they faced remind us of the importance of context for understanding women's experience of cultural change. Life could be messier, much messier, than studies of cultural transformation by themselves sometimes indicate.

Liubov' Aleksandrova

Constraints provide the dominant theme in the story of Liubov' Aleksandrova. I regard her story as a good starting point, featuring as it does a literate young woman, capable of supporting herself economically, who displayed a manifest desire for pleasure and play – precisely the sort of woman for whom urban culture was likely to be enticing. But in her case, the pursuit of pleasure and desire to live as she chose was repeatedly thwarted by not only the legal constraints imposed by marriage but also limited opportunities and family and community strictures that operated even in urban areas, where women's conduct was both controlled and scrutinized far more intensively than men's.

The twenty-year old Liubov', daughter of a townswoman, petitioned the tsar in October 1882, seeking separation from Platon, her husband of two years. Platon was a widower thirty-four years Liubov''s senior, a retired soldier and member of the hairdressers' guild in Novgorod, the capital city of Novgorod province. He had been chosen by Liubov''s

---

24. Sheila Fitzpatrick, 'Editor's Introduction: Petitions and Denunciations in Russian and Soviet History', *Russian History/Histoire Russe*, 24 (1997), 1–9 (4, 6).

mother in a marriage the mother arranged and to which Liubov', although then earning her own living as a telegraph worker, dutifully acceded. Two years later, the dutifulness was no longer in evidence. Still very young and, in the opinion of the governor of Novgorod province, 'not unattractive', married to a man almost old enough to be her grandfather, Liubov' had a taste for good times that she indulged as best she could in a relatively small city such as Novgorod (primarily an administrative centre, with a population numbering just under 25,000). She visited the circus, drank more than was seemly during public gatherings and basked, if not more, in the attentions of other men, sometimes returning to her husband's roof in the small hours of the morning.[25] Such behaviour flagrantly violated the rules of female sexual decorum, for which male heads of households, in this instance her husband Platon, held responsibility. But when Platon sought to fulfill his masculine duty and discipline the wayward Liubov', chastising her physically as was customary in their milieu, she fled his household.

This is not the story Liubov' told the authorities, of course. In her petition seeking separation, Liubov', like other women appealing for relief, presented herself as an innocent and helpless victim of abuse. Platon beat and mistreated her and insulted her in public, she alleged. Once he even declared in the presence of others that Liubov' led 'an adulterous life'. So offensive to her was this statement that Liubov' had sued Platon for insult, an actionable offence in Russia, where a person's public standing depended upon her or his reputation.[26] Although Liubov' claimed to have won the case, the decision showed that in fact the couple had reconciled, probably as a result of evidence that came to light in the course of the trial which cast Liubov' in a very negative light.

Chief among that evidence were two undated letters from Liubov''s own mother, endeavouring in vain to bring the fun-loving Liubov' to heel. The letters offer vivid evidence of the modest public pleasures available in a small city as well as of the opprobrium attached to women who succumbed to them. Asserting the importance of female propriety, self-denial and self-command, the letters also bear witness to the ways that individual behaviour remained far from an individual matter. Subject to intensive community scrutiny, a person's misconduct might cast a shadow

---

25. *Rossiiskii gosudarstvennyi istoricheskii arkhiv* (RGIA), f. 1412, op. 212, d. 103 (Aleksandrova, 1881), l. 22.
26. RGIA, f. 1412, op. 212, d. 103, l. 1.

on others, on members of the offender's family first and foremost. 'Can it be that you don't value your reputation? Why do you let people judge you so harshly? Don't you know that our entire neighborhood condemns you for your drinking bout [*kutezh*] at the circus?' the mother rhetorically inquired.

'It is base and shameful of you to forget yourself that way and then to drag yourself home at three in the morning [...] It's sinful Liuda and God won't forgive you for the indecent way you behave. You're a young woman who should keep herself decent so that people will respect you and regard you as honourable and noble [*blagorodnaia*]. Don't you know that the very men who invite you for a drink at the buffet make fun of you behind your back? [...] Sooner or later you'll lose your good name and people will despise you!'[27]

The mother urged the daughter to accept her lot in life. In the mother's opinion Platon had been too gentle rather than too brutal with the errant Liubov': 'Platon is stupid and weak; someone else would have cast you off and everyone would have said good riddance'. The solution, in the mother's opinion, was strict adherence to domestic virtues and abandonment of unseemly pleasures. 'If you have the slightest family feeling towards me', the mother urged, 'then give up your foolishness and take a different path [...]. Stay closer to home and spend less time with your girlfriends [...]'. Most important of all: to make the best of one's circumstances, rather than trying to change them: 'Not everyone lives in heaven, and family happiness depends upon "our sister [*nasha sestra*]"'.[28]

Liubov', however, was unwilling to accept her circumstances or forsake her pleasures. Indeed, if the report of an investigator can be trusted – and it is by no means clear that it can – she continued to pursue those pleasures with characteristic verve. By 1886, Liubov' had made her way to St Petersburg and was living with her stepfather, having managed to obtain, either from her husband or from local authorities, the documents she needed to live temporarily on her own. Once again she asked the chancellery to intervene on her behalf, as her most recent passport was nearing expiry. The investigator recommended against it, certain that Liubov' had transgressed the porous boundary that separated a night on the town from sexual commerce.

---

27. RGIA, f. 1412, op. 212, d. 103, ll. 35–36.
28. RGIA, f. 1412, op. 212, d. 103, ll. 35, 36.

Women who violated sexual norms risked more than their reputation. Since 1843, Russian law, modelled on that of France, had required all women who 'traded in vice' to register with the police, carry a special passport (the 'yellow ticket') and submit to regular venereal examinations; women who peddled their favours without registering were classified as clandestine or 'secret' prostitutes, and if discovered, were often forced to register. A 'secret prostitute' was what the investigator called Liubov', although he provided no evidence that she obtained money in exchange for her favours or had sex with more than two men, at most. After she left her husband, he reported, Liubov' had invited one Solov'ev to spend time with her at a hotel; after that she lived with and was supported by a telegraph worker named Osipov in what appears (to this reader) to have been a consensual union.[29] All this was more than sufficient to convince officials that Liubov' was unworthy of the emperor's mercy. 'Although some of the evidence showed that she lived honourably in St Petersburg, investigation revealed that she engaged in "secret prostitution" and besides, cohabits with Osipov, on whose means she lives… On account of her immoral behaviour, she does not deserve sympathy', the report dated 28 October 1886 concluded, instructing the authorities to revoke Liubov''s temporary passport and deny her one thereafter.[30]

Over the months that followed, Liubov''s desperate attempts to reopen her case led nowhere. Since leaving Platon, Liubov' claimed she had reformed completely and had not taken a drink for nearly six years, as her former employer, a Mr Fall in the city of Novgorod, could attest. The investigation upheld her story. Various St Petersburg authorities affirmed that Liubov' now conducted herself in 'exemplary' fashion and was known to have done nothing 'disreputable'. Nevertheless, having made up their minds as to her immoral character, officials denied her petition. 'The petitioner cried bitterly', reported the policeman who conveyed the bad news to Liubov'. He endeavoured in vain to convince her to acknowledge her 'frivolous behaviour' and return to her husband. And on that gloomy note, the file ends.[31]

---

29. RGIA, f. 1412, op. 212, d. 103, l. 22. On regulated prostitution, see Laurie Bernstein, 'Yellow Tickets and State-Licensed Brothels: The Tsarist Government and the Regulation of Urban Prostitution', in *Health and Society in Revolutionary Russia*, ed. by Susan Gross Solomon and John F. Hutchinson (Bloomington: Indiana University Press, 1990), pp. 45–65 and Engel, *Between the Fields and the City*, pp. 166–97.
30. RGIA, f. 1412, op. 212, d. 103, ll. 42, 45.
31. RGIA, f. 1412, op. 212, d. 103, ll. 51, 54, 56.

Zinaida Agafonova

Constraints proved decisive in the case of Zinaida Agafonova, too. However, in her story the impact of urban culture is far more palpable, not only because the story unfolded in Moscow, a major urban centre where the possibilities for pleasure were more abundant, but also because it took place a decade later, when the cultural changes that accompanied urbanization and industrialization were considerably more advanced. In addition, Agafonova was in a far better position than Aleksandrova to take advantage of the opportunities the city offered. A woman who loved to enjoy herself – to dress in the latest fashions, dance, drink, and have a good time in the company of friends – Zinaida Agafonova also possessed the means to do so. This was a consequence of Russian property law, which by contrast with the laws of many Western countries, preserved married women's right to own and manage their own property rather than granting that right to the husband.[32] The daughter of a coachman and, like her husband, barely able to read and write, Zinaida had inherited a substantial sum of money at her wealthy grandmother's death in 1893.

At the same time, the milieu from which Zinaida derived was exceedingly traditional. Both she and Mikhail, the twenty-seven-year-old townsman she wed at her grandmother's behest at the age of seventeen, belonged to the branch of the priestless Old Believer faith attached to the Rogozhskii cemetery in Moscow. Old Belief was a schismatic branch of Orthodoxy barely tolerated by the government. Its family practices were even more hierarchical and rigid than those that prevailed elsewhere in the lower-middle class milieu. Following their marriage in 1889, the couple moved in with Mikhail's parents, traders in iron products who owned three houses in the city; the young couple remained there even after the birth of two daughters. When she inherited a fortune from her grandmother in 1893, Zinaida began to chafe at the ways that her husband and in-laws limited her pursuit of pleasure and a lavish lifestyle. Eager to obtain total control of her inheritance, of which her husband had been appointed guardian until she reached the age of thirty, Zinaida sought the freedom to arrange her life as she chose.

Zinaida's aspirations are evident even in her petition. It not only presented her as an innocent and helpless victim, but also asserted

---

32. Michelle Lamarche Marrese, *A Woman's Kingdom: Noblewomen and the Control of Property in Russia, 1700–1861* (Ithaca, NY: Cornell University Press, 2002).

rights to selfhood that fit rather awkwardly with the self-presentation of victimhood. 'I married Mikhail S. Agafonov and from the moment of my marriage my husband demanded that I transfer to him the capital that belongs to me. When I refuse, he insults me in a variety of ways', the petition began.[33] Submitted on 9 September 1894, it was composed by Zinaida and rewritten by a scribe, or so the petition claimed. In addition to emphasizing Zinaida's suffering at her husband's hands, the petition employed terms that echoed the language of the 'woman question', the movement for women's equality that began in the reign of Alexander II (1855–81) and reverberated ever more widely over the following decades. By the 1890s, watered-down versions of its ideas could be found even in popular magazines such as the widely read *Messenger of Fashion* (*Vestnik mody*), which questioned notions of women's inferiority and extolled women's achievements in fields such as medicine.[34] Comparable ideas had clearly reached Zinaida Agafonova. Her husband's cruel treatment was 'the result of [Mikhail's] ineradicable understanding that he is a man, and supposedly, this gives him the right to do with me as he pleases', the petition asserted. Abusing his authority, he had denied her 'the most ordinary pleasures', mistreating her even when she 'just wanted to leave the house to breathe fresh air or be with my acquaintances'. Invoking a 'freedom' to which she felt sufficiently entitled to refer to it in a petition to the tsar, she complained that Mikhail did everything in his power to wrest it from her.[35]

Zinaida's sense of entitlement and her desire to enjoy the 'ordinary pleasures' available to those with money, and consume as conspicuously as her resources allowed, elicited decidedly mixed reactions from those who knew her. That some responded critically was surely due, in part, to the undeniable fact that Zinaida's behaviour occasionally violated the rules governing female propriety and appeared disconcertingly unrefined. But then again, it is the opportunities for self-fashioning, rather than the forms that self-fashioning assumed, that for some historians constitute a positive dimension of urban culture.[36] The investigation of the case, which involved the summoning of multiple witnesses, unfolded over the course of fifteen

---

33. RGIA, f. 1412, op. 212, d. 30 (Agafonova, Z. 1894), l. 1.
34. Carolyn Marks, '"Providing Amusement for the Ladies": The Rise of the Russian Women's Magazine in the 1880s', in *An Improper Profession: Women, Gender and Journalism in Late Imperial Russia*, ed. by Barbara T. Norton and Jehanne Gheith (Durham, NC: Duke University Press, 2001), pp. 93–119 (110–12).
35. RGIA, f. 1412, op. 212, d. 30, l. 1.
36. McReynolds, *Russia at Play*, pp. 6–10.

months and yielded roughly two hundred pages of evidence retained in the chancellery's archive. It revealed not only the impact of urban culture on Zinaida Agafonova but also the anxieties that her behaviour aroused.

Zinaida's efforts to refashion her life required freeing herself from the constraints of her traditional, Old Believer milieu. Once she obtained her inheritance, she persuaded Mikhail to move out of his parents' dwelling and into an apartment of their own. There, free of her in-laws' restraining influence, Zinaida drew upon her wealth to mimic the lifestyle of her social betters. Thus, having been denied a 'nursemaid [*niania*]' for her two daughters while living with her husband's family, she hired not only a *niania* but also the more fashionable 'nursery governess [*bonna*]' and a governess – a noblewoman, no less. Zinaida frequently entertained guests in the evening with wine and snacks at the couple's apartment or at the dacha, that emblem of an urban middle-class leisured lifestyle, which they rented in Khimki during the summer, also at Zinaida's insistence, where someone played the piano and guests danced well into the night.[37] From the dacha, Zinaida frequently travelled by train to Moscow to spend the evening visiting pleasure gardens, restaurants and other commercial places of amusement. Her efforts to transform her way of life eventually extended to religion itself: a year after she petitioned, she left the Old Belief and formally converted to Russian Orthodoxy.

Zinaida's lavish lifestyle and pursuit of her own pleasure became a source of increasingly bitter conflict with her husband Mikhail, who, because he was still guardian of her fortune, was presented with the bills. Raised in a strict and parsimonious Old Believer milieu, poorly educated and 'undeveloped [*nerazvityi*]', as many witnesses put it (and indeed, his correspondence is filled with misspellings), Mikhail preferred to continue his parents' way of life. This meant spending money only when necessary and only on essentials, and investing the rest in his parents' business and the repair of their various properties. It enraged him when his wife engendered 'huge expenses', to use his words, 'throwing enormous balls, and buying various expensive drinks like port and Malaga wine, and cognac at six roubles a bottle or more, and other drinks, too'. Mikhail also suffered from jealousy. The presence of young men at the couple's evening parties provoked that feeling, as did his wife's habit of spending time alone with one Sergei Alekseev, a married merchant in whose company Zinaida travelled on trains and visited restaurants and

---

37. Stephen Lovell, *Summerfolk: A History of the Dacha, 1710–2000* (Ithaca, NY: Cornell University Press, 2003), pp. 4–5.

pleasure gardens. This behaviour prompted Mikhail to suspect that she was involved with Alekseev in a love affair (*amurnichala*, as Mikhail put it, creating his own verb from a noun). But Mikhail proved helpless to banish the man from his wife's presence.[38]

In his dismay at Zinaida's lifestyle, Mikhail was far from alone, however. Zinaida's self-indulgence and her flouting of gender proprieties troubled others as well. Their reactions suggest, at the very least, that in the view of many people the new emphasis on individual gratification had by no means displaced the long-standing insistence on female propriety and self-command. Zinaida openly spent lots of money, and '[refused] herself nothing', disapprovingly commented the man from whom the couple rented their dacha. Maria Vereshchagina, nineteen years of age and a distant relative of Zinaida's, who attended the dacha parties and sometimes played the piano for the assembled guests, came to dislike the 'lifestyle of that company' and thereafter ceased her visits. In the opinion of retired captain Sergei Mironov, a recent acquaintance of the Agafonovs, Zinaida's evening parties at the couple's apartment were more like 'drunken orgies'. The company was carelessly chosen and exclusively by the wife. At one such gathering, Mironov observed, Mikhail Agafonov knew only a single guest sufficiently well to introduce Mironov to him.[39]

But it was Zinaida's behaviour in Alekseev's company that elicited the most opprobrium. Alekseev often accompanied Zinaida on her evening outings to town, in the absence not only of Mikhail but also of Alekseev's own wife. Such behaviour flagrantly defied the norms of female propriety, not only those current in the Agafonovs' own highly conservative milieu, but also those set forth in the literature of advice aimed at those who aspired to gentility, which forbade married women even to attend dinner parties or the theatre unaccompanied by their husbands. If circumstances forced a respectable woman to appear in public with another man, he must be 'as respectable an escort as possible', literary guardians of propriety decreed.[40] Most witnesses in the Agafonov case expressed their doubts about Alekseev's respectability. Their critical comments suggest the stringent criteria applied to female behaviour and a level of public scrutiny comparable to that applied to Liubov' Alexandrova. Thus, the seventy-year-old townswoman

---

38. RGIA, f. 1412, op. 212, d. 30, ll. 60–2, 128, 145.
39. RGIA, f. 1412, op. 212, d. 30, ll. 100–01, 133, 155.
40. *Khoroshii ton: sbornik pravil i sovetov na vse sluchai zhizni obshchestvennoi i semeinoi*, 5th edn. (St Petersburg: German Goppe, 1910), p. 53.

who, with her son, lived at the neighbouring dacha expressed shock at how freely Zinaida conducted herself in public. The woman was in the habit of sitting on the terrace of her dacha knitting all day and so was privy to the goings-on next door. She witnessed how Zinaida sat right next to Alekseev in a carriage, tussled with him on the ground, and seemed always to be imbibing alcoholic beverages in his presence. She complained that on holidays, when guests would come from Moscow to visit, the company made lots of noise, drank cognac and carried on all night. Zinaida conducted herself 'quite indecently', in the neighbour's opinion. Such behaviour troubled several other dacha dwellers, too.[41]

But others disagreed. They found nothing amiss in Zinaida's conduct: in their view, she was enjoying the benefits of wealth in a socially appropriate fashion. If the couple were experiencing difficulties, these people blamed Mikhail, not Zinaida. Poorly educated, 'undeveloped', he was simply incapable of fulfilling the demands of his wife's more sophisticated lifestyle. Thus, in the opinion of Ivan Kulikov, another townsman, Mikhail's lack of education was at the root of the couple's problems: 'As an uneducated man, he was dissatisfied when his wife entertained guests with wine and snacks'. The children's governess criticized Mikhail, too: 'He considers her every little expenditure excessive, every meal an orgy and a glass of wine, drunkenness'. Some even defended Zinaida's habit of consuming alcohol, a matter on which the literature of advice had no light to shed. Judging moderate drinking perfectly acceptable, these witnesses regarded one, two or, even three glasses of spirits (*vino*) consumed in good company as nothing to make a fuss about. And while no one, with the notable exception of Alekseev's wife, condoned Zinaida's forays in the company of Alekseev alone, most of the witnesses who spoke in her favour chose to ignore that aspect of her conduct.[42]

So did chancellery officials, agents of a paternalistic and autocratic state though they were. While acknowledging the 'frivolity' of Zinaida's conduct in the company of Alekseev, they rejected allegations that the two were sexually involved. They also observed but refrained from judging her 'gay character, hospitality and love of company' and the lifestyle that reflected it, while deeming Mikhail coarse, uneducated, undeveloped and 'calculating to the point of miserliness'. What troubled them was Zinaida's extravagance, the 'superficial attitude towards life' that led her to spend enormous amounts of money pursuing her own pleasures to the neglect of

---

41. RGIA, f. 1412, op. 212, d. 30, ll. 133, 141, 142.
42. RGIA, f. 1412, op. 212, d. 30, ll. 145, 154, 155.

her children's economic future. This was the reason officials gave for denying Zinaida the 'freedom' she so ardently sought. Emphasizing the primacy of long-term family interests over the right of the individual to enjoy her property, they denied Zinaida's request for a passport and restored her to her husband's authority. However crude and stingy Mikhail might have been, he nevertheless displayed a 'much more serious attitude towards life' than his wife, in the view of officials. He would thus be far better able than she to guard the 'material interests' of their children and instil in them a comparable seriousness. And with that decision, the case came to a close.[43]

Lidiia Semenova

The case of Lidiia Semenova unfolded in a cultural environment in which the strictures on female conduct appear to have lessened in noteworthy ways. Although only slightly over a decade had passed since officials denied Agafonova a passport, these were the very years when the social and cultural changes associated with industrialization and urbanization became really palpable. They were reflected in the revolutionary upheavals of 1905 and intensified thereafter, as sex displaced politics at the centre of public debates.[44] After 1905, too, institutional restrictions on individual mobility, such as the stringent requirements for divorce and rules governing the internal passport, eased without disappearing entirely. In March 1914, for the first time, married women gained the right to an internal passport in their own name simply by requesting it.

Lidiia Semenova's story reflects both continuities and changes. Born in Riga, Latvia, her father a Latvian machinist on the railroad, her mother the daughter of a carpenter, she is the first of our subjects to have taken her marital fate in her own hands and defied the long-standing tradition that empowered parents or guardians to arrange the marriages of the young. In 1900, at the age of nineteen, she married over her parents' opposition a man ten years her senior, a supplier (*postavshchik*) for the Riga-Orel railroad line. Nikolai Semenov had won his bride by appealing to her thirst for pleasure and adventure. Although lacking the wherewithal to follow through, he enticed her with promises of a luxurious future and travel to the world renowned Paris Exhibition of 1900. Lidiia's misjudgement quickly became

---

43. RGIA, f. 1412, op. 212, d. 30, ll. 185–87.
44. Laura Engelstein, *The Keys to Happiness: Sex and the Pursuit of Modernity in Fin-de-Siècle Russia* (Ithaca, NY: Cornell University Press, 1992).

apparent. Poorly educated, crude and prone to violence, Nikolai made their marital life a misery. After six years, Lidiia left him to live with her parents, briefly reconciled with him for the sake of their two children, and then fled again, this time to live with her lover. The details of Lidiia Semenova's story and the outcome of her appeal reflect the changed atmosphere of the times, including the growing acceptance of individual gratification, most significantly sexual gratification, by important sectors of the public; even as her story demonstrates the continuing significance of institutional constraints on individual behaviour, these changes notwithstanding.[45]

As it had in the previous cases, the issue of women's sexual propriety figured prominently in the case of Lidiia Semenova. That Lidiia had become sexually involved with a man other than her husband there could be no question. The lover, N.M.K, as he is referred to in the chancellery's documents, was a townsman like the husband, employed by the Konshin textile magnates in Moscow. When exactly he became Lidiia's lover remains unclear, but that they were passionately involved is evident in the letters K. sent her, and which Nikolai purloined: 'I kiss you in the place that only I can kiss and press you to my breast', K. declared in one of them. Encouraging Lidiia to abandon Nikolai for good, K. instructed her on how best to obtain her freedom. First, she must gain Nikolai's permission to travel abroad; then, 'using all your knowledge and cleverness' demonstrate to him that if he could allow her to go off (*udirat'*) without him abroad, then Nikolai could also approve a long-term internal passport for her at home.[46] Several witnesses concurred that Lidiia had begun living with NMK after leaving her husband's roof.

But people also withheld judgment of this behaviour, perhaps because strictures had eased or perhaps because Semenova lived 'respectably' with K. Having conducted undercover surveillance of Lidiia's conduct, a Moscow police officer reported that she 'has a good character, and lives on the support of the Moscow townsman N.M.K., who is her lover'. Emphasizing that she had become involved (*soshlis'*) with her lover only *after* parting from her husband, the testimony of witnesses, too, indicates a greater hesitancy to condemn extra-marital sexual conduct, or at least extra-marital conduct eventuating in a stable union, than was evident in the previous cases. A retired Major-General, resident in Riga, declared 'categorically' that Lidiia had remained chaste before leaving her husband. And if she took a lover afterwards, he continued, 'then that is completely normal, a natural result of the coarse and vulgar behaviour

---

45. RGIA, f. 1412, op. 228, d. 35 (Semenova, 1906), ll. 1, 11, 26, 27.
46. RGIA, f. 1412, op. 228, d. 35, ll. 20–21.

of the husband'. A collegiate secretary resident in Moscow, another witness, likewise acknowledged without negative commentary her involvement with K., of whom the witness had 'the highest opinion'. The two planned to marry once Lidiia gained a divorce, he asserted.[47]

The change was even evident in the language of chancellery officials, albeit to a far lesser degree. Initially, they were staunch defenders of the chastity of wives whether or not they cohabited with their husbands and prepared to punish women who strayed by refusing them a passport, however brutal and neglectful the husband may have been and however 'respectable' the new relationship. In the mid-1890s, however, officials had begun to moderate their stance. The new moderation is evident in the language with which they described Semenova's behaviour and in the resolution of her case. After leaving Nikolai, the officials' decision declared, she had become involved in an 'illicit [*nezakonnaia*] attachment with K., with whom she continues to live', but otherwise had done 'nothing reprehensible'. As for Nikolai Semenov, he too had been unfaithful in 1907, having formed a 'criminal [*prestupnaia*] connection' with a domestic servant. In view of Semenova's own 'reprehensible conduct' (a reference to the liaison), officials were unwilling to approve her passport. But they did ensure that she would be able to live separately from her husband, obtaining permission for this from the Moscow City governor.[48] It thus remained difficult for Lidiia to travel about freely and impossible for her to go abroad as she had requested several times. But the governor's permission did preserve her from the police harassment so often endured by wives who lacked an internal passport in their own name.

Lidiia's individual freedom was further constrained by the stringent requirements for divorce. To be sure, these, too, had eased significantly by the early years of the twentieth century. Divorce had become far more accessible to moneyed couples prepared to collude in demonstrating adultery, the most common grounds for divorce.[49] But Nikolai Semenov was unwilling to collude, despite his wife's ardent appeals. In a letter of 24 October 1907, Lidiia had pleaded with him not to obstruct her divorce suit. Appealing to Nikolai's heart for the sake of the 'happy moments' that

---

47. RGIA, f. 1412, op. 228, d. 35, ll. 27, 31, 34.
48. RGIA, f. 1412, op. 228, d. 35, l. 36.
49. Gregory Freeze, 'Profane Narratives about a Holy Sacrament: Marriage and Divorce in Late Imperial Russia', in *Sacred Stories: Religion and Spirituality in Modern Russia*, ed. by Mark D. Steinberg and Heather J. Coleman (Bloomington: Indiana University Press, 2007), pp. 146–78.

perhaps she had provided him during their years together, she declared her unwillingness to return to him under any circumstances, in light of 'the hell that arose' when they lived together, especially towards the end. Since cohabitation was impossible, she requested her 'freedom' and begged Nikolai not to contest a divorce: 'Why should you cause me extra trouble, extra expenses – there is already a lot of grief and tears in this world. For the last time, I ask you not to oppose a divorce, and return my freedom to me'. Nikolai evidently refused. In 1910, when Lidiia appealed to the chancellery one final time, Nikolai was still her husband, and she was living on the short-term passports he permitted her.[50]

These three stories bear witness to the social mobility engendered by the changes of the late nineteenth century and offer support for both the positive and negative assessments of urban culture and its impact on women in Russia. On the positive side, the new and more individualized values of the marketplace appear to have fostered new desires and encouraged Agafonova and Semenova to assert them, much as consumer culture did for Tania, the young peasant woman whom Worobec depicts. But urban life and its blandishments offered all three of these pleasure-loving townswomen far more varied opportunities to indulge their desires than were to be found in a peasant village, and encouraged the three to break free of the constraints imposed by family and community and refashion their lives better to suit themselves. On the negative, the stories of Aleksandrova and Agafonova, in particular, provide evidence of the anxieties aroused by unattended – 'unowned' – women in the city, while that of Semenova suggests that over time, such anxieties may have eased.

But these three stories also draw attention to factors affecting the lives of women that cultural historians often neglect. It is true that the source base for this essay, women's appeals for marital separation, has a built-in bias towards structural limitations on freedom. These are not only failed marriages, but failed marriages in which the husband, for whatever reason, refused to permit his wife to live as she pleased. The sample omits couples that lived happily or parted amicably and leaves out single women altogether. Still, if the source base is biased, the limitations these stories reveal were real enough. They remind us that while cultural change may offer new ways of conceiving and expressing the self, individuals also act within the social and institutional structures of their particular time and place, which, like material realities, constrain as well as enable their choices.

---

50. RGIA, f. 1412, op. 228, d. 35, ll. 25, 41.

3. Russian Peasant Women's Culture: Three Voices

Christine D. Worobec

Beginning in the mid-1980s, the task of uncovering the culture of nineteenth-century Russian peasant women involved a search for women's voices in the ethnographic and literary sources of the time. Folk songs, proverbs, folktales and other expressions of oral culture, as well as the ritual practices associated with the life-cycle – baptism, courtship and marriage and death – recorded by educated observers and utilized in prose writing, infused life into otherwise faceless government statistics. In the period before the emancipation of the serfs in 1861, serfowners' accounts regarding taxpayers and their obligations, property, as well as household composition, performed a similar service.[1] After emancipation, records

---

The author would like to thank Stella Rock for her perceptive comments on an earlier draft and Christine Ruane for her invaluable advice about peasant women's clothing in the late Imperial period.

1. See Christine D. Worobec's revision of her 1984 dissertation *Peasant Russia: Family and Community in the Post-Emancipation Period* (Princeton: Princeton University Press, 1991), chapters 4 and 5 and her 'Death Ritual among Russian and Ukrainian Peasants: Linkages between the Living and the Dead', in *Cultures in Flux: Lower-Class Values, Practices, and Resistance in Late Imperial Russia*, ed. by Stephen P. Frank and Mark D. Steinberg (Princeton: Princeton University Press, 1994), pp. 11–33; Barbara Alpern Engel, 'Peasant Morality and Pre-Marital Relations in Late Nineteenth-Century Russia', *Journal of Social History* 23.4 (1990), 695–714 and M. M. Gromyko, *Mir russkoi derevni* (Moscow: Molodaia gvardiia, 1991). Even Steven L. Hoch who complained about the unreliability of ethnographic sources found himself utilizing them to explain the practice of brideprice on the Gagarin estate of Petrovskoe. See his *Serfdom and Social Control in Russia: Petrovskoe, a Village in Tambov* (Chicago: University of Chicago Press, 1986), pp. 97–103. David L. Ransel eschewed the use of ethnographic sources in his *Mothers of Misery: Child Abandonment in Russia* (Princeton: Princeton University Press, 1988), but eventually did an important

from newly-established *volost'* (township) courts supplemented both official sources and ethnographic materials. These transcripts provided a sense of the issues that concerned peasant women, including spousal abuse, personal and familial reputation, control over their dowries and their children's parental obligations.[2] In navigating rich ethnographic sources, historians understood those sources' limitations. The static nature of the written form had obviously robbed the materials of their creativity and constantly evolving use of wordplay. Furthermore, recorded oral traditions represented sanitized versions of the originals. Not only had Russia's strict censorship laws prohibited the printing of anything that smacked of a bawdy or political nature, but peasants wary of the educated observers' intrusion into their lives had tailored their responses to what they thought the ethnographers wanted and expurgated information that might have had adverse implications for their communities.[3]

Systematic examination of evolving ethnographic practices and the representations of peasant culture by an educated elite had to wait until the post-structural turn began to influence Russian historical writing in the West, beginning in the 1990s. Works by Cathy Frierson and Stephen P. Frank, for example, demonstrated the fact that observers of the countryside had their own agendas and prejudices that dictated which oral sources they would record and how exactly they would portray Russian peasant life. Contradictory images of peasant women as temptresses and viragos, on

---

edition and translation (with the help of Michael Levine) of the ethnographer Ol'ga Semenova Tian-Shanskaia's *Zhizn' Ivana: ocherki iz byta krest'ian odnoi iz chernozemnykh gubernii* (St Petersburg: Imperatorskoe russkoe geograficheskoe obshchestvo po otdeleniiu etnografii, 1914) together with some of her unpublished writings under the title *Village Life in Late Tsarist Russia: An Ethnography by Olga Semyonova Tian-Shanskaia* (Bloomington: Indiana University Press, 1993). Ransel found Tian-Shanskaia's writings more reliable than those of other Russian ethnographers because she provided a fairly bleak description of Russian peasant life.

2. For work on the township courts (which were presided over by peasant judges who were supposed to rule on the basis of both the written law and customary law) and peasant women's issues, see in particular Jane Burbank, *Russian Peasants Go to Court: Legal Culture in the Countryside, 1905–1917* (Bloomington: Indiana University Press, 2004); Beatrice Farnsworth, 'The Litigious Daughter-in-Law: Family Relations in Rural Russia in the Second Half of the Nineteenth Century', *Slavic Review* 45.1 (1986), 49–64; 'The Soldatka: Folklore and Court Record', *Slavic Review* 49.1 (1990), 58–73; Gareth Popkins, 'Code vs. Custom? Norms and Tactics in Peasant Volost Court Appeals, 1889–1917', *Russian Review* 59.3 (2000), 408–24 and Worobec, *Peasant Russia*, chapter 6.

3. Aleksandr N. Afanas'ev's collection of bawdy tales, *Russkie zavetnye skazki*, could not be published in Russia, but rather had to be published anonymously in Geneva in 1872. See 'Translator's Foreward', in Afanas'ev's *Erotic Tales of Old Russia*, ed. and trans. by Yury Perkov (Oakland: Scythian Books, 1988), p. 13.

the one hand, and as meek virgins, on the other hand, coexisted uneasily with one another, both within peasant culture and in representations of that culture.[4] While most contemporary descriptions of the late nineteenth century decried these women's backwardness, others (often from the one and the same author) complained about women's brazen independence and growing consumerism, which the educated elite believed was threatening traditional peasant culture.

Of a more serious nature was the fact that the dominant ethnographic representations of the nineteenth century focused on what their authors considered to be 'traditional' or 'authentic' peasant culture, a culture that had to be stripped of any associations with, or influences from, elite and official cultures. In retrospect that sanitization appears to be an impossible task.[5] In essence, this search for authenticity translated into recording cultural artefacts supposedly untainted by written culture, on the one hand; on the other hand, it dictated a focus on rituals and practices that were denounced by the Russian Orthodox ecclesiastical hierarchy as being 'superstitious' and even 'pagan' (a term that churchmen used very loosely). At the same time, non-clerical writers searching for pagan remnants and magical practices left unrecorded those 'superstitious' religious practices, such as excessive veneration of saints' uncorrupted bodies, which they deemed to be too Christian for their tastes.[6] The resulting partial

---

4. Stephen P. Frank, 'Confronting the Domestic Other: Rural Popular Culture and Its Enemies in *Fin-de-Siècle* Russia', in *Cultures in Flux*, pp. 74–107 and Cathy Frierson, *Peasant Icons: Representations of Rural People in Late Nineteenth-Century Russia* (Oxford: Oxford University Press, 1993), chapter 8. See also Nathaniel Knight, 'Science, Empire, and Nationality: Ethnography in the Russian Geographical Society, 1845–1855', in *Imperial Russia: New Histories for the Empire*, ed. by Jane Burbank and David L. Ransel (Bloomington: Indiana University Press, 1998), pp. 108–41 and Christine D. Worobec, 'Temptress or Virgin? The Precarious Sexual Position of Women in Post-Emancipation Ukrainian Peasant Society', *Slavic Review*, 49.2 (1990), 227–38. For a critical analysis of the populist writer Gleb Uspenskii's writings on Russian peasant women (1843–1902), see Henrietta Mondry, *Pure, Strong and Sexless: The Peasant Woman's Body and Gleb Uspensky* (Amsterdam: Rodopi, 2006) and her comparison of Uspenskii's and Anton Chekhov's writings in her 'Peasant Women's Sexualities in the Writings of Gleb Uspenskii and Anton Chekhov', *Essays in Poetics*, 31 (2006), 258–71. For a pioneering examination of Russian medical doctors' belief in the sexual purity of Russian peasant women, see Laura Engelstein, 'Morality and the Wooden Spoon: Russian Doctors View Syphilis, Social Class, and Sexual Behavior, 1890–1905', *Representations*, 14 (1986), 169–208.
5. Carlo Ginsburg's classic *The Cheese and the Worms: The Cosmos of a Sixteenth-Century Miller*, trans. by John Tedeschi and Anne Tedeschi (Baltimore: Johns Hopkins University Press, 1980) demonstrates the ways in which a miller brought before the Inquisition was influenced by written culture.
6. Ironically, revolutionary groups after emancipation were more sympathetic to the religious practices and rituals of Old Believers and sectarians than those of Orthodox

sanitization of nineteenth-century Russian peasant culture and the artificial binary opposition between peasant and elite cultures have had unfortunate ramifications for our understanding of nineteenth-century peasant culture in general and peasant women's culture in particular.

Uncritical readings of nineteenth-century ethnographic materials have resulted in the perpetuation of the myth that Russian peasant society subscribed to *dvoeverie* or dual faith, in which pagan beliefs co-existed with Christian beliefs, or, worse yet, in which Christian beliefs amounted to nothing more than a veneer overlaying ancient beliefs. 'The persistence and ubiquity' of this concept of dual faith 'have encouraged an unhelpful preoccupation' in scholarship 'with identifying latent paganism in Russian culture and spirituality'.[7] On the basis of nineteenth-century sources, Joanna Hubbs, a specialist in Russian cultural studies, has, for example, argued for the existence in that century of a resistant matriarchal peasant women's culture that had its foundations in the goddess culture of the pre-Christian era. According to Hubbs, the Mother of God and St Paraskeva, as well as other Christian elements, were merely evolutionary stages that involved the assimilation of pagan deities.[8]

Eve Levin's seminal critique of the notion of dual faith, and her invitation to scholars of early modern Russia to learn from their Western European counterparts in understanding the ways in which Christianity co-opted paganism and transformed it, have largely succeeded in dampening enthusiasm for the concept, at least among historians.[9] Through textual

---

peasants, but only insofar as they believed that these peasant groups, by virtue of their being divorced from the official church, were revolutionary by nature and, therefore, more likely to follow calls for the overthrow of the autocracy. See Alexander Etkind, 'Whirling with the Other: Russian Populism and Religious Sects', *Russian Review* 62.4 (2003), 565–99.

7. Stella Rock, *Popular Religion in Russia: 'Double Belief' and the Making of an Academic Myth* (London: Routledge, 2007), p. 1.
8. Joanna Hubbs, *Mother Russia: The Feminine Myth in Russian Culture* (Bloomington: Indiana University Press, 1988), pp. 100–23. For other uncritical readings of nineteenth-century ethnographic materials and acceptance of dual faith as reflective of peasant beliefs, see Linda J. Ivanits, *Russian Folk Belief* (Armonk, NY: M. E. Sharpe, 1989) and Elizabeth A. Warner, 'Russian Peasant Beliefs and Practices Concerning Death and the Supernatural Collected in Novosokol'niki Region, Pskov Province, Russia, 1995', *Folklore* 111.1–2 (2000), 67–90.
9. Eve Levin, '*Dvoeverie* and Popular Religion', in *Seeking God: The Recovery of Religious Identity in Orthodox Russia*, ed. by Stephen K. Batalden (DeKalb: Northern Illinois University Press, 1993), pp. 29–52. For examples of work that eschew the concept of *dvoeverie* underlying popular religiosity, see Chris Chulos, *Converging Worlds: Religion and Community in Peasant Russia, 1861–1917* (DeKalb: Northern Illinois University Press, 2003); Gregory L. Freeze, 'Institutionalizing Piety: The Church and Popular

evidence and that of material culture, she has demonstrated that the cult of St Paraskeva, prevalent not only in Russia but also in the Balkan Peninsula, had medieval Christian origins and was emphatically not 'a manifestation of living paganism'. Neither was Paraskeva 'just a pagan goddess with a new name'. Russian peasant women who venerated St Paraskeva and associated her with spinning, among other domestic duties, 'staunchly identified themselves as Christian'. Furthermore, popular and ecclesiastical representations of the saint were closely linked.[10] Similarly, Vera Shevzov's exploration of Marianism in late Imperial Russia demonstrates conclusively the ways in which 'a rich liturgical tradition' helped construct a 'Marian-centred culture'. The lay veneration of Mary, particularly among women who found in Mary a sympathetic intercessor and protectress who understood their positions as virgins, pregnant women and mothers, was not confined to peasant women. However, rural women figured prominently in the miracle tales associated with the Mother of God icons. Those stories 'allow us to see Mary working among those who at the time had little voice in the Church's establishment and whose experiences and thoughts are thereby harder to unearth'.[11] Finally, Stella Rock's definitive exposé of dual faith should lay to rest folklorists' obsession with trying to uncover pagan and 'indigenous' elements in contemporary Russia, when folklorists of other cultures have largely abandoned the attempt to 'reconstruct [...] pre-Christian belief system[s]'. Rock convincingly argues that in the medieval and early modern periods the term did not pertain to dual belief as being an amalgam of paganism and Christianity but rather to Christian 'believers who accept[ed] the validity of other denominations [mainly catholicism and later lutheranism], or parts of their doctrine, and believers who [cast] doubt [upon] aspects of the one true Orthodox faith'. As in Western Europe, Rock points out, 'medieval clerics were more

---

  Religion, 1750–1850', in *Imperial Russia*, pp. 210–49; Robert H. Greene, *Bodies Like Bright Stars: Saints and Relics in Orthodox Russia* (DeKalb: Northern Illinois University Press, 2010); Brenda Meehan, 'To Save Oneself: Russian Peasant Women and the Development of Women's Religious Communities in Prerevolutionary Russia', in *Russian Peasant Women*, ed. by Beatrice Farnsworth and Lynne Viola (New York: Oxford University Press, 1992), pp. 121–33; Vera Shevzov, *Russian Orthodoxy on the Eve of Revolution* (New York: Oxford University Press, 2004) and Christine D. Worobec, *Possessed: Women, Witches and Demons in Imperial Russia* (DeKalb: Northern Illinois University Press, 2001).

10. Eve Levin, 'The Christian Sources of the Cult of St Paraskeva', in *Letters from Heaven: Popular Religion in Russia and Ukraine*, ed. by John-Paul Himka and Andriy Zayarnyuk (Toronto: University of Toronto Press, 2006), pp. 126–45 (126–28).
11. Shevzov, *Russian Orthodoxy*, Chapter 5, pp. 217, 233.

concerned with pastoral matters and ecclesiastical discipline than with fighting obdurate paganism'.[12]

In addition to perpetuating myths about peasants' spirituality, the separation out of supposedly 'pure' indigenous peasant practices from other influences, including high culture, obscures the dramatic changes of the nineteenth century. Peasant migration was fairly widespread already in the late stages of serfdom and development of capitalist relationships. As Boris Gorshkov reminds us, 'many scholars remain unaware that observers of the late eighteenth- and early nineteenth century often portrayed Russia's peasants as habitually on the move'. These 'observers, [both] Russian and foreign, described roads jammed at various times of the year with peasants heading in all directions for trade and work'.[13] They were day-labourers, entrepreneurs, and middle men and women engaged in a variety of cottage industries, including wet-nursing. Rural communities of coachmen and women were established as early as the fifteenth century and existed late in the nineteenth century to deliver government officials and information from community to community.[14] Travel on Russia's roads only increased after emancipation, as did the growing interconnectivity between urban centres and the rural hinterlands. Peasant families increasingly supplemented agricultural and domestic industry with trades associated with outmigration, and the steamboat and railroad made travel to distant religious sites, as well as urban centres, cheaper and safer, although groups of peasants still made the trek on foot. By the end of the nineteenth century, as Barbara Alpern Engel has demonstrated, women's migration to the cities increased considerably, in response to a surplus rural population and as

---

12. On the folklorists' quest for 'indigenous' elements in the post-Soviet period, see Natalie Kononenko, *Slavic Folklore: A Handbook* (Westport, Conn.: Greenwood, 2007), p. 6. Quotations from Rock: *Popular Religion*, pp. 85, 140. Elizabeth Warner explains folklorists' emphasis on 'the unusual tenacity' of pagan practices as resulting from 'the sheer vastness of the Russia that lay beyond the centres of civilisation and the relative lack of missionary zeal of the Orthodox Church'. See her *Russian Myths* (Austin: University of Texas Press, 2002), p. 78. There is a tendency, however, to underestimate the knowledge that believers had of Orthodox principles and the effect of extraliturgical work that Orthodox clerics undertook in the nineteenth-century. For a discussion of extraliturgical activities see Gregory L. Freeze, 'The Rechristianization of Russia: the Church and Popular Religion, 1750–1850', *Studia Slavica Finlandensia*, 7 (1990), 101–36 and Shevzov, *Russian Orthodoxy*, pp. 78–79.
13. Boris B. Gorshkov, 'Serfs on the Move: Peasant Seasonal Migration in Pre-Reform Russia, 1800–61', *Kritika*, 1.4 (2000), 627–56.
14. John Randolph, 'The Singing Coachman or, The Road and Russia's Ethnographic Invention in Early Modern Times', *Journal of Early Modern History* 11.1–2 (2007), 33–61.

urban job opportunities, especially in the service industries, expanded.¹⁵ Increasing literacy (even if at a lower rate among peasant women than among men) and an exploding print culture facilitated peasants' mobility for religious and labour reasons. They also created a bridge between urban and rural cultures.¹⁶ Even an illiterate person could profit from information read out loud in the home or tavern.

In the current scholarship, whilst far more sensitive to the religiosity of the Russian peasantry in daily life than the social histories written prior to the late 1990s, there is nonetheless a tendency to separate out religious from the economic and social history.¹⁷ In spite of the demand for ever growing interdisciplinarity, scholars of religion and scholars of the Russian peasantry are trained differently and focus on different things. Social historians, for example, are far more sensitive to class divisions than scholars of religion, when discussing lived religion or religion as practiced among a variety of classes.¹⁸ It is the rare person who crosses all the disciplines, yet cross we must if we are to obtain a holistic sense of Russian peasant culture and the influences upon it.

Finding women's voices among the nineteenth-century Russian peasantry remains the historian's goal to this day, a goal that is made exceedingly difficult by the fact that peasant women did not leave memoirs, and that too much time has passed for scholars to carry out

---

15. Barbara Alpern Engel, *Between the Fields and the City: Women, Work, and Family in Russia, 1861–1914* (Cambridge: Cambridge University Press, 1995).
16. For works on the impact of literacy see Jeffrey Brooks, *When Russia Learned to Read: Literacy and Popular Culture, 1861–1917* (Princeton: Princeton University Press, 1985) and Chulos, *Converging Worlds*. Peasant women's literacy rate was approximately one quarter that of men. See David Moon, *The Russian Peasantry, 1600–1930: The World the Peasants Made* (London: Longman, 1999), p. 348.
17. For a pioneering book that integrates religious with other aspects of Russian village life, see M. M. Gromyko and A. V. Buganov, *O vozzreniiakh russkogo naroda* (Moscow: Palomnik, 2000). The historical anthropologist Douglas Rogers has reintegrated religious thinking with social and economic history by focusing on the ethical choices that Old Believers of the town Sepych in Perm' region made as they confronted major economic and social changes from the founding of the community in the late seventeenth-century until the present day. See his pathbreaking *The Old Faith and the Russian Land: A Historical Ethnography of Ethics in the Urals* (Ithaca: Cornell University Press, 2009).
18. Chulos's *Converging Worlds* is a model of looking at the changing religious practices of peasants in a dynamic world. Vera Shevzov is sensitive to the rural parish but argues rightly that the ecclesial community embraced more than peasants; it included all believers, including clerics. See her *Russian Orthodoxy*, p. 10. Nadieszda Kizenko is sensitive to class but notes that in deciphering written confessions, it is often difficult to determine class identity. See her 'Written Confessions and the Construction of Sacred Narrative', in *Sacred Stories: Religion and Spirituality in Modern Russia*, ed. by Mark D. Steinberg and Heather J. Coleman (Bloomington: Indiana University Press, 2007), pp. 93–118 (104–07).

oral histories for generations born before the 1917 revolutions.[19] Peasant women's biographical details still have to be teased out of sources that they did not create entirely on their own and that were mediated by others, be they miracle tales recording the healing of various diseases and bodily afflictions through the intercession of saints and the Mother of God; be they medical or, by the late nineteenth and early twentieth century, psychiatric case studies; or be they lengthy trial depositions and divorce narratives, sources that have only recently become the subject of analysis.[20]

At least now, however, secular and magical folkloric materials, the provenance of which is not always known, are being supplemented by these other types of sources, some of them religious in nature. As David Ransel has pointed out in his oral histories of peasant women's childbearing and rearing practices in the twentieth century, women have insisted upon their infants' baptism for the religious safety it accorded the children. In the case of a difficult birth, 'if the women did not shout "Ours!" then the "evil spirit" would take it'. Because Russian ethnographers usually exclude non-canonical folk beliefs from the classification 'religious', Ransel argues, 'they misread this behaviour as something other than baptism – and baptism, in turn, as something other than this decisive claim of a child for the faith'.[21] Furthermore, there is a growing realization among scholars that beliefs in magic and the sacred could and did 'coexist' in believers' minds and that the line between the two was often blurred.[22] A study of practices and rituals among Russian peasant women has accordingly to be sensitive

---

19. David Ransel's *Village Mothers: Three Generations of Change in Russia and Tataria* (Bloomington: Indiana University Press, 2000) is a pioneering oral history of Russian peasant and Tatar women's experiences of birthing and mothering that can serve as a model for future oral history projects for generations born after 1917. Ransel's first cohort of interviewees included women born before 1912, while the second and third generational cohorts were born between 1912 and 1930, and after 1930 respectively.
20. For use of these types of sources see Barbara Alpern Engel, 'Freedom and Its Limitations: A Peasant Wife Seeks to Escape Her Abusive Husband', in *The Human Tradition in Imperial Russia*, ed. by Christine D. Worobec (Lanham, Maryland: Rowman and Littlefield, 2009), pp. 115–27; Barbara Alpern Engel, 'In the Name of the Tsar: Competing Legalities and Marital Conflict in Late Imperial Russia', *Journal of Modern History*, 77.1 (2005), 70–96; Gregory L. Freeze, 'Profane Narratives about a Holy Sacrament: Marriage and Divorce in Late Imperial Russia', in *Sacred Stories*, pp. 146–78; Christine D. Worobec, 'Miraculous Healings', in *Sacred Stories*, pp. 22–43 and Worobec, *Possessed*, chapter 4.
21. Ransel, *Village Mothers*, p. 177.
22. In describing the content of written confessions of sin, Kizenko subscribes to the notion of the magic and sacred coexisting with one another but would not agree with my premise that the line between magic and the sacred was sometimes blurred: Kizenko, 'Written Confessions', 109. For a fuller explanation of my argument with regard to the connection between demonic possession and sorcery, see my *Possessed*, pp. 64–68, 69–86.

not only to folkloric elements, but also to canonical and non-canonical beliefs. Thus, for example, Andrei Toporkov has demonstrated the ways in which Russian 'charms reside at the intersection of [the] Christian church and folkloric knowledge'. There are 'canonical and non-canonical prayers [apocrypha]' on one end of the continuum and 'folkloric-magical texts on the other'. Charms that fall in the middle of the two extremes, Toporkov argues, reflect influences of both.[23] Furthermore, Alla Astakhova notes that 'canonical prayers always accompany the charms intoned in the process of curing', and the charms themselves may be akin to prayers if they are founded upon 'spiritual verse' and invoke 'Christian personae'. Even the charms' recitation on the part of women healers follows clerical practice.[24] Such recognition of the potency of Christian beliefs among peasant women in spite of occasional nineteenth-century clerical pronouncements to the contrary, and absence from most ethnographic records, can only move our research on Russian peasant women forward.

An extremely rare source – correspondence by three literate Russian peasant women of two generations – has come to light through the perseverance of linguist Professor Olga T. Yokoyama, who found in the Tiumen' branch of the Russian State Archive an unusual set of letters written between 1881 and 1896 mainly by members of the Zhernokov family. The correspondents, Elizaveta Dmitr'evna Zhernokova (née Bekhtereva, 1839–1918), her sister Liubov' Dmitr'evna Rodigina (née Bekhtereva, 1845–1926), and her daughter Tat'iana Lavrovna (b. 1876; married name Stefanova) were Russian Orthodox believers residing in the southern part of Viatka province in the northeast corner of European Russia. The Zhernokovs, Bekhterevs, and Rodigins had all been state peasants prior to emancipation, which meant that they had not experienced serfdom. The three women and their menfolk sent letters to Elizaveta's son Vasilii, who worked in the Western Siberian town of Tiumen', located on the Tura River.[25] Although the three women cannot be representative of all peasant women, their letters' content illuminates

---

23. A. Toporkov, 'Russian Love Charms in a Comparative Light', trans. by Sibelan E. S. Forrester, in *Charms, Charmers and Charming: International Research on Verbal Magic*, ed. by Jonathan Roper (Basingstoke: Palgrave, 2009), pp. 121–44 (125).
24. Alla Astakhova, '"Sound Shaping" of East Slavic Zagovory', *Oral Tradition*, 7.2 (1992), 365–72 (371).
25. *Russian Peasant Letters: Texts and Contexts*, ed. and trans. by Olga T. Yokoyama, 2 vols (Wiesbaden: Harrassowitz, 2008). My analysis of these letters is indebted to the painstaking work of Yokoyama and her assistants. All translations of the letters that I cite are by Yokoyama from this source. Volume and page numbers follow the quotations in the text.

a rapidly changing socio-economic world and a broader culture than one that is distinctly peasant, some of the contours of which are familiar to scholars and some of which are less familiar.

The correspondence, as we shall see, documents a culture that mixes the sacred and profane. As was typical of the formal writing of Orthodox believers of other classes, religious salutations and references to God are ubiquitous. Elizaveta was a devout woman who often went on pilgrimage, but when she gave one of her sons marital advice she quoted the text of a popular nineteenth-century Russian poem and song. Her daughter Tat'iana was well-educated for a peasant girl. Being of marrying age, she was more preoccupied by the figure that she cut in society, the clothes that she wore, and her dowry's content. However, she too made religious references and eventually married a cleric. The single letter of Elizaveta's sister Liubov' reflects only a pious nature, befitting a woman who, after her husband's death, founded a women's religious community.

Through an analysis of these letters, I would like to demonstrate ways in which peasant women's culture needs to be investigated further. We need to eschew our older searches for the 'authentic' peasant and arguments about whether traditionalism, individualism, or collectivism characterized the Russian peasantry. We may even have to abandon our notion that there is such a thing as a 'peasant culture' or a 'peasant world view'. So many influences were at play on peasant villages. These localities were never the isolated oases that we have sometimes imagined them to be. There was always a great deal of peasant movement, which manifested itself either in travel outside the village for work, to markets and on pilgrimages to religious sites both near and far, or in movement from one occupational status to another in the social hierarchy.

In the Zhernokovs we see a family that experienced economic hardship as well as upward mobility, so even in peripheral places near and in Western Siberia, there was incredible dynamism. Capitalist consumerism had certainly penetrated Tiumen' and raised expectations among peasants of an upwardly mobile life. The Zhernokovs lived in the modest fishing and agricultural village of Pazdery in the south of Viatka province, a village that had previously 'belonged to the royal household'. By 1914 it had a population of over 1,000 and had had a *zemstvo* (secular elementary) school for several decades. The town of Sarapul, 50 *versts* (about 50 kilometres) away, and its 'leather dressing industry' served as a magnet for migrant labourers (II, 407–08). When we meet the Zhernokovs in the early 1880s, Elizaveta and her husband Lavr Andreevich (1836–1909) had moved down the social ladder. Shortly after their marriage in 1863, Lavr had a certificate identifying him as a temporary merchant. However, by the early 1880s Elizaveta and Lavr were extremely poor farmers, and had started up a supplementary business transporting goods by river (I, 16). According to Lavr, writing on 16 February 1882, 'We live not wealthily. We have no horse.... The delivery [business] brings little profit, there isn't even enough for household expenses'. He had to ask his itinerant second son Vasilii (1864–1936) for 'money by Easter, because we must buy seeds of wheat, oats, and various other seeds for sowing' (II, 230, 231). That business would, nevertheless, result in the family's growing prosperity, the opening of a village dry-goods store in 1883 and the purchase and renting of steamboats in the late 1880s to transport liquor and potatoes (I, 16, 18). By the mid-1880s the eldest son Aleksei, who had returned from Tiumen', was increasingly in charge of the family business as his father developed a drinking problem. Even with these changes, the parents' economic circumstances were precarious enough that they were dependent on their second son for spending money (II, 285). In another upward move in 1892 the Zhernokovs were able to open their own liquor store and pub in Pazdery. Shortly thereafter, Aleksei moved his nuclear family (wife and seven children) to Sarapul, the base of the family's expanding transportation business. By 1894 the family's enterprises in Pazdery were shut down and their agricultural land and horses sold, leaving the parents Elizaveta and Lavr renting land and 'almost completely dependent on their children' for money and management of their household economy (I, 20, 22).

In 1881, the beginning of the extant correspondence, Elizaveta and Lavr's household was of the extended variety, a not uncommon structure for peasants whose aging parents were widowed. It continued to grow for several years. Apart from two older sons living in Tiumen', they had three younger sons ranging between the ages of nine and fourteen and a daughter, aged four, as well as Lavr's sixty-six-year-old mother, Praskov'ia Vasil'evna Stefanova (d. 1889), who had had Lavr out of wedlock and had never married, living with them. The three-generational family expanded again in 1882 when Lavr's elderly stepmother Tat'iana Grigor'evna Zhernokova (family name at birth unknown) joined them. That same year Elizaveta gave birth to a baby girl, but the child did not survive.[26] Finally, Elizaveta and

---

26. Lavr had been adopted by Andrei Iakimovich Zhernokov.

Lavr's son Aleksei returned to Pazdery in 1883, soon brought a wife from Perm' into the household and yet another son was born to Elizaveta and Lavr in 1884 (I, 15, 16). Eventually, Aleksei and his wife had seven children, all of whom found a place in the patrilocal extended household. By 1889, the family's significant growth required the expansion and renovation of the house so that it had two stories. The more spacious home still, however, required Aleksei and his nuclear family to sleep in one room.

Both Elizaveta and Lavr identified themselves in the 1897 all-national census as 'self-taught [and] literate', although in their correspondence they generally relied on peasant relatives as scribes (I, 2). Most of their letters were addressed to their second son, Vasilii, who by the early twentieth century was an entrepreneur and Hereditary Honorary Citizen in Tiumen' (I, 2–3). Elizaveta's language indicates that she had familiarity with, if not mastery of, the liturgical language, Church Slavonic and biblical passages (II, 21, 163, 165). In this respect, she was more typical of peasant believers than historians have assumed. Familiarity with liturgical language and the Bible was not confined to Old Believers and evangelical groups within Imperial Russia. All of Elizaveta's sons had secular primary education, while the daughter Tat'iana had finished all but the highest class in the Sarapul gymnasium, as well as the teacher preparation programme, which tended to attract women from the middle and upper rather than peasant classes.[27] In the end, Tat'iana did not teach but moved back and forth 'between Pazdery and Sarapul, helping her parents run the household and her sister-in-law take care of the children' (I, 22). She wrote rather than dictated her letters.

In all the correspondence from various family members, references to God and use of pious language are commonplace. Some of these salutations and comments exemplify the more formal language that Orthodox believers of all classes believed was necessary in this type of communication, but others are a reminder that on a daily basis oral greetings, many sayings and references to time were religiously based. In April 1894 Tat'iana, for example, sent her brother Vasilii and her sister-in-law Evdokiia Prokop'evna a commercial Easter card, which contained the following printed message: 'I have the honour of greeting you with the high and solemn holiday of Christ's luminous resurrection, and I wish you to celebrate it and many

---

27. Christine Ruane, *Gender, Class, and the Professionalization of Russian City Teachers, 1860–1914* (Pittsburgh: University of Pittsburgh Press, 1994), p. 66.

future ones in good health and in perfect well-being' (II, 339). In a letter received by the same recipients on 20 April 1894, Tania (the diminutive of Tat'iana) modified and personalized the card's greeting, after providing the requisite Paschal greeting '*Khristos voskrese*' ('Christ is risen') by saying: 'I *congratulate you* with the high and solemn holiday of Christ's luminous resurrection and *from my soul* I wish you good health and *all the best in this life*'. Asking after their health, she informs them in common everyday speech, 'We are, thank God, healthy' (II, 337). In similar but more extensive pious language, Elizaveta's sister and Tania's maternal aunt, Liubov' sent her nephew and godson Alesha (the diminutive of Aleksei) greetings on 14 July 1881 connected to a family gathering in Sarapul to celebrate 'the feast of Our Lady of Kazan' (celebrated on 8 July). She extended to him her 'blessing and wish you wholeheartedly from my whole soul salvation for your soul and health for your body, as well as success in your soul-saving undertakings'. Before wishing him 'from God, all the best' and signing her name, she asks that he not 'forget me in your prayers' (II, 215, 216–17). Prayers were clearly important for not only Liubov', but also her sister Elizaveta. On 16 February 1882, the day after Elizaveta gave birth to a daughter, being vulnerable to complications associated with childbirth and perhaps worried about the baby's survival, Elizaveta dictated three prayers she wanted her son Vasilii to say 'at least once every day'. The first prayer in Church Slavonic was addressed to Jesus Christ, asking that 'our world' be saved 'from great disaster', while the second, more popular one to the Mother of God beseeched her to 'save us from sudden death'. Finally, Elizaveta, undoubtedly due to anxiety that her son was climbing the social ladder too quickly, added a 'prayer to get rid of arrogance'. The latter ('I denounce you, O Satan, [with] all your arrogance. I united with you, O Christ. Amen') was 'closely related to the pledge recited by a person undergoing the sacrament of baptism' (II, 231; I, 21–22).

Elizaveta expresses her understanding of her son's obligations to his parents and to God because of his financial success as a merchant in a series of letters written almost a decade later, in the latter half of 1891 and early 1892. On 23 July Elizaveta mentions that 'when I was sick I made a pledge to go to Kazan' to pray' and in this connection requests twenty-five roubles 'for good deeds'. She goes on to report the poor nature of their crops, as well as lack of money, noting, too, that 'father drinks on and off, but thank God, less now. […] It would be good to send money to some monastery […] to ask that they pray for him' (II, 284, 285). It is only in the third letter, dated 1 January 1892, when no money had been forthcoming, that the mother identifies the exact nature of her illness, 'a mild stroke'. This time she adds that she made an additional pledge 'on my own behalf, as well as on behalf of all of you, to send to the Holy Sepulchre in Jerusalem an affordable donation' (II, 289). In the second letter of 3 December 1891, Elizaveta reminds her son that money for religious purposes will do him 'good, too, in the sense that your labour will be used for good deeds and the Church. I'm confident that you will not begrudge satisfying your mother's request with what comes from your labour, for which God will reward you threefold' (II, 288).

Elizaveta's letters exemplify a number of Russian Orthodox practices that believers of all classes shared. It was customary for ill men and women, regardless of class, to make vows to God that they would visit a particular holy site to give thanks for their recovery. In Elizaveta's case, she had made her first pilgrimage in fulfillment of a pledge in the summer of 1889 to the popular Sviato-Nikolaevskii monastery in Verkhotur'e in northern Perm' province where she paid respects to the relics of St Simeon.[28] The correspondence does not indicate whether she had made that vow in the midst of her own illness, or whether Lavr's drinking had already prompted her to seek spiritual help for him. Given the saint's reputation for healing alcoholism, it is possible that Elizaveta was acting on behalf of her spouse (II, 273).[29] Often pilgrims timed their visits to saints' shrines in coordination with their feast days, times when their relics were believed to have the highest efficacy in terms of healing properties. Elizaveta did not do so on this occasion, as St Simeon's feast days are celebrated on 12 September and 18 December. Later in 1892 she did, however, make a pilgrimage to Sviiazhsk (just west of Kazan') to participate in the solemn celebration of the translation of St German's relics on 26 September (II, 307). In 1894, this time in connection with her own health, she embarked on an ambitious pilgrimage circuit to major holy sites, some at a distance from Pazdery. According to her own description, she went to 'Kazan', and from Kazan' to Raifa, and Raifa to Sviiazhsk, and from Sviiazhsk to Nizhnii Novgorod and to Murom, to Sarov, and Diveevo, and Ponetaevka' (II, 349). Elizaveta did not go into

---

28. By the turn of the twentieth century Verkhotur'e attracted up to 120,000 pilgrims annually. See the website of the Novo-Tikhvin women's monastery, http://www.sestry.ru/church/content/pilgrim/sviat/zss/index_html#verkh [Last accessed 19 January 2010].

29. A posting dated 29 October 2009 on 'The Byzantine Forum' connects St Simeon to the healing of alcoholics, http://www.byzcath.org/forums/ubbthreads.php/topics/336488/Lives_of_Little%20Known_Saints [Last accessed 21 October 2011].

any detail about the relics and miracle-working icons housed at these sites, presumably because she did not need to. These were popular pilgrimage destinations that were described in the religious pamphlet literature and pilgrimage magazine *Russkii palomnik* (*The Russian Pilgrim*). We do not know if Elizaveta had companions on these occasions but, given concerns of safety, she in all likelihood would have travelled in the company of either family members or neighbours, or a combination of the two. In summer 1895, we learn, her month-long pilgrimage to Kazan', Sviiazhsk, and the Raifa monastery included one of her grandchildren and members of her sister's family (II, 362). If Elizaveta and her companion pilgrims went by foot rather than rail and cart on any of these trips, they would have been consciously strengthening the sincerity of their pledge. If they did travel by rail, they would have joined peasant migrants in crammed third-class carriages.

The pilgrimages would have given Elizaveta respite from her alcoholic husband and her domestic duties. They would have also allowed her to communicate with other female pilgrims (from various classes) who sought relief from their own or their children's and spouses' illnesses, or sought spiritual counselling. Through their prayers for the intercession of the Mother of God, Christ, saints and other holy persons, and through vows to visit saints' graves, the ill, handicapped and sick at heart could hope to attain God's mercy and grace. Even if their physical illnesses were not cured, they came away renewed from having entered holy space and having shared in the miraculous, i.e. the spiritual presence of a saint and the Mother of God. Although men also went on pilgrimages, late nineteenth-century observers' descriptions suggest that women, particularly from the peasantry, predominated among these worshippers. Indeed, Lavr's spiritual journeys pale in number in comparison to those of his wife Elizaveta: he did seek out the spiritual help of the charismatic priest Ioann of Kronshtadt in mid-1894, and in summer 1895 he headed off to a monastery in Tobolsk, but these were the extent of his forays (II, 344, 362). Elizaveta did not travel with her husband on these occasions, for what reasons we do not know. It appears that Elizaveta herself travelled to Kronshtadt earlier in spring 1893, since she asked Vasilii to finance such a trip in her letter dated 19 September 1892 (II, 307).[30]

The money that Elizaveta requested from her children for her pilgrimages would have been used for any transportation she might have used, food

---

30. Note that not all letters were saved.

and lodging along the way, although sleeping under the open sky was not uncommon for peasants. She would also have made cash donations as well as offerings of ribbons, towels and cloth at the monastic sites in exchange for candles and special prayer services. She probably purchased holy water, holy oil, religious pamphlets and other paraphernalia from peddlers who set up stalls outside the monastery gates. Such donations represented pilgrims' sincerity, while the souvenirs functioned as an indispensable part of the rituals of thanksgiving and remembrance. The monastic institutions would have provided basic tea and bread and possibly a night's accommodation (if they were not inundated with pilgrims).

Elizaveta's request of her son Vasilii in January 1895 that he provide her with money so that she could 'go to Kiev to pray' indicated not only her concern with her health ('I am constantly ill'), but also with her mortality. Her desire to visit the most ancient Orthodox city in the empire was part of her quest for salvation (II, 348). Her monetary donations to holy sites in Jerusalem and Mount Athos in lieu of physical pilgrimages sought additional intercessional prayers for herself and her family members (II, 321). Women were not allowed, of course, on Mount Athos, so an actual trip there was out of the question for Elizaveta. A voyage from Odessa to Jerusalem would have been not only costly but time-consuming for this devout woman. Elizaveta was also clearly unable to follow the example of those pious single women who, free from family responsibilities, became full-time pilgrims. For example, in 1897 an elderly, illiterate, and impoverished noblewoman described herself to an observer as a pilgrim by profession. As a teenager she had fled an unconsummated marriage forced upon her by her mother, dedicating her life to wandering from one religious site to another. For the next thirty-three years she supported her travels to such far away places as Solovki (in the White Sea region) and Jerusalem by selling lace that she had made herself.[31] In the mid-nineteenth century the *keleinitsa* (self-proclaimed religious person) Anis'ia Romanova of the *sloboda* (large settlement) Dedilovskaia, Tula province, went on numerous pilgrimages. She travelled several times to holy sites in Kiev, Moscow and Voronezh. She also ventured out to monasteries in Zadonsk and Solovki in 1852, and again in 1858, to Jerusalem. In all of these places she studied the contemplative way of life and purchased icons, as well as books recounting

---

31. *Kto pomogaet gorodskiia popechitel'stva?* (Moscow: Gorodskaia tipografiia, 1897), pp. 47–48. The pilgrim interpreted the death of her husband six weeks after the wedding as God's punishment.

the lives of the saints and containing prayer cycles. Upon her return to Russia from a year in Jerusalem, Romanova attracted people of all ranks to her with her tales of the Holy Land and the mementos – candles that she had burned in Christ's tomb at Easter, crosses and other religious paraphernalia from the Holy Land – that she was prepared to sell them.[32] Scores of other professional women pilgrims, some of them peasants, traversed the Russian countryside, bringing communion bread, candles, holy water and oil, and other material items from monasteries to the rural and urban faithful and carrying the donations, ribbons, cloth and requests of these same faithful, who themselves could not go on pilgrimage, to monastic shrines. Elizaveta's husband Lavr makes a reference to such a pilgrim in a letter of 22 September 1889, noting that the woman had stayed with Lavr and Elizaveta in Pazdery, a week after having stayed with Vasilii in Tiumen' for a similar length of time (II, 275).

Elizaveta outlived the dates of the saved correspondence, as a result of which we do not know what type of preparations she made for her death. However, we can assume from her concern for her salvation and her remark that 'you know that however old you are you must be preparing to go to our heavenly homeland' that she would have asked her sons to set aside donations to at least one monastic institution to say eternal prayers for her (II, 348). Her husband Lavr gives us a detailed report of his own mother's bequests. Never having married, and having had Lavr out of wedlock, Praskov'ia Vasil'evna had saved substantial sums for eternal prayers. Lavr informs Vasilii on 25 September 1889 that his grandmother 'was properly administered the Eucharist and underwent a chrisming […] in Pazdery village, 40-day memorial prayers for her soul were commissioned for 50 rubles, 60 rubles were sent to Mount Athos, and 182 rubles of her own money were left for her funeral' (II, 273–74).[33] Similarly, a childless peasant widow of Podcherkov township, Dmitrov district, Moscow province, left her 'net capital […] to be placed in one of the credit institutions in the name of the holy Church servants of the parish Chernogriazh for the eternal memory of my and my husband's souls'. She also bequeathed 'two pieces of linen to the poor and miserable' to pave her way to a peaceful death. And finally, she left 'ten measures of rye to the Nikolopestush monastery for the remembrance

---

32. Gromyko and Buganov, *O vozzreniiakh*, pp. 149–50.
33. I changed Yokoyama's use of the word 'viaticum' to 'the Eucharist' to reflect more clearly Russian Orthodox terminology.

of my and my husband's souls'.³⁴ In imitation of medieval princesses and noblewomen known for their charitable works, the former serf Praskov'ia Ivanovna Kovaleva (1768–1803), who eventually married Count Nikolai Petrovich Sheremetev (1751–1809), was insistent on her deathbed that charitable work be conducted in her name, in this instance 'to help poor and orphaned girls and to see that the hospital at Sukharev Tower be finished'.³⁵

While Elizaveta became more preoccupied with things spiritual as she aged, she was prone to secular influences as well. In the 1 January 1892 letter to Vasilii in which she asked a third time for money to fulfil her spiritual vow of sending money to Jerusalem's Holy Sepulchre, she also gave him motherly advice about choosing a bride. In fact, in other letters we learn a good deal about matchmaking and expectations regarding the choice of spouse. After several failures in matchmaking, Elizaveta was concerned that her son would remain a bachelor: 'It won't be forever, I think, that you intend to remain and live as such, and perhaps you may be thinking of selecting for yourself a helpmeet and uniting [with her] in the ties of holy matrimony'. The advice she gives him comes from a poem by A. V. Timofeev, entitled 'Vybor zheny' ('Choosing a Wife'), which was also the text of several popular songs (I, 87 n. 24):

> Don't marry a clever woman, you will lose your mind; if you marry a widow, the old husband will come. Don't marry gold, the father-in-law's fortune! Don't marry status, the wife's relatives! If you marry gold, you will be selling yourself; if you marry status, forget about your wife! There are many songbirds in God's woods; there are many pretty maidens in the tsar's towns. Chase a nightingale into your cage; pick from among the maidens a little birdie wife (II, 290).

In order to underscore the fact that she was worried about her son's upward mobility and the arrogance that she felt came with prosperity, Elizaveta added: 'This is wonderful advice from a poet, and mine is the same, [just] so that the chosen birdie be religious and modest, even if [she is] not rich' (II, 290). The mother could have heard the song at a local or regional fair or had a copy of the text in 'a cheap *lubok* [popular print] version'.³⁶

---

34. *Trudy Kommisii, po preobrazovaniiu volostnykh sudov: slovesnye oprosy krest'ian, pis'mennye otzyvy razlichnykh mest i lits i resheniia: volostnykh sudov, s"ezdov mirovykh posrednikov i gubernskikh po krest'ianskim delam prisutstvii*, 7 vols (St Petersburg: [Kommisiia po preobrazovaniiu volostnykh sudov], 1873–74), II, 525–26.
35. Douglas Smith, *The Pearl: A True Tale of Forbidden Love in Catherine the Great's Russia* (New Haven: Yale University Press, 2008), p. 233.
36. Laura J. Olson, *Performing Russia: Folk Revival and Russian Identity* (London: Routledge, 2004), p. 22.

As Robert Rothstein has pointed out, the influence of literary poetry led to more regular metrical schemes and the increasing use of rhyme in folk songs, and the sway of the urban ballad brought to peasants' vocabulary new words associated with ready-to-wear clothing and other consumer products such as 'sports coat', 'galoshes', 'blouse', 'dress', 'card table', and 'factory-made napkin'. Songs, he concludes, reflected not only changes in rural culture, 'but were also a force for change' as they 'spread subversive ideas like greater sexual equality, more independence for youth, or even criticism of the mistreatment of workers'.[37] Even as a member of an older generation, Elizaveta could not but be affected by urban culture. She often travelled to the market town of Sharkan (where her sister lived) and Sarapul. A portrait photograph of her taken in 1905 shows a matronly woman dressed in a dark, ready-to-wear dress with puffed sleeves, lacework on the bodice and a high collar with covered buttons. Her hair is parted in the middle and partially covered with a cap, from which lace is cascading downward, rather than with a kerchief (II, 487). Although her dress is not of the latest fashion and not likely borrowed from the photographer's studio, Elizaveta definitely shows off an urban appearance. While her lack of a smile was indicative of the seriousness of having one's picture taken, it may also have been a result of the uncomfortable dentures with which she had been fitted (II, 364). Elizaveta, too, was not immune from the influences of upward mobility.

Consumer goods were, nonetheless, far more important to Elizaveta's children. Her son Ivan wrote to his brother Vasilii in February 1891 about an unsuccessful betrothal to a literate village girl whose upwardly mobile father is described as 'a Gogoli peasant', 'a Sarapul burger' and 'an Osa temporary second-guild merchant'. In order to impress the potential bride from this 'thrifty village-style household', whom Ivan describes somewhat tellingly as 'not very pretty [...], but not ugly either', he and his cousins visited her several times, having rented several pairs of troikas. He noted that they bought the bride's various dowry items at N. I. Osipov's in Sarapul, including 'gold, silver, copper and dishes, mirrors and a dressing table'. Ivan also reported that they had their photograph, a copy of which he included with the letter, taken at the Virpsha Studio (II, 275, 277–78). Material objects and photographs demonstrated a new sensibility of individual success and independence, a blending-in with lower-middle-class society.

---

37. Robert A. Rothstein, 'Death of the Folk Song?', in *Cultures in Flux,* pp. 108–20 (112–13).

Elizaveta's daughter Tania was very conscious of her appearance and complained about the lack of clothing, of an allowance for clothing and of a suitable dowry. Already at the age of fifteen, she dismissively announces in a letter to her brother Vasia (the diminutive for Vasilii) that her parents 'probably already think that it's time to get me ready for marriage. So, well, now all that's left to me is to remain in this stupid state, i.e. to be fattening my body and my dowry. Isn't this disgusting, isn't my situation ridiculous!' (II, 291–92). At the same time, she uses her new status as a marriageable young woman to claim that she needs to have a room of her own: 'And aren't I a maiden, don't I need a place to sleep or to change clothes?' (II, 293). Almost two years later, in November 1893, she complains about her brother Aleksei's and sister-in-law's miserliness, noting that she 'needs money for perfume for pomade, and for needles, pins and hairpins, and whatever else may be necessary for a lady's grooming. It's simply embarrassing to fall behind others'. She laments that she possesses only one dress, one shawl, and one 'ninety-kopeck knit hat', which 'I have been wearing [...] for a second year'. To make her point, she itemizes the numerous scarves and dresses that her sister-in-law Raisa Davidovna Zhernokova (née Kirkkhof) possesses (II, 324, 325). Finally, at the age of nineteen, when Tania expresses the notion that she 'will soon [be] enroll[ing] among the old maids', she is able, with her brothers' help, to buy a suitable dowry chest, a photographic album of 'very good paper', a ten-rouble shawl, 'a fashionable sash', a silk scarf, 'tablecloths, napkins, and linen scarves for factory prices' near Iaroslavl', 'a stylish autumn jacket, a very pretty parasol, an autumn hat, a small rug for next to the bed, and in short, some (other) small stuff' (II, 368). In the same letter she describes the 'gorgeous dowry' of a gymnasium friend who was marrying 'a widowed physician's assistant' – 'all silk and velvet, three seamstresses have been working on it day and night – and some money, and tons of golden jewellery' (II, 367). The turn in her fortune as a result of her brothers' willingness to finance her dowry even allowed Tania to consider buying a 200-rouble piano! (II, 354). Long gone were the days when peasant girls embroidered their own trousseaus and when peasant women wove their own cloth and sewed their own clothes. Owning ready-to-wear clothing and other factory- made items represented upward mobility and attracted potential suitors as familiarity with urban goods became common.[38]

---

38. For a discussion of the impact of ready-to-wear clothing on peasant women, see Christine Ruane, *The Empire's New Clothes: A History of the Russian Fashion Industry, 1700–1917* (New Haven: Yale University Press, 2009), pp. 74–80.

The late-nineteenth-century correspondence of the Zhernokov family thus provides us insights into what was important to upwardly mobile Russian peasant women of the time. Events connected to the life cycle are ever present in the descriptions, including the birth and christening of children, but not the rituals surrounding the events. It would appear, for example, that working bees, where marriageable peasant women did handiwork while suitors entertained them with song, were no longer part of the non-agricultural calendar. Formal betrothals still occurred and parents were very much involved in their children's matchmaking, although choice lay now with the potential bride and groom. The need to purchase consumer goods to compete in an evolving, more fluid, class marriage market, had displaced rituals and activities that might have once been confined to a rural if not always purely peasant milieu, when gentry and clergy would have participated in some of these events.

Religious sensibilities, at least among the members of the Zhernokov and Rodigin families, especially Elizaveta and her sister, were paramount to their identities and understanding of their world. Elizaveta's sister, in fact, sometime after her husband's death took the veil and established a women's religious community, which became a women's monastery in late 1917.[39] While it was unusual for a peasant woman to have the resources to establish such a community, peasant women dominated among those who decided to take up the contemplative life and did occasionally serve as abbesses. Seeking 'an alternative to domesticity', and inspired by the Mother of God, many of these women joined women from other classes in seeking a life of serving God, one that celebrated compassion, humility, intercession on behalf of the poor and social engagement.[40] A surfeit of single and widowed women in late nineteenth-century villages that resulted from the economic and social dislocations of increasing male out-migration to the cities, where mortality rates were higher than in the countryside, also contributed to the phenomenal growth of women's religious communities. Those who did not wish ultimately to take up the rigours of cloistered life could, nonetheless, find employment and shelter

---

39. Liubov', who took the name Sofiia, financed her community from the estate of her husband and late son Aleksei, as well as donations from her son Panteleimon and one of her nephews, a Tiumen' merchant (II, 397).
40. Gary Marker, 'The Enlightenment of Anna Labzina: Gender, Faith, and Public Life in Catherinian and Alexandrian Russia', *Slavic Review* 59.2 (2000), 369–90 (369).

in these institutions.[41] Interestingly, however, Liubov''s path was one she shared with her contemporary, the Grand Duchess Elizaveta Fedorovna, sister of the last tsarina Alexandra, who founded the Saints Mary and Martha women's monastery in Moscow after her husband's assassination in 1905. Class was not as important as we might think in dictating women's options and practices. More interdisciplinary work needs to be done on peasant women's evolving cultural aspirations and the influences that were at work in their lives during the dramatic decades of economic and social change after emancipation. Only then will we have a better sense of the everyday experiences and the choices that these women enjoyed.

---

41. Brenda Meehan, 'Popular Piety, Local Initiative, and the Founding of Women's Religious Communities in Russia, 1764–1907', in *Seeking God*, p. 99; William G. Wagner, 'Parodoxes of Piety: The Nizhegorod Convent of the Exaltation of the Cross, 1807–1935', in *Orthodox Russia: Belief and Practice Under the Tsars*, ed. by Valerie A. Kivelson and Robert H. Greene (University Park: Pennsylvania State University Press, 2003), pp. 211–38 (222).

4. Mary and Women in Late Imperial Russian Orthodoxy

Vera Shevzov

In a recent collection of essays on people's sacred worlds and the academic study of them, historian Robert Orsi has suggested that we think about religion in terms of relationships that believers form with holy figures. 'These relationships have all the complexities', he maintains, 'of relationships between humans'.[1] If we apply this approach to modern Russia, it quickly becomes evident that the study of women in Orthodox Christianity inevitably leads to, if not begins with, a study of women's relationship with Mary, the Birth-giver of God (*Bogoroditsa*). Ubiquitously present through her countless images that were located in homes, churches, roadside chapels, marketplaces and sometimes even taverns, Mary was a steadfast reference point in the lives of Orthodox women in the late Imperial period. Supported by an Orthodox belief that her intercessional powers alone could be more effective than the prayers of the entire faith community, Orthodox women turned readily to Mary in moments of need,

---

Research for this essay was conducted with the generous support of a grant from the National Endowment for the Humanities. Any views, findings and conclusions expressed in this essay do not necessarily reflect those of the National Endowment for the Humanities.

1. Robert A. Orsi, *Between Heaven and Earth: The Religious Worlds People Make and the Scholars Who Study Them* (Princeton, NJ: Princeton University Press, 2005), p. 2.

distress and thanksgiving.[2] Though often confined to oral culture, women's experiences with Mary and her icons were also recorded in petitions to Church authorities regarding the special veneration of Marian images, and in logs kept in churches that housed her miracle-working icons.[3] In this sense, Russia's Orthodox women from all social and economic backgrounds contributed to sustaining Mary's life in modern Russia no less than her image contributed to sustaining theirs.

Relationships between women and Mary in modern Russia, however, were highly complex and remain difficult to characterize, in part because of their personal nature. To a large extent, they were formed by associations visually prompted by Marian icons and by the stories associated with them. They also depended in large part on each woman's individual disposition, hopes, fears, and desires. At the same time, Orthodox women's conceptions of the woman whom they so revered and the devotional relationship they developed with her were also informed by a broader array of sources. Women's notions about Mary were animated by a rich, though eclectic, narrative culture that included scripture, liturgical celebrations honouring specific events in Mary's life, prayers and hymns in her honour, sermons, and, by the mid-nineteenth century, a growing body of devotional literature. In order to gain a sense of the narrative pool from which Russian Orthodox believers in general, and women in particular, might have drawn in forging their relationships with Mary, this essay focuses on a body of hagiographical Marian literature widely circulated in the late nineteenth and early twentieth centuries, commonly entitled *The Earthly Life of the Most-Holy Birth-Giver of God* (*Zemnaia zhizn' presviatoi Bogoroditsy*).

This genre of literature warrants attention for several reasons. First, numerous accounts of Mary's life were published in Russia in the nineteenth

---

2. *Pokhvala Presviatoi Deve Bogoroditse. Izbrannyie dushepoleznyie prosheniia, stikhotvoreniia, povesti i primery iz zhizni i tvorenii sviatykh otets*, comp. by Igumen Sergii (Novgorod: Tip. M. O. Selivanova, 1905). For descriptions of Mary in local folk customs, see Linda Ivanits, *Russian Folk Belief* (Armonk, NY: M.E. Sharpe, 1989), pp. 20–24. Joanna Hubbs has pointed out that women's readings of the Christian story were often expressed in 'spiritual verses' that often circulated among, and were composed by, women from various social classes, especially the peasantry: Joanna Hubbs, *Mother Russia: The Feminine Myth in Russian Culture* (Bloomington, IN: Indiana University Press, 1988), p. 95. George Fedotov briefly analysed the image of Mary in such spiritual verses: G. Fedotov, *Stikhi dukhovnye* (Paris: YMCA Press, 1935), pp. 47–58.
3. Vera Shevzov, *Russian Orthodoxy on the Eve of Revolution* (New York: Oxford University Press, 2004), pp. 222–36.

century, and the number of editions and versions significantly increased during the second half of that century. Sold in villages by itinerant peddlers, the work was commonly found in peasant homes and rural libraries, along with the expected saints' lives, Psalters and prayer books.[4] In addition, Mary's life was a customary topic in preaching and periliturgical discussions (*vnebogosluzhebnye besedy*). Indeed, a review of one version of such a *Life,* that appeared in 1891 in the *Theological Bibliographical Bulletin* (*Bogoslovskii bibliograficheskii listok*), maintained that clergy would find it a rich source for their sermons.[5]

These texts are also notable in that they compel us to reconsider the notion of Mariology in late Imperial Russia and the relationship between images of Mary and the expected roles of women in family, church and society. Most Orthodox Christians at that time probably would have agreed with the view of the dean of the Moscow Theological Academy, Archimandrite Aleksei Rzhanitsyn, who maintained that the essence of the Orthodox teaching on Mary, the *Bogoroditsa*, was best expressed in the words of a familiar prayer, 'More honourable than the cherubim, and beyond compare more glorious than the seraphim, who without defilement gave birth to God the Word, true Birth-giver of God, we magnify you'.[6] Yet in contemplating the meaning of these words, not all believers would necessarily have followed the classical, doctrinal direction he took in an 1848 essay, in which he analysed the titles, Birth-giver of God (*Bogoroditsa*) and Ever-Virgin (*Prisnodeva*), only in light of her son and the Incarnation. While probably no one would have argued against that approach, we can well imagine that many nineteenth-century women would have been inspired to expound upon Mary's sanctity in a different way, namely by considering her life as she may have lived it. Published accounts of Mary's life offered believers narratives that helped to cultivate such inspiration

---

4. For examples, see Rossiiskii etnograficheskii muzei, f. 7 (Tenishev), d. 1252, l. 4 (diocese of Orel, rural public library); d. 801, l. 14; l. 20 (Novgorod, private peasant holdings); d. 821, l. 72 (Novgorod, local school library); d. 452, l. 35 (Viatka, this topic was the subject of public readings at the local zemstvo school); d. 61, l. 9 (diocese of Vladimir, private peasant home). Also see *Chto chitat' narodu? Kriticheskii ukazatel' knig dlia narodnogo i detskogo chteniia, sostavlen uchitel'nitsami Khar'kovskoi chastnoi zhenskoi voskresnoi shkoly* (St Petersburg: Tip. V. S. Balashova, 1888), pp. iii; 6.
5. M. E., *Bogoslovskii bibliograficheskii listok za 1891. Prilozhenie k zhurnalu Rukovodstvo dlia sel'skikh pastyrei*, 12 (1891), 462–65.
6. Part of a well-known Byzantine hymn in honour of the Mother of God; usually attributed to St Cosmas the Hymnographer (d. 737). The entire hymn 'It Is Truly Meet' (*Dostoino Est'*) is a standard daily prayer in the Orthodox tradition.

and the imagination that it fuelled. Moreover, the fact that the *Lives* were welcomed by clergy and laity suggests that they exerted pressure neither from above, nor from below, on Marian beliefs and piety, but reflected a tacitly accepted, and in many ways 'standard' impression of her in late Imperial Russia.

This essay examines the images of Mary, particularly in terms of her motherhood, as presented in the published *Lives* in the late nineteenth and early twentieth centuries, in order to appreciate the variety of associations regarding her powerful image that were available to Orthodox women during this period. Because these *Lives* were composed and published at the same time that currents from the feminist movement in the West were impressing Russian society, this essay also considers the image of Mary as presented in Orthodox – mainly clerical – responses to that movement. Read in the light of these clerical responses, the published *Lives* of Mary take on added meaning in terms of defining the traditional Orthodox depiction of Mary and explaining Mary's unabated appeal among Russia's women of faith.

The published *Lives* of Mary: Sources and Inspiration

Published accounts of Mary's life in nineteenth-century Russia were not original in the usual understanding of that term. As early as the mid-second century, curiosity concerning the woman who bore and raised Jesus, as well as disputes about that woman's identity, led to the formulation of early Christian accounts of Mary's early life.[7] By the late fourth and fifth centuries Christians also told stories about her death.[8] Throughout

---

7. 'The Protevangelium of James', ed. by Oscar Cullmann, in *New Testament Apocrypha*, I, ed. by Wilhelm Schneemelcher and trans. by R. McL.Wilson (Louisville, KY: 1991), pp. 421–39. For historical background to the text, see Nicolae Roddy, 'The Form and Function of the Protevangelium of James', *Coptic Church Review*, 14 (1993), 35–45; Mary F. Foskett, *A Virgin Conceived: Mary and Classical Representations of Virginity* (Bloomington, IN: Indiana University Press), pp. 141–63; Pieter W. van der Hosrt, 'Sex, Birth, Purity and Asceticism in the *Protevangelium Jacobi*', in *A Feminist Companion to Mariology*, ed. by Amy-Jill Levine with Maria Mayo Robbins (New York: T & T Clark International, 2005), pp. 56–66; Stephen J. Shoemaker, 'Between Scripture and Tradition: The Marian Apocrypha of Early Christianity', in *Reception and Interpretation of the Bible in Late Antiquity: Proceedings of the Montreal Colloquium in Honor of Charles Kannengiesser, 11–13 October*, ed. by Charles Kannengiesser, Lorenzo DiTommaso and Lucian Turcescu (Boston: Brill, 2008), pp. 491–510.
8. Vladimir Sakharov, 'Apokrificheskie i legendarnyie skazaniia o Presviatoi Deve Marii, osobenno rasprostranennyie v drevnei Rusi', *Khristianskoe chtenie*, no. 3–4 (1888), 281–

the Byzantine period, select stories and episodes from her life shaped the Christian understandings of Mary by their influence on preaching, iconography, and hymnody. The homilies of such well known patristic authors as Ephrem the Syrian (d. 373), John Chrysostom (d. 407), Andrew of Crete (d. 720 or 740), Germanus, archbishop of Constantinople (d. 733 or 740) and John of Damascus (d. 749), all reflected the influence of such apocryphal accounts. Given their widespread influence in Byzantium, it is not surprising that stories concerning Mary's life, including the *Protevangelium of James* and narratives concerning her death, were part of the 'international collection' of apocryphal texts that ancient Russia inherited from Byzantium following the Christianization of Rus' in the ninth and tenth centuries.[9]

Apocryphal texts in general, including those concerning Mary, were ambiguously positioned in Orthodox Christianity in nineteenth-century Russia. On the one hand, the Church recognized the distinction between canonical and non-canonical texts and maintained that the latter often contained fabricated embellishments to biblical narratives. Some churchmen went even further and attempted to demythologize certain Marian-related apocryphal accounts since they only 'supported fabrications which were intolerable in the Christian Church'.[10] In his history of Mount Athos, for instance, the archaeologist and bishop Porfirii (Uspenskii) challenged a story about a reported visit of Mary to Mount Athos following the death and resurrection of Jesus, a story often included in nineteenth-century *Lives* of Mary. By demonstrating that the story was a popular local Athonite legend on which Georgian monks from the Iveron monastery on Athos had capitalized in the late sixteenth and early seventeenth centuries, Uspenskii hoped to curtail any damage that 'pious falsehoods' might inflict on the 'holy truth'.[11]

---

331 (307–20); Stephen J. Shoemaker, *Ancient Traditions of the Virgin Mary's Dormition and Assumption* (New York: Oxford University Press, 2002).

9. Protierei I. Smirnov, 'Apokrificheskie skazaniia o Bozhiei Materi i deianiiakh apostolov', *Pravoslavnoe obozrenie* (April, 1873), 569–614; N. F. Sumtsov, *Ocherki istorii iuzhno-russkikh apokrificheskikh skazanii i pesen* (Kiev: Tip. A. Divdenko, 1888), pp. 3–4; V. V. Mil'kov, *Drevnerusskie apokrify* (St Petersburg: Izd. Russkogo Khristianskogo gumanitarnogo instituta, 1999), p. 18. Francis Thomson, however, has noted although aprocryphal gospels such as the *Protevangelium of James* were among the earliest translated into Slavonic, the earliest existing manuscripts in Russia date only to the fourteenth-century: Francis Thomson, 'The Nature of the Reception of Christian Byzantine Culture in Russia in the 10th-13th centuries', *Slavic Gandensia*, 5 (1978), 107–38 (108).

10. Episkop Porfirii (Uspenskii), *Istoriia Afona v dvukh tomakh*, 2 vols (1892; reprint, Moscow: DAR, 2007), I, 201.

11. Episkop Porfirii, *Istoriia Afona*, I, 201–12.

On the other hand, such caution could only go so far. Various apocryphal stories dating from the second to the tenth centuries, as well as patristic writings concerning the life and character of Mary, were woven into the analytically elusive yet palpable fabric of Orthodoxy known as tradition. In ancient Russia, such apocryphal stories were embedded in collections with canonical texts, including biblical texts, suggesting that the boundary between the two often had been vague at best.[12] In the first part of the sixteenth century, the future metropolitan of Moscow, Makarii, oversaw the gathering of such sacred writings along with hundreds of texts concerning saints and feasts into a monumental collection of daily readings – the *menologion* (*Chet'i-Minei*). Subsequently, in the early eighteenth century, the bishop of Rostov, Dimitrii, completed his own version of the *menologion* that also contained material drawn from Western sources, such as the Gospel of Pseudo-Matthew. By including apocryphal stories associated with Mary in their collections, Metropolitan Makarii (Bulgakov) of Moscow (d. 1563) and Metropolitan Dimitrii (Tuptalo) of Rostov (d. 1709) sanctioned and reaffirmed their place in Orthodox devotional knowledge.

While stories concerning Mary's early life and death developed independently early in the history of Christianity, as a literary genre, the hagiographical *Life* of Mary appeared later. Marian hagiographies that combined descriptions of her early years, as depicted in the *Protevangelium of James*, with those of her later years, as depicted in stories about her death, appeared in Byzantine monastic circles as early as the sixth or seventh century and subsequently found their way to the medieval West.[13] In Russia, the genre of Mary's *Life* was known by at least the fourteenth century, with some scholars indicating its importance in the composition of lives of medieval and early modern Russian saints.[14]

In the modern period, inspiration to pen these lives in Russia came primarily from the Ukraine, through the work of the seventeenth-century preacher and archimandrite of the Chernigov monastery, Ioannikii

---

12. Mil'kov, *Drevnerusskie apokrify*, pp. 59–60; Henry J. Cooper, *Slavic Scriptures: The Formation of the Church Slavonic Version of the Holy Bible* (Teaneck, NJ: Fairleigh Dickinson University Press, 2003), p. 127.
13. Stephen Shoemaker, 'The Virgin Mary in the Ministry of Jesus and the Early Church according to the Earliest Life of the Virgin', *Harvard Theological Review* 98.4 (2005), 441–67; Sakharov, 'Apokrificheskie i legendarnyie skazaniia o Presviatoi Deve Marii', 295, 314.
14. *Slovar' knizhnikov i knizhnosti Drevnei Rusi*, ed. by D. S. Likhachev, vyp. 1 (Leningrad: Nauka, 1987), pp. 137–38; D. V. Sosnitskaia, 'Zhitie Bogoroditsy v russkoi rukopisnoi traditsii', *Russkaia rech'*, 5 (2007), 70–73; T. R. Rudi, 'Pravednye zheny drevnei Rusi (K voprosu o tipologii sviatosti)', *Russkaia literatura*, 3 (2001), 84–92.

Galiatovskii (d. 1688). His well-known collection of Marian miracles, *The New Heaven* (*Nebo novoe*), incorporated not only ancient Byzantine and Russian narratives about Mary, but also details of her life that had come to be known primarily in the Roman catholic West.[15] It is noteworthy that Russia's nineteenth-century interest in Mary's life also found a parallel in Europe, where during the first half of that century a well-received *Life* of Mary composed in France by Abbot Orsini was published and subsequently translated into English, Italian, Spanish, and German.[16] It is difficult to establish for certain, however, the extent to which this work or others like it were known or read in Russia.

By the nineteenth century, then, stories about Mary's life had already enjoyed quasi-canonical status in Russia for centuries insofar as they had informed liturgical hymnody and iconography. Consequently, Russia's believers would have attributed a semblance of authority to them. To question the authenticity of even select strands of such narratives could potentially call into question the authority ascribed to tradition more broadly speaking. Not surprisingly, therefore, in describing his source base, one author of a *Life* of Mary, composed in 1845, maintained that the Orthodox church 'preserves' and 'respects' such stories about Mary 'because they carry the imprint of apostolic times and are entirely compatible with the Word of God', thereby attributing to them a sense of authenticity, if not historical accuracy.[17]

What might explain the resurgence and popularity of this genre in nineteenth-century Russia? In part, these *Lives* exemplified the broader upsurge in the production of devotional literature in Russia in the second half of the nineteenth century and, in particular, of Marian devotional literature. Such an interest in her life might also be viewed as part of broader devotional

---

15. The complete title of Goliatovskii's work, initially published in Polish, was *Nebo novoe, s novymi zvezdami sotvorennoe, t. e. Preblagoslovennaia Deva Mariia s chudami Svoimi, soch. Ioannikiia Goliatovskogo* (L'vov, 1665). The work was translated into Russian in 1677; Sumtsov, *Ocherki istorii*, p. 57; N. F. Sumtsov, *Ioannikii Goliatovskii* (Kiev: Tip. G. V. Gorchak-Novitskogo, 1884); I. I. Ogienko, *Legendarno-Apokrificheskii element v 'Nebe Novom' Ioannikiia Goliatovskago, iuzhno-russkago propovednika XVII-go veka* (Kiev: Tip. T. G. Meinandera, 1913).
16. M. L'Abbé Orsini, *Life of the Blessed Virgin Mary, Mother of God, taken from the Traditions of the East, the Manners of the Israelites, and the Writings of the Holy Fathers*, trans. Rev. Patrick Power, 2nd American edn (New York: Edward Dunigan and Brother, 1851). For a brief overview of the life of Abbot Orsini, see N. Tomasini, *L'abbé Orsini, 1801–1875* (Paris: P. Balitout, 1875).
17. *Velichie Presviatyia Bogoroditsy i Prisno-Devy Marii* (Moscow: Universitetskaia tipografiia, 1845), p. 7.

trends sweeping through Europe, in which Mary figured prominently. With the reports of appearances of Mary in La Salette (France, 1856), Lourdes (1858), Marpingen (Germany, 1876) and Knock (Ireland, 1879), the nineteenth century has been referred to as the start of the 'age of Mary'. Believers' experience of Mary in nineteenth-century Russia, especially through her countless icons, was no less evident. Her *Life* provided a background and character to the woman who was portrayed on these revered images and helped to facilitate a relationship with her.[18] Evgenii Poselianin, a compiler of such a *Life*, reminded his readers that they 'did not have to sail from Antioch to Jerusalem in order to enter into a relationship with the Mother of God'. Such a relationship was possible through meditation and prayer, imaginative recollection and an 'exalted gaze' upward from 'worldly strife'.[19]

Imagination played a key role in these devotional texts. They documented centuries of imaginative Christians thinking from such diverse places as Constantinople, Syria, Jerusalem, Crete and Rome, as well as encouraged creative thought on the part of their readers. The genre's very raison d'être – filling in the conspicuous lacunae left by canonical scriptures – motivated devotional elaboration. By 'piously exerting their imaginations', wrote Evgenii Poselianin, readers could surmise what might have taken place in Mary's life.[20] Moreover, the fact that many of these *Lives* often told similar, yet not identical, stories, tacitly encouraged and sanctioned such creative reflection. Not only was such meditation not harmful or frivolous; it was, in fact, a matter of devotional etiquette. Compilers of Mary's life insisted that given the extent to which believers turned to her for guidance and inspiration, believers were 'obligated to know the circumstances of her [own] life'.[21] Such knowledge would be both 'comforting and edifying'.[22]

The popularity of the genre might also be explained by a spirituality that encouraged an imitation of Mary. Such imitation was a common theme in Orthodoxy in pre-revolutionary Russia. Clergy especially addressed this

---

18. Thomas A. Kselman, *Miracles and Prophecies in Nineteenth-Century France* (New Brunswick, NJ: Rutgers University Press, 1983); David Blackbourn, *Marpingen: Apparitions of the Virgin Mary in Bismarckian Germany* (Oxford, Oxford University Press, 1993); Ruth Harris, *Lourdes: Body and Spirit in the Secular Age* (New York: Penguin Compass, 1999); Eugene Hynes, *Knock: The Virgin's Apparition in Nineteenth-Century Ireland* (Cork: Cork University Press, 2008).
19. E. Poselianin, *Bogomater' na zemle* (St Petersburg, Izd. 'Sel'skogo vestnika', 1913), p. 4.
20. Poselianin, *Bogomater' na zemle*, p. 50.
21. *Zemnaia zhizn' Presviatoi Bogoroditsy* (Odessa: E. I. Fesenko, 1896), pp. i-ii. For a later edition, see *Zemnaia zhizn' Presviatoi Bogoroditsy s risunkami*, 3rd edn (Odessa: E. I. Fesenko, 1914).
22. *Velichie Presviatyia Bogoroditsy i Prisno-Devy Marii*, p. 3.

topic on the occasions of her feast days, when they encouraged such imitation in their sermons. Only by imitating the 'inner image' of Mary, Bishop Iustin (Polianskii) of Riazan' stated in 1900, could believers 'maturely' fulfill Christ's directives.[23] In 1894 the widely-distributed journal, the *Russian Pilgrim* (*Russkii palomnik*), even republished a modified and highly-edited translation of an eighteenth-century work by the French Jesuit Alexander-Joseph de Rouville called *The Imitation of Mary* (*O podrazhanii Presviatoi Deve Marii*), a sequel of sorts to Thomas à Kempis' famous *Life of Christ*. To some extent, the longing to know more about Mary's life was related to a desire to imitate her.[24]

Furthermore, the proliferation of versions of Mary's *Life* in the nineteenth and early twentieth centuries took place at a time when the quest for the historical Jesus among Western biblical scholars was well underway. In Russia, these influences were felt on the more popular level by means of the circulation of such books as Ernest Renan's famous *The Life of Jesus* in 1863 (Russian translation abroad, 1864) and Lev Tolstoi's various essays regarding Christianity that followed his *Confession* (*Ispoved'*) in 1879. While the authors of the versions of the *Life* of Mary did not refer to the modern *Lives* of Jesus, their compositions, nevertheless, reflect sensitivity towards history and a desire to present their accounts as 'factual', despite their mythological character. For instance, in order to give his account added authority, one anonymous compiler made sure to identify the authors of relevant ancient sources as historians.[25] In addition, such *Lives* frequently described the environment of the Holy Land, often including illustrations to ground their narratives geographically. Some compilers also attempted to provide broader historical contexts for their stories. In relating the story of the wedding at Cana, for example, one compiler described what he considered to be a typical Jewish wedding of the time. Another presented evidence for consecrated virgins living in the temple during this period as a context for the story of Mary's presentation into

---

23. Episkop Iustin, *Pouchenie v chest' i slavu Presviatyia Bogoroditsy* (Moscow: Afonskii russkii Panteleimonov monastyr, 1900), p. 90; *Besedy o presviatoi Bogoroditse* (St Petersburg [n.p], 1901), pp. 3, 19. Occasionally, a compiler of a life of Mary would mention the importance of imitating Mary as a guide to salvation. For example, S. D. Stul'tsev, *Zhizn' presviatyia vladychitsy nasheia Bogoroditsy i prisno Devy Marii* (Moscow: Manukhin, 1873); *Zemnaia zhizn' Presviatoi Bogoroditsy*, comp. by Ioann Kuzmicheev (Moscow: Izd. Morozova, 1894), p. 4.
24. Alexandre-Joseph de Rouville, *Imitation de la très Sainte Vierge: sur le modèle de l'imitation de Jésus-Christ* (Paris: A. Delalain, 1819); *O podrazhanii Presviatoi Deve Marii, po primeru posledovaniia Iisusu Khristu*, trans. by Iakov Utkin (St Petersburg: Tip. A. Baikova, 1820).
25. *Zemnoe zhitie Bogoroditsy Devy – upovaniia khristianom* (Moscow: Tip. Pogodina, 1871).

the temple.[26]

Finally, the late nineteenth century offered greater opportunity for authorship of such texts. No longer was the compilation of such publications a predominantly monastic occupation. Among more than two dozen accounts of Mary's life, only four can be directly identified with a monastic context: two were penned by monastics and two others were published by monastery presses.[27] Several texts remain anonymous. The identifiable compilers include an interesting mix of urban and rural priests, deacons, a professor at a theological academy, lay men and even two lay women who were known for their careers in the literary world: the translator and devotional writer Avdot'ia Pavlovna Glinka (1795–1863) and Sof'ia Ivanovna Snessoreva (1816–1904).[28] The experience of marriage and family in many of these cases introduced a new working context for the narration of Mary's life.

We can see some of the motivations that led to the compilation of these *Lives* in the foreword that Avdot'ia Glinka, wife of the poet and essayist Fedor Glinka, provided to her book, *The Life of the Most Holy Virgin Mother of God According to the Books of the Menalogion* (*Zhizn'*

---

26. *Zemnaia zhizn' Presviatoi Bogoroditsy i Prisno – Devy Marii sostavlennaia na osnovanii sviashchennogo pisaniia, sviashchennogo predaniia i pisanii otsov tserkvi* (Moscow: Tip. Orlova, 1876), p. 18; *Zhizn' Presviatoi Bogoroditsy s prilozheniem skazanii o chudotvornykh ikonakh eia* (Moscow: Tip. Sytina, 1903).
27. *Zhizn' preblagoslovennoi vladychitsy nasheia Bogoroditsy Prisnodevy Marii*, comp. by Ieromonakh Stefan, 3rd edn (Moscow: Tip. I. D. Sytina, 1898); *Zemnaia zhizn' Presviatoi Devy Marii Bogoroditsy* (Moscow: Izd. Afonskogo sv. Proroka Ilii skita, 1899); Arkhimandrit Ioann Veriuzhskii, *Beseda s russkimi bogomol'tsami o zemnoi zhizni Bozhiei Materi i eia blazhennom uspenii* (St Petersburg: Pravoslavnoe Palestinskoe obshchestvo, 1908); Vasilii, episkop Mozhaiskii, *Zhizn' presviatyia i preblagoslovennyia Bogoroditsy i Prisnodevy Marii: Dushespasitel'nyia besedy* (Sergiev Posad: Tip. Sv. Tr. Sergievoi Lavry, 1914).
28. Although it is impossible to identify the compilers of all of the versions of the published *Lives* in late imperial Russia, in addition to Avdot'ia Glinka and Sof'ia Snessoreva, some of the compilers include: Petr Simonovich Kaznaskii, (d. 1878), a layman, historian and graduate from the Moscow Theological Academy; I. V. Krasnitskii, a layman, devotional writer, and bibliographer (d. 1900); P. Losev, a layman, devotional writer and author of a catechetical textbook; E. N. Poselianin (Pogozhev), a layman, devotional writer from a noble family; executed 1931; Ivan Evgen'evich Rozanov, a deacon; Mikhail Il'ich Sokolov (d. 1885), a priest and devotional writer who published in *Rukovodstvo dlia sel'skikh pastyrei* and *Tserkovnyi vestnik*; Arkhimandrit Ioann Veriuzhskii (d. 1907), superior of the Kirillo-Novozerskii monastery: 'Nekrolog', *Vologodskie eparkhial'nye vedomosti*, no. 2 (1907), 40–41. It is noteworthy that Avdot'ia Glinka was also a composer of akathist hymns, a genre of devotional hymnody that became extraordinarily popular in nineteenth-century Russia. For akathist hymns to the Mother of God, see Vera Shevzov, 'Between Popular and Official: *Akafisty* Hymns and Marian Icons in Late Imperial Russia', in *Letters from Heaven: Popular Religion in Russia and Ukraine*, ed. by John-Paul Himka and Andriy Zayarnyuk (Toronto: University of Toronto Press, 2006), pp. 251–77.

presviatoi Devy Bogoroditsy po knigam Chet'i-Mineiam), first published in 1840.[29] Having compiled her work from the references to Mary in the *Menalogion (Chet'i-Minei)* by Dimitrii, Metropolitan of Rostov, Glinka stated that she had been inspired to take on this project for two reasons.[30] First, she believed such a text would provide people with a relatively complete *Life* of the Mother of God, which could serve as spiritual inspiration and edification. She noted that she had enjoyed spiritual benefit while working on this project. As she wrote, the scenes frequently brought tears of compunction to her eyes: 'I acknowledge – no one secular book [...] has had such a touching effect on me'.[31]

Second, Glinka was sensitive to the dilemmas of Christianity in a modernizing world, a sentiment shared by Abbot Orsini with regard to his compilation of a *Life* of Mary in France.[32] Glinka wished to make Mary's life more accessible to the common, secular ear; hence, she translated the relevant passages from the Slavonic *menalogion* into modern Russian, an effort Orthodox clergy found commendable.[33] Glinka's progressive efforts proved fruitful. Her version of the *Earthly Life* was an immediate success; by 1915 it had gone through sixteen editions.

Sof'ia Snessoreva, whose *Life* of Mary (*Zemnaia zhizn' presviatoi Bogoroditsy i opisanie sviatykh chudotvornykh ee ikon*) was published some fifty years later (1891), seems to have been motivated by similar sensibilities. A translator, Snessoreva had worked for such well-known publications as *Library for Reading* (*Biblioteka dlia chteniia*), *Collection of Foreign Novels* (*Sobranie inostrannykh romanov*), and *Notes of the Fatherland* (*Otechestvennye zapiski*).[34] Her life path eventually led her to become a

---

29. For biographical information on Avdot'ia Pavlovna Glinka, see N. L., *O zhizni i konchine Avdot'i Pavlovny Glinki* (St Petersburg: Tip. Imp. Akad. Nauk, 1863).
30. *Zhizn' presviatoi devy Bogoroditsy po knigam Chet'i-Mineiam*, comp. by Avdot'ia Glinka, 14th edn (Moscow: Tip. Stupina, 1904), pp. 5–7. The *Chet'i-Minei* is a twelve-volume collection of the lives of saints and readings for feasts for every day of the liturgical year.
31. Glinka, *Zhizn' presviatoi devy Bogoroditsy*, p. 7.
32. In the preface to his work, Abbot Orsini had indicated that one of the reasons for compiling the life of Mary concerned the need to modernize the appeal of the Christian faith: *Life of the Blessed Virgin Mary*, pp. v-ix.
33. V. Grechulevich, 'Skazaniia o zemnoi zhizni Presviatoi Bogoroditsy s izlozheniem ucheniia Tserkvi', *Strannik*, Otdel III Bibliograficheskii, 3 (1869), 55–59.
34. For Snessoreva's autobiographical reflections, see S. I. Snessoreva, 'Avtobiograficheskiia zapiski', in *Sviatitel' Ignatii Brianchaninov. Polnoe sobranie tvorenii*, 5 vols (Moscow: Palomnik, 2003), 5, 239–54; E. M. Aksenenko, 'Avtobiograficheskii ocherk S. I. Snessorevoi "Na Pamiat' Drugu"', *Ezhegodnik Rukopisnogo otdela Pushkinskogo doma na 2001* (St Petersburg: Dmitrii Bulanin, 2006), pp. 158–68.

spiritual daughter of the well-known monastic writer and later bishop, Ignatii Brianchaninov. He, in turn, drew upon her connections to the literary world and became indebted to her for the publication of many of his works.³⁵ Though she clearly loved her work as a translator of secular European literature, under the encouragement and influence of Brianchaninov, Snessoreva began writing spiritual works, culminating with the publication of a *Life* of Mary when she was 83. Like Glinka, she too, was moved by Mary. As one reviewer of her book wrote, her work 'is permeated with and warmed by the religious sensibilities of its author'.³⁶ Yet unlike Glinka, whose work drew almost exclusively on Metropolitan Dimitrii of Rostov's *menologion*, Snessoreva culled from a wide variety of sources, including the fourteenth-century Byzantine historian Nicephorus Callistus Zanathopoulos (d. 1335). Comparable to the work of hagiographers in late antiquity, Glinka's and Snessoreva's work with Mary's life became a means of not only expressing their own devotion but, as Derek Kruger has observed, 'a technology for its cultivation'.³⁷

The Byzantine predecessors of Russia's nineteenth-century *Lives* of Mary exhibited two tendencies with respect to her portrayal. According to the historian of Christianity, Stephen Shoemaker, the first tendency appeared in a *Life of the Virgin*, dating back as early as the seventh century; it emphasized Mary's active presence during Jesus' ministry and in the early Christian community after his death. According to this seventh-century *Life*, Mary was active during her son's ministry as a leader and guardian of the women who followed him. This early text also depicted her as the sole witness to the resurrection. She announced the glad tidings to the disciples and to the myrrh-bearing women. Finally, this *Life* placed the Mother of God at the centre of the Christian community following Jesus' ascension: 'She was a leader and a teacher to the holy apostles', the text states.³⁸

Another *Life* of Mary that appeared later in monastic circles (in the ninth and tenth centuries) exhibits a second tendency. The extent to which it minimises Mary's role, both during Jesus' ministry and in the early years

---

35. For correspondence between Ignatii Brianchaninov and Sof'ia Snessoreva, see 'Pis'ma sviatitelia Ignatiia Brianchaninova k S. I. Snessorevoi, *Sviatitel' Ignatii Brianchaninov. Polnoe sobranie tvorenii*, V, 487–554.
36. *Bogoslovskii bibliograficheskii listok*, 463.
37. Derek Krueger, *Writing and Holiness: The Practice of Authorship in the Early Christian East* (University of Pennsylvania Press, 2004), p. 4.
38. Shoemaker, 'The Virgin Mary in the Ministry of Jesus', p. 455.

of the Christian community, is striking. This *Life* of Mary, composed by Epiphanius the Monk in Constantinople in the ninth century, did not even mention her presence at the wedding at Cana. Similarly, Mary neither bore witness to the resurrection, nor was among the women who found the empty tomb. Instead, this *Life* portrayed her as having stayed at home because her grief was too great.[39]

The numerous *Lives* of Mary published in nineteenth-century Russia generally fall between these two types. Some versions of her *Life* stray little from the Gospel texts.[40] The majority of *Lives*, however, follow the chronology of the biblical narrative, but draw to one degree or another on the apocryphal narratives that describe Mary's birth, childhood and death, as well as writings attributed (sometimes falsely) to such well-known Christian authors as Ignatius of Antioch, Andrew of Crete, John Chrysostom and Ambrose of Milan, among others. The *Lives* also sometimes make extensive use of liturgical texts, hymnody and whatever else their compilers assumed as belonging under the canopy of 'tradition', and therefore worthy of communication. In the end, the *Lives* are distinguished from one another not only by the stories the compilers chose to include, but also by the compiler's own intermittent interpretation and commentary.

The *Life* of Mary: Vocation and Motherhood

The *Lives* of Mary, though often similar in terms of chapter composition, varied in style and emphasis. Some compilers, for instance, wove their narrative voices freely into the text; others chose a more reserved approach and focused more strictly on the New Testament and traditional liturgical texts.[41] Some compilations read as weighty panegyrics that meditated on Mary as an 'imprint of perfection', upon whom God continually gazed 'with eyes of favour'.[42] Such *Lives* often opened with a review of the classical biblical prefigurations and prophecies that ancient Christians believed

---

39. Shoemaker, 'The Virgin Mary in the Ministry of Jesus', p. 458.
40. *Zemnaia zhizn' Tsaritsy Nebesnoi* (Moscow: Sinodal'naia tipografiia, 1913).
41. As examples, see P. S. Kazanskii, *Zemnaia zhizn' Presviatoi Bogoroditsy* (St Petersburg: Izd. Elagina, 1870); M. I. Sokolov, *Zhizn' Bozhiei Materi* (St Petersburg: Tip. Tovarishchestva 'Obshchestvennaia pol'za', 1873); *Zemnaia zhizn' Tsaritsy Nebesnoi* (Moscow: Sinodal'naia tipografiia, 1913).
42. *Raduisia Blagodatnaia, Gospod' s Toboiu. Blagochestivyia razmyshleniia o rozhdenii, zemnoi zhizni, i vziatii na nebo Presviatoi Devy Marii*, 8th edn (Moscow: Universitetskaia tip., 1859), pp. 14–15 and chapter 4.

had foretold Mary's role in salvation history.[43] Others, while never losing sight of her perceived unique role in salvation history, steered their readers toward considering the complications, dilemmas, challenges and dangers that Mary humanly faced despite that role. Amid the sometimes subtle differences in presentation and emphases, three characteristic features of Mary in these *Lives* come into relief when considering images of Mary in pre-revolutionary Russia: her character, her maternal experiences and her leadership role.

In addition to depicting Mary as educated, hard-working (especially after Joseph's death), courageous (*muzhestvennaia*) and, in some instances, even politically aware, the *Lives* consistently portray Mary as a woman very much attuned to her own vocation, willing to defy convention in order to follow that perceived calling, despite the seemingly contradictory ways it led her.[44] For instance, her self-imposed vow of virginity, which resulted from this sense of vocation, functioned as a sign of independence from hierarchical structures. According to most nineteenth-century accounts of Mary's *Life*, the temple priests were confounded by Mary's decision to forego marriage in order to remain a virgin. Glinka and Snessoreva, along with other compilers, maintained that the high priests were caught off-guard by her 'strong determination' and 'firm response', as well as by the 'novelty' of her decision.[45] They recalled no precedent for such a decision.[46] Similarly, the *Lives* state that even after her betrothal to the eighty-year-old widower

---

43. *Raduisia Blagodatnaia, Gospod' s Toboiu* (Moscow: Universitetskaia tip, 1859); *Zemnaia zhizn' Presviatyia Bogoroditsy: Blagochestivyia razmyshleniia khristianina* (Moscow: Tip. A. Semena, 1863), p. 12; Sokolov, *Zhizn' Bozhiei Materi*.
44. For examples where compilers emphasized Mary's intellectual acumen and enlightened mind, see *Zemnaia zhizn' Presviatoi Bogoroditsy i Prisno-Devy Marii* (Moscow: Tip. Orlova, 1876), p. 15; *Zhizn' Presviatoi Bogoroditsy* (Moscow: Tip. Sytina, 1903), p. 9; Poselianin, *Bogomater' na zemle*, p. 26. For compilers who mentioned her work ethic, see *Zemnaia zhizn' Presviatoi Bogoroditsy* (Moscow: Izd. Gubanova, 1886), p. 25; *Zemnaia zhizn' Presviatoi Bogoroditsy* (Odessa: E. I. Fesenko, 1896), p. 94; Poselianin, *Bogomater' na zemle*, pp. 50, 61. For Mary's courage, see *Zemnaia zhizn' presviatyia Bogoroditsy* (Moscow, 1863), p. 30; Glinka, *Zhizn' presviatoi devy Bogoroditsy*, p. 57. For Mary's political awareness, see *Zhizn' Presviatoi Bogoroditsy* (Moscow: Tip. Sytina, 1903), pp. 88–89.
45. S. I. Snessoreva, *Zemnaia zhizn' Presviatoi Bogoroditsy* (St Petersburg: I. L. Tuzov, 1898), p. 20; *Zemnaia zhizn' Presviatoi Bogoroditsy* (Moscow: Sytin, 1892), pp. 43–44; I. Krasnitskii, *Zemnaia zhizn' Presviatoi Bogoroditsy* (Novocherkassk: Donskaia tipografiia, 1893), p. 7; *Zemnaia zhizn' Presviatoi Devy Marii* (Moscow: Izd. Afonskago sv. Proroka Il'ii skita, 1899), p. 26; *Zemnaia zhizn' Presviatoi Bogoroditsy* (Odessa: E. I. Fesenko, 1914), p. 32; *Zemnaia zhizn' Presviatoi Bogoroditsy*, comp. by Sviashchennik Pokrovskii (Moscow: Tip. Sytina, 1915), p. 15.
46. For examples, see Glinka, *Zhizn' presviatoi devy Bogoroditsy* p. 45; *Zemnaia zhizn' Presviatoi Bogoroditsy i Prisno-Devy Marii* (Moscow: Tip. Orlova, 1876), p. 14.

Joseph, Mary continued to live according to her perceived calling and did not unequivocally conform to the life of Joseph's busy household. She seems to have lived in Joseph's home but did not, at least at first, forego her aspirations in order to cultivate family bonds.[47] Her vocation took precedence.

At the same time, in contrast to the Gospel texts in which family was redefined largely in terms of discipleship, many of the *Lives* are significantly more sensitive to traditional family bonds. The deacon, I. E. Rozanov, for example, emphasized the spiritual benefits and joys of family life and considered the nature of human bonding unique to the parent-child relationship.[48] This is also evident with respect to the portrayal of Mary's alleged parents. Some versions of Mary's life depict Joachim and Anna hesitating to fulfil their vow of dedicating Mary to the temple. Instead, a determined three-year-old Mary convinces them to let her go. Similarly, in some versions, Anna not only regularly visits Mary, but, along with Joachim, eventually moves to Jerusalem in order to be closer to her daughter and to participate in her upbringing. When Joachim dies, some *Lives* note that Anna moves in with Mary and spends the last two years of her life with her.[49] In her compilation, Glinka included a discussion of the feast of the Annunciation by the Archbishop of Tver, Grigorii (Postnikov), in which he linked the power of Mary's prayer to the lack of parental love. She engaged in prayer, he maintained, 'when the emptiness of her heart desired fullness'.[50]

The Gospel texts offer scant insights into Mary's life and disposition during the years of Jesus' youth and ministry. Only two, the Gospel according to Matthew and the Gospel according to Luke, relate any details about Mary and her infant son. After their brief mention of Jesus' birth and, in Matthew, the family's flight to Egypt and eventual return to Nazareth, these texts offer readers only four glimpses of Mary for the duration of Jesus' short life.[51] The nineteenth-century *Lives* of Mary often recognize

---

47. As examples, see Glinka, *Zhizn' presviatoi devy Bogoroditsy*, p. 48; *O zemnoi zhizni Presviatoi Bogoroditsy: Narodnyie chteniia* (St Petersburg: Tip. Straufa, 1890); *Zemnaia zhizn' Presviatoi Bogoroditsy* (Odessa: E. I. Fesenko, 1896), pp. 23, 25; Pokrovskii, *Zemnaia zhizn' Presviatoi Bogoroditsy*, p. 15.
48. I. E. Rozanov, *Zemnaia zhizn' Presviatyia Bogoroditsy*, 2nd edn (Moscow: L. F. Snegirev, 1885).
49. *Zemnaia zhizn' Presviatoi Bogoroditsy* (Moscow: Tip. Orlova, 1876), p. 18; Rozanov, *Zemnaia zhizn' Presviatyia Bogoroditsy*, p. 10; *Zemnaia zhizn' Presviatoi Bogoroditsy* (Odessa: E. I. Fesenko, 1896), p. 37; Veriuzhskii, *Beseda s russkimi bogomol'tsami*, p. 6.
50. Glinka, *Zhizn' presviatoi devy Bogoroditsy*, p. 236.
51. The four scenes include: 1) Mark 3:31–35 with parallels in Matthew 12:46–50 and Luke

this conspicuous lacuna in Scripture and address it. Several compilers reflected upon the anonymity of motherhood and its consequences. As an 'invisible' period in a mother's life, the years of child-rearing generally escape historical attention. Mary, in this sense, was no different from other mothers.[52] In an attempt to rehabilitate this anonymity, one version of Mary's life reminded its readers that often it was not the most conspicuous actions in history, but the 'inner', not immediately evident, ones that ultimately proved historically most significant.[53]

Other authors attempted to dispel the 'deep anonymity' and 'impenetrable veil' of silence surrounding Mary's motherhood by encouraging readers to imagine her hypothetical conversations with Jesus, when they 'inclined their heads together'. It was at these moments that he may have disclosed mysteries known to her alone.[54] While some versions of Mary's *Life* predictably maintain that Jesus, as the Word of God incarnate, needed no instruction, others emphasize that he followed the development laws of all children. Hence, Mary's and Joseph's roles were not superfluous in his upbringing.[55] Evgenii Poselianin emphasized that the holy family was a working family and that Mary, too, worked. As a single mother following Joseph's death, her work only increased so as to be able to support her son.[56] Another compiler, who composed a *Life* for public reading groups among 'the people', specifically noted that Mary took on the education of her son and served as an example to parents in child-rearing.[57]

Texts are more divided with respect to Mary's role during Jesus' ministry. Some versions of Mary's *Life* maintain that, despite scriptural silence on

---

8:19–21; 2) Mark 6:1–6 with parallels in Matthew 13: 53–58 and Luke 4:16–30; 3) Luke 2:41–52 and 4) John 2:1–2.

52. Poselianin, *Bogomater' na zemle*, p. 51; *Zemnaia zhizn' Presviatoi Bogoroditsy* (Moscow, Tip. A. Semena, 1863), p. 31; Ieromonakh Stefan, *Zhizn' preblagoslovennoi vladychitsy nashei Bogoroditsy*, p. 45.

53. *Zemnaia zhizn' Presviatoi Devy Marii Bogoroditsy* (Moscow: Izd. Afonskago sv. Proroka Il'ii skita, 1899), p. 57.

54. *Zemnaia zhizn' Presviatyia Bogoroditsy* (Moscow, Tip. A. Semena, 1863), pp. 30–31; Snessoreva, *Zemnaia zhizn'*, p. 47; *Zemnaia zhizn' Presviatoi Devy Marii Bogoroditsy* (Moscow: Izd. Afonskago sv. Proroka Il'ii skita, 1899), p. 56; *Zhizn' Presviatoi Bogoroditsy s prilozheniem skazanii o chudotvornykh ikonakh ee* (Moscow: Tip. Sytina, 1903), p. 89; *Zemnaia zhizn Tsaritsy Nebesnoi* (Moscow: Sinodal'naia tipografiia, 1913), p. 19.

55. *Zemnaia zhizn' Presviatoi Bogoroditsy i ee chudesa* (Moscow: Izd. Gubanova, 1886), p. 25; *O zemnoi zhizni Presviatoi Bogoroditsy* (St Petersburg: Tip. Straufa, 1890), p. 18; *Zemnaia zhizn' Presviatoi Bogoroditsy* (Odessa: E. I. Fesenko, 1896), p. 94; *Zhizn' Presviatoi Bogoroditsy* (Moscow: Tip. Sytina, 1903), p. 89.

56. Poselianin, *Bogomater' na zemle*, pp. 50–51, 54.

57. *O zemnoi zhizni Presviatoi Bogoroditsy* (St Petersburg: Tip. Straufa, 1890), p. 56.

the matter, Mary was undoubtedly among the women who followed Jesus throughout his ministry.[58] The version of Mary's *Life* that originated in the Skete of the prophet Elijah on Mount Athos, for instance, agrees that while Mary was present in Jesus' company throughout his ministry and served as an inspiration for the other women in the group, she at no time manifested her 'maternal rights' over him. In other words, the compiler of this text made a point to emphasize that Mary's sphere of influence did not extend to the content of Jesus' ministry.[59] Other versions of Mary's life, such as Snessoreva's, left Mary outside the purview of Jesus' ministry altogether, maintaining that Mary spent very little time with him during those years.[60] While authors often attempted to decipher the meaning of scriptural silence regarding this period in Mary's life, few actually interpreted it as an overt virtue, as did the rural priest M. Sokolov from the Smolensk diocese. In his version of Mary's *Life*, he maintained that 'nothing better demonstrated the Holy Virgin's humility and meekness than her silence during Jesus' ministry'.[61]

Despite their views on Mary's whereabouts during the three years of Jesus' active ministry, all versions of Mary's *Life* have her joining him in Jerusalem for his final days. From this point, as Snessoreva reported, Mary remained as close to her son as possible and if she did not visually witness the events that unfolded, then at least she heard what transpired.[62] Accordingly, compilers often retained the ancient tradition that considered Mary a unique witness to the last days of Jesus' life.

Mary's motherhood comes into particular relief in descriptions of her experiences during the final hours of her son's life. All of the texts dwell on her maternal agony in the face of the excruciating torture of her only child. Some *Lives* depict her as making a desperate appeal to Pilate in person.[63] The depth of this agony explains why, according to many compilers, Jesus did not address Mary as 'mother' in his last words to her on the Cross; instead he

---

58. As examples, see Stul'tsev, *Zhizn' presviatyia vladychitsy nasheia Bogoroditsy*, p. 67; *Zemnaia zhizn' Presviatoi Bogoroditsy* (Moscow: Tip. Orlova, 1876), p. 45. *Zemnaia zhizn' Presviatoi Bogoroditsy* (Moscow: Tip. Sytina, 1892); *Zemnaia zhizn' Presviatoi Bogoroditsy* (Odessa: E. I. Fesenko, 1896), p. 100.
59. *Zemnaia zhizn' presviatoi devy Marii Bogoroditsy* (Moscow: Izd. Afonskago sv. Proroka Il'ii skita, 1899), p. 58.
60. Snessoreva, *Zemnaia zhizn'*, p. 51; *Zhizn' Presviatoi Bogoroditsy* (Moscow: Tip. Sytina, 1903), p. 93.
61. Sokolov, *Zhizn' Bozhiei Materi*, p. 22.
62. Snessoreva, *Zemnaia zhizn'*, p. 55.
63. *O zemnoi zhizni Presviatoi Bogoroditsy: Narodnye chteniia* (St Petersburg: Tip. Straufa, 1890), p. 36; Kuzmicheev, *Zemnaia zhizn' Presviatoi Bogoroditsy* (Moscow: Izd. Morozova, 1894), p. 90; Poselianin, *Bogomater' na zemle*, p. 60.

chose the more formal 'woman', trying to spare her grief.⁶⁴ Several versions even attempt to penetrate the character of that suffering. The well-known devotional writer, Evgenii Poselianin, described in most compelling terms the inner turmoil and anguish of a woman torn between a deep faith in, and understanding of, the cause for which her son chose to die and her profound, unique and unrepeatable bond with an only child. Even at this final stand, according to Poselianin, 'a secret, silent conversation, never recognized by the world', took place between mother and son.⁶⁵

Because of the power and privilege of motherhood, the majority of the *Lives* did not accept at face value Scripture's silence regarding Mary's witness of the resurrection. After all, claimed one anonymous compiler, 'she undoubtedly had more right to see the Saviour' than anyone else.⁶⁶ Accordingly, the *Lives* of Mary often follow the ancient tradition that places Mary as the first witness to the resurrection. Some versions also included the ancient explanation of why such an important 'fact' was not included in the Gospel accounts. Compilers maintained that this detail was omitted so as not to give anyone pause to doubt the resurrection, since mothers can be biased. For this reason Mary herself forbade the disciples to speak about her or her testimonies directly.⁶⁷

Finally, the nineteenth-century *Lives* of Mary included those scenes from ancient narratives that depicted her as an influential teacher and administrator in the life of the early Church. One version refers to her as the 'focal point' of the young Christian community.⁶⁸ Fearlessly, claimed Snessoreva, 'she directed the first steps of the infant church' and guided the apostles on their missionary itineraries. According to the nineteenth-century *Lives*, Mary also reportedly participated in missionary work, which, in one account, earned her the title of 'holy preacher' (*sviataia propovednitsa*).⁶⁹ The

---

64. *Zemnaia zhizn' Presviatyia Bogoroditsy* (Moscow: Tip. A. Semena, 1863), pp. 40–41; *Zemnaia zhizn' Presviatyia Bogoroditsy*, 16th edn (St Petersburg, Izd. A. A. Kholmushina, 1897), pp. 21–22; Snessoreva, *Zemnaia zhizn'*, p. 56; *Zemnaia zhizn' Presviatoi Devy Marii Bogoroditsy* (Moscow: Izd. Afonskago sv. Proroka Il'ii skita, 1899), p. 65.
65. Poselianin, *Bogomater' na zemle*, pp. 56, 61. Also see, *Zemnaia zhizn' Presviatoi Bogoroditsy* (Moscow: Tip. Orlova, 1976), p. 43; Rozanov, *Zemnaia zhizn' Presviatoi Bogoroditsy*, p. 40; P. Losev, *Zemnaia zhizn' presviatoi Bogoroditsy* (Moscow, 1897), p. 43.
66. *Zemnaia zhizn' Presviatoi Devy Marii Bogoroditsy* (Moscow: Izd. Afonskago, sv. Proroka Il'ii skita, 1899), p. 76.
67. Snessoreva, *Zemnaia zhizn'*, p. 60. Other examples where Mary was portrayed as the first witness to the Resurrection, *Raduisia Blagodatnaia, Gospod' s Toboiu*, (Moscow: Universitetskaia tip., 1859), p. 85; *Zemnoe zhitie Bogoroditsy Devy – upovaniia khristianom* (Moscow: Tip. Pogodina, 1871), p. 31; *Zemnaia zhizn' Presviatoi Bogoroditsy* (Odessa: E. I. Fesenko, 1896), p. 107.
68. Poselianin, *Bogomater' na zemle*, p. 70.
69. *O zemnoi zhizni Presviatoi Bogoroditsy* (St Petersburg: Tip. Straufa, 1890), p. 35. For

apostles routinely turned to her for guidance and support, seeing in her 'the face of their Lord'.⁷⁰ Moreover, because she was the first to comprehend the significance of the events surrounding the life and death of her son, she was the 'Apostle to the apostles', speaking words as if from the lips of the Lord himself.⁷¹ New members of the young community would travel from afar to hear her speak. As the primary source of information concerning the life and teachings of Jesus that were known only to her as his mother, she was not only a source of inspiration but, as Glinka's compilation suggests, one of the primary sources for the Gospel narrative.⁷²

Throughout most of the nineteenth century, the published *Lives* of Mary typically end with her death or dormition. Occasionally, authors added a chapter on Mary's appearances after her death, and one version added a chapter on posthumous miracles attributed to her.⁷³ During the second quarter of the nineteenth century, however, accounts of Mary's life increasingly began to include a compendium of images of Russia's most specially-revered Marian icons and the miracle stories associated with them. Prior to this time, Mary's life and the compendia of her miracle-working images were for the most part published separately. Combining the two genres offered an added dimension, both to Mary's life, and to her miracle-working images. On the one hand, the combined genre expanded the scope and meaning of Mary's life and motherhood. With Mary's life now encompassing the chronicles associated with her icons, her authority, identity and meaning were no longer simply a part of the past, but were confirmed as relating to the

---

other examples see, *Zemnoe zhitie Bogoroditsy Devy – upovaniia khristianom* (Moscow: Tip. Pogodina, 1871), p. 32; Rozanov, *Zemnaia zhizn' Presviatoi Bogoroditsy*, p. 46; Krasnitskii, *Zemnaia zhizn' Presviatoi Bogoroditsy*, p. 30. Many of the descriptions of Mary as a missionary are based on a narrative describing Mary's visit to Mt. Athos and her interaction with its non-Christian inhabitants. In the late nineteenth-century, in a desire to purge Christianity of 'lies to which it is intolerant', the archeologist and Bishop Porfirii (Uspenskii) maintained that the story was a popular local Athonite myth on which Georgian monks from the Iveron monastery on Mount Athos had capitalised in the late sixteenth- and early seventeenth-century in order to give added weight to their own community. See Episkop Porfirii (Uspenskii), *Istoriia Afona v dvukh tomakh*, 2 vols (1892; reprint, Moscow: DAR, 2007), I, 212.

70. Glinka, *Zemnaia zhizn' Bogoroditsy*, p. 149.
71. Snessoreva, *Zemnaia zhizn'*, p. 60; *Zemnaia zhizn' Presviatoi Bogoroditsy* (Odessa: E. I. Fesenko, 1896), p. 112.
72. Glinka, *Zhizn' presviatoi devy Bogoroditsy*, p. 146–47; *Zemnoe zhitie Bogoroditsy Devy – upovaniia khristianom* (Moscow: Tip. Pogodina, 1871), pp. 32–33; *O zemnoi zhizni Presviatoi Bogoroditsy* (St Petersburg: Tip. Straufa, 1890), p. 35; *Zemnaia zhizn' Presviatoi Bogoroditsy* (Moscow: Tip. Sytina, 1892), p. 133. *Zemnaia zhizn' Presviatoi Devy Marii Bogoroditsy* (Moscow: Izd. Afonskago sv. Proroka Il'ii skita, 1899), p. 77.
73. *Zemnaia zhizn' presviatoi Bogoroditsy i ee chudesa* (Moscow: E. A. Gubanov, 1886).

present.[74] The life of Mary in the devotional imagination did not cease with her death. On the other hand, the combined genre also effectively dispelled modern inclinations to separate the 'unmodern' or perceived superstitious phenomenon of miracle-working icons from the Orthodox tradition of Marian veneration. Finally, by being linked to a narrative of Mary's life that was based primarily on scripture, patristic writings and hymnography, as well as on generally accepted ancient apocryphal stories, Russia's myriad of miracle-working icons of Mary, though visually manifold, were unified in light of Mary's life. The *Life* of Mary, in other words, focused the believer's gaze before the believer's attention became redirected to the multitude of her icons, each with its own complex story.

The Appeal of Mary's *Life* in late Imperial Russia

The popular appeal of Mary's life for Russia's Orthodox women in the nineteenth and early twentieth centuries is difficult to gauge. The direct testimonies of Glinka's and Senssoreva's work and the indirect evidence that these *Lives* were sold by traveling peddlers, found in peasant homes and in rural and urban libraries suggests that Orthodox women in Russia were familiar with these accounts. Moreover, since clergy turned to Mary's life as a source for preaching and public discussion, many women would have been comfortable with the process of imagining the character of her life. One way to consider the potential impact of these accounts is to read them in light of Orthodox responses to the women's movement in the late Imperial period.[75] In what way did the image of Mary, as presented in the *Lives*, correspond to the ideals and images of women, in particular Mary, described in these responses to the women's movement?

In essays and sermons that directly addressed issues the women's movement raised, churchmen generally agreed on the essential equality by nature of men and women, basing their views either on the creation

---

74. As examples, see Sokolov, *Zhizn' Bozhiei Materi* (St Petersburg: Tip. Tovarishchestva 'Obshchestvennaia pol'za', 1873), p. 28.
75. For an excellent and insightful overview of Orthodox clergy's views on the nature and roles of women in late imperial Russia, see William G. Wagner, '"Orthodox Domesticity": Creating a Social Role for Women', in *Sacred Stories: Religion and Spirituality in Modern Russia*, ed. by Mark D. Steinberg and Heather J. Coleman (Bloomington, IN: Indiana University Press, 2007), pp. 119–45. For a history of the women's movement in Russia, see Richard Stites, *The Women's Liberation Movement in Russia: Feminism, Nihilism, Bolshevism, 1860–1930* (Princeton: Princeton University Press, 1978); Linda Edmondson, *The Feminist Movement in Russia: 1900–1917* (Stanford: Stanford University Press, 1984).

story in Genesis (1:26–31; 2:4–25) or on Paul's assertion in his letter to the Galatians (3:29), that there is neither male nor female 'in Christ'. In the essential matters of redemption, salvation and the Kingdom of God, they thus maintained no differences between men and women.[76] Such essential equality, they often argued, was a unique trait of Christianity that set it apart from other religions in the world of late antiquity.[77]

At the same time, however, churchmen differed in their evaluations of the distinction between the sexes in this life.[78] On the one hand, some churchmen did not share the Orthodox establishment's view that the image of God shone directly only through men – women reflecting that image only indirectly, by means of their husbands.[79] Some clergy dismissed feminist demands for equal rights in the workforce by insisting on women's inferior intellectual and physical strength.[80] As the priest N. Steletskii wrote in 1909, 'we are convinced that to no female is it given to develop genuinely creative activity, to pave the way for new paths in the sciences or the arts, or to produce something that would have true significance in the history of culture and that would facilitate progress'.[81]

On the other hand, in attempting to embrace modern ideals and aspirations, other churchmen were significantly more moderate in their consideration of distinctions between men and women. Describing women as 'equal participants' in life and equal helpmates on the home front, they also recognized the intellectual acumen of women and argued strongly for their professional education.[82] In his support for women's education, a lay

---

76. As an example, see I. Galakhov, 'Zhenskii vopros, ego prichiny i otsenki s khristianskoi tochki zreniia', *Khristianskoe chtenie* (July, 1903), pp. 102–03; *Zhenshchina-khristianka* (Moscow: Sinodal'naia tipografiia, 1905), p. 23; *Zhenshchina-khristianka* (Kaluga: Tip. Gubernskago pravleniia, 1912).
77. *Velikoe vospitatel'noe znachenie Khristianskoi zhenshchiny: rech' vospitannitsam, okonchivshim kurs v 3i zhenskoi gimnazii v 1893 godu* (Moscow: Univeritetskaia tipografiia, 1893); A. V. Nikitin, 'Khristianskii vzgliad na znachenie i prava zhenshchiny', *Vera i tserkov'*, 1.5 (1899), 718–56; Episkop Vissarion, 'Polozhenie lits zhenskago pola v zhizni khristianskoi, semeinoi i obshchestvennoi', *Dushepoleznoe chtenie* (November, 1902), 344–45; *Zhenshchina-khristianka* (Moscow, 1905).
78. Preosviashchennyi Nikanor, episkop Ufimskii, 'Ideal zhenshchiny khristianki: Pouchenie v den' Prechistyia devy Bogoroditsy Kazanskago Eia obraza, oktiabria 22', *Pravoslavnoe obozrenie* (November, 1882), 579–93.
79. A. N., 'Uchenie apostola Pavla o zhenskom pokryvale i zhenskom tserkovnom uchitel'stve', *Chtenie v obshchestve liubitelei dukhovnogo prosveshcheniia* (November–December, 1872), 357–85 (360).
80. Episkop Vissarion, 'Polozhenie lits zhenskago pola', pp. 346–48.
81. Nikolai Steletskii, *Khristianskoe naznachenie zhenshchiny i zhenskaia emansipatsiia nashego vremeni* (Kiev: Kievskoe Sviato-Vladimirskoe bratstvo, 1909), p. 1.
82. Aleksei Kliucharev, 'O naznachenii zhenshchiny. Slovo v den' rozhdeniia

physician writing in the devotional journal, *Beneficial Reading for the Soul* (*Dushepoleznoe chtenie*), argued that Christ himself had chosen to discuss complex theological issues with women.[83] In a similar vein, the Bishop of Tomsk, Makarii (Nevskii), maintained that women would not only benefit from theological education but from philosophical, mathematical and scientific education as well: 'From among the main fields of human knowledge, there is not one which would not be beneficial to women'.[84]

Despite their diverse evaluations of the differences between men and women, most churchmen in late Imperial Russia agreed that by divine design the two were responsible for different social spheres.[85] Writing in 1873, the priest Aleksei Kliucharev described these spheres as two 'worlds' – a 'macrocosm' (*mir velikii*) and a 'microcosm' (*mir malyi*). The macrocosm entailed the public social and political spheres of life, while the microcosm referred to the private and familial spheres.[86] Few churchmen would have disagreed that a woman's world – her 'innate kingdom' and the 'cornerstone of state and society' – was the family.[87] Churchmen differed only as to the degree of the permeability of the two worlds and the extent to which women were free to move between them.

In their efforts to define women's roles, clergy drew primarily on the images of women as mothers and helpmates as the main antidote to the growing women's movement in their midst. Despite Orthodoxy's traditional estimation of monasticism as the higher form of lifestyle, churchmen paid remarkably little attention to its ideals and virtues when it came to modern women. Instead, they insisted that motherhood and the family belonged to the essence of womanhood.

Attempting to empower women in their traditional roles, clergy countered associations of family life and marriage with confinement, by arguing for the immense potential influence (social and political) of

---

blagochestiveishiia gosudaryni imperatritsy Marii Aleksandrovny', *Dushepoleznoe chtenie*, part 3 (1873), pp. 75–85; Dimitrii Sokolov, *Naznachenie zhenshchiny po ucheniiu Slova Bozhiia* (St Petersburg: Izd. A. Katanskago, 1899), pp. 5–6.

83. Nikolai Piaskovskii, 'Istinnaia emansipatsiia i vysshee obrazovanie zhenshchin s khristianskoi tochki zreniia' *Dushepoleznoe chtenie*, part 1 (1902), 145–55 (145).
84. Makarii, Episkop Tomskii, *Obrazovanie, prava i obiazannosti zhenshchiny* (St Petersburg: Obshchestvo razprostraneniia religiozno-nravstvennogo prosveshcheniia v dukhe pravoslavnoi tserkvi. 1902), p. 5.
85. For a thorough overview of this issue, see Wagner, 'Orthodox Domesticity'.
86. Kliucharev, 'O naznachenii zhenshchiny', 75–85; *Velikoe vospitatel'noe znachenie*; Steletskii, *Khristianskoe naznachenie zhenshchiny*.
87. Kliucharev, 'O naznachenii zhenshchiny', p. 78; Piaskovskii, 'Istinnaia emansipatsiia', p. 148; Protierei Ioann Sergiev, 'Naznachenie i mesto zhenshchiny v mire i tserkvi', *Vera i tserkov'*, 10 (1902), 649–52; *Zhenshchina-khristianka* (Moscow: Sinodal'naia tipografiia, 1905), p. 10.

mothers and wives.[88] For instance, given the potential that women held to 'shape the character of the human race', one priest wondered why a woman would instead desire to participate in government life.[89] Another priest maintained that because of women's associations with life, and the creation of life, as mothers, they were meant to direct culture and history.[90]

In 1864, an anonymous, Orthodox woman voiced similar sentiments in an unusual essay published in the devotional journal, *Beneficial Reading for the Soul*. Voicing her concerns about the potential complications the women's movement might have for children and family life, she advocated a higher social, political and civic evaluation of motherhood. Alluding to her own experiences as a mother, she spoke of the unique position she held, and of the freedom and independence that role gave her, with respect to social influence.[91] As mothers and overseers of the 'microcosmic' or 'inner' sphere of human life, she maintained, women were positioned at the very core of society, the very functioning of which depended on them.

Remarkably, in their response to the women's movement and their deliberations on the role of women in contemporary society, Orthodox churchmen did not routinely draw on the image of Mary in support of their views or as a model to imitate. When they did introduce her, they spoke of her most often theologically and meta-historically in light of the Incarnation.[92] Her role as God-bearer in salvation history, they argued, placed her at the forefront of any discussion of women and liberation for several reasons. Because God had chosen to clothe himself in the humanity of a woman, reasoned Aleksandr Nadezhdin in 1872, there could be no doubt about women's dignity and glory. Given Mary's role in salvation history, he argued, any contempt and disrespect for women was 'abnormal'.[93] In maintaining that Mary's role in salvation history ensured the high esteem of women at large, Orthodox churchmen also sometimes considered the classical Christian view of the relationship between Mary and Eve. Through her love and humility, Mary, in this view, willfully 'accepted God into herself' and thereby restored

---

88. *Velikoe vospitatel'noe znachenie*.
89. *Zhenshchina-Khristianka* (Kaluga: Tip. Gubernskago pravleniia, 1912).
90. *Zhenshchina-Khristianka*, p. 33.
91. E. P-a., 'Emansipatsiia zhenshchin', *Dushepoleznoe chtenie*, part 2 (1864), 317–38. It was highly unusual for women to publish in Orthodox periodicals at the time.
92. Dmitrii Derzhavin, 'Doblestnaia zhena po izobrazheniiu Solomona Prit. 31: 10–32', *Dushepoleznoe chtenie*, part 2 (1866), 226–43; Episkop Vissarion, 'Polozhenie lits zhenskago pola', p. 245.
93. Aleksandr Nadezhdin, 'Zhenshchiny v istorii khristianskoi tserkvi', *Strannik*, 12 (1872), 141–86.

to all of creation what Eve had lost – namely, a life in communion with God.[94] In so doing, Mary was the first genuinely-emancipated woman who not only enjoyed such communion herself, but enabled it for all of creation.[95] Writing in 1873, the priest A. Khoinatskii even suggested that in the person of Mary, women might be imagined as occupying a higher place than men in the Kingdom of God, since Mary had proven herself more honourable than even the angelic hosts.[96]

While churchmen readily hailed Mary theologically as the first genuinely emancipated woman, they found more difficulty in convincingly translating that role into their depiction of Mary as a mother in first-century Palestine and as a member of the earliest Christian community. Especially striking was churchmen's minimization of any potential public leadership roles that Mary might have held among the earliest followers of Jesus. Given the Orthodox understanding of Jesus as the incarnate Logos of God, it is not surprising that neither the *Lives* of Mary nor churchmen's responses to the women's movement offered her a prominent role in Jesus' ministry. Yet clerical responses to the women's movement also rarely considered such a role for her in the Christian community even following Jesus' death and resurrection. Despite their general lauding of what they deemed characteristically female traits – multi-tasking and effective managerial skills – Mary, in their estimation, had 'no independent significance' in the management of the earliest Christian community.[97]

In part, churchmen's minimization of Mary's role in the post-resurrectional Christian community may have stemmed from their concerns regarding a growing discussion about the ordination of women.[98] In an 1873 essay devoted to this topic, the priest A. Khoinatskii insisted that even though Mary lived in the temple during her childhood and had access to the Holy of Holies, she never had a priestly function, nor presided over

---

94. Sokolov, *Naznachenie zhenshchiny*, p. 7.
95. Piaskovskii, 'Istinnaia emansipatsiia', p. 145.
96. A. F. Khoinatskii, 'O pritiazaniiakh nekotorykh sovremennykh zhenshchin na sviashennosluzhenie v tserkvi Khristianskoi', *Dushepoleznoe chtenie*, part 1 (1873), 57–75.
97. Sokolov, *Naznachenie zhenshchiny*, p. 10; Ioann (Sokolov), episkop Smolenskii, *Khristianskoe naznachenie zhenshchiny* (St Petersburg: Pechatnia A. I. Snegirevoi, 1914) [sermon delivered in 1868].
98. It is noteworthy that among the earliest writings addressing women and the priesthood among Orthodox churchmen were those penned against the role of women in communities of priestless Old Believers. See 'O zhenskom sviashchennodeistvovanii', *Pravoslavnyi sobesednik* (June, 1864), 177–97; (July, 1864), 263–306; (August, 1864), 331–54.

the Eucharistic meal.[99] In 1882, the Bishop of Ufa, Nikanor (Brovkovich), reminded his readers that Mary never performed any liturgical functions in church.[100] Furthermore, she did not preach. 'Finding herself in the company of the first Christians', wrote one anonymous author, she never came forward with a public sermon or public teaching, 'leaving this right to men'.[101]

When read in light of churchmen's reflections on issues stemming from the women's movement, the *Life* of Mary takes on added meaning and potential significance. Its inherent appeal for Orthodox women, especially mothers, becomes readily evident. Presented as no less traditional and authoritative than contemporary pastoral voices, stories from these *Lives* often presented alternative images of the life of the woman and intercessor, to whom most Orthodox women turned in their daily lives. Although on occasion some compilers narrated their version of Mary's life in light of conventional, clerical sensibilities of the time – stating, for instance, that Mary did not 'mix' her voice with the voice of the apostles – even these versions usually portrayed Mary as a teacher and missionary following Jesus' death and resurrection.[102] The scattered glimpses of Mary struggling between her will and the divine will, and between her will and established social conventions; bearing the challenges of household and family that seemed at odds with her own vocational calling; facing the anonymity of motherhood; suffering alongside a child and finding herself in an entirely new public role in the later years of her life, offer more existentially gripping images for meditation and imitation, than the somewhat more elusive theological depictions of Mary as a 'vessel' (*sosud*) or 'seal of perfection'.

Conceivably, certain episodes in the *Lives* could have also reverberated with progressive Christian thinking on the 'women's question' at that time. One of Russia's earliest feminist theologians, E. Liuleva, hinted at the sensibilities with which at least some Orthodox women in late Imperial Russia might have approached their faith. In her essay 'The Free Woman and Christianity', for instance, Liuleva argued that Christ established the foundation for the liberation of women by giving them full access to the Kingdom of God. In so doing, he consistently regarded women as free, independent persons who enjoyed the same rights and

---

99. Khoinatskii, 'O pritiazaniiakh nekotorykh sovremennykh zhenshchin'.
100. Preosviashchennyi Nikanor, episkop Ufimskii, 'Ideal zhenshchiny', pp. 579–93.
101. A. N., 'Uchenie apostola Pavla o zhenskom pokryvale'; Sokolov, *Naznachenie zhenshchiny*, p. 7.
102. Sokolov, *Zhizn' Bozhiei Materi* (St Petersburg, 1873), pp. 22–23.

capabilities as men in matters of eternal life and the discernment of truth. Liuleva dismissed the conventional argument that women could not be preachers because, according to canonical Scripture, Christ had not chosen women as apostles. Because of historical circumstances, she argued, women preachers would not have been possible in his day. At the same time, Liuleva maintained, the Gospel texts testify that women were heard. Women were 'apostles to the apostles' since they were the first witnesses to Christ's resurrection; 'There could be no stronger confirmation of women's full rights and independence'.[103]

Similarly, in Liuleva's estimation, traditional Orthodox views of marriage did not reflect the liberating values expressed by Christ in the gospel texts. Since their first responsibility was to their husbands, married women were denied not so much their right as their responsibility to pursue the gospel mandate to seek the Kingdom of God.[104] In light of such views, Mary's *Life* generally offered a counter image of marriage. In virtually all of these accounts, Mary's personal vows and 'calling' remained formative in her relationship with Joseph, though not without causing strain, as the well-known scene of Joseph's struggles at Mary's pregnancy illustrates. Indeed, Liuleva singled out Mary as having gained independence on account of her vow of virginity. Generally, those who were familiar with episodes from various versions of Mary's *Life* might have easily drawn on them in support of Liuleva's views.

In his essay on the earliest texts of the *Life of the Virgin*, historian Stephen Shoemaker, considers the potential audiences of the *Lives* he examined. He wonders, for instance, why the narratives of Mary's life, that so strongly emphasized her leadership, arose and were popular in all-male monastic circles. 'One might not expect to find such traditions favoured', he states, 'in an environment as traditionally unwelcoming to women as Mount Athos'.[105] Indicating that a *Life* of Mary did not circulate widely outside monastic circles in the seventh to the tenth centuries, he wonders about the kind of influence such narratives, with their strong emphasis on Mary's leadership, might have had in a parish setting, where they could have provided models and precedents for women's roles in the Church.

The resurgence of the genre of the *Life* of Mary in nineteenth- and early twentieth-century Russia gives new life to Shoemaker's hypothetical query

---

103. E. Liuleva, *Svobodnaia zhenshchina i khristianstvo* (Moscow, 1906), p. 7.
104. Liuleva, *Svobodnaia zhenshchina*, pp. 17–22.
105. Shoemaker, 'The Virgin Mary in the Ministry of Jesus', 466–67.

and begs questions regarding the transposition of ancient texts into modern times. Although drawing mostly on ancient and medieval narratives – some of which were no less challenging to social and political norms in their own day – Mary's *Life* in the late nineteenth and early twentieth centuries takes on new shades of meaning in the context of modernity.[106] Although humility, meekness and purity still graced Mary dutifully and dependably in these narratives, these features often receded before, or yielded to, a search for Mary's more adaptive human qualities as demanded by the notion of earthly life in nineteenth- and early twentieth-century Russia. Consequently, while not devotionally dismissive of Mary's unique role in salvation history and of the praise with which she is often lauded, women, and mothers in particular, might, nevertheless, have also identified with, and been emboldened by, her fierce sense of vocation and the fervent way she pursued it, despite the social precepts and political pressures of her times.

At the same time, the potential appeal and influence of many episodes in these *Lives* for nineteenth- and early twentieth-century Orthodox women from various social backgrounds may well have stemmed not from any perceived novelty in the features of Mary's life, but precisely from their foundations in what they knew as tradition. Often grounded in the same stories that inspired Church hymnography, Marian feasts and Marian iconography, these *Lives* encouraged the stirring of the imagination and thereby fostered women's 'living contact' with Mary on their terms, while still resonating with the faith community of which they were a part.[107] Such freedom within the bounds of tradition not only potentially quickened personal ties between women and Mary, but also showed those bounds to be more yielding than historians often assume.

The widespread circulation of her *Life* and the inclusion of the stories associated with specially-revered icons of Mary as part of her life narrative prevent historians of Orthodoxy in Russia from unequivocally accepting the tempting view that the image of Mary in Russian Orthodoxy was hopelessly chained to a male, clerical and ascetic culture and

---

106. For an example of ancient writing on Mary that challenged social and political norms in their own day, see Susan Ashbrook Harvey, 'On Mary's Voice: Gendered Words in Syriac Marian Tradition', in *The Cultural Turn in Late Ancient Studies: Gender, Asceticism and Historiography*, ed. by Dale B. Martin and Patricia Cox Miller (Durham, NC: Duke University Press, 2005), pp. 63–86.
107. For a rich discussion of the role of the imagination in the religious life, see Paul Avis, *God and the Creative Imagination: Metaphor, Symbol, Myth in Religion and Theology* (New York: Routledge, 1994).

theology.[108] Mary was a far more complicated figure in Russia's Orthodox culture. Finding inspiration from the ancients and confirmation in countless stories associated with her miracle-working icons, Mary's life with all of its imaginable nuances and variations continued to have irresistible appeal for Russia's women, even in a rapidly modernizing age.

---

108. Elizabeth Schüssler Fiorenza, 'Feminist Theology as a Critical Theology of Liberation', in *Churches in Struggle: Liberation Theologies and Social Change in North America*, ed. by William K. Tabb (New York: Monthly Review Press, 1986), pp. 46–66 (57, 59).

5. Women and the Visual Arts

Rosalind P. Blakesley

In 1800, the French artist Marie Louise Elisabeth Vigée-Lebrun, then resident in St Petersburg, was elected an honourary free associate of the Imperial Academy of Fine Arts. The first woman painter to be honoured in this way, the artist responded by painting what she later considered to be the best of her many self-portraits and presented it to the Academy, where it hung in the Council Chamber until 1922 (Fig. 1).[1] Vigée-Lebrun depicted herself at work on a portrait of Empress Maria Fedorovna, who was not only consort of the Emperor of all the Russias, but also an artist in her own right. Conveniently marking the start of the period under consideration in this book, the painting could be construed as testament to the achievement of women artists in Russia at the time, as Vigée-Lebrun celebrates acceptance into the bastion of the Russian artistic establishment by depicting herself carrying out a prestigious Imperial portrait of another woman artist. The painting's composition could be seen to enforce this multi-layered reading of female artistic agency. The planar structure, in which the outline of Maria Fedorovna hovers above the shadow which Vigée-Lebrun casts on the canvas, might be read as a metaphor for the established, professional woman artist both standing apart from, and buttressed by, amateur practice. At the same time, the way in which both sitters look directly at the (female) artist who painted them sets up a dialogic encounter between women, which subverts the more familiar objectification of female subjects for a male gaze.

This essay is dedicated to Alison Hilton, whose insightful research and intellectual generosity have supported so many scholars of Russian art. I am also grateful to Wendy Salmond, Jordana Pomeroy, and Jane Sharp for their many helpful comments and advice.

1. See Pierre de Nolhac, *Madame Vigée Le Brun, peintre de la reine Marie-Antoinette, 1755–1842* (Paris: Manzi, Joyant and Co., 1908). For Vigée-Lebrun's experiences in Russia, see *Vospominaniia g-zhi Vizhe-Lebren: o prebyvanii ee v Sankt-Peterburge i Moskve 1795–1801*, ed. by Damir V. Solov'ev (St Petersburg: Iskusstvo-SPB, 2004).

Fig. 1   Marie Louise Elisabeth Vigée-Lebrun, *Self-portrait*, 1800. © The State Hermitage Museum, St Petersburg.

Yet any inference from Vigée-Lebrun's painting that women artists were an established part of the cultural fabric of Russia would be misleading. With the exception of the occasional acclaimed foreigner or woman of Imperial status, female practitioners of painting, sculpture, or architecture were practically invisible in Russia at the time. Denied access to the formal artistic education provided by the Academy as well as to any official routes of exhibiting and selling their work, they tended to produce amateur work in media such as watercolour and pastel which was enjoyed in the domestic rather than the public sphere. The same was true of music and theatre, where women tended to focus on those forms of song, instrumental works, or amateur dramatics suitable for performance in the home, as Philip Bullock and Julie Cassiday explore in their chapters here. As far as the upper classes are concerned, it would be simplistic to draw too clear a correlation between gender and amateurism, as throughout the first half of the nineteenth century painting and drawing, like literature, were practised by noblemen as much as by noblewomen almost exclusively as dilettantes, as professional work was deemed beneath them. Nonetheless, recognition for female artistic achievement outside the home was negligible. Even Vigée-Lebrun, a portraitist of international repute, was given only an honorific title by the Academy, as the formal rank of Academician, which would have been appropriate to her status and experience, was not granted to women at the time.

By 1917, however, women were not only practising as professional artists, but, in the likes of Natal'ia Goncharova, Ol'ga Rozanova and Liubov' Popova, constituted a powerhouse within the Russian avant-garde. Research on Russian women artists has focused understandably on these and other women who emerged in the final decades of Imperial rule and played a vital role in the formal innovation and move towards abstraction for which the avant-garde is famed. Indeed, if Russian art historians have been relatively slow to engage critically with the nature of women's artistic production in the eighteenth and nineteenth centuries, they have come into their own in their scholarship of the avant-garde. It is important, nonetheless, to consider the earlier period of relative inactivity as much as the high-profile artists at the dawn of the twentieth century, as charting the transition of women artists in Russia from marginal figures to world-renowned practitioners raises significant questions about the role of women in Russia's creative and cultural life. In this chapter the balance is deliberately weighted in favour of the nineteenth century, whose women artists have suffered from relative scholarly neglect, though the iconic artists of the pre-revolutionary period receive due mention.[2] A recurrent theme is the relationship between painting and the applied arts – an opposition which has been fundamental to feminist art history in general, as women were long excluded from the institutions which taught and supported the fine arts, but excelled in applied arts and crafts. As Alison Hilton noted in her seminal essay of 1996, this issue acquires especial resonance in Russia where the change in

---

2. In broad surveys of Russian art, Jeremy Howard alone has made women artists prior to the late nineteenth century a focus of his work. See Jeremy Howard, *East European Art 1650–1950* (Oxford: Oxford University Press, 2006), pp. 97–119.

status of women artists from an outsider minority to a central force was closely linked to their activity in the applied and decorative arts, as these foreshadowed the move in the revolutionary period to integrate art into everyday life.[3] Much Western scholarship has accordingly been driven by the desire to rehabilitate areas of art and design in which Russian women flourished, rather than labouring a male standard in the 'higher' arts against which women artists are found wanting. Taking its cue from such concerns, this account charts shifting tensions between the categories of fine and applied arts in order to shed light on certain habits of mind which have influenced the production, consumption, and interpretation of Russian women's art.

Maria Fedorovna (1759–1828), Vigée-Lebrun's subject in her self-portrait, offers an interesting starting point. Born and educated in Germany as Princess Sophia Dorothea Augusta Luisa of Württemberg, she took the name Maria Fedorovna on her conversion to the Russian Orthodox faith, and moved to Russia after her marriage to Grand Duke Paul (later Paul I) in September 1776. There, she became a stylish and influential patron of the fine and decorative arts at Pavlovsk, the palace which Catherine the Great had commissioned for Paul and his wife in 1781, as well as an accomplished artist in many different media. If her early work involved the sort of still-life painting in pastels which was customary of many aristocratic women, Maria Fedorovna soon went beyond the subjects and techniques expected of her sex, securing tuition with an Academy professor (the German medallist and engraver Karl Leberecht) and acquiring her own lathe in order to fashion cameos, medals, engravings, and decorative objects in ivory, amber, and other semi-precious stones.[4] Particularly thought-provoking are a set of drawings of architectural monuments at Pavlovsk and Tsarskoe Selo which Maria Fedorovna mounted onto buttons in 1790, and presented in a frame to Catherine the Great (Figs. 2 and 3). There is an intriguing dialectic

---

3. Alison Hilton, 'Domestic Crafts and Creative Freedom: Russian Women's Art', in *Russia, Women, Culture*, ed. by Helena Goscilo and Beth Holmgren (Bloomington and Indianapolis: Indiana University Press, 1996), p. 347.
4. For Maria Fedorovna's activities as an artist and patron, see Dmitrii F. Kobeko, 'Imperatritsa Mariia Fedorovna, kak khudozhnitsa i liubitel'nitsa iskusstva', *Vestnik iziashchnykh iskusstv*, II, 6 (1884), 399–410; *Imperatritsa Mariia Fedorovna*, ed. by Sergei V. Mironenko and Nikolai S. Tret'iakov (Pavlovsk: Art-Palas, 2000) and Rosalind P. Blakesley, 'Sculpting in Tiaras: Grand Duchess Maria Fedorovna as a Producer and Consumer of the Arts', in *Women and Material Culture*, ed. by Jennie Batchelor and Cora Kaplan (London: Palgrave Macmillan, 2007), pp. 71–85.

at play here between different art forms and their gendered associations. Architecture, represented by various follies and temples in a classical Greek style, was an historically male preserve. (That depicted here was largely the work of Charles Cameron, the Scottish architect employed by the Empress at Tsarskoe Selo and subsequently commissioned to design the palace and many of the garden structures at Pavlovsk.) Its figuration in drawing – an acknowledged and respected component of the fine arts – was the work of another man, as Maria Fedorovna's drawings are copies of originals by the miniaturist François Viollier. In copying one man's drawings of another man's architecture, Maria Fedorovna's work might thus seem derivative, with an inferred deference to the greater originality and artistic prowess of men. Yet she uses her sources to create an entirely new artistic artefact in the form of the buttons which, as part of costume and dress as well as an applied art, speak to interests and pursuits typically associated with women. A process of gradual transformation is under way, negotiating a visual journey from the masculine connotations of the architecture to a highly inventive, feminine art form.

Fig. 2 Grand Duchess Maria Fedorovna, three Imperial buttons comprised of drawings in graphite on vellum, mounted in gold frames, 1790. Lot no. 424, The Russian Sale, Sotheby's, London, 1 December 2004. © Sotheby's.

Fig. 3 Grand Duchess Maria Fedorovna, three Imperial buttons, 1790 (detail of fig. 2). © Sotheby's.

Such visual playfulness apart, the buttons have an important documentary function, as they provide a rare record of the appearance of Pavlovsk before a fire devastated the palace in 1803. They also offer an insight into the dynamic between Maria Fedorovna and her mother-in-law, not least in the inscription which they bear: 'Ces boutons sont presentés à la plus chérie des Mères par celle qui est à ses pieds en vous suppliant d'agreér ses Voeux et ses hommages pour la journée d'aujourd'hui. Le 25, Juin 1790 Marie F.I'.[5] Relations between the two

---

5. 'These buttons are presented to the most beloved of mothers, by one kneeling at your feet beseeching you to accept her wishes and respect on this day, today 25th June 1790

women were far from easy: Paul was openly antagonistic towards his mother and Catherine tested Maria Fedorovna's forbearance to an extreme when she took the couple's two oldest sons, Alexander and Konstantin, away from their mother to be raised under the Empress's own supervision. Maria Fedorovna, nevertheless, regularly presented her mother-in-law with examples of her artistic work, especially that which depicted subjects close to the Empress's heart, such as cameos and silhouettes of family members, or – as with the buttons – the landscape architecture of Catherine's estates. Such gifts were often accompanied by respectful and affectionate texts. In keeping with contemporary notions of the importance of women as nurturers and peace-makers within the home – values which had been strongly impressed on Maria Fedorovna during her childhood and upbringing in Germany, and which in Russia were enforced by the clergy at times, as Vera Shevzov shows in her essay here – the Grand Duchess thus used her creative work as a form of diplomatic offering to foster good familial relations within the Imperial court. Certainly, her artistic endeavour in no way transgressed any norms of social behaviour, but instead sat comfortably with the conservative family values which Maria Fedorovna upheld.

Along with her daughters and the offspring of certain academic professors, Maria Fedorovna was one of only a handful of women receiving tuition from members of the Academy of Arts at the time – a privilege which reflected her status as wife of the heir to the Russian throne.[6] Other than drawing lessons in the few existing educational institutions for girls, or tuition under private art tutors in wealthy households, there was little formal artistic training available to Russian women. However, students at the Smol'nyi Institute for Young Ladies of the Nobility, which Catherine the Great had established in 1764, were taught painting, drawing, how to work with clay and the craft of turning on a lathe in which Maria Fedorovna excelled (these alongside other prized female accomplishments such as music which were 'designed to improve the marriage prospects of girls from

---

Marie F.I'. Catalogue of *The Russian Sale*, Sotheby's, London (1 December 2004), p. 262.

6. It is reasonable to suppose that Elizaveta and Sofiia, the daughters of the professor of sculpture, Nicholas Gillet, and Ekaterina, the daughter of Karl Leberecht, received some form of artistic education thanks to their personal connections, as they feature in Academy records, in 1774 and 1807 respectively. See Sergei N. Kondakov, *Iubileinyi spravochnik Imperatorskoi Akademii khudozhestv, 1764–1914*, 2 vols (St Petersburg: P. Golike and A. Vil'borts, 1914), II, 69, 112.

the nobility and gentry', to quote from Bullock's chapter).[7] From the final quarter of the eighteenth century, although they were unable to study there, women were also able to submit examples of their work to the Academy, which might respond by awarding an official title, a medal, or dispensation to pursue related professional work. In 1796, Maria Fedorovna's daughters Elena and Aleksandra, who studied under the renowned portraitist Orest Kiprenskii, each presented the Academy with a wax profile portrait in relief depicting, respectively, Peter the Great and Catherine the Great as Minerva.[8] Marking the annual celebration of Catherine's accession to the Russian throne, these works were an act of homage to the Empress rather than a quest for official recognition from the Academy: the celebration records noted Catherine's delight at being depicted as Minerva and as Peter's successor by her granddaughters, who were only eleven and twelve years old at the time.[9] But other women, professors' daughters among them, were granted the right to teach on the basis of works submitted to the Academy and in 1812, Marfa Dovgaleva became the first woman known to be awarded an Academy medal, winning a second-class silver medal for her proficiency in engraving.[10] (Such was the importance of academic recognition that in 1869, Pelageia Zhukova petitioned the Academy for a copy of the certificate confirming her right to teach after the original was lost in a house fire.)[11] Little of these women's work survives, and the brief mention in Academy records of their submissions is often all we know of their careers. Even A. M. Bakunina, who in 1835 became the first Russian woman artist to be sponsored to travel abroad (in her case as a scholar of the Imperial Society for the Encouragement of the Arts), disappeared almost without trace. If they

---

7. Elena F. Petinova, *Freiliny ee Velichestva: portrety vospitannits Imperatorskogo vospitatel'nogo obshchestva blagorodnykh devits Dmitriia Levitskogo* (St Petersburg: Avrora, 2000), p. 16. For the Smol'nyi Institute under Maria Fedorovna's direction, see Nikolai P. Cherepnin, *Imperatorskoe Vospitatel'noe obshchestvo blagorodnykh devits: istoricheskii ocherk, 1764–1917*, 2 vols (Petrograd: Gosudarstvennaia tipografiia, 1914), I, 297–620.
8. P. N. Petrov, *Sbornik materialov dlia istorii Imperatorskoi S.-Peterburgskoi Akademii khudozhestv za sto let ee suchchestvovaniia*, 3 vols (St Petersburg: Gogenfel'den and Co., 1864), I, 351–52.
9. See *Iskusstvo zhenskogo roda: Zhenshchiny-khudozhnitsy v Rossii XV-XX vekov*, ed. by Lidia I. Iovleva (Moscow: State Tret'iakov Gallery/Creative Laboratory INO, 2002), pp. 68–69.
10. See Petrov, *Sbornik materialov*, II (1865), 36.
11. Russian State Historical Archive, St Petersburg (RGIA), f. 789, *opis'* 14, *delo* 18-Zh, pp. 1, 1, ob, 2.

pursued a career in the visual arts at all, most women worked as art tutors for children in aristocratic households. Academic recognition certainly gave no guarantee of future success, as the case of Mariia Kurt, the wife of a St Petersburg merchant, attests. In 1839, Kurt was made an Unclassed Artist (the lowest of various titles which the Academy awarded at the time) and was firmly set on an artistic career, writing to the Academy: 'having studied painting for ages, all my aspirations are focused on attracting the attention of the public and, sooner or later, counting myself among the profession of Russian artists'. Yet twenty-six years later, by which time she was in her mid-seventies, Kurt was still supplicating the Academy for financial aid, suggesting that her hopes of earning a living as a professional artist had not been realized.[12]

Fig. 4   Ekaterina Khilkova, *The Interior of the Women's Department of the St Petersburg Drawing School for Auditors*, 1855. © 2011, State Russian Museum, St Petersburg.

---

12. RGIA, f. 789, *opis'* 14, *delo* 110-K, ff 1, pp. 1, 6.

Fig. 5 Christina Robertson, *Portrait of Grand Duchess Maria Nikolaevna*, 1841.
© The State Hermitage Museum, St Petersburg.

The 1840s, however, witnessed a turning point in the artistic education of women in Russia. A growing number began to frequent the Academy in the capacity of 'free attendants' (*vol'noprikhodiashchie*), who were excluded from official competitions and exams, but could win medals and awards.[13] A few women also attended the few small art schools which were appearing in the provinces, though they tended to be related to the men running these schools.[14] More formally, in 1843 the Stroganov School of Drawing in Moscow opened a drawing section for women, complementing the teacher training and instruction in the applied arts that it already provided; and the St Petersburg Drawing School for Auditors, founded by the Society for the Encouragement of the Arts in 1840, established a separate women's department in 1842. This facility offered the most comprehensive, officially-sanctioned artistic training for women in Russia to date, though it still lagged well behind developments in France, where the state-funded Ecole Nationale de Dessin pour les Jeunes Filles had been founded in 1803.[15] In a report to Nicholas I of May 1842, the Minister of Finance Count Egor Kankrin argued that the initiative at the Drawing School for Auditors would be of use in training women 'not only to be self-sufficient workers, but also, in their capacity as wives and mothers, to be future helpers and educators of men'.[16] Such views sat well with the tsar's own views on women's education at the time, and he appointed his daughter, Grand Duchess Maria Nikolaevna, as the department's first patroness. Girls could enrol from the age of twelve, but had to be accompanied from the age of fourteen until such time as they married, whereupon they could come once more on their own. Classes took place twice a week and largely followed the

---

13. For the Academy's increasing recognition of women artists in the early 1850s, see Rosalind P. Blakesley, 'A Century of Women Painters, Sculptors, and Patrons from the Time of Catherine the Great', in *An Imperial Collection: Women Artists from the State Hermitage*, ed. by Jordana Pomeroy, Rosalind P. Blakesley et al. (London: Merrell Publishers in association with the National Museum of Women in the Arts, Washington DC, 2003), pp. 70–71.
14. Aleksandra Venetsianova studied at the school that her father, Aleksei Venetsianov, established on his estate in Tver Province and Ekaterina Demidova and Elizaveta Nadezhina attended their father Afanasii Nadezhin's art school in Kozlov, Tambov Province. See Nina Moleva and Elii Beliutin, *Russkaia khudozhestvennaia shkola pervoi poloviny XIX veka* (Moscow: Iskusstvo, 1963), pp. 313, 382–83.
15. For the Ecole Nationale de Dessin pour les Jeunes Filles and its emphasis on teaching vocational skills in industrial design, see Tamar Garb, '"Men of Genius, Women of Taste": The Gendering of Art Education in Late Nineteenth-Century Paris', in *Overcoming All Obstacles: The Women of the Académie Julian*, ed. by Gabriel P. Weisberg and Jane R. Becker (New York: The Dahesh Museum in association with Rutgers University Press, New Brunswick, New Jersey and London, 1999), pp. 121–23.
16. Elena Antonova-Borovskaia, 'Zhenskoe khudozhestvennoe obrazovanie v Rossii', *Russkoe iskusstvo*, II (2010), pp. 124–29 (125).

same programme as that set for male students, with the exception of 'technical drawing', which was not deemed appropriate for women. Conversely, female students studied 'landscape drawing' which was forbidden the men, on the grounds that the relative ease of the exercise could lead them to 'inaccuracies and superficial drawing'. Girls and women from the upper classes were freely admitted, while those of lower social status had to acquire special permission to take part. When the department opened on 24 September 1842, fourteen women had enrolled, comprising the daughters of a nobleman, three civil servants, two townsfolk (*meshchane*), two army captains and one colonel, an archpriest, a doctor, a court servant, a coppersmith and a ploughman. By December that year the number had swollen to forty and by 1846 there were 169 attenders, of whom 112 came from the nobility and 28 from the merchant class (this preponderance of students from the upper classes setting the pattern for many years). The following year women featured on the list of the school's prize winners for the first time. Teaching faculty later included figures as renowned as Ivan Kramskoi, the Realist painter who spearheaded the famous student revolt against the Academy in 1863 and set up an independent commune of artists known as the *Artel khudozhnikov*. (Significantly, women were welcome at the social and artistic gatherings which took place every Thursday at the *Artel*.)[17] Such instruction was solid enough to launch many women on careers as drawing teachers, just as the conservatoires were to produce a large number of female music teachers in later years (see chapter six).

Ekaterina Khilkova's painting of 1855 provides a vital visual record of activities in the women's department at the St Petersburg Drawing School for Auditors, just over a decade after classes began (Fig. 4). With the exception of one man on the far left, whose role is unclear, all of the figures in Khilkova's painting are female and women, in fact, provided instruction as well as attending as students (Khilkova herself worked as a drawing teacher there for a while, as well as in other women's educational institutes). There are also indications of a pedagogic methodology that revolved around two distinct teaching models: study lithographs (then a popular form of instruction), which are pinned to the walls and displayed above the desks; and classical models in the form of the different orders of column capital arranged along the far wall and the cast of the celebrated antique statue *Laocöon* glimpsed through the open door. It is

---

17. For these and other details of the women's classes in the St Petersburg Drawing School for Auditors, as well as the careers of some of the women who studied there, see Antonova-Borovskaia, 'Zhenskoe khudozhestvennoe obrazovanie v Rossii', pp. 124–29.

clear that students were encouraged to draw from these models to acquaint themselves with their formal properties and expressive language, as a copy of one of the lithographs lies on a desk to the right and a seated figure on a stool in the end room appears to be sketching the *Laocöon*. Another woman in the foreground, flanked by two others, seems to be drawing either an image of, or an actual bas-relief of, a decorative motif, but the applied arts are otherwise absent from Khilkova's painting. It may be that these were taught in another room, and the vignette with the bas-relief was included here as a token of the curriculum's inclusion of the applied and decorative arts. There is no sense, however, that the students' energies were directed towards the sort of craftwork deemed appropriate for women. On the contrary, the focus on the study of the human head, and on classical models, suggests a clear ambition to master some of the more demanding skills required of a successful draughtsman or painter.

Khilkova's image is carefully constructed, with good knowledge of the rules of perspective (the striped carpet on the left rather crudely emphasizing this), and the confident placement of figures in an interior setting. The rendition of the different materials of the women's outfits is also convincing, from the silken texture of the skirts, to the lace of the collars and the diaphanous white blouse in the centre. One might, nevertheless, perceive limitations to her work in the similarity of the facial expressions and postures; in the polished but unadventurous use of paint; and in the lack of excitement to the composition as a whole. Here, though, the feminist art historian would caution against linking qualitative evaluations to gender on the basis of visual evidence in one painting alone. Is Khilkova's work really inferior to that of her male peers, or simply typical of the vast majority of Russian interior painting at the time? Similar questions might be asked of Sof'ia Sukhovo-Kobylina (1825–67), who in 1854 overcame the obstacles posed by both her gender and her higher social class to become the first woman to win the Academy's top award of a gold medal (an event which she chose to commemorate on canvas) and subsequently set up a fashionable studio in Rome.[18] The few surviving landscape paintings for which Sukhovo-Kobylina was feted may show little innovation in terms of technique or style, but was not the same true for most contemporary male

---

18. Many artists wrote of the hospitality that they received in Sukhovo-Kobylina's Italian home, and of their impressions of her work. For further information, if still scant, on her life and work, see Varvara Ponomareva and Tatiana Zuikova, 'Sof'ia Vasil'evna Sukhovo-Kobylina', *Russkoe iskusstvo,* II (2010), pp. 131–34.

landscape artists?[19] In other words, the very *ordinariness* of the paintings of Khilkova and Sukhovo-Kobylina (both of which won academic medals) can serve as an index of their achievement in meeting the expectations of the artistic establishment at the time. Among women, only Christina Robertson (1799–1854), a Scottish artist who worked in St Petersburg from 1839 to 1841 and again in the late 1840s, stood out for her parade portraits of Russia's aristocratic elite for which she became one of the highest paid portraitists in the Russian capital. The subject of extensive research by Elizaveta Renne, Robertson specialized in full-length state portraits of Imperial women (Fig. 5), in which the evocative brushwork of the outfits, the suggestiveness of the poses and the combination of grandiose architecture and intimate detail, established Robertson's success in her chosen genre. (Robertson became only the second woman painter, after Vigée-Lebrun, to be elected an honorary free associate of the Academy of Arts in 1841.)[20] Otherwise, Russian women's contribution to the fine arts until the mid-nineteenth century (which largely entailed painting alone, as women's work in sculpture or architecture was practically unheard of) is noteworthy for the circumstances of the producer and for its typicality, rather than for any marked originality or aesthetic impact which set it apart.[21]

From the late 1850s a different picture began to emerge. In 1857 and 1858, Natal'ia Makukhina and Julie Hagen-Schwarz (1824–1902) were elected Academicians of Portrait Painting, the title which had been unavailable to Vigée-Lebrun half a century before. Hagen-Schwarz, the daughter of a German Balt artist, seems to have enjoyed particular success in official circles,

---

19. For examples of Sukhovo-Kobylina's work, including a landscape, a self-portrait and the artist's visual record of receiving her gold medal at the Academy, see *Iskusstvo zhenskogo roda*, pp. 77–79.
20. For Elizaveta Renne's work on Robertson, see 'A British Portraitist in Imperial Russia: Christina Robertson and the Court of Nicholas I', *Apollo* (September 1995), pp. 43–45; 'Christina Robertson in Russia', in *Christina Robertson: A Scottish Portraitist at the Russian Court*, ed. by Amanda Farr (Edinburgh: City Art Centre, 1996), pp. 14–29; 'Pridvornyi khudozhnik Kristina Robertson', *Nashe nasledie*, 55 (2000), 35–37 and 'Bridging Two Empires: Christina Robertson and the Court of St Petersburg', in *An Imperial Collection*, pp. 87–99.
21. The only woman sculptor to achieve renown in Russia before the late nineteenth century was Marie-Anne Collot, the Frenchwoman who came to St Petersburg with Etienne-Maurice Falconet when he was commissioned by Catherine the Great to sculpt the equestrian monument to Peter the Great. See Irina G. Etoeva, '"Brilliant Proof of the Creative Abilities of Women": Marie-Anne Collot in Russia', in *An Imperial Collection*, pp. 77–85 and Alexander M. Schenker, *The Bronze Horseman: Falconet's Monument to Peter the Great* (New Haven and London: Yale University Press, 2003), pp. 111–16 and *passim*.

winning a three-year foreign scholarship from the Cabinet of His Imperial Highness in 1853, despite already being resident in Rome and having spent much of her career to date living and studying in Western Europe.[22] A rare extant work is *Young Italian with Pistol in Hand* of 1851–54 (State Tret'iakov Gallery, Moscow), which forms part of a group of paintings produced by mainly academically-trained artists from various European countries who studied or worked in Italy in the first half of the nineteenth century. There, they were inspired by the strong Italian light and by the different customs that they encountered to produce local portraits and scenes of everyday life in a distinct style, which became known as the 'Italian genre'. Highly popular with Russian artists after Karl Briullov's excursions in the genre in the 1830s, the Italian genre was characterized by an emphasis on regional character and by strong tonal contrasts, both of which are manifest in Hagen-Schwarz's painting. There is a particularly strong affinity between her work and that of Vasilii Shternberg, such as *Card-playing in a Neapolitan Hostelry* (1840s, State Tret'iakov Gallery, Moscow), notably in the attention to costume and facial hair and in the pronounced chiaroscuro.[23] That Hagen-Schwarz produced her painting after the heyday of the Italian genre suggests that her work was relatively conservative. However, her canvas does not comfortably meet either the 'lyrical' or the 'festive' categories into which a recent scholar has divided the Italian genre.[24] Rather, it evinces a moody, menacing air in keeping with the critical realism that was emerging among Russian artists of the 1850s and 1860s, placing Hagen-Schwarz's work in the interstices between two very different approaches to genre painting at the time.

Judging from her correspondence, Hagen-Schwarz later produced over five hundred portraits, between 1872 and 1898.[25] These are almost all now lost, which may suggest that they were of little aesthetic interest, though it might equally illustrate the struggle which women still faced to have their work appreciated and preserved. Their access to artistic training in the school system certainly remained firmly gendered, as the Ministry of Education's statute on women's gymnasiums and progymnasiums of 1870

---

22. *Gosudarstvennaia Tret'iakovskaia galereia: katalog sobraniia*, ed. by Ian V. Bruk and Lidia I. Iovleva (Moscow: Skanrus, 2005), III (*Zhivopis' pervoi poloviny XIX veka*), 90.
23. See *Plenniki krasoty: Russkoe akademicheskoe i salonnoe iskusstvo 1830–1910-kh godov*, ed. by Lidia I. Iovleva (Moscow: State Tret'iakov Gallery/Skanrus, 2004), p. 148.
24. Ekaterina A. Bobrinskaia, 'Ital'ianskii zhanr v russkoi zhivopisi pervoi poloviny XIX veka', in *Plenniki krasoty*, pp. 138, 142.
25. Ludmila A. Markina, 'Woman Artists in Russia: from the Baroque to the Modern', in *Iskusstvo zhenskogo roda*, pp. 59, 323.

reveals: the only compulsory subject with any reference to the visual arts was 'needlework essential for practical application in the home', while drawing was offered as an elective subject.[26] The final three decades of the nineteenth century, nevertheless, marked a period of increasing opportunity, activity and recognition for women artists in Russia. In 1868 Mariia Ivanova-Raevskaia (1842–1912), a recipient of the title of Unclassed Artist, set up a school of drawing and painting in Kharkov, Ukraine, whose students were soon winning special mentions and medals for the works that they submitted to the Academy's exhibitions.[27] Ivanova-Raevskaia deviated from orthodox teaching methods by encouraging her pupils to study drawing and painting simultaneously (rather than mastering the skill of drawing before working in paint, as was normal academic practice) and by prioritizing the study of anatomy: her application to the Academy for material assistance in opening the school requested not the drawings and studies for students to copy, which were standard fare at the time, but a skeleton and a skull.[28] Such an approach raised no hackles at the Academy, which elected Ivanova-Raevskaia an honorary free associate in recognition of her teaching activities in 1872. By then, the status of women within the Academy was subject to intense debate, and the Academy finally agreed to admit women as full-time, fully-registered students in 1873.[29] The Moscow School of Painting, Sculpture and Architecture followed suit, admitting growing numbers of women both as full-time students and as auditors from the 1870s onwards.[30]

The path of women students at the Academy was far from smooth, as I have discussed elsewhere.[31] While initially taught alongside male students, from 1876 they were segregated into women-only classes, which provided a

---

26. See *Russian Women, 1698–1917: Experience and Expression. An Anthology of Sources*, comp. by Robin Bisha, Jehanne M. Gheith, Christine Holden and William G. Wagner (Bloomington and Indianapolis: Indiana University Press, 2002), p. 183.
27. For the Kharkov School, see Kondakov, *Iubileinyi spravochnik*, pp. 238–42. Ivanova-Raevskaia's school was reorganized in 1896 as the Kharkov City Painting School, which in turn became the Kharkov Art-Technical Institute in the early Soviet era. See Howard, *East European Art*, p. 112.
28. RGIA, f. 789, *opis'* 14, *delo* 1-Iu, p. 8 and Nina Moleva and Elii Beliutin, *Russkaia khudozhestvennaia shkola vtoroi poloviny XIX-nachala XX veka* (Moscow: Iskusstvo, 1967), pp. 153–54.
29. *Sbornik postanovlenii Soveta Imperatorskoi Akademii khudozhestv po khudozhestvennoi i uchebnoi chasti s 1859 po 1890 god* (St Petersburg: Tipografiia D-ta Udelov, 1890), p. 181.
30. Nina Dmitrieva, *Moskovskoe uchilishche zhivopisi, vaianiia i zodchestva* (Moscow: Iskusstvo, 1951), p. 109.
31. Blakesley, 'A Century of Women Painters, Sculptors, and Patrons', pp. 74–75.

more limited curriculum than that available to the men. Further restrictions were imposed in 1884, when the number of women permitted to study in the Academy in any one year was limited to fifty, of whom only twenty-five could be registered as full-time students, the other twenty-five attending as auditors, without being formally registered or taking official examinations. Such developments mirror those in women's education more widely in late nineteenth-century Russia, in which initial decisions in favour of women's access to tertiary education or vocational training were later tempered or rescinded, particularly after the clampdown on institutes of higher learning which followed the assassination of Alexander II in 1881.[32]

Yet regardless of such limitations, by the end of the century women were increasingly prominent in both numbers and achievement at the Academy. They found a valuable champion in Il'ia Repin, the great Realist artist who welcomed women into his studio at the Academy as soon as he began to teach there in 1894. Particularly significant is that Repin allowed women to work from female models alongside men, as photographs and paintings of sessions in his studio in the 1890s confirm.[33] This countered the almost complete exclusion of women from the genre of the nude life-study, which was a practice deeply embedded in the high-art establishment. (In America, such was the strength of feeling surrounding female contemplation of the naked body that Thomas Eakins was forced to resign as head of the Pennsylvania Academy of the Fine Arts in 1886 after exposing women students to a nude male model.) Graduates of Repin's studio included Ol'ga Della-Vos-Kardovskaia (1875–1952), whose *Portrait of Anna Akhmatova* conveys a compelling sense of introspection in the poet's arresting profile; and Elizaveta Zvantseva (1864–1921), who set up an art school in Moscow and, later, St Petersburg, which numbered Valentin Serov, Lev Bakst, and Kuz'ma Petrov-Vodkin among its teachers and Ol'ga Rozanova among its pupils. Like Repin, Zvantseva also employed female nude models in the life classes held at her school. The same period produced Russia's first great woman sculptor, Anna Golubkina (1864–1927), who, following

---

32. See Richard Stites, *The Women's Liberation Movement in Russia: Feminism, Nihilism, and Bolshevism, 1860–1930* (Princeton NJ: Princeton University Press, 1978), pp. 168–73 and Christine Johanson, *Women's Struggle for Higher Education in Russia, 1855–1900* (Kingston and Montreal: McGill-Queen's University Press, 1987), pp. 95–103.
33. See Hilton, 'Domestic Crafts and Creative Freedom', p. 350; G. I. Pribul'skaia, 'Repin i Akademiia khudozhestv. Po materialam biografii khudozhnika', in *Il'ia Efimovich Repin: k 150-letiiu so dnia rozhdeniia. Sbornik statei*, ed. by Vladimir Leniashin (St Petersburg: State Russian Museum/Palace Edition, 1995), p. 104 and Alison Hilton, '"Bases of the New Creation": Women Artists and Constructivism', *Arts Magazine*, 55.2 (1980), 42.

a stint as Rodin's assistant in Paris, won commissions as high-profile as a bas-relief for the façade of the Moscow Art Theatre.[34] Entire articles on women artists began to appear in the Russian press. High-born women in the capital city set up the First Ladies' Art Circle (1882–1917) and the St Petersburg Society for the Encouragement of Female Artistic and Craft Work (1892–1914), both of which supported women artists by organizing practical studio sessions, exhibitions, trading outlets and social gatherings at which lectures, *tableaux vivants* and musical or theatrical performances would take place.[35] These initiatives had a central philanthropic purpose to raise money for struggling artists and their families, the beneficiaries of which included none other than Mikhail Zoshchenko, the writer who later acquired unrivalled popularity for his satirical observation of the incongruities of modern Soviet life.

These various developments in Russia set up an interesting comparison with practices elsewhere. In France, women – though usually rich women – had been admitted to some professional studios from the 1830s and were able to study nude models in a few ateliers from the late 1860s and at the Académie Julian (the famous commercial art school established in Paris in 1868) from 1873.[36] Social conventions persuaded Rodolphe Julian to set up separate studios for women at the Académie Julian, as had been the case at the Russian Academy, but women in his establishment continued

---

34. Golubkina trained at the Moscow School of Painting, Sculpture and Architecture from 1890–94 and at the Academy from 1894–95. On her work, see Aleksandr Kamenskii, *Anna Golubkina: lichnost', epokha, skul'ptura* (Moscow: Izobrazitel'noe iskusstvo, 1990); Édouard Papet, '"La poésie de l'antiquité nationale": céramique émaillée et bois sculpté en Russie, 1890–1914', in *L'Art russe dans la seconde moitié du XIXe siècle: en quête d'identité* (Paris: Musée d'Orsay, 2005), pp. 344–50; Ol'ga Kalugina, *Skul'ptor Anna Golubkina: opyt kompleksnogo issledovaniia tvorcheskoi sud'by* (Moscow: Galart, 2006) and Ol'ga Kalugina, 'Moskovskaia akademiia Anny Golubkinoi: k 100-letiiu masterskoi skul'ptora', *Russkoe iskusstvo*, II (2010), 138–43.
35. See, for example, Andrei I. Somov, 'Zhenshchiny khudozhnitsy', *Vestnik iziashchnyk iskusstv*, I, no. 3 (1883), pp. 356–83 (which focuses entirely on foreign women artists) and Anon, 'Russkie khudozhnitsy', *Niva*, 1 (1891), 16–18. On the First Ladies' Art Circle and the St Petersburg Society for the Encouragement of Female Artistic and Craft Work, see Dmitrii Severiukhin, *Staryi khudozhestvennyi Peterburg: rynok i samoorganizatsiia khudozhnikov* (St Petersburg: Mir, 2008), pp. 344–50.
36. For French painters who taught women in their ateliers, and for early opportunities for women to study from the nude, see Germaine Greer, '"A tout prix devenir quelqu'un": the women of the Académie Julian', in *Artistic Relations: Literature and the Visual Arts in Nineteenth-Century France*, ed. by Peter Collier and Robert Lethbridge (New Haven and London: Yale University Press, 1994), pp. 40–45, 54. For women's access to life drawing in France more generally, see Tamar Garb, 'The Forbidden Gaze: Women Artists and the Male Nude in Late Nineteenth-Century France', in *The Body Imaged: The Human Form and Visual Culture Since the Renaissance*, ed. by Kathleen Adler and Marcia Pointon (Cambridge: Cambridge University Press, 1993), pp. 33–42.

to enjoy similar training to that offered to the men.[37] In contrast, the Ecole des Beaux-Arts in Paris (France's main, state-sponsored school of fine arts which dated from the seventeenth century) did not admit women until 1897. In England, a Government School of Art for Females had been established in 1859 and women were permitted to attend the Royal Academy from the 1860s, but their exclusion there from life-drawing classes barred their progress in any form of narrative painting (those life models that they were finally allowed to study in the 1890s were carefully draped) and mixed classes were not established until 1903.[38] The Academy in St Petersburg, then, was far from reactionary, as concerns official artistic education for women, compared to its better-known European counterparts. On the contrary, in admitting women almost a quarter of a century before its august French predecessor and allowing mixed classes (albeit intermittently), it was arguably at the forefront of state provision in women's fine art education.

The burning question is whether we should construe women's acceptance into the Academy as a victory; for by the time they were admitted the institution was in disarray. Shaken by the Revolt of the Fourteen in 1863, when fourteen students had left their *alma mater* in protest of the limitations of its medal competitions, the Academy had been further undermined by the Society of Travelling Art Exhibitions whose members, the *Peredvizhniki*, developed a popular Realist style. As they finally achieved full acceptance at the Academy, women were thus gaining access to an institution which was widely seen as moribund and retrograde (an irony which, as Germaine Greer has observed, was equally the case in France).[39] In Russia, the proximity of the dates of the formation of the Society of Travelling Art Exhibitions (1870) and the admission of women to the Academy (1873) is particularly conspicuous. Did the Academy vote to include women precisely (if tacitly) as part of their strategy to counteract the success of the Society, which did not admit a woman artist, Emiliia Shanks, until 1894? (Shanks, who had exhibited with the Society since 1891, was a popular candidate, winning one more vote in the election of members that year than the acclaimed artist Valentin Serov – fifteen, to Serov's fourteen).[40] In the absence of firm evidence,

---

37. See Greer, '"A tout prix devenir quelqu'un"', pp. 53–54 and Catherine Fehrer, 'Women at the Académie Julian in Paris', *The Burlington Magazine*, 136, no. 1100 (November 1994), 752–57.
38. Hilton, 'Domestic Crafts and Creative Freedom', p. 351.
39. 'When women were clamouring for the right to attend the Ecole des Beaux-Arts, they were struggling to board a sinking ship'. Greer, '"A tout prix devenir quelqu'un"', p. 57.
40. *Tovarishchestvo peredvizhnykh khudozhestvennykh vystavok: pis'ma, dokumenty 1869–1899*, ed. by Sofiia N. Gol'dshtein, 2 vols (Moscow: Iskusstvo, 1987), II, 387, 445. For an example of Shanks' work, see *Iskusstvo zhenskogo roda*, p. 105.

we can only hypothesize on the Academy's motives, but the acceptance of women would have helped maintain healthy application and admission figures during the first flush of the *Peredvizhniki*'s success. Moreover, the supposition that the Academy may have been actively courting women is supported by the minutes of a council meeting of 1876, which noted that the number of female applicants would increase 'once they find out that a separate section of women's classes has been established'.[41] As for the women themselves, we are largely ignorant of their awareness of and response to the Academy's fluctuating reputation. It is nonetheless telling that, despite changes in academic policy and approach, which ranged from the inclusion of women to far-reaching reforms in 1893, many women still elected to study in private studios abroad.[42] Perhaps those with neither the money, nor the opportunity to travel, chose to hold their counsel, for the Academy remained the only place in Russia where they could acquire an official and comprehensive education in the fine arts.[43]

If the relative benefits of the fine art training offered to women by the Academy are up for debate, women's practice in the applied and decorative arts in the final quarter of the nineteenth century was thriving. Spearheaded by Alison Hilton, Wendy Salmond and other scholars in the United States, such work has become the subject of outstanding research in recent years.[44] Particularly remarkable were the female patrons and artists, many of aristocratic background, who set up and managed ambitious initiatives to revive the cottage handicraft activities that in Russia are known as *kustar*

---

41. Minutes of the Academy Council meeting of 27 February 1876: *Sbornik postanovlenii*, pp. 181–82.
42. The Académie Julian proved particularly popular, attracting Marie Bashkirtseff from 1877–81, Ekaterina Zarudnaia-Kavos from 1885–86 and Mariia Iakunchikova from 1889–92. For rising interest in the Ukrainian Bashkirtseff (Mariia Bashkirtseva, 1858–84), see Jane R. Becker, 'Nothing like a Rival to Spur One On: Marie Bashkirtseff and Louise Breslau at the Academie Julian', in *Overcoming All Obstacles*, pp. 69–113; *The Journal of Marie Bashkirtseff*, trans. by Mathilde Blind (London: Virago, 1985); Colette Cosnier, *Marie Bashkirtseff: un portrait sans retouches* (Paris: Pierre Horay, 1985); *Marie Bashkirtseff: peintre et sculpteur & écrivain et témoin de son temps* (Nice: Musée des Beaux-Arts, 1995) and Hilde Hoogenboom, 'The Famous White Box: The Creation of Mariia Bashkirtseva and Her Diary', in *Gender and Sexuality in Russian Civilisation*, ed. by Peter I. Barta (London: Routledge, 2001), pp. 181–204.
43. For independent institutions where women could receive an artistic education in late nineteenth-century Russia, see Aleksei Novitskii, *Istoriia russkogo iskusstva*, 2 vols (Moscow: V. N. Lind, 1903), II, 518–19.
44. See, for example, Alison Hilton, *Russian Folk Art* (Bloomington and Indianapolis: Indiana University Press, 1995); Wendy Salmond, *Arts and Crafts in Late Imperial Russia: Reviving the Kustar Art Industries, 1870–1917* (Cambridge: Cambridge University Press, 1996) and Karen Kettering, 'Enamels from the Moscow Workshop of Mariia Semenova', *The 49th Washington Antiques Show: Women of Metal* (2004), pp. 81–88.

crafts. This *kustar* production, which ranged from objects as practical as ploughs and nails, to traditionally feminine handicrafts such as lace-making and weaving, formed a vital part of the peasant economy. Under pressure from Russia's rapid industrialization (see chapter two) and the migration to the cities and cheap factory goods which resulted, however, the *kustar* industries were in serious danger of decline. Galvanized by the threat to the peasant craft heritage which such a situation presented, women in cities and more distant provinces opened workshops to revive and nurture traditional craft skills. Most famous are the activities at the estates of Abramtsevo, near Moscow and Talashkino, near Smolensk, which have been explored in depth. Yet there is a welcome new focus on little-studied aspects of women's work at these communities, such as the vibrant personal enamelling practice of Mariia Tenisheva, the patron and chatelaine at Talashkino.[45] Wendy Salmond has also brought critical attention to lesser-known enterprises, such as the embroidery workshops which operated in the village of Solomenko in Tambov Province from 1891–1917.[46] In providing training and employment and simultaneously encouraging high-quality handicraft, these and other workshops created an important intersection between artistic endeavour and social work.

The most influential woman associated with the *kustar* revival was Elena Polenova (1850–98), who had studied in the women's department at the St Petersburg Drawing School for Auditors (under Kramskoi from 1864 and again in the late 1870s) and directed the workshops at Abramtsevo from 1885. Inspired by vernacular architecture and peasant artefacts, which she collected for a museum on the estate, Polenova formulated designs for carved and painted furniture and decorative objects which would appeal to modern aesthetic sensibilities. Realized by local men and boys in the woodwork and joinery workshops, these found a ready market in Moscow and beyond and played a major role in the commercial viability of the Abramtsevo project. Frustrated by the lack of time for personal creative exploration, however, Polenova left the workshops in 1893 to focus on her own work, primarily in the fields of embroidery (she contributed designs to the Solomenko workshops) and graphic design. Highly articulate about

---

45. See Jesco Oser, *Mir emalei kniagini Marii Tenishevoi* (Moscow: private publisher, 2004). For Tenisheva's life, see Larisa Zhuravleva, *Kniaginia Mariia Tenisheva* (Smolensk: Poligramma, 1994).
46. Wendy Salmond, 'The Solomenko Embroidery Workshops', *The Journal of Decorative and Propaganda Arts*, Russian/Soviet Theme Issue, 5 (1987), 126–43.

her need to be a working, *earning* artist and about professionalism in the visual arts in general, Polenova was vocal in her frustration at the difficulties in getting exhibited with the *Peredvizhniki*.[47] At the end of the century, however, her work in many media featured prominently in the exhibitions of the World of Art group and its associated journal, which dedicated a lengthy article to the artist and held a retrospective after Polenova's untimely death from a brain tumour in 1898.[48] In her monograph of 1952, Elena Sakharova anticipated by half a century the current enthusiasm for Polenova's work.[49] Indeed, Polenova is now acclaimed as a major force in Russian modernism for the variety of her creative experience, the brilliance of her sense of pattern and rhythm in illustrations and other graphic work, the inventiveness of her visual interpretation of folktales, as well as her stylized plant and animal motifs and the wide application of her designs.[50]

Polenova was far from the only woman to make an impact with the World of Art group. On the contrary, it is with the advent of this famous galaxy of artists that coalesced around Sergei Diaghilev in *fin-de-siècle* Russia that women began to constitute a critical mass in the vanguard of Russian art. Mariia Vasil'evna Iakunchikova (1870–1902: not to be confused with her relation by marriage, Mariia Fedorovna Iakunchikova, who ran the Solomenko workshops) shared Polenova's mental and creative flexibility, working in media ranging from painting, embroidery and poker-work to book and toy design and orchestrating the celebrated Russian handicraft section at the Exposition Universelle in Paris in 1900.[51] Zinaida Serebriakova (1884–1967) probed gender stereotypes in her intimate self-portraits, in which the artist traces a fluctuating binary of artist/model and mother/wife by depicting the rituals of self-adornment

---

47. See Polenova's correspondence with Pelageia Antipova, Sergei Ivanov, and Mariia V. Iakunchikova in *Vasilii Dmitrievich Polenov, Elena Dmitrievna Polenova: khronika sem'i khudozhnikov*, ed. by Elena V. Sakharova (Moscow: Iskusstvo, 1964), pp. 382, 450, 455.
48. 'E. D. Polenova', *Mir iskusstva*, II/18–19 (1899), 97–120.
49. Elena Sakharova, *Elena Dmitrievna Polenova, 1850–1898* (Moscow: Iskusstvo, 1952).
50. For a recent account of Polenova's oeuvre, see Kristen M. Harkness, 'The Phantom of Inspiration: Elena Polenova, Mariia Iakunchikova and the Emergence of Modern Art in Russia', PhD thesis, University of Pittsburgh, 2009. For appreciation in Britain of Polenova's work, see Rosalind P. Blakesley, '"The Venerable Artist's Fiery Speeches Ringing in my Soul": The Artistic Impact of William Morris and his Circle in Nineteenth-Century Russia', in *Internationalism and the Arts*, ed. by Grace Brockington (Oxford: Peter Lang, 2009), pp. 96–99.
51. See Mikhail Kiselev, *Mariia Vasil'evna Iakunchikova 1870–1902* (Moscow: Iskusstvo, 1979).

and domestication that can weave through a woman's life.⁵² Particularly notable is the contribution of women to printmaking and book design, in which the likes of Anna Ostroumova-Lebedeva (1871–1955) and Elizaveta Kruglikova (1865–1942) excelled. Both women played a critical role in the transformation of printmaking from a technique largely appreciated for its reproductive qualities, to an autonomous art form esteemed for its own expressive potential and aesthetic peculiarities. These and other areas of graphic design figured among the most fertile fields of artistic exploration at the turn of the century and were seized on and pushed in ever more innovative and daring directions by members of the avant-garde. Indeed, the flair for pattern and structure, the stylized, linear approach and the flat use of colour, which characterized the best graphic design of the period, spilt over into other areas of women's artistic endeavour. Suffice to mention Natal'ia Goncharova's costume designs for the Ballets Russes, Aleksandra Ekster's sets and costumes for theatre and film and the textile designs by Varvara Stepanova and Liubov' Popova, as well as the ground-breaking non-objective painting for which all four women are famed.⁵³ Indeed, the only sphere of the visual arts in which women did not make a critical contribution at this time was architecture, a subject unavailable to them until the Women's Polytechnical Courses opened in 1906 and the Academy finally admitted women to its architecture department in 1908.⁵⁴

The reception afforded to women artists in early twentieth-century Russia was mixed. At an extreme, Goncharova was put on trial for obscenity in 1910 after exhibiting paintings of female nudes – an event which, in Jane Sharp's brilliant analysis, illustrates an attempt by the courts to discipline a woman for venturing into a genre of painting that was the exclusive domain

---

52. See Alison Hilton, 'Zinaida Serebriakova', *Women's Art Journal* III/2 (1982/83), 32–35; Tatiana A. Savitskaia, *Z. Serebriakova: izbrannye proizvedeniia* (Moscow: Sovetskii khudozhnik, 1988); *Zinaida Serebriakova: pis'ma, sovremenniki o khudozhnitse*, ed. by Valentina Kniazeva (Moscow: Izobrazitel'noe iskusstvo, 1987) and Alla Rusakova, *Zinaida Serebriakova, 1884–1967* (Moscow: Iskusstvo-XXI vek, 2006).
53. For textile and clothing designs, see Natalia Adaskina, 'Constructivist Fabrics and Dress Design', *The Journal of Decorative and Propaganda Arts*, Russian/Soviet Theme Issue, 5 (Summer 1987), pp. 144–59.
54. Wendy Salmond, 'Training and Professionalism: Russia', in *Dictionary of Women Artists*, ed. by Delia Gaze, 2 vols (London: Fitzroy Dearborn, 1997), I, 119. Salmond's article (115–21) remains the richest account in English of the education of Russian women artists. For women's architectural training more generally, see Nina Smurova, 'Iz istorii vysshego zhenskogo arkhitekturnogo obrazovaniia v Rossii', *Problemy istorii sovetskoi arkhitektury (Sbornik nauchnykh trudov)* (Moscow: TsNIIP gradostroitel'stva, 1980), pp. 110–18.

of men. For Sharp, 'Goncharova's identity as a woman and as a producer of images of female nudity was seen as contradictory, and her behaviour therefore as criminally "sexed"'.[55]

Other commentators were openly enthusiastic, but even they struggled to reconcile the strength and novelty of the women's output with their gender and resorted to investing the women with 'masculine' traits. Thus, Iakov Tugendkhol'd wrote of Goncharova: 'Her personality, as strange as it seems, is more masculine than feminine. [...] The basic characteristic of Goncharova's talent is her masculine, sharp, energetic expressivity. [...] In essence, her analytic abilities dominate her gift for synthesis; her masculine eye dominates over her feminine lyricism'.[56] Konstantin Somov, a stalwart of the World of Art group, shared Tugendkhol'd's belief that powerful, visual expression and the fact of being female were largely incompatible, writing of Iakunchikova in 1902: 'She is now an interesting artist, which is a great exception for women. She draws well, has a fine feeling for colour which is *assez personelle*. Her technique is masculine'.[57] As Helena Goscilo and Elena Kornetchuk, authors of one of the more penetrating articles on contemporary Russian women's art, observe: 'then, as now, "masculine" operated as the standard Russian code word for excellence, so the statement intended a compliment, however backhanded and condescending'.[58] Notions of originality were so firmly gendered that the only way these commentators could accommodate forceful innovation in a woman artist was by equating her to a man.

In contrast, and thanks in no small part to the momentum of feminist art history, the final three decades of the twentieth century witnessed a surge of interest in the women of the Russian avant-garde – a development which owes as much to books, exhibitions, and reference works on women artists as it does to Russian studies.[59] The 1990s marked a particular watershed,

---

55. Jane A. Sharp, 'Redrawing the Margins of Russian Vanguard Art: Natalia Goncharova's Trial for Pornography in 1910', in *Sexuality and the Body in Russian Culture*, ed. by Jane T. Costlow, Stephanie Sandler and Judith Vowles (Stanford, CA: Stanford University Press, 1993), p. 98.
56. Iakov Tugendkhol'd, 'Vystavka kartin Natalii Goncharovoi', *Apollon*, 8 (October 1913), 72: cited in Sharp, 'Redrawing the Margins of Russian Vanguard Art', pp. 120–21.
57. Letter from K. A. Somov to A. A. Somov, Paris, 1897, in *Konstantin Andreevich Somov. Pis'ma, dnevniki, suzhdeniia sovremennikov*, comp. and annotated by Iu. N. Podkopaeva and A. N. Sveshnikova (Moscow: Iskusstvo, 1979), p. 61.
58. Helena Goscilo and Elena Kornetchuk, 'Canvassing Gender: Recent Women's Art', in *Iskusstvo zhenskogo roda*, p. 169.
59. Exhibition catalogues include *Women Artists 1550–1950*, ed. by Ann Sutherland Harris

starting with Miuda Yablonskaya's *Women Artists of Russia's New Age, 1900–1935* of 1990 and culminating (at least in terms of international exposure and publicity) with *Amazons of the Avant-Garde*, the large travelling exhibition dedicated to Ekster, Goncharova, Popova, Rozanova, Stepanova and Nadezhda Udal'tsova, which the Guggenheim Museum, New York, organized in 1999/2000.[60] Grappling with the issue as to why these artists achieved the heights of artistic expression and influence which they did, John E. Bowlt argued in the exhibition catalogue that we cannot use the linguistic trope of repression and submission common to discourses on women's art elsewhere, as the Russian 'amazons' enjoyed freedoms in their personal, creative and social lives which were unknown in the West. This is not to deny the practical obstacles and critical aggression which they faced (Bowlt himself mentions the reviewer of Goncharova's 1913 retrospective for whom 'the most disgusting thing is that the artist is a woman'.)[61] But women in Russia's pre-revolutionary avant-garde benefited from the relative absence of gendered, professional jealousy in their immediate milieu; from supportive creative partnerships which did not subordinate the work of the woman to that of the man, as was – and is – often the case; and from the availability of spaces of experimentation in the form of studios, theatres, exhibitions, performances, installations and street events. Their extraordinary creative energy was thus bolstered by places and systems of support, both practical and emotional, which had been long denied their sex. That *Amazons of the Avant-Garde* focused on studio

---

and Linda Nochlin (Los Angeles: Los Angeles County Museum of Art, 1976), which included Bashkirtseff, Goncharova, Udal'tsova, Ekster, Rozanova and Popova; and those of broader scope, such as *International Arts and Crafts*, ed. by Karen Livingstone and Linda Parry (London: V&A Publications, 2005), which included works by Polenova and Tenisheva. For reference works, see *Dictionary of Women Artists: An International Dictionary of Women Artists born before 1900*, ed. by Chris Petteys (Boston, Mass.: G. K. Hall & Co., 1985) and especially *Dictionary of Women Artists*, ed. by Delia Gaze, which contains substantial entries on many of the women mentioned in this account.

60. As examples, see Miuda Yablonskaya, *Women Artists of Russia's New Age, 1900–1935* (New York: Rizzoli, 1990); Dmitri Sarabianov and Natalia Adaskina, *Popova*, trans. by Marian Schwartz (London: Thames and Hudson, 1990); *Aleksandr Rodchenko. Varvara Stepanova. Budushchee – edinstvennaia nasha tsel'*, ed. by Peter Never (Munich: Prestel, 1991); Georgii Kovalenko, *Aleksandra Ekster. Put' khudozhnika. Khudozhnik i vremia* (Moscow: Galart, 1993); Dmitrii Sarab'ianov, *Liubov' Popova* (Moscow: Galart, 1994) and *N. A. Udal'tsova: zhizn' russkoi kubistki. Dnevniki, stat'i, vospominaniia*, comp. by Ekaterina Drevina and Vasilii Rakitin (Moscow: RA, 1994).

61. John E. Bowlt, 'Women of Genius', in *Amazons of the Avant-Garde. Alexandra Exter, Natalia Goncharova, Liubov Popova, Olga Rozanova, Varvara Stepanova, and Nadezhda Udaltsova*, ed. by John E. Bowlt and Matthew Drutt (New York: Guggenheim Museum Publications, 2000), pp. 24–26.

painting to the exclusion of these artists' formidable output in applied art and design, nevertheless, perpetuated those hierarchical distinctions which have militated against female artistic recognition. Indeed, the exhibition's remit stands as a stark reminder of where our values still lie.

The twenty-first century looks set to continue to interrogate the distinctive nature, production and context of Russian women's art. In 2002, the State Russian Museum in St Petersburg held a vast retrospective of Goncharova's oeuvre,[62] and the same year the State Tret'iakov Gallery in Moscow held the first exhibition in Russia dedicated to the work of women artists from the fifteenth to the twentieth centuries. The Tret'iakov exhibition made significant inroads in the quest to recover the work of neglected women painters of the nineteenth century, though its decision to concentrate on 'visual art proper, i.e. painting, sculpture and graphics, avoiding a wide area of feminine creation – decorative applied art' again ratified the age-old hierarchy between the fine and the 'lesser' arts (though, paradoxically, the exhibition included an entire section on fine needlework in ancient Russia).[63] In the West, women artists were integral to the 2002 exhibition on *The Russian Avant-Garde Book 1910–1934* at the Museum of Modern Art, New York, which reiterated the significance of this non-fine-art medium in modern art. Three years later, Jane Sharp set a new benchmark in the critique of Russian women artists in *Russian Modernism between East and West: Natal'ia Goncharova and the Moscow Avant-Garde* (2005), which argued for Goncharova's centrality in reclaiming Russia's 'Eastern' cultural heritage.[64] Christina Kiaer and Margarita Tupitsyn have also produced important new intellectual frameworks for the study of pre- and post-revolutionary women artists as well as, in Tupitsyn's case, pioneering work on contemporary women's art.[65]

Of particular import is Tupitsyn and Kiaer's collaboration on the exhibition *Rodchenko & Popova: Defining Constructivism*, which opened at Tate Modern, London, in 2009. If in 1999, the sex of the artists determined the conceptualization of *Amazons of the Avant-Garde*, a decade later the gender

---

62. *Natal'iia Goncharova. Gody v Rossii* (St Petersburg, Palace Editions, 2002).
63. *Iskusstvo zhenskogo roda*, pp. 11, 34–51.
64. Jane A. Sharp, *Russian Modernism between East and West: Natal'ia Goncharova and the Moscow Avant-Garde* (Cambridge: Cambridge University Press, 2005).
65. See, for example, Margarita Tupitsyn, 'Unveiling Feminism: Women's Art in the Soviet Union', *Arts Magazine* (December 1990), 63–67 and Christina Kiaer, *Imagine No Possessions: The Socialist Objects of Russian Constructivism* (Cambridge, Mass.: MIT Press, 2005).

difference between Popova and Rodchenko was no longer prioritized. Rather, Popova was presented along with Rodchenko as one of the signal artists of the Russian avant-garde and given an equal platform for the presentation and critical discussion of her work.[66] The value of this relative inattention to sexual difference is a moot point. What provides the most profitable route for the exploration of women's art – an emphasis on their distinctiveness, as in the *Amazons* exhibition, or the projection of parity, as in the Rodchenko and Popova show? Whatever the case, the sex of Russian, women artists and their supposedly unique characteristics will continue to shape assessments of, and responses to, their work. For Yablonskaya, writing in 2002, 'the peculiar predisposition of women to visual analysis of reality has its own characteristic features that are no less valuable than those shown by men. The penetrating sensitivity of women, the sharpness of their intuitive reactions, the powerful and diverse structure of their sensations, particularly of the tactile ones, are the qualities especially valuable for creative activity'.[67] At the same time, the liberation of a woman artist in *Rodchenko & Popova* from methods of display predicated on gender, heralds new avenues of enquiry, in which the apparent specificities of the female sex, if not disregarded, are at least downplayed. Such shifts of focus may portend ever keener concern to give women artists and their work the same level of exposure and critical enquiry as that afforded to men.

---

66. If Popova's identity as a woman artist within constructivism is not foregrounded in the exhibition, it is addressed in the catalogue. See Christina Kiaer, 'His and Her Constructivism', in *Rodchenko & Popova: Defining Constructivism*, ed. by Margarita Tupitsyn (London: Tate Publishing, 2009), pp. 143–59.
67. Miuda Yablonskaya, 'A "New" Phenomenon? An Essay on Systematization', in *Iskusstvo zhenskogo roda*, p. 134.

6. Women and Music

Philip Ross Bullock

In comparison to the related fields of literature and the visual arts (examined by Rosalind Blakesley and Arja Rosenholm and Irina Savkina in this volume),[1] the place of women – whether individually or collectively, – in modern Russian music has barely begun to be studied. The rise of the so-called 'new musicology' in Anglo-American criticism, which has done so much to foreground discussion of gender and sexuality, has thus far, had relatively little impact on Russian studies. Despite the transformation of academic priorities that followed the collapse of the Soviet Union in 1991, Russian musicology remains to a great extent occupied by issues relating to the life and works of canonical male composers, such as the homosexuality of Petr Chaikovskii (1840–93) or the alleged anti-Soviet opinions of Dmitrii Shostakovich (1906–75). Even where scholars have begun to reassess the historiography of Russian music, as in the case of work by Marina Frolova-Walker and Richard Taruskin on the discourses of nationalism, the role of gender in cultural production has received scant attention.[2] Yet, whether as

---

1. See, for instance, *A History of Women's Writing in Russia*, ed. by Adele Marie Barker and Jehanne M. Gheith (Cambridge: Cambridge University Press, 2002); *An Anthology of Russian Women's Writing, 1777–1992*, ed. by Catriona Kelly, trans. by Catriona Kelly et al. (Oxford: Oxford University Press, 1994); Catriona Kelly, *A History of Russian Women's Writing, 1820–1992* (Oxford: Clarendon Press, 1994); Jordana Pomeroy et al., *An Imperial Collection: Women Artists from the State Hermitage Museum* (New York: National Museum of Women in the Arts; London: Merrell; 2003) and *Amazons of the Avant-Garde: Alexandra Exter, Natalia Goncharova, Liubov Popova, Olga Rozanova, Varvara Stepanova, and Nadezhda Udaltsova*, ed. by John E. Bowlt and Matthew Drutt (London: Royal Academy of Arts; New York: Solomon R. Guggenheim Foundation, 1999).
2. Marina Frolova-Walker, *Russian Music and Nationalism: From Glinka to Stalin* (New Haven, CT, and London: Yale University Press, 2007) and Richard Taruskin, *Defining Russia Musically: Historical and Hermeneutical Essays* (Princeton, NJ: Princeton University Press, 1997).

teachers, performers, scholars, composers or patrons, women have played a central role in the development of modern Russian musical culture, even if this role has not enjoyed the prominence it deserves. As Rosalind Blakesley argues in her chapter on the visual arts:

> It is important [...] to consider the earlier period of relative inactivity as much as the high-profile artists at the dawn of the twentieth century; as charting the transition of women artists in Russia from marginal figures to practitioners of world renown raises significant questions about the role of women in Russia's creative and cultural life.

Of course, many of the barriers that have prevented women from participating fully in the cultural sphere were not unique to Russia and the conventional narrative of European women's increased involvement in aspects of public and professional life from the eighteenth century onwards is one that can be told of Russia too (albeit with constant reference to specific, local factors).

Before the beginning of the eighteenth century, female participation in Russia's musical institutions was necessarily limited by the fact that women were confined to the *terem* (separate quarters). Women could not appear on the stage (especially in the religious dramas that formed the core of the pre-Petrine theatrical repertoire) and Nikolai Findeizen's survey of 'singers, composers, and music theorists of the sixteenth and seventeenth centuries' implies an entirely male tradition (at least as revealed by the study of official documents).[3] Such restrictions (usually motivated by considerations of ecclesiastical propriety) did not, though, apply to popular culture. Contemporary accounts of the *skomorokhi* (minstrels) suggest that women often took part in dancing and revelry. Giles Fletcher (1548–1611), the sixteenth-century English diplomat, observed that the Tsar would entertain himself 'with jesters and dwarfs, men and women that tumble before him and sing many songs after the Russian manner'.[4] Similarly, Adam Olearius (1603–71), who visited Muscovy in the middle of the seventeenth century, noted: 'The dancers, particularly the women, hold varicoloured, embroidered handkerchiefs, which they wave about

---

3. Nikolai Findeizen, *History of Music in Russia from Antiquity to 1800*, trans. by Samuel William Pring, ed. and annotated by Miloš Velimorović and Claudia R. Jensen, with the assistance of Malcolm Hamrick Brown and Daniel C. Waugh, 2 vols (Indianapolis and Bloomington: Indiana University Press, 2008), I, 259–66.
4. Cited in Catriona Kelly, 'The Origins of the Russian Theatre', in *A History of Russian Theatre*, ed. by Robert Leach and Victor Borovsky (Cambridge: Cambridge University Press, 1999), pp. 18–40 (20).

while dancing although they themselves remain in place almost all the time'.[5] Women were also deeply involved in the musical manifestations of peasant culture, such as seasonal songs, marriage rituals, laments, spells, charms and divinations (many of which would – like performances by the *skomorokhi* – be censured by the Church on account of their pagan origins).[6]

The roots of women's modern involvement in secular and society music-making, however, go back to the beginning of the eighteenth century. Indeed, it was three of Russia's three eighteenth-century empresses – Anna (1693–1740, reigned from 1730), Elizabeth (1709–62, reigned from 1741) and Catherine the Great (1729–96, reigned from 1762) – who did much to establish Western-style music and music-making at the heart of the cultural life of the court and the capitals (Peter the Great's interest in music was limited largely to ceremonial functions). It was during Anna's reign that music first became 'an indispensable part of court life – an embellishment and a required entertainment'.[7] This can be seen most obviously in her decision to invite a series of Italian opera troupes to visit Russia from 1731. The tradition of female imperial patronage was continued by Catherine the Great, who brought a French opera company to Russia and, conversely, encouraged Russian composers to study in Western Europe. She also supported the nascent institutions of Russian opera, as well as writing the libretti for five comic operas on folk themes and *The Beginning of Oleg's Reign* (*Nachal'noe upravlenie Olega*), an historical pageant that made extensive use of choruses and songs.[8] Music soon became one of the social accomplishments of the all-round enlightenment citizen, as can be seen in the case of Ekaterina Dashkova (1742–1810), the first president of the Russian Academy of Sciences, who sang at Catherine's court, kept an album of favourite pieces and took a lively interest in the musical issues of the day.[9] The important role played by the salon in establishing norms of civilized behaviour and cultural intimacy meant that if women did turn their hand to composition, it was in the form of songs and small instrumental works

---

5. Cited in Findeizen, *History of Music in Russia from Antiquity to 1800*, I, 119.
6. Natalie Kononenko, 'Women as Performers of Oral Literature: A Re-Examination of Epic and Lament', in *Women Writers in Russian Literature*, ed. by Toby W. Clayman and Diana Greene (Westport, CT: Greenwood Press, 1994), pp. 17–33.
7. Findeizen, *History of Music in Russia from Antiquity to 1800*, II, 1.
8. Lurana Donnels O'Malley, *The Dramatic Works of Catherine The Great: Theatre and Politics in Eighteenth-Century Russia* (Aldershot: Ashgate, 2006), especially Chapter 5, 'Comic Operas', pp. 169–200.
9. *E. R. Dashkova i muzyka*, ed. by M. P. Priashnikova (Moscow: MGI imeni E. R. Dashkovoi, 2001).

suitable for domestic performance.[10] Of those that made it into print, such as the *Huit romances, composées et arrangées pour le harpe par la princesse Natalie de Kourakin* (1795), a few were attributable to a particular composer. Yet many other works were published either anonymously or behind a series of initials (where only the grammatical ending allows us to discern the gender but not the identity of the author).[11]

A further factor in inhibiting women's compositional activities may have been the absence of comparable role models in Western Europe more generally. Figures such as Elisabeth Vigée-Lebrun (1755–1842) or Madame de Staël (1766–1817) – both of whom visited Russia – offered examples of female creativity in painting and literature,[12] yet there were few, if any, well-known women composers who might serve as archetype and inspiration. Indeed, it would not be until well into the late nineteenth century that women would achieve any degree of prominence as composers in Europe. Chaikovskii, for instance, was impressed by the abilities of the British composer, Ethel Smyth (1858–1944), whom he met in 1888:

> Miss Smyth is one of the comparatively few women composers who may be seriously reckoned among the workers in this sphere of music. She had come to Leipzig a few years before and studied theory and composition very thoroughly; she had composed several interesting works (the best of which, a violin sonata, I heard excellently played by the composer herself and Mr Brodsky), and gave promise in the future of a serious and talented career.[13]

Yet what appear to modern critics as distinct constraints on feminine creativity may, nonetheless, have granted women some greater freedom of manoeuvre than at first seems to be the case. With the shift from sentimentalism and neo-classicism to a form of romanticism in the early

---

10. A selection of such works can be heard on *Music of Russian Princesses from the Court of Catherine the Great* (Dorian Recordings DOR-93244).
11. M. G. Dolgushina, *U istokov russkogo romansa: kamernaia vokal'naia kul'tura aleksandrovskoi epokhi* (Vologda: Knizhnoe nasledie, 2004), p. 80.
12. Malcolm V. Jones, 'Flirting Her Way round the Court of St Petersburg: Some Thoughts on Vigée-Lebrun's Russian Period and Her Portrait of Varvara Nikolaevna Golovina', in *Diagonales dostoïevskiennes: mélanges en l'honneur de Jacques Catteau*, ed. by Marie-Aude Albert (Paris: Presses de l'université de Paris-Sorbonne, 2002), pp. 273–89. Esteem for de Staël was far from universal, however, and a number of (male) commentators blamed her for 'damaging women's morals or simply for monopolizing the admiration for women readers at the expense of young (male) Russian writers'. See Alessandra Tosi, *Waiting for Pushkin: Russian Fiction in the Reign of Alexander I (1801–1825)* (Amsterdam and New York: Rodopi, 2006), pp. 141–42.
13. Cited in Rosa Newmarch, *Tchaikovsky: His Life and Works, with Extracts from His Writings, and the Diary of His Tour Abroad in 1888* (London: Grant Richards, 1900), p. 194.

nineteenth century, the salon was no longer necessarily the realm of the accomplished society amateur and hostesses could aspire to more than simply the modes of politeness and patronage that had been their lot previously. The Moscow salon of Zinaida Volkonskaia (1792–1862) – one of the greatest admirers of de Staël in Russia – became one of the most significant musical and literary venues of the 1820s.[14] Her opera – *Giovanna d'Arco* – was performed in her Roman salon in 1821 (with Volkonskaia herself taking the lead role), and she staged a private performance of Paisiello's *La bella molinara* during the Congress of Vienna in 1822.[15] Another important Russian salon was that held in St Petersburg by the virtuoso Polish pianist and composer Maria Szymanowska (1789–1831), who toured extensively through Russia and Europe, and was eventually appointed 'court' or 'first' pianist.[16] It was in such quasi-domestic settings – as much as in the public spaces of the court and the theatre – that Russia first consolidated its status as a cultural power, and women played a crucial role in this process.

Nevertheless, a professional career in music long remained closed to Russian women of the nobility or gentry, and public performance long remained the domain of foreigners, or of serfs and townspeople (*meshchane*), whose presence on the stage was less likely to upset Russia's feudal code or to transgress social propriety. Indeed, the relationship between class and gender was crucial to the world of musical theatre, governed as it was by what one scholar has dubbed 'the erotic bond linking serf-performer and master-spectator'.[17] One leading actress and singer from serf background was Praskov'ia Kovaleva (1768–1803), nicknamed the 'Pearl' ('Zhemchugova').[18] The mistress of Count Nikolai Sheremetev (whom she married clandestinely in 1801), she performed extensively at the Sheremetev family theatre at Kuskovo (one of Russia's leading musical venues) throughout the 1780s and 1790s. Another leading singer of the era was Elizaveta Uranova (1772–1826), who trained at the St Petersburg

---

14. Thomas P. Hodge, *A Double Garland: Poetry and Art-Song in Early-Nineteenth-Century Russia* (Evanston, IL: Northwestern University Press, 2000), pp. 225–26.
15. *Lives in Letters: Princess Zinaida Volkonskaya and her Correspondence*, ed. by Bayara Aroutunova (Columbus, OH: Slavica, 1994) and Maria Fairweather, *Pilgrim Princess: A Life of Princess Zinaida Volkonsky* (London: Robinson, 1999).
16. Anne Swartz, 'Maria Szymanowska: Contemporary Accounts from Moscow and St Petersburg', *New Journal for Music*, 1.1 (1990), 38–64.
17. Laurence Senelick, 'The Erotic Bondage of Serf Theatre', *Russian Review*, 50.1 (1991), 24–34 (29).
18. Douglas Smith, *The Pearl: A True Tale of Forbidden Love in Catherine the Great's Russia* (New Haven, CT, and London: Yale University Press, 2008).

theatrical academy, known principally by her married name of Sandunova. Her marriage to the actor Sila Sandunov (1756–1820) was achieved only after a struggle with one of Catherine's ministers, Aleksandr Bezborodko (1747–99), who desired the singer for himself. Although the Sandunovs were eventually allowed to marry as a result of Catherine's direct intervention (a case of female imperial benefactor defending a female performing artist), the case, nonetheless, illustrated that even the most talented and popular artists could still be treated as little more than the property of noble patrons.[19] (The position of women actresses in this period is treated in greater detail by Julie Cassiday elsewhere in this volume.)

The emphasis placed by Russia's rulers on the values of enlightenment and civilized behaviour (in both public and private) had significant consequences for women's involvement in culture more generally. Led by Aleksandra Fedorovna (1798–1860), wife of Nicholas I (1796–1855), the imperial household took a keen interest in music, giving a lead to members of the nobility, gentry and middle classes to do the same. As Richard Wortman writes: 'Alexandra was an active patron of the musical life of the court and the capital. She organized numerous family musicals, where she played the piano and Nicholas played the trumpet'.[20] In particular, women's education (whether at home, or at boarding schools such as the Smol'nyi Institute in St Petersburg, the Ekaterininskii Institute in Moscow, or similar institutions in provincial cities) came to include not only formal literacy, but also a whole range of accomplishments – music, as well as drawing, dancing, a rudimentary knowledge of history and geography and a command of modern foreign languages – that were explicitly designed to improve the marriage prospects of girls from the nobility and gentry. Well into the nineteenth century, girls acquired often impressive abilities as singers and instrumentalists (whether on the harp, guitar or the keyboard), something reflected in the literature of the time. As Richard Stites notes: 'Few Russian novels about the gentry failed to feature a piano performance

---

19. Lurana Donnels O'Malley, 'Signs from Empresses and Actresses: Women and Theatre in the Eighteenth Century', in *Women in Russian Culture and Society, 1700–1825*, ed. by Wendy Rosslyn and Alessandra Tosi (Basingstoke and New York: Palgrave Macmillan, 2007), pp. 9–23 (15–16) and Wendy Rosslyn, 'Female Employees in the Russian Imperial Theatres (1785–1825)', in *Women and Gender in 18th-Century Russia*, ed. by Wendy Rosslyn (Aldershot: Ashgate, 2003), pp. 257–77.
20. Richard S. Wortman, *Scenarios of Power: Myth and Ceremony in Russian Monarchy*, 2 vols (Princeton, NJ: Princeton University Press, 1995–2000), I: *From Peter the Great to the Death of Nicholas I*, 342.

or song by a young marriageable girl'.[21] From the late eighteenth century onwards, cheap and accessible collections of song texts circulated, evidence of the extent to which the cultivation of the arts in polite company had begun to spread, both socially and geographically. As their titles make clear *The Latest Songbook for Tender Maids and Amiable Women* (*Noveishii tualetnyi pesennik dlia milykh devits i liubeznykh zhenshchin*) (Orel, 1820), or *The Latest Songbook for Beautiful Girls and Amiable Women* (*Noveishii pesennik dlia prekrasnykh devushek i liubeznykh zhenshchin*) (Moscow, 1820) – there was a distinct association between femininity and music. Indeed, the emphasis placed on the cultivation of polite conversation, the unmediated expression of tender emotion and the role of women as teachers meant that culture more generally underwent a process of feminization, even if female creativity itself was constrained.[22] As Arja Rosenholm and Irina Savkina suggest about the impact of sentimentalism on women in the late eighteenth century: 'on the one hand it legitimized femininity as publicly significant and creative; on the other, it laid down strict limits for the creative representation of the female'.

The cultivation of amateurism and the association of music-making with a feminine (or feminized) sensibility began to be challenged around the middle of the nineteenth century. Talented musicians from the nobility such as Vladimir Odoevskii (1803–69) and the Viel'gorskii brothers (Matvei, 1787–1863, and Mikhail, 1788–1856) had already moved in this direction, but the most decisive step came in 1859 with the foundation of the Russian Music Society, whose primary aim was 'the development of musical education and musical taste in Russia and the encouragement of native talents'.[23] Russian musicians had long been aware that they lacked the kind of professional training and institutional identity offered by the Imperial Academy of Fine Arts. Only with the opening of the St Petersburg conservatoire in 1862 (the Moscow Conservatoire followed in 1866) could musicians – both men and women – aspire to some sort of professional status in Russian society (see, for instance, Blakesley's discussion of the evolving position of women in the Imperial Academy of Fine Arts, also in

---

21. Richard Stites, *Serfdom, Society, and the Arts in Imperial Russia: The Pleasure and the Power* (New Haven, CT and London: Yale University Press, 2005), p. 59.
22. Gitta Hammarberg, 'The Feminine Chronotope and Sentimentalist Canon Formation', in *Literature, Lives and Legality in Catherine's Russia*, ed. by A. G. Cross and G. S. Smith (Nottingham: Astra, 1995), pp. 103–20.
23. Cited in Philip S. Taylor, *Anton Rubinstein: A Life in Music* (Bloomington and Indianapolis: Indiana University Press, 2007), p. 83.

this volume). Although much of the credit for these achievements belongs to Anton Rubinshtein (1829–1894), nothing could have been done without the support of his imperial patron, Grand Duchess Elena Pavlovna (1807–73), who lent the official authority of the state to the new undertaking and encouraged other patrons and subscribers to participate.[24] The most obvious beneficiaries of this new form of conservatoire training were largely men, whether composers such as Chaikovskii, or the many native performers who could now aspire to a professional career (not least former peasants and members of the urban lower classes who studied orchestral instruments).[25] Yet the majority of conservatoire students were in fact young women of talent and dedication, but who were unlikely – because of considerations of wealth, gender and class – to embark on public careers.[26] Such women went on instead to make up the large and largely unsung body of music teachers who were so central to Rubinshtein's overall aim of developing 'musical education and musical taste'. Just as Elena Pavlovna illustrated the persistence of eighteenth-century notions of aristocratic patronage in the service of Russia's liberalization under Alexander II, so too did an appeal to women's pedagogical abilities constitute a modernization of traditional feminine accomplishments and gender roles.

It would thus be some time before women came to play a more visible role in Russia's musical life, and even when women were able to cultivate their skills as teachers and performers, the ultimate beneficiaries of this process would often still be men; many male musicians received their earliest musical education at home from their mothers. A further way of supporting the careers and aspirations of men was by providing the kind of substantial financial support that could not yet be provided by fees and royalties alone. In the case of Chaikovskii, it was the assistance of Nadezhda fon Mekk (1831–94) that proved essential in dealing with a succession of personal and professional difficulties. The widow of a recently deceased railway magnate, and consequently extremely wealthy, she first approached Chaikovskii in 1876 with a request to provide arrangements of his own works for violin and piano for her to play (she was a gifted amateur violinist). In the wake of his disastrous marriage to Antonina Miliukova (1849–1917)

---

24. Anne Swartz, 'The Romanov Family's Patronage of Music, 1820–1880', in *Encomium Musicae: Essays in Memory of Robert J. Snow*, ed. by David Crawford (Hillsdale: Pendragon, 2002), pp. 717–32.
25. Lynn Sargeant, 'A New Class of People: The Conservatoire and Music Professionalization in Russia, 1861–1917', *Music and Letters*, 85.1 (2004), 41–61 (49–52).
26. Sargeant, 'A New Class of People', pp. 48–49, 52–54.

in 1877, Chaikovskii suffered a breakdown and fled to Western Europe. It was at this point that fon Mekk stepped in, offering not only to pay off his outstanding debts, but also to provide a regular monthly allowance. This allowance – which would be paid until 1890 – was instrumental in allowing Chaikovskii to give up his position at the Moscow Conservatoire in 1878 and thus establish himself as Russia's first full-time professional composer. By mutual arrangement, the two never formally met (although they did encounter each other occasionally in society and at her country estate) and their relationship was conducted through a series of long and demonstrative letters (in his, Chaikovskii gave some of the most detailed commentaries on his own works).[27] A commonplace in the secondary literature (derived ultimately from Chaikovskii's earliest biographers) has been the juxtaposition of the selfless and devoted supported of fon Mekk and the hysterical distractions of the egotistical Miliukova, a juxtaposition in which the traditional gendered opposition of women as either angelic or malevolent can clearly be discerned.[28]

Known variously as the Balakirev circle, the New Russian School, or the Mighty Handful (*moguchaia kuchka*), the five members of the 'nationalist' school were all men: Milii Balakirev (1837–1910), Aleksandr Borodin (1833–87); Tsezar' Kiui (1835–1918); Modest Musorgskii (1839–81); and Nikolai Rimskii-Korsakov (1844–1908). Opposed to conservatoire training and often earning their livelihoods by other means (at least during the heyday of the movement in the 1860s and 1870s), they did without the kind of female patronage observed in the cases of Rubinshtein and Chaikovskii. Nonetheless, as Vladimir Stasov (1824–1906) observed, two sisters – Aleksandra and Nadezhda Purgol'd (1845–1929 and 1848–1919 respectively) – played a crucial role in the artistic life of this close-knit group:

> Mention must also be made of two gifted women who played an important rôle in the fortunes of the new Russian school. These were the Purgold sisters, both of whom were exceptionally talented musicians and quite unique among the multitude of women who pursued this art in the days of Glinka and Dargomïzhsky, or, in fact, who pursue it today. The elder sister, Alexandra Nikolayevna (Alexandra Molas, by marriage) was a singer who

---

27. '*To My Best Friend*': *Correspondence between Tchaikovsky and Nadezhda von Meck, 1876–1878*, ed. by Edward Garden and Nigel Gotteri, trans. by Galina von Meck (Oxford: Clarendon Press, 1993).
28. For a 'revisionist' account of the marriage from Chaikovskii's wife's point of view, see Valerii Sokolov, *Antonina Chaikovskaia: istoriia zabytoi zhizni* (Moscow: Muzyka, 1994).

was taught first by Dargomïzhsky and later by Mussorgsky. Her singing style, not being of the conventional operatic variety, was excellently suited to the interpretation of honest and unaffected music, whether passionate, tragic, comic or tender – to the recitative style which forms the basis of all the songs and much of the operas written by our new school. Indeed, her singing was so true to the spirit of the music that now and then one of these composers would say that his work had two authors – himself and the performer. The other sister, Nadezhda Nikolayevna (later the wife of Rimsky-Korsakov), was not only more highly educated musically than any of our other women engaged in music; she not only had an instinctive grasp of music and its forms but she was, herself, a gifted composer. Her compositions include an orchestral fantasy *Night* based on Gogol's story *St. John's Eve*, and a piano fantasy. She transcribed many of her friends' orchestral compositions for piano four-hands and orchestrated several passages of *The Maid of Pskov*. Moreover, even while under Dargomïzhsky's tutelage, she as such an excellent accompanist that Musorgsky constantly referred to her as 'our orchestra'. From the end of the sixties and beginning of the seventies, the Purgold sisters took part in preliminary readings of all the songs and operas being composed by the members of the group and afterwards also participated in full rehearsals of their works.[29]

Stasov's approval of the Purgol'd sisters (notwithstanding Nadezhda's gifts as a composer) is based largely on their noble and altruistic support for the male composers of the nationalist school (although the influence of Nadezhda's thorough academic training on her husband was also treated with suspicion by Stasov and Balakirev, who felt she was leading him away from the nationalist cause).[30] Stasov's admiration of the Purgol'd sisters was, moreover, in inverse proportion to his dislike of 'the multitude of women who pursued this art in the days of Glinka and Dargomïzhsky, or, in fact, who pursue it today'. Despite the widespread sympathy for female emancipation among members of the radical intelligentsia in the second half of the nineteenth-century (Stasov's own sister, Nadezhda Stasova (1822–95), was a leading member of the women's movement and was involved in philanthropic work to improve the material conditions of working women),[31] Stasov appears to be expressing here a distaste for

---

29. Vladimir Vasilevich Stasov, 'Twenty-five Years of Russian Art: Our Music', in *Selected Essays on Music*, trans. by Florence Jonas (London: Barrie and Rockliff, 1968), pp. 66–116 (110).
30. Marina Frolova-Walker, 'Nikolay Andreyevich Rimsky-Korsakov', in *The New Grove Dictionary of Music and Musicians*, ed. by Stanley Sadie and John Tyrrell, 2nd edn, 29 vols (London: Macmillan, 2001), XXI, 400–23 (401).
31. Barbara Alpern Engel, *Mothers and Daughters: Women of the Intelligentsia in Nineteenth-Century Russia* (Cambridge: Cambridge University Press, 1983), pp. 57–61, and Richard Stites, *The Women's Liberation Movement in Russia: Feminism, Nihilism, and Bolshevism, 1860–1930* (Princeton: Princeton University Press, 1978), p. 66.

the feminization of musical life (whether in dilettante society or the lower levels of the profession) that was then widespread.[32] The distinctive role played by women in supporting the work of the nationalist composers can in fact be traced back to Liudmila Shestakova (1816–1906), the sister of Mikhail Glinka (1804–57). Not only did she organize Glinka's own indolent and disorderly life, but she also assiduously promoted his posthumous reputation by preserving and publishing his scores, compiling biographical material about him (indeed, she had earlier encouraged him to write his own memoirs) and encouraging renewed interest in the performance of his compositions. Moreover, through her close relationships with Stasov and the nationalists, she contributed to the historiography of Russian music by endorsing them as heirs to Glinka's legacy (one commentator has even dubbed her the 'handmaid to Russian music').[33] If Shestakova did much to encourage these composers at the beginning of their careers, then their subsequent popularity owes much to Mariia Olenina d'Al'geim (1869–1970), who studied with Aleksandra Purgol'd-Molas in 1887 and did much to promote the songs of Musorgskii, first in France and then in Russia itself, around the turn of the century.[34]

If women were adept at playing the role of handmaids to masculine creativity (in a way that parallels the patronage of figures such as Mariia Tenisheva at Talashkino, discussed by Blakesley elsewhere in this volume), then they were also beginning to explore their own talents more confidently, whether as performers or (less frequently) composers. The position of foreign women in Russian musical life remained, as before, prominent. Clara Wieck Schumann (1819–96) had toured Russia in 1844 and again in 1864 as one of Europe's leading virtuoso pianists, but perhaps the most durable impression made by a female musician from Europe was that made by Pauline Viardot (1821–1910), who arrived in St Petersburg in 1843 (with her husband, Louis) to sing in a series of Italian operas. It was at this time that she met Ivan Turgenev (1818–83), who immediately fell in love with her and who was to spend the rest of his life living with or near to the Viardots (who left Russia in 1846).[35] Despite her association with the Italian opera in St Petersburg, Viardot, nonetheless, made a significant contribution to

---

32. Sargeant, 'A New Class of People', pp. 52–53.
33. Serge Bertensson, 'Ludmila Ivanovna Shestakova – Handmaid to Russian Music', *The Musical Quarterly*, 31.3 (1945), 331–38.
34. Alexander Tumanov, *The Life and Artistry of Maria Olenina-d'Alheim*, trans. Christopher Barnes (Edmonton: University of Alberta Press, 2000).
35. April Fitzlyon, *The Price of Genius: A Life of Pauline Viardot* (London: John Calder, 1964).

Russian music itself. In the singing-lesson scene in Rossini's *Barber of Seville*, she famously inserted a Russian romance – Aliab'ev's *Nightingale* (*Solovei*) – as well as setting a number of verses by Russian poets as songs herself. Her most famous collaboration with a Russian writer, however, took the form of the operettas which she composed to librettos (in French) by Turgenev, such as *Trop de femmes* (1867), *L'ogre* (1868), *Le conte de fées* and *Le dernier sorcier* (both 1869), which were performed at her home in Baden-Baden.

The position – whether social or material – for Russian performers had also begun to improve around the middle of the century. An important element in the establishment of a professional system of conservatoire training was the fact that graduates obtained the title of 'free artist' (*svobodnyi khudozhnik*), which granted them an increasingly secure sense of social status than had been the case under the former system of feudal patronage. Alongside professional respect came a greater sense of aesthetic worth. As the national arts began to play an even larger part in Russian life and it became ever more possible for individual artists to make a living on the basis of their creative work, native performers began to enjoy more of the respect once accorded to foreign virtuosi. Anna Vorob'eva-Petrova (1816–1901) – herself the daughter of two of Russia's leading singers – created the roles of Vania and Ratmir in Glinka's *A Life for the Tsar* (*Zhizn' za tsaria*, 1836) and *Ruslan and Liudmila* (*Ruslan i Liudmila*, 1842) respectively. Iuliia Platonova (1841–92) claimed to have brought about the staging of the revized version of Musorgskii's *Boris Godunov*, first by creating the role of Marina Mniszek in the partial version of the opera that was performed in 1873 and then by using the occasion of a benefit concert to insist on a full production of the work (although scholars have since disputed her version of the story).[36] Aleksandra Panaeva (1853–1942) was the first to sing the role of Tat'iana in Chaikovskii's *Eugene Onegin* (*Evgenii Onegin*) in a performance at the Moscow Conservatoire in 1879 (he would dedicated his *Seven Romances*, op. 47 to her the following year). Around the turn of the century, Nadezhda Zabela-Vrubel' (1868–1913) sang in many of the premieres of Rimskii-Korsakov's operas at the private opera house belonging to Savva Mamontov (1841–1918) in Moscow and created the part of Sirin in the first performance of Rimskii-Korsakov's *The Legend of the Invisible City of Kitezh and the Maiden Fevroniia* (*Skazanie o nevidimom grade Kitezhe i deve Fevronii*) at the Mariinskii Theatre in St Petersburg in 1907.

---

36. Caryl Emerson and Robert Oldani, *Modest Musorgsky and Boris Godunov: Myths, Realities, Reconsiderations* (Cambridge: Cambridge University Press, 1994), pp. 82–84.

Women also enjoyed successful careers as teachers, with professorships at the conservatoires offering a particularly visible marker of professional success (often alongside operatic and concert careers). The Swedish mezzo-soprano Henriette Nissen-Saloman (1819–79) had taught singing at the St Petersburg Conservatoire from its very opening. There, her pupils included Natal'ia Iretskaia (1845–1922), who later taught at the St Petersburg Conservatoire, and Elizaveta Lavrovskaia (1845–1919), who also studied with Viardot. Lavrovskaia went on to sing the roles of Vania and Ratmir that had been created by Vorob'eva-Petrova, and famously suggested *Eugene Onegin* as a suitable subject for an opera to Chaikovskii (she also taught at the Moscow Conservatoire). These direct connections between generations of female teachers and performers did much to establish a distinct Russian vocal tradition that was to last well into the next century. If a career as a singer had always been a possibility (however constrained by social convention) for a musical woman, then that of a concert pianist was somewhat more unusual, as can be seen by the career of Anna Esipova (1851–1914), who toured Europe extensively in the late nineteenth century before being appointed professor at the St Petersburg Conservatoire, where her pupils included Sergei Prokof'ev (1891–1953). A performing career was not without its perils, though, as can be seen from the career of Evlaliia Kadmina (1853–81), whose fate can be seen as an example of what Julie Cassiday refers to, in her chapter in this volume on nineteenth-century actresses, as 'a distinctively Russian tendency to blend art and life, often to the tragic detriment of the latter'. Of mixed merchant and gypsy origin, she was educated initially at the Elizavetinskii Institute for the daughters of the nobility, before going on to study singing with Aleksandra Aleksandrova-Kochetova (1833–1903) at the Moscow Conservatoire. After a successful career in both the capitals and the provinces, and a period studying in Italy, she was, nonetheless, subject to increasing criticism and eventually gave up singing in favour of acting. An unhappy love affair led her to take her own life – she took poison and collapsed on stage, dying a few days later. The potency of her myth was fictionalized in a number of literary versions of her suicide, including Turgenev's 'Klara Milich' (1882), Anton Chekhov's 'Tat'iana Repina' (1889) and Aleksandr Kuprin's 'Her Final Debut' ('Poslednii debiut', 1889).[37]

---

37. Julie Buckler, 'Her Final Debut: The Kadmina Legend in Russian Literature', in *Intersections and Transpositions: Russian Music, Literature, and Society*, ed. by Andrew B. Wachtel (Evanston, IL: Northwestern University Press, 1998), pp. 225–52. More generally, see Julie A. Buckler, *The Literary Lorgnette: Attending Opera in Imperial Russia* (Stanford, CA: Stanford University Press, 2000), especially Chapter 3, 'Embodying Opera: The Prima Donna in Russia', pp. 57–94.

If Kadmina's life and death were memorialized in a number of works of Russian fiction, then the careers of a number of singers of popular music were facilitated by the development of new technologies. Early-twentieth-century artistes such as Nadezhda Plevitskaia (1884–1940), Varia Panina (1872–1911) and Anastas'ia Vial'steva (1871–1913) engaged with ever wider audiences through concerts, recordings, photography and the often melodramatic stories that circulated about their lives (although it is only recently that the study of urban middle-brow culture has attracted serious academic study).[38]

The legend of Kadmina illustrates both the possibilities and perils of a performing career in the mid-nineteenth century. Yet if the role of diva and teacher was increasingly (although not entirely) an accessible, acceptable and attractive one for educated women in nineteenth-century Russia, then that of composer was altogether more difficult, although not entirely impossible. Valentina Serova (née Bergman, 1846–1924) had joined the St Petersburg Conservatoire in 1862 in order to study the piano with Rubinshtein. The following year, she married the composer and critic, Aleksandr Serov (1820–71), with whom she also studied. Her debut as a composer came in 1871, when she completed (along with Nikolai Solov'ev (1846–1916)) the final act of her husband's opera, *The Power of the Fiend* (*Vrazh'ia sila*), which had been left incomplete on his sudden death. She went on to write four operas of her own, including *Uriel Acosta* (1885, performed at the Bolshoi in Moscow) and *Il'ia Muromets* (performed at Mamontov's private opera in 1899).[39] Another important woman composer was Ella Shul'ts (1846–1926), who took the pseudonym Adaevskaia. A virtuoso pupil of pianist Adolf Henselt (1814–89), she went on to study at the newly-founded St Petersburg Conservatoire from 1864 to 1868, thanks to the generosity of Grand Duchess Elena Pavlovna (something she was forbidden to reveal). Her first opera – *The Homely Girl* (*Neprigozhaia*, 1873), also known as *The Boyar's Daughter* (*Doch' boiarina*) – was followed by *The Dawn of Freedom* (*Zaria svobody*, 1877). However, this was turned down by the censor – despite being dedicated to the reformist tsar Alexander II – on the grounds that it included a depiction of a peasant uprising. Having undertaken a number of European concert tours,

---

38. Louise MacReynolds, '"The Incomparable" Anastassia Vial'tseva and the Cult of Personality', in *Russia – Women – Culture*, ed. by Helena Goscilo and Beth Holmgren (Bloomington: Indiana University Press, 1996), pp. 273–94.
39. Malcolm Hamrick Brown, 'Serova, Valentina Semyonovna', in *The New Grove Dictionary of Music and Musicians*, XXIII, 140.

Adaevskaia eventually settled in Western Europe, first in Venice, and then – from 1911 – in Germany, where she was part of the circle of women surrounding Elisabeth, Queen of Rumania (1843–1916), who published poetry in a variety of languages under the pen-name of Carmen Sylva. That the first monograph about Adaevskaia was published only in 2005 suggests just how belated the study of Russia's women musicians has been.[40]

Adaevskaia was also a keen ethnomusicologist and studied not only Russian folksong, but also Orthodox Church music and even the music of Ancient Greece (she perceived affinities between Greek music and Slavonic chant and one of her most significant compositions is her *Greek Sonata* (*Grecheskaia sonata*) for clarinet or violin and piano of 1880, which draws on her studies of musical modes). Indeed, some of the earliest studies in Slavonic folk music were pioneered by women, such as Ol'ga Agreneva-Slavianskaia (1847–1920). But the most prominent female musicologist of the time was Evgeniia Lineva (1853/4–1919). Having begun her career as a professional singer (and, indeed, as a clandestine revolutionary, responsible for translating some of the works of Marx and Engels into Russian), she then became one of the first people to employ the phonograph in order to transcribe Russian folksongs.[41] Famed for their accuracy (recording for the first time the multiple parts of a folksong in performance rather than a single melody), they also provided Igor' Stravinskii (1882–1971) with material that was to be incorporated into his *Rite of Spring* (*Vesna sviashchennaia*, 1913). In addition to further researchers into Slavic folk music, Lineva helped found the People's Conservatoire in Moscow (1905–18) in order to give lessons in choral singing to the less well-off.

Lineva also enjoyed a prominent reputation in the West. Between 1890 and 1896, she lived in emigration in the UK and the USA (where she raised money for the émigré community by organizing performance of Russian folksongs by her own choir). Even after her return to Russia she participated in international musicological congresses and published her research in international journals. The part played by women in promoting Russian national music (whether in the form of ethnomusicological research or the composition of art-music) was noted

---

40. Renate Hüsken, *Ella Adaïewsky (1846–1926): Pianistin, Komponistin, Musikwissenschaftlerin* (Cologne: Dohr, 2005).
41. E. Lineva, *Velikorusskiia pesni v narodnoi garmonizatsii*, 2 vols (St Petersburg: Imp. akademiia nauk, 1904–09), trans. Eugenie Lineff, *The Peasant Songs of Great Russia as They Are in the Folk's Harmonization*, 2 vols (St Petersburg: Imperial Academy of Science; London: D. Nutt, 1905–12).

by one British critic in 1914: 'The student of Russian music will notice ere his researches are far advanced that the development of Russian musical nationalism owes very much to the efforts of women'.[42] The list included not only the Purgol'd sisters, fon Mekk, Olenina-d'Alheim and Lineva, but also two Western women who had done much to popularize Russian music in Europe. The first was the Countess Mercy-Argenteau (1837–90), who organized a series of concerts of Russian music in Belgium from 1885, translated a number of opera libretti and song texts and whose 1888 book on Kiui was one of the first works devoted to Russian music in any Western language.[43] The other was Rosa Newmarch (1857–1940), who studied with Stasov at the Imperial Library in St Petersburg, helped promote the performance of Russian works throughout Britain (especially at the Queen's Hall Promenade Concerts) and published a great number of books and articles on aspects of Russian music (and the arts more generally).[44] In many ways, Newmarch's career was a successful fusion of the traditional feminine accomplishments prized in British middle-class society (in particular, modern languages and music) and modes of female participation in the cultural sphere (patronage, popularization and education) that had also evolved within the context of nineteenth-century Russian society.[45]

By the start of the twentieth century, then, Russian women had begun to participate more fully in various aspects of musical life: not just as lower-class entertainers, or noble patrons and amateurs; but as teachers, composers, musicologists and performers. Many of the transformations that had taken place in the late Imperial era were to be consolidated and further built upon by the nominal commitment to female emancipation and equality that characterized the whole of the Soviet era (although as Marxism-Leninism was a class-based system of social and economic analysis,

---

42. M. Montagu-Nathan, 'The Influence of Women on the Russian School', *The Musical Times* (1 July 1914), 442–44 (442).
43. Ctesse de Mercy-Argenteau, *César Cui: Esquisse critique* (Paris: Librairie Fischbacher, 1888).
44. These include *Tchaikovsky: His Life and Works, with Extracts from His Writings, and the Diary of His Tour Abroad in 1888* (London: Grant Richards, 1900), *Poetry and Progress in Russia* (London and New York: John Lane, 1907), *The Russian Opera* (London: Herbert Jenkins, 1914), *The Russian Arts* (London: Herbert Jenkins, 1916) and *The Devout Russian* (London: Herbert Jenkins, 1918), as well as translations of Alfred Habets, *Borodin and Liszt* (London: Digby, Long & Co., 1895) and Modest Chaikovskii, *The Life and Letters of Peter Ilich Tchaikovsky* (London and New York: John Lane, 1906).
45. On Newmarch more generally, see Philip Ross Bullock, *Rosa Newmarch and Russian Music in Late Nineteenth and Early Twentieth-Century England* (Farnham and Burlington, VT: Ashgate, 2009).

gender issues as such were often marginalized or even repudiated altogether under the heading of 'bourgeois feminism'). One of the clearest instances of continuity between the pre-revolutionary radical tradition and the Soviet period can be seen in the career of Nadezhda Briusova (1881–1951), sister of the poet Valerii Briusov (1873–1924). Briusova and Lineva had been the only two women involved in the foundation of the People's Conservatoire in Moscow. Moreover, Briusova shared both Lineva's interest in the folk music repertoire, and her commitment to educating the masses in the performance and appreciation of music more generally. Not only was Briusova active as a teacher (first at the People's Conservatoire, then at the Moscow Conservatoire), but she was also one of the few women to achieve prominence in the Commissariat of Enlightenment and other agencies of state and political power. As a woman, Briusova was able to contribute in the cultural sphere because of durable notions of women as educators and enlighteners, especially in the arts. At the same time, however, she was confronted with attendant prejudices against the system of professional music education in Russia, which was often denigrated on account of its perceived gender bias. As Amy Nelson argues: 'Briusova struggled both to overcome the stigma associated with teaching music as a profession and to orient the pedagogy programme to the needs of Soviet popular education programmes. Before the revolution, teaching was considered a fall-back option for failed performers and a money-making pastime for bourgeois women'.[46] If the advancement of women in Soviet academic institutions had its roots in the achievements of the pre-revolutionary intelligentsia, then the possibilities open to Soviet women composers also had a direct link to the late Imperial age. Rimskii-Korsakov's wife, Nadezhda Purgol'd, had given up her own ambitions to serve her husband (and the nationalist cause more generally), but his daughter-in-law, Iuliia Veisberg (1880–1942) was able to embark on a more independent career. After studying in St Petersburg and Berlin, she married Andrei Rimskii-Korsakov (1878–1940) and together they edited the journal, *The Musical Contemporary* (*Muzykal'nyi sovremennik*), from 1915 to 1917. After the Revolution, Veisberg would become a leading member of the Association of Contemporary Music (a modernist grouping of composers that maintained close links with the West), although it would be her compositions for children (operas and songs) for which she was most praised; clearly, female creativity continued to be linked with notions of social enlightenment.

---

46. Amy Nelson, *Music for the Revolution: Musicians and Power in Early Soviet Russia* (University Park, PA: Pennsylvania University Press, 2004), p. 166.

If histories of Soviet and post-Soviet musical life contain the names of some of Russia's most illustrious female figures – think, for instance, of composers such as Galina Ustvol'skaia (1919–2006) or Sof'ia Gubaidulina (b. 1931), of performers such as Galina Vishnevskaia (b. 1926) or Mariia Iudina (1899–1970), or the immense contribution made by women to twentieth-century Russian musicology[47] – then it is nonetheless important not to view developments before 1917 as little more than a preparatory act for the achievements that were to follow. As can be seen, the history of women's on-going involvement in Russian music is a complex and evolving one. Gender is far from being an absolute or essential category which rigidly determines the participation of any single group within the institutions and expectations of a given society. Exactly what constitutes appropriate behaviour for women differs from generation to generation, as do women's own attitudes to whether their gender shapes their place in the social realm or not (and if so, to what extent and in what specific ways). What is clear is that women have made a series of vital contributions to Russian musical culture, and that the impact of gender on the intricate interplay between individuals and the broader social context remains to be studied in detail.

---

47. Ellon D. Carpenter, 'Women Music Scholars in the Soviet Union', in *The Musical Women: An International Perspective*, ed. by Judith Lang Zaimont et al., 3 vols (New York and London: Greenwood Press, 1984–91), III, 456–516.

7. The Rise of the Actress in Early Nineteenth-Century Russia

Julie A. Cassiday

By the close of the nineteenth century, the performing arts had not only taken firm root across the vast expanse of the Russian empire, but also become one of the country's most notable exports.[1] Operatic bass Fedor Shaliapin, ballerina Anna Pavlova, choreographer Sergei Diagilev and actor-director Konstantin Stanislavskii all toured outside Russia in the early twentieth century, securing personal fame and establishing their country's pre-eminence in the performing arts. Among these cultural exports were Russia's most popular dramatic actresses, such women as Mariia Savina, Lidiia Iavorskaia and Vera Komissarzhevskaia, who drew crowds of curious spectators to see their unique Russian style of acting, in spite of a significant language barrier. While on tour in Western Europe and the United States, these Silver Age actresses elicited passionate responses from spectators and critics, who viewed their performances as the product of a

---

An earlier version of this article was presented as '"The Precious Pearl of Our Theater": The Early-Nineteenth-Century Russian Actress as Public Woman' at the National Conference of the American Association for the Advancement of Slavic Studies in 2006. The author would like to thank the State Central Theatrical Library in St Petersburg for providing her with materials vital to her research; Williams College for supporting this and other projects and Gitta Hammarberg, Marcus Levitt and Douglas Smith for their comments on the paper out of which this article has grown. All translations are the author's own unless otherwise noted.

1. For overviews of the development of the dramatic and performing arts in nineteenth-century Russia, see Catherine A. Schuler, *Theatre and Identity in Imperial Russia* (Iowa City: University of Iowa Press, 2009) and Richard Stites, *Serfdom, Society and the Arts in Imperial Russia: The Pleasure and the Power* (New Haven: Yale University Press, 2005).

distinctively Russian tendency to blend art and life, usually to the tragic detriment of the latter.

Catherine Schuler, whose study of the Silver Age actress documents the careers of Russia's first female superstars, suggests that Savina, Iavorskaia, Komissarzhevskaia and their contemporaries created the particular fusion of art and life, of sexuality and soulfulness, that earned them celebrity both abroad and in Russia.[2] Indeed, the rise of mass media, the popularity of women's issues and increased cultural exchange between Russia and the West created unprecedented opportunities for Russian actresses in the last third of the nineteenth century: in addition to choosing their own roles, many Silver Age actresses all but controlled the repertoire of the theatres where they performed, or opened their own private theatres in the country's two capitals. However, the particularly feminine blend of art and life, which Schuler links directly to 'the destabilization of conventional femininity' had, in fact, already taken shape on the Russian stage almost a century before.[3]

Although Silver Age actresses took advantage of the implications that blending art on the stage with life beyond the footlights held for Russian women, this particular paradigm of the actress first took shape in the Golden Age of Russian theatre during the reign of Alexander I (1801–1825). The Alexandrine stage was arguably the most important cultural institution in early nineteenth-century Russia, even though its dramatic repertoire, typified by plays translated from French and German, the sentimental tragedies of Vladislav Ozerov and satirical comedies by Prince Aleksandr Shakhovskoi, fell out of fashion by mid-century. Both supported by the state and widely attended by members of multiple social classes, the Alexandrine theatre 'was vaunted as a "school for morals" and a "school for the people", but in a sense it was more akin to a "school for citizens", contributing to the development of civil society', as Murray Frame aptly describes.[4] In addition to providing a powerful venue for literally enacting Russian national identity, the Alexandrine theatre created the country's first female stars, whose cult status both rivalled and prefigured that of their sisters several

---

2. Catherine A. Schuler, *Women in Russian Theatre: The Actress in the Silver Age* (London: Routledge, 1996). Schuler dates the '"golden age" of Russian actresses' from the 1870s to 1910 (p. 2).
3. Schuler, *Women in Russian Theatre*, p. 8.
4. Murray Frame, *School for Citizens: Theatre and Civil Society in Imperial Russia* (New Haven: Yale University Press, 2006), p. 8. Schuler's *Theatre and Identity in Imperial Russia* also explores the ways in which the country's dramatic theatre fostered new forms of national identity during the nineteenth-century.

decades later. Examining the rise of the Alexandrine actress reveals not only the specific ways in which Russian women blended art in the theatre with life beyond the footlights throughout the nineteenth and well into the twentieth centuries, but also the vital role of the actress's sexual availability in constructing her emotional and artistic authenticity. As 'the precious pearls of our theatre', such actresses as Praskov'ia (Parasha) Zhemchugova and Ekaterina Semenova created a specifically feminine form of artistic legitimacy, which initiated the destabilization of gender roles picked up by Russia's Silver Age actresses at the century's end.[5]

Public Women and the Anti-Theatrical Prejudice

The prostitute and the actress share the distinction of being the first women to take on public professions in many European countries.[6] Despite clear differences between sex work and the performing arts, the two professions share a deep connection in the Western imagination, since both prostitutes and actresses earn their living by displaying their bodies publicly for the enjoyment of a largely male audience.[7] Spectators of different times and places have readily conflated these two types of performance in a single identity of the public woman, occasioning perennial accusations of actresses' impropriety, licentiousness and harlotry. As a result, the dubious nature of the actress's profession has provided a convenient target for anti-theatrical diatribes, such as Jean-Jacques Rousseau's 'Lettre à M. d'Alembert sur les spectacles' ('Letter to d'Alembert on the Theatre', 1757), in which the author asks 'how an estate, the unique object of which is to show oneself off to the public and, what is worse, for money, could agree with decent

---

5. The phrase 'the precious pearls of our theatre' paraphrases S. P. Zhikharev's description of Ekaterina Semenova, which will be quoted at length and discussed below.
6. For studies that examine the association of the actress with the prostitute, see Lenard R. Berlanstein, *Daughters of Eve: A Cultural History of French Theater Women from the Old Regime to the Fin de Siècle* (Cambridge: Harvard University Press, 2001); Tracy C. Davis, *Actresses as Working Women: Their Social Identity in Victorian Culture* (London and New York: Routledge, 1991) and Deborah C. Payne, 'Reified Object or Emergent Professional? Rethoerizing the Restoration Actress', in *Cultural Readings of Restoration and Eighteenth-Century English Theater*, ed. by J. Douglas Canfield and Deborah C. Payne (Athens and London: University of Georgia Press, 1995), pp. 13–38.
7. As Kirsten Pullen states, 'At particular historical moments, the body of the actress (assumed to be an object onto which male desires were projected) and the body of the prostitute (assumed to be an object onto which male desires were enacted) slipped discursively into one: whore/actress'. *Actresses and Whores: On Stage and in Society* (Cambridge: Cambridge University Press, 2005), p. 2.

women and be compatible with modesty and good morals: is there even need to dispute about the moral differences between the sexes to feel how unlikely it is that she who sets herself for sale in performance would not soon do the same in person and never let herself be tempted to satisfy desires that she takes so much effort to excite?'[8] As his rhetorical question implies, Rousseau assumes that feminine morality can exist only in private and that any woman who displays her body in public in return for money is destined, sooner or later, to become a whore. The anxiety of Rousseau and his contemporaries at the thought of an attractive actress boldly returning the spectator's gaze from the stage indicates the extent to which the female performer's identity as a public woman challenged eighteenth-century assumptions about gender-appropriate behaviour and the clear separation of the public from the private sphere.[9]

With the introduction of professional theatre into Russia in the eighteenth-century, Western European attitudes towards the actress began to merge with Russians' own pre-existing anti-theatrical prejudice. However, as semiotician Iurii Lotman has shown, with other ideological imports from the Parisian centre of enlightenment to its periphery, Western European notions of the actress as public woman were not simply grafted on to Russian culture.[10] In fact, despite clear familiarity with the 'Lettre à M. d'Alembert sur les spectacles' and widespread enthusiasm for Rousseau, Russians rejected the ultimate conclusion of his antitheatrical invective that theatre be banned from any well-ordered society.[11] Instead, professional drama came to

---

8. Jean-Jacques Rousseau, 'Letter to d'Alembert on the Theater', ed. by Allan Bloom and Christopher Kelly, trans. by Allan Bloom, in *The Collected Writings of Rousseau*, 13 vols, ed. and trans. by Allan Bloom, Charles Butterworth and Christopher Kelly, ed. by Roger D. Masters and Christopher Kelly (Hanover and London: Dartmouth College and University Press of New England, 1990–2010), X (2004), 251–352 (317).
9. For examinations of the ways in which actresses experienced this particular anxiety in eighteenth-century Britain, see Kimberly Crouch, 'The Public Life of Actresses: Prostitutes or Ladies?', in *Gender in Eighteenth-Century England: Roles, Representations and Responsibilities*, ed. by Hannah Barker and Elaine Chalus (London and New York: Longman, 1997), pp. 58–78 and Kristina Straub, 'The Construction of Actresses' Femininity', in her *Sexual Suspects: Eighteenth-Century Players and Sexual Ideology* (Princeton: Princeton University Press, 1992), pp. 89–108. Virginia Scott demonstrates the widespread nature of Rousseau's view of the actress as a sexual predator in 'The Actress and Utopian Theatre Reform in Eighteenth-Century France: Riccoboni, Rousseau, and Restif', *Theatre Research International*, 27.1 (2002), 18–27.
10. Iu. M. Lotman, 'Arkhaisty-prosvetiteli', in *Tynianovskii sbornik: vtorye tynianovskie chteniia*, ed. by A. Chudakov (Riga: Zinatne, 1986), pp. 192–207 (198).
11. For evidence of Russians' familiarity with the 'Lettre à M. d'Alembert sur les spectacles', see Marcus C. Levitt, 'The Polemic with Rousseau over Gender and Sociability in E. S. Urusova's *Polion* (1774)', *Russian Review*, 66 (2007), 586–601; N. M. Karamzin, *Pis'ma*

Russia at the behest of the state and with the support of the gentry, becoming 'not simply a form of entertainment, but a powerful means of education'.[12] Consequently, when Western European-style theatre, ballet and opera arrived on Russian soil, the terms and significance of the debate about the theatre's social utility were significantly transformed. With the patronage of Russia's most noble and public women – including the empresses Anna Ioannovna, Elizaveta Petrovna and Catherine the Great – and without the need to satisfy the tastes of the ticket-paying rabble, Russian actresses at first did not experience the disrepute that their French and British sisters did during the eighteenth century, and 'acting was initially a respectable profession for women' in Russia.[13] However, memoirs from the end of the century attest to a deep-seated suspicion of the theatre held by many noble Russians, who, in the words of Barbara Alpern Engel, 'were profoundly hostile to women's presence in public and regarded such women as fair game', as did lower class men.[14] As a result, young noblewomen were only reluctantly allowed to attend public theatrical productions, let alone perform on stage.[15]

By the close of the eighteenth century, the Russian theatre exhibited the same division of labour along lines of social class and gender as in Western Europe, only in exaggerated form. A thriving culture of amateur and domestic theatricals allowed both men and women of the Russian nobility to take part in all aspects of the theatre, including acting, in the

---

russkogo puteshestvennika, ed. by Iu. M. Lotman, M. A. Marchenko, and B. A. Uspenskii (Leningrad: Nauka, 1984), pp. 161, 223, 275 and F. Z. Kanunova and O. B. Levedeva, 'Pis'mo Russo k d'Alemberu v vospriiatii V. A. Zhukovskogo', *Russkaia literatura*, no. 1 (1982), 158–68. For broader discussion of Russians' reception of Rousseau, see Lotman, 'Russo i russkaia kul'tura XVIII - nachala XIX veka', in Jean-Jacques Rousseau, *Traktaty*, ed. and trans. by V. S. Alekseev-Popov et al. (Moscow: Nauka, 1969), pp. 555–604 and 'Russo i russkaia kul'tura XVII veka', in *Epokha prosveshcheniia: iz istorii mezhdunarodnykh sviazei russkoi literatury*, ed. by M. P. Alekseev (Leningrad: Nauka, 1967), pp. 208–81.

12. Frame, p. 1.
13. Wendy Rosslyn, 'The Prehistory of Russian Actresses: Women on Stage in Russia (1704–1757)', in *Eighteenth-Century Russia: Society, Culture, Economy. Papers from the VII International Conference of the Study Group on Eighteenth-Century Russia, Wittenberg 2004*, ed. by Roger Bartlett and Gabriela Lehmann-Carli (Münster: LIT Verlag, 2007), pp. 69–81 (79).
14. Barbara Alpern Engel, 'Women and Urban Culture', in this volume.
15. D. Blagovo, *Rasskazy babushki iz vospominanii piati pokolenii, zapisannye i sobrannye ee vnukom*, ed. by T. I. Ornatskaia (Leningrad: Nauka, 1989), pp. 152, 154 and M. S. Shchepkin, *Zapiski aktera Shchepkina*, ed. by N. N. Panfilova and O. M. Fel'dman (Moscow: Iskusstvo, 1988), p. 51. See also V. Mikhnevich, *Russkaia zhenshchina XVIII stoletiia: istoricheskie etiudy* (Kiev: Tip. I. I. Chokolova, 1895), p. 269; Wendy Rosslyn, 'The Prehistory of Russian Actresses', pp. 69–71 and Prince M. M. Schcherbatov, *On the Corruption of Morals in Russia*, ed. and trans. by A. Lentin (Cambridge: University Press, 1969), pp. 252–53.

privacy of their own homes. But in public theatres, which were located almost exclusively in St Petersburg and Moscow, the vast majority of actors and actresses had begun life in Russia's lowest classes, often as serfs. They constituted a caste subject to a state-run theatrical administration dominated by male elites, whose attitude towards their employees was both paternal and patronizing. In addition, early nineteenth-century Russia's culture of spectatorship centred on young men of the gentry, called *teatraly*, whose love of drama found its fullest expression in the pursuit of attractive actresses, ballerinas and opera singers. Pushkin paints a vivid picture of the typical *teatral* in a description of Russia's theatre-going public from 1820:

> Before the beginning of an opera, tragedy, or ballet, a young man wanders through all ten rows of the stalls, treads on the feet of everyone, chit-chats with all of his familiars and non-familiars. "Where are you coming from?" – "From Sem...[enova], from Sosn...[itskii], from Kol...[osova], from Ist...[omina]", – "Lucky for you!" – "Today she's singing, she's acting, she's dancing – let's applaud her – let's call her! she's so sweet! she has such eyes! such talent!" – And the curtain rises. The young man and his friends, going from seat to seat, are carried away and give a round of applause.[16]

Although Pushkin's satirical description of the *teatral* merely hints at the sexual dimension of young noblemen's admiration of the era's most famous female performers, numerous memoirs attest to the regularity with which male nobles took actresses as mistresses, as well as to the theatrical administration's involvement in what Wendy Rosslyn has identified as a system of covert prostitution.[17] By the early nineteenth century, the professional Russian theatre had become a thinly veiled but socially acceptable brothel, in which actresses' dramatic performance in public implied a sexual performance in private with male spectators and superiors in the theatrical administration. Thus, the ascent of female performers, such as Zhemchugova and Semenova, out of serfdom to the

---

16. A. S. Pushkin, 'Moi zamechaniia ob russkom teatre', in his *Polnoe sobranie sochinenii*, 17 vols, ed. by Maksim Gor'kii (Moscow: Izd. Akademii Nauk SSSR, 1937–1959), XI (1949), 9–13 (9).
17. Wendy Rosslyn provides an insightful and comprehensive analysis of the working conditions of Russian actresses in the early nineteenth-century in 'Female Employees in the Russian Imperial Theatres (1785–1825)', in *Women and Gender in 18th-Century Russia*, ed. by Wendy Rosslyn (Aldershot: Ashgate, 2003), pp. 257–77 and 'Petersburg Actresses On and Off Stage (1775–1825)', in *St Petersburg, 1703–1825*, ed. by Anthony Cross (Basingstoke: Palgrave, 2003), pp. 119–47. Schuler documents the prevalence of sexual patronage and prostitution among Russian actresses later in the nineteenth-century in *Women in Russian Theatre* (pp. 26–27).

heights of theatrical fame, and into the Russian nobility via marriage to their owner/patron, demonstrates the ways in which 'expressive culture generated pleasure as it deployed power' in Alexandrine Russia.[18]

Although the sexual availability of Russian actresses at the turn of the eighteenth century arose from assumptions about, and prejudices against, the public display of the female body analogous to those of Rousseau, the discourse surrounding Russian actresses differs in several respects from that found in the 'Lettre à M. d'Alembert sur les spectacles'. When critics of the theatre in England and France directly denounced women on stage as wanton, Western European actresses themselves took up their pens to counter or corroborate such attacks, both of which increased their celebrity and income. On the contrary, Russians preferred to skirt around the issue of actresses' suspect morals and female performers of the era had little, if any, opportunity to take part in the discussion of their profession. However, the seemingly greater tact of Russians' attitude toward the sexually-available actress belies a profound cultural anxiety about her role as public woman and created a discourse in which poetic language, redolent metaphor and a sentimental master plot distinguish the actress's place in the Russian cultural imagination of the time.

Suffering, Tears and Feverish Insomnia

Since the female stars of the Alexandrine stage did not leave their own stories behind, we can never know how Zhemchugova and Semenova constructed and understood their acting careers themselves. The literary genre of the theatrical memoir, which has proven popular in Russian culture, crystallized only in the mid-nineteenth century, providing later generations of performers with the means to narrate their lives.[19] Although the Alexandrine actress left no autobiography behind, two works of fiction purport to tell her story in her own words and offer a vivid account of her distinctly sentimental biography. Aleksandr Gertsen (Herzen)'s 'The Thieving Magpie' ('Soroka-vorovka', 1846) and Nikolai Leskov's 'The

---

18. Stites, p. 5.
19. Maude F. Meisel, 'Self-Presentation on Stage and Page in the Memoirs of Russian Women Performers', in *Mapping the Feminine: Russian Women and Cultural Difference*, ed. Hilde Hoogenboom, Catharine Theimer Nepomnyashchy, and Irina Reyfman (Bloomington: Slavica, 2008), pp. 51–66. For a fuller discussion of the genre of the theatrical memoir in Russia, see Meisel's 'Russian Performers' Memoirs', Ph.D. diss., Columbia University, 1993.

Toupée Artist' ('Tupeinyi khudozhnik', 1883), despite differences in the authors' styles and concerns, paint a unified picture of what brought the actress in early nineteenth-century Russia to the pinnacle of fame, as well as what inexorably caused her downfall.[20] Both convey the tragic tale of a serf actress in her own voice and place her tear-jerking story within a larger narrative told by an upper-class man.

'The Thieving Magpie' establishes the archetypal trajectory of the actress's life from enserfed obscurity, through artistic triumph, and ultimately to personal tragedy. Based on the real-life story of the serf actress Kuz'mina, who performed in the private theatre of the tyrannical Count S. M. Kamenskii, Herzen's story conflates the actress's tormented life off-stage with her ability to depict authentic suffering on stage.[21] Herzen's actress impresses his narrator, a performer considering employment in the fictional Prince Skalinskii's troupe, with a moving rendition of the role of Aneta in 'The Thieving Magpie' (a Russian translation of Caigniez and d'Aubigny's melodrama 'La Pie Voleuse', 1815). In spite of the artificiality of the Prince's theatre, Aneta's sincere performance rivets the narrator and establishes the emotional range and intensity of the 'great Russian actress'.[22] When she first comes on stage, he is struck by 'a weak female voice; in it was expressed such terrible, deep suffering. [...] Where did such sounds come from in that young bosom; they are not made up, not learned from solfèges, but achieved through suffering, [and] come as the reward of terrible trials'.[23] As the play reaches its climax, the narrator grasps the significance of these sounds: 'her voice and appearance were a loud protest — a soul-rending protest revealing the world's absurdity and at the same time softened by a kind of warm, meek femininity'.[24] Most impressively, Aneta's performance moves our narrator to weep openly, making him 'sob like a child' and 'purging the soul of its rubbish'.[25] The actress's genuine

---

20. A. Gertsen, 'Soroka-vorovka. Povest'. (Posviashcheno Mikhailu Semenovichu Shchepkinu)', in *Povesti i rasskazy* (Leningrad: Khudozhestvennaia literatura, 1974), pp. 271–92. N. S. Leskov, 'Tupeinyi khudozhnik. Rasskaz na mogile. (Sviatoi pamiati blagoslovennogo dnia 19-go fevralia 1861 g.)', *Sobranie sochinenii*, 11 vols (Moskva: Khudozhestvennaia literature, 1856-58), vii (1858): 220–42.
21. For a description of the actor Mikhail Shchepkin's performance of the anecdote on which Herzen's story is based, see T. S. Grits, 'K istorii "Soroki-vorovki"', *Literaturnoe nasledstvo*, vol. 63 (*Gertsen i Ogarev, III*, ed. by V. Vinogradov, I. S. Zil'bershtein, S. A. Makarov and M. V. Khrapchenko) (Moscow: Izd. Akademii Nauk SSSR, 1956), 655–60.
22. Gertsen, p. 279.
23. Gertsen, p. 279.
24. Gertsen, p. 280.
25. Gertsen, p. 281.

depiction of suffering on stage moves the narrator to an equally genuine experience of suffering, which culminates in a night of feverish insomnia as 'a thousand variations on the theme of "The Thieving Magpie" wandered through [his] head'.[26]

Aneta's performance so impresses the narrator that he decides to meet her the next day, which allows us not only to see her acting through his eyes but also to hear her life story through his ears. Aneta's career on the stage began with a kind but spendthrift master, who took her to Italy and France as part of her theatrical training. However, after her master's death, his entire troupe was sold, to pay off his debts, to the cruel and lascivious Skalinksii, who prizes Aneta for her artistic virtuosity and wants to exploit her feminine charms. Typical of the peculiarly Russian institution of serf theatre, Prince Skalinskii's privately owned stage functions as both public entertainment and private harem. Yet the virtuous Aneta fends off the Prince's advances at the price of becoming a prisoner on his estate. Realizing she cannot escape, she exacts revenge on Skalinskii by becoming pregnant with another man's child, destroying her health and, as the narrator learns afterwards, dying once her child is born. Aneta ends her story by describing the terrible toll that this revenge has taken on her: the actress's life has become a perpetual state of the same feverish insomnia experienced by the narrator and she can only 'play a single role [...] And so, everything is finished — both my talent and my life... farewell, art, farewell, passions on the stage!'[27] The narrator ends his interview with Aneta in a bitter lament, bursting into tears as he leaves her room.

Interestingly, the actress's two performances — on stage as Aneta before a full auditorium and in her boudoir as herself before the story's narrator — differ only in their venue and audience. She tells her lachrymose life story in 'that voice which so strongly shook [the narrator] yesterday', conveying with her face 'a terrible tale: in every feature it was possible to read that confession which sounded in her voice yesterday'.[28] Aneta's personal suffering as the chattel of a lecher gives rise to her genuine performance of suffering on stage and any boundary between art and

---

26. Gertsen, p. 282. These expectations for the great Russian actress bear comparison with what Rosenholm and Savkina describe as 'the reciprocal permeability of life and art by appealing to the authenticity of women's inner intonation' in women's prose at mid-century: Arja Rosenholm and Irina Savkina, '"How Women Should Write": Women's Writing in the Nineteenth Century' in this volume.
27. Gertsen, p. 289.
28. Gertsen, p. 285.

life disappears as the narrator 'admired her as a work of art'.[29] The great actress's sacrifice of her soul, her body and even her life guarantees the authenticity of her theatrical performance and her spectator's empathic mirroring of suffering, tears and sleeplessness demonstrates the efficacy of Aneta's art.

Leskov's 'The Toupée Artist' repeats, with minor variations, the same plot as Herzen's 'The Thieving Magpie'. Once again, the narrator listens to the story of a serf actress in Kamenskii's theatre and, once again, the actress succeeds on stage only to find herself the victim of her master's unwanted sexual advances. However, Leskov's actress, Liubov' Onisimovna, finds an admirer and would-be saviour in the story's title character, Kamenskii's make-up artist and personal barber. The very night that Liubov' Onisimovna becomes Kamenskii's star actress, the toupée artist Arkadii is instructed to dress her as Saint Cecilia and to adorn her with the aquamarine earrings in which the Count seduces each of his 'odalisques'.[30] Liubov' Onisimovna and Arkadii run away together but are quickly captured and returned to the Kamenskii estate. Although Leskov's actress almost escapes with Arkadii twice, her promising stage career ends neither in marriage to the toupée artist, nor in her master's bed, but in Kamenskii's cattle yard, where repeated loss and suffering eventually force her to seek solace in alcohol every night to relieve her insomnia. Although Leskov's story offers little description of Liubov' Onisimovna's theatrical virtuosity, her faded beauty, her 'honest, meek and sentimental' character and her moving narration of her chaste love for Arkadii create the same equation between personal suffering and authentic acting as in 'The Thieving Magpie'.[31]

The striking similarity of Herzen's and Leskov's stories illuminates the sentimental nature of the Alexandrine actress's biography. Much like Nikolai Karamzin's heroine in the Russian sentimentalist classic, 'Poor Liza' ('Bednaia Liza', 1792), both Aneta and Liubov' Onisimovna are lower-class women sexually victimized by an upper-class man. Like Liza, both sacrifice everything they have for the sake of an idealized amalgam of art and love and both reach the height of their theatrical fame at the very moment and by the very means, that bring their acting and life to a tragic demise. In addition, both stories use the same framing device as 'Poor Liza', a narrator whose emotional receptivity to the heroine's tragic tale both introduces

---

29. Gertsen, p. 285.
30. Leskov, p. 225.
31. Leskov, p. 221.

and concludes the story as a whole. In 'The Thieving Magpie', Aneta's monologue (marked as her quoted speech) follows a debate among four young men about the dearth of good Russian actresses and it ends with the actor-narrator wiping tears from his eyes as 'he and [his companions] represented a fine group of mourners for Aneta'.[32] In much the same way, Leskov's story begins with a morbid description of the embalmer's art, conveys Liubov' Onisimovna's tale over her dead lover's grave through *skaz* and then closes with the narrator's lament: 'I never witnessed, in my entire life, a more terrible and soul-rending death watch'.[33] Despite these stories' claims to speak on behalf of the Alexandrine actress, their framing makes each of them 'a twice-told story, an utterance of a trivocal structure', which, as Gitta Hammarberg demonstrates, shifts the tale's focus from the actress to the narrator.[34] The sentimental frame around 'The Thieving Magpie' and 'The Toupée Artist' place the 'narrator's emotive involvement' at centre stage: he vicariously experiences the emotional trajectory of the actress's tragedy, revels in his aesthetic and ethical sensitivity and urges his narratee, as well as the reader, to empathize with the actress as he does.[35] Both Herzen and Leskov make the actress, narrator, narratee and reader of their stories into what Hammarberg aptly calls 'sensitive "clones"' of each other, linked by their shared suffering, tears and sleeplessness.[36]

The content and form of these two stories reveal the fundamentally sentimental nature of what would become, in the second half of the nineteenth century, the biographical cliché of the great Russian actress. Indeed, as Maude Meisel describes in her survey of women's theatrical memoirs, the Russian actress has typically been understood as 'expressing her inner being in public'.[37] In addition, Herzen and Leskov's tales bring to light the combined aesthetic and ethical imperative that these women's tragic careers imply. The actress's ability to offer an authentic representation of suffering arises out of her victimization as a serf and woman, the lowest of the low in Russia's hierarchical social order, while the very authenticity of her acting demands an empathic emotional response from her typically noble

---

32. Gertsen, p. 292.
33. Leskov, p. 242.
34. Gitta Hammarberg, 'Poor Liza, Poor Èrast, Lucky Narrator', *Slavic and East European Journal* 31.3 (1987), 305–21 (306). Hammarberg expands her analysis of 'Poor Liza' in *From the Idyll to the Novel: Karamazin's Sentimentalist Prose* (Cambridge: Cambridge University Press, 1991), pp. 138–59.
35. Hammarberg, 'Poor Liza, Poor Èrast, Lucky Narrator', p. 307.
36. Hammarberg, 'Poor Liza, Poor Èrast, Lucky Narrator', p. 312.
37. Meisel, 'Self-Presentation on Stage and Page', p. 160.

and male spectators. Although doomed to perish, the great Russian actress has the power to initiate an aesthetic, emotional and ethical chain reaction, which binds her audience together in a shared, soul-purging experience of spectatorship.

The Precious Pearl

When we turn from Herzen's and Leskov's fictions to the two most legendary actresses of the Alexandrine era, we encounter female performers who inspired the sentimental master plot outlined above, as well as the inevitable snags in this narrative caused by real life. In spite of the differences in their careers, the serf actress, Zhemchugova, and Russia's greatest tragedienne, Semenova, both of whom earned the epithet of 'pearl', experienced a meteoric rise to fame and were eventually elevated through marriage to the highest ranks of the Russian nobility. Their combined story reveals, even more clearly than Herzen's and Leskov's fictions, the specific nature of the anxiety posed by the Russian actress's identity as public woman, as well as the era's attempt to contain this anxiety. Zhemchugova's career predates that of Semenova by some fifteen years and, in effect, articulates the terms in which the later actress's celebrity would take shape. Because no documents from Zhemchugova herself and little indisputable information about her life and career survives, she appears to be a *tabula rasa* on which largely male spectators, critics, and historians have inscribed their own fantasies and fears about the Russian actress.[38]

Zhemchugova lived a truly exceptional life for a serf woman, as her appearance in three of the seven essays in this volume attests.[39] The daughter of a blacksmith, she was born Praskov'ia Kovaleva in 1768 on one of the wealthy Sheremetev family's vast estates. She left home at the age of seven to receive the 'instruction in genteel manners, diction, singing, gestures, foreign languages, and music' necessary for the stage, entering the Sheremetevs' vast network of serf theatricals soon afterwards.[40] Graced

---

38. The one exception to this trend is Douglas Smith's recent and masterful study of Zhemchugova, which represents a unique attempt to cull the actual facts of her life from the seemingly countless legends and acknowledges the extreme difficulty of reconstructing her story from what little remains of her life: Douglas Smith, *The Pearl: A True Tale of Forbidden Love in Catherine the Great's Russia* (New Haven: Yale University Press, 2008).
39. For other discussions of Zhemchugova-Kovalova, see Christine D. Worobec, 'Russian Peasant Women's Culture: Three Stories' and Philip Ross Bullock, 'Women and Music' in this volume.
40. N. A. Elizarova, *Teatry Sheremetevykh* (Moscow: Izd. Ostankinskogo dvortsa-muzeia,

with beauty, talent and an outstanding voice, Kovaleva made her debut in the Sheremetevs' Kuskovo theatre before her eleventh birthday and she quickly rose to become the star of Count Nikolai Petrovich Sheremetev's troupe. She was best known for the cross-dressing role of Eliana in André Grétry's opera *Les Mariages samnites* (1768), which she performed for several royal personages, including Catherine the Great, who was so pleased by Kovaleva's performance that she presented the actress with a diamond ring.

Count Sheremetev treated the over two hundred performers he owned as empty vessels to be filled with the language, manners and gestures necessary for neo-classical theatre, giving them stage names that signalled this elevation in status. He typically replaced peasants' plebeian surnames with more refined speaking names that referred, in the case of women, to precious stones, and in that of men, to minerals. Among his performers were Anna Izumrudova, 'the emerald', Tat'iana Granatova, 'the garnet', Fekla Biriuzova, 'the turquoise', Kuz'ma Serdolikov, 'the carnelian', Andrei Kremnev, 'the flint' and Nikolai Mramorov, 'the marble'.[41] Sheremetev gave Kovaleva the stage name Zhemchugova, or 'the pearl', an appellation which, like its French counterpart 'perle', refers not only to a gemstone produced by molluscs, but also to an object of great value or a person of extraordinary talent. However, in addition to describing the esteem in which he held his prized diva, Sheremetev may have also borrowed a metaphor common in French libertine literature for female genitalia in his renaming. Even more explicit than Denis Diderot's first novel, *Les bijoux indiscrets* (1747), in which women's personal 'jewels' recount their owners' sexploits, the count's choice of 'the pearl' for Zhemchugova may refer to the clitoris, often labeled 'la perle' in French erotic argot of the time.[42]

Given the conflation of Zhemchugova's artistic and sexual worth signalled by her gemstone epithet, an equation we have already seen in the aquamarine earrings of Leskov's 'The Toupée Artist', it hardly comes as a surprise that she lived as Sheremetev's mistress for approximately a

---

1944), p. 300.
41. Elizarova, p. 307.
42. For French sources documenting this meaning of 'perle', see Pierre Guiraud, *Dictionnaire historique, stylistique, rhétorique, étymologique, de la littérature érotique* (Paris: Éditions Payot et Rivages, 1993), pp. 42, 490; Jean-Marc Richard, *Dictionnaire des expressions paillardes et libertines de la littérature française* (Paris: Filipachhi, 1993), p. 188 and Marie-Françoise Le Pennec, *Petit glossaire du langage érotique aux XVIIe et XVIIIe siècles* (Paris: Éditions Borderie, 1979), p. 50.

decade. Liberating her from serfdom in 1798, Sheremetev devised a dubious account of her family's descent from Polish nobility to justify a secret marriage in 1801. The 'pearl' of his theatre gave birth to Sheremetev's sole male heir in 1803 and died several weeks later. He made their union public only after Zhemchugova's death, leaving monuments to her memory in both Moscow and Petersburg, as well as a testament to their son, in which Nikolai Petrovich declared his abiding love for the actress, who possessed 'reason adorned with virtue, sincerity, philanthropy, constancy, loyalty [...] an attachment to holy faith, and the most zealous reverence of God'.[43]

The facts of the liaison between Sheremetev and Zhemchugova are colourful but few, due to the fact that 'someone's "solicitous hand" [...] painstakingly removed everything relating to Sheremetev's intimate life from the family archives'.[44] Nonetheless, Russian and Soviet historians writing about Zhemchugova concur on three points that go far beyond the scant information outlined above and that rationalize Zhemchugova's combined status as Sheremetev's chattel, concubine and actress by framing her story much as Herzen's and Leskov's. First, biographers agree that Zhemchugova's greatest roles required her to portray women who rebelled against social convention because they loved men outside their social class. They claim that her ability to play these roles convincingly arose from the fact that they 'found an echo in Parasha's soul, in her personal feelings engendered by the forbidden liaison and love for the count'.[45] As in 'The Thieving Magpie' and 'The Toupée Artist', the power of Zhemchugova's acting relies on the authenticity of her feelings: the sincerity of the actress's private life determines the power and truth of her public performance.

Second, some historians insist that Zhemchugova and Sheremetev fell in love at first sight, that their love was genuine and that both suffered deeply because they dared to challenge social custom; they thereby justify Sheremetev's sexual relationship with a star actress still in her teens through a supposedly profound spiritual bond.[46] However, according to

---

43. 'Iz bumag i perepiski grafa Nikolaia Petrovicha Sheremeteva', *Russkii arkhiv*, 34 (1896), 457–520 (512). As Smith points out, Sheremetev's own use of sentimental language to describe his relationship with Zhemchugova had a profound impact on her legacy, in effect transforming her into a saint immediately after her untimely death (pp. 61–63, 72, 254).
44. Elizarova, p. 299.
45. Elizarova, p. 303. See also, S. V. Istomin, 'Praskov'ia Ivanovna Zhemchugova, 1768–1803', in *Samye znamenitye artisty Rossii* (Moscow: Veche, 2000), pp. 14–20 (16–19).
46. Elizarova, p. 305; Istomin, p. 19. Evreinov even goes so far as to reconstruct the conversation in which the two first met, while Sukhodolov exclaims, 'Yes, she was

other accounts, Sheremetev 'knew no law other than lust'; one story even describes how 'every day he would forget his handkerchief in the room of one or another of his peasant actresses, and at night he would show up to claim his property'.[47] Like the fictionalized Count Kamenskii, Sheremetev appears to have treated his troupe of actresses as a personal harem and the fact that he took another former actress (and one of Zhemchugova's personal maids) as his mistress a year after his beloved's death seriously undermines the sentimental narrative of a unique and all-consuming love touted by historians and Sheremetev himself.[48]

Third, historians state that Zhemchugova's death in 1803 happened neither as a result of the tuberculosis she inherited from her father, nor due to complications during childbirth, but rather because of the soul-rending grief occasioned by the sacrifices both she and her husband made for their love. Zhemchugova is repeatedly described as having given her life to an idealized combination of love and art, which left a legacy not only in the theatre, but also in the popular imagination in the form of the folksong, 'Vechor pozdno iz lesochka ia korov domoi gnala' ('Late one evening I drove the cows home from the forest'), which, some biographers claim, 'Parasha [...] the first Russian poetess' herself composed.[49] These three instances of

---

happy! And although by the ideas of that time and even later, love could not exist between a female serf and a grandee, love existed nonetheless, an unusual, if you wish – fairytale [love], but it existed'. N. N. Evreinov, *Krepostnye aktery: Populiarnyi istoricheskii ocherk (vtoroe, zanovo pererabotannoe i znachitel'no dopolnennoe izdanie)* (Leningrad: Izd. Kubuch, 1925), pp. 13–14; V. N. Sukhodolov, 'Graf N. P. Sheremetev i Praskov'ia Zhemchugova', *Otechestvo* (1994), pp. 99–108 (100). See also E. S. Kots, *Krepostnaia intelligentsiia* (Leningrad: Knigoizd. Seiatel', 1926), p. 160.

47. Kots, p. 160. Smith confirms Sheremetev's preference for serf women, as well as his propensity to exercise his *droit du seigneur* among his serf actresses (pp. 26–27).

48. One historian even feels the need to fend off possible accusations of paedophilia: 'It is impossible to suppose that Nikolai Petrovich, who was already thirty years old in 1781 [when Zhemchugova was only thirteen], could take an interest at this time in Praskov'ia Ivanovna as a woman'. Vladimir Staniukovich, *Domashnii krepostnoi teatr Sheremetevykh XVIII veka* (Leningrad: Izd. Gosudarstvennogo russkogo muzeia, 1927), pp. 32–33. Sheremetev's testament to his son also emphasizes that Zhemchugova was the unique love of his life. 'Iz bumag i perepiski Grafa Nikolaia Petrovicha Sheremeteva', pp. 510–19. Stites has astutely pointed out in his study of the arts in nineteenth-century Russia that sometimes '"theatre" was simply a ruse for maintaining a collection of concubines. The female body, in some cases, served multiple functions as an acting device, a sexual object, and a target for the knout' (p. 240).

49. Kots, p. 161. Emmanuil Beskin repeats this claim in *Krepostnoi teatr* (Moscow-Leningrad: Kinopechat', 1927), p. 19. In addition, Evreinov connects the folksong ' ... U Uspenskogo sobora / V bol'shoi kolokol zvoniat. / Nashu miluiu Parashu / Venchat' s barinom khotiat...' [... By the Uspenskii cathedral / in the great belltower rings the bell. / Our dear Parasha / they want to marry to a gentleman...] to Zhemchugova (p. 16).

mythologizing Zhemchugova's experience demonstrate the need to couch the narrative of the serf actress in sentimental terms, to use the actress's public performance as a justification of her master's sexual excess and to rewrite the economic, artistic and erotic hierarchy of master and serf as a utopian performance of loving equals.[50]

Body and Soul

Semenova's story repeats much of the sentimental discourse surrounding Zhemchugova, however, with greater nuance and increased ambiguity. The fifteen years separating their careers had brought about significant changes in the Russian theatre, including the decline of privately-owned serf theatres and the growth of the state-owned imperial theatre in which Semenova was raised, trained and earned her fame. However, the wealth of materials documenting the actress's life, as well as the remarkable power she herself exercd throughout her stage career, prevents Semenova from becoming a *tabula rasa* for biographers' fears and fantasies. Rather, her story resembles a palimpsest in which the sentimental narrative of the Russian actress is written over the bluntly non-sentimental facts of her life.

Semenova was born into serfdom in 1786 and her unmarried peasant mother gave her at the age of ten to the imperial theatre school in St Petersburg, where she lived and studied until she made her debut on the professional stage in 1803, at the age of seventeen.[51] Semenova quickly established herself as Russia's premiere tragic actress through tear-jerking performances in the leading female roles of Ozerov's sentimental tragedies. However, her career was interrupted several times by enmity and rivalry, most notably when the French tragedienne Marguerite-Joséphine Weimer (known as Mlle. Georges), a former favourite of Napoleon, came to Russia for an extended tour. In the years before 1812, spectators in both St Petersburg and Moscow weighed the respective talents of the French and Russian actresses as they performed in parallel French and Russian productions of the same plays

---

50. Although Schuler describes Zhemchugova as 'a sort of fairy-tale princess', the clear parallels between her story and those in Herzen's 'The Thieving Magpie' and Leskov's 'The Toupée Artist' point to its fundamentally sentimental nature. Catherine Schuler, 'The Gender of Russian Serf Theatre and Performance', *Women, Theatre, and Performance: New Histories, New Historiographies*, ed. by Maggie B. Gale and Vivien Gardner (New York: Palgrave, 2000), pp. 216–35 (229).
51. Biographical information about Semenova comes primarily from N. Medvedeva, *Ekaterina Semenova: Zhizn' i tvorchestvo tragicheskoi aktrisy* (Moscow: Iskusstvo, 1964) and R. Ben'iash, *Katerina Semenova* (Leningrad: Iskusstvo, 1987).

until 'the competition between them, which arose seemingly involuntarily [...] exceeded the limits of the theatre and turned into an event of general significance'.[52] *Teatraly* were sharply divided between fans of Semenova and followers of Mlle. Georges until the Napoleonic invasion, when Russia's theatre-going public declared their own actress the victor.

Semenova's constant efforts to improve her acting, as well as her tremendous popularity among spectators, secured her pre-eminence in the Russian theatre of her day, and she was widely acclaimed as the quintessence of tragedy on the Russian stage, even by Pushkin:

> When speaking of Russian tragedy, one speaks of Semenova, and perhaps, only of her. Endowed with talent, beauty, lively and true feeling, she was educated of her own accord [...] Her acting, always free and clear, the nobility of her animated movements, her pure, even, and pleasant voice, and her frequent surges of true inspiration, all this belongs to her and is borrowed from no one. Semenova never had imitators [...] Semenova has no rival [...] She remained the autocratic queen of the tragic stage.[53]

In addition to talent and beauty, Semenova also had the patronage of Prince Ivan Gagarin, a permanent member of the imperial theatre's repertory committee, who provided her with a level of influence in theatrical affairs that no Russian actress had known before. Although Gagarin began courting Semenova soon after her debut, she became his mistress only in 1807, in an apparently calculated attempt to acquire the most reliable and powerful patron possible. After living with Gagarin for almost twenty years and bearing his children, Semenova retired from the theatre in 1826 to become Gagarin's lawful spouse, and she spent the rest of her life in relative obscurity, raising her family and squandering Gagarin's vast wealth on various legal entanglements until her death in 1849.

Semenova's spectacular rise from serfdom to celebrity clearly falls within the sentimental master plot of the Russian actress. However, critics and historians could not repeat the simple equation made in Zhemchugova's case, between the actress's art and life, when confronted with the ambiguous facts of Semenova's career. Rather than claiming that Semenova's art blossomed out of her life circumstances, they describe how she realized her profound artistic talent *in spite of* the numerous obstacles she encountered, *in spite of* her lack of true love for Gagarin and *in spite of* the fact that she left the stage at the height of her powers to live privately as a Russian

---

52. Ben'iash, p. 93.
53. Pushkin, p. 10.

noblewoman. This reformulation of the Russian actress's sentimental narrative not only acknowledges, but requires the artist's failure to realize perfection in her performance. Semenova's authenticity as a tragic actress finds its rationalization in the supposedly tragic compromises forced upon her by an unworthy and unfeeling world. Both her steadfast love of the stage and her refusal to demean her talent justify Semenova's willingness to sham love for Gagarin, providing 'an instructive example [...] of how even the greatest natural talent is spoiled, and in some instances even perishes'.[54]

The inherent ambivalence of this version of the actress's sentimental narrative finds its reflection in the many epithets that Semenova earned during her career. On the one hand, the actress's devotees called her Melpomene (the muse of tragedy), 'a goddess of beauty' (a phrase from Konstantin Batiushkov's encomium to Semenova), or Tragedy Itself. On the other hand, one of her less enthusiastic fans, the *teatral* Stepan Zhikharev, uses the appellation 'pearl' to cast doubt on Semenova's greatness:

> Semenova is a beauty; Semenova is the precious pearl of our theatre; Semenova has everything in order to become one of the greatest actresses of her time; but will she fulfill her destiny? Will she preserve that constant love of art, which compels the chosen few to scorn the advantages of a tranquil and sumptuous life in order to give themselves up to the tireless labours to acquire necessary knowledge? Did she not too soon array herself in velvet robes, clothe herself in Turkish shawls, and adorn herself with various costly trifles? From what I hear from everyone, and indeed have experienced in part myself at the rehearsal of *Dimitrii Donskoi*, when she so rudely insulted me with her haughty 'What?' – she lacks education, simplicity of heart, and that warm-heartedness, which the French mean by the word *aménité*; and these qualities, with little exception, are always the property of great talents [...] Sweet Semenova, you are indisputably a beauty, indisputably the precious pearl of our theatre, and the entire public admires you for good reason; but tell me why I, an amateur, do not weep while watching you act, as I usually weep thanks to your colleague Iakovlev?[55]

By all accounts, Semenova's behaviour offstage was distinguished by arrogance, vanity and aloofness, qualities that a young Russian nobleman apparently did not expect from a sexually-available actress.

More interesting than Zhikharev's desire to put Semenova in her

---

54. A. N. Sirotinin, 'Ekaterina Semenovna Semenova (Ocherk iz istorii russkogo teatra)', *Istoricheskii vestnik* (Sept. 1886), 474–508 (480).
55. S. P. Zhikharev, 'Dnevnik chinovnika', in *Zapiski sovremennika. Vospominaniia starogo teatrala*, 2 vols, ed. by A. V. Lisitsyn (Leningrad: Iskusstvo, 1989), II, 3–328 (265–66). Batiushkov's encomium to Semenova can be found in Sirotinin, p. 479.

place is his use of rhetorical questions in this diary entry, which bears a noteworthy resemblance to Rousseau's antitheatrical diatribe quoted above. Both Rousseau and Zhikharev use rhetorical questions to condemn the behaviour of actresses. However, if Rousseau chastises the actress for making her body publicly available at all, Zhikharev rebukes Semenova for the unavailability of her body and her soul to spectators.[56] Semenova's lack of *aménité* prevents Zhikharev from becoming her 'sensitive "clone"' and mirroring the actress's suffering and tears during a tragic tirade. Zhikharev's critique differs sharply from the praise of Petr Pletnev, who lauds Semenova's ability to move the entire audience to tears in the role of Medea: 'Looking at her, almost everyone cried throughout the entire fourth act. In this way Semenova has surpassed all the best known actresses of her kind'.[57] In contrast to Rousseau, who argues against women ever leaving the private sphere to perform publicly on stage, Zhikharev's and Pletnev's comments confirm the value of the aesthetic, emotional and ethical chain reaction triggered by the actress's public performance.

The sentimental stories of Zhemchugova and Semenova demonstrate that the early nineteenth-century Russian actress's function as a public woman, in effect, inverts that of the prostitute. If the whore provides the individual with a private and potentially shameful means of libidinal release, then the actress gives her audience a public and artistically legitimated means of doing essentially the same thing. The precious pearl of the Russian theatre accumulates and expresses the affective energy of male elites, taking it out of the private sphere and placing it in the era's most important public venue, the professional theatre. Although the expression of repressed emotion inevitably has tragic consequences for the actress herself, her sacrifice constitutes the community of *teatraly* and Russian national identity through a collective act of sublimation. Zhemchugova and Semenovna provide particularly vivid real-life examples of the discourse surrounding the precious pearl, yet other female stars of the Alexandrine era, such as Aleksandra Karatygina, Mariia Val'berkhova and Aleksandra Kolosova, were praised or panned using the same sentimental terms, as

---

56. Aksakov repeats a similar critique of Semenova in his description of her acting in S. T. Aksakov, 'Iakov Emel'ianovich Shusherin i sovremennye emu teatral'nye znamenitosti', in his *Sobranie sochinenii*, 4 vols, ed. by S. Mashinskii (Moscow: Gos. Izd. Khudozhestvennoi literatury, 1955–56), II (1955), 337–99.
57. P. A. Pletnev, 'Dramaticheskoe iskusstvo g-zhi Semenovoi', in *Sochineniia i perepiska P. A. Pletneva*, 3 vols, ed. by Ia. K. Grot (St Petersburg: Tip. Imperatorskoi Akademii Nauk, 1885), I, 44–53 (50).

were male stars, including Iakov Shusherin, Stepan Mochalov, Aleksei Iakovlev and Ivan Sosnitskii. As a result, the precious pearl of the Russian theatre defined the actor's profession as a whole in Alexandrine Russia, playing a key role in the actual process of, as well as heated debates about, the feminization of Russian culture in the early nineteenth century.[58]

From Subject to Author

If Zhemchugova and Semenova were the subjects of a sentimental narrative written largely, if not entirely, by others, a few of their peers managed to author their own stories as sentimentalism gave way to romanticism, Realism, Naturalism and Modernism in the nineteenth-century theatre. The memoirs of two of Semenova's contemporaries on Petersburg's imperial stage appeared in print several decades after the end of the Alexandrine era. Much like Zhemchugova's and Semenova's biographers, Aleksandra Asenkova and Aleksandra Karatygina asserted, 'the actress, regardless of her nationality, is a special, an exceptional being. All of her belongs entirely, body and soul, to the theatre'.[59] At the same time, however, these retired leading ladies wrote about backstage intrigues, romantic scandals and pragmatic necessities that complicated the sentimental narrative of the precious pearl. Most notable in this regard is the autobiography of Liubov' Nikulina-Kositskaia, who began her life in serfdom and her career as an actress in the Russian provinces in mid-century. On the one hand, Nikulina-Kositskaia describes her introduction to the theatre as a transcendental experience leading to a mystical vocation: '[…] my soul left my body and passed up there, onto the stage. I was lost to the everyday world. I didn't see or hear anything; it was like everything had died for me. When the curtain fell, I no longer asked why

---

58. For more detailed discussions of acting in the Alexandrine era, see *Istoriia russkogo dramaticheskogo teatra*, ed. by E. G. Kholodov, 7 vols (Moscow: Iskusstvo, 1977–87), II (1977), 148–90, 361–98 and T. Rodina, *Russkoe teatral'noe iskusstvo v nachale XIX veka* (Moscow: Izd. Akademii nauk SSSR, 1961), pp. 61–104, 211–274. Stites also provides an insightful overview of nineteenth-century acting and the century's dramatic repertoire in the imperial theatres of Moscow and Petersburg (pp. 173–220), as well as a useful description of the country's growing network of provincial theatres (pp. 221–80).

59. A. E. Asenkova, 'Kartiny proshedshego. Zapiski russkoi artistki. Glava 1-ia', *Muzykal'nyi i teatral'nyi vestnik*, no. 36 (1857), pp. 492–94 (492). For the remainder of Asenkova's memoirs, see the following 1857 editions of *Muzykal'nyi i teatral'nyi vestnik*:, no. 37, pp. 492–95; no. 39, pp. 529–32; no. 42, pp. 578–80; no. 44, pp. 606–07; no. 46, pp. 642–44; no. 49, pp. 699–700; no. 50, pp. 709–13 and no. 51, pp. 720–25. Karatygina's memoirs appear as 'Vospominaniia A. M. Karatyginoi', in P. A. Karatygin, *Zapiski*, 2 vols, ed. by B. V. Kazanskii (Leningrad: Academia, 1929), II, 121–330.

and what it was for. Now I understood everything; I even understood that my life was there, and there was none for me here. I was trembling all over'.[60] On the other hand, Nikulina-Kositskaia's arduous path from the provinces to Moscow, a path on which many would-be stage stars embarked throughout the nineteenth century, disabused her of any sentimental or romantic notions she might have had about a woman's life in the theatre. Like many aspiring actresses in nineteenth-century Russia, Nikulina-Kositskaia endured haphazard training, a gruelling schedule of tours and male spectators' importunate advances before the opportunity to perform in Moscow, let alone audition for the imperial stage, even arose. In spite of the many ways in which their stories failed to conform to the sentimental prescriptions of the precious pearl, Russia's first actress-autobiographers insistently preserved the master narrative established for Zhemchugova and Semenova.

The opportunity for actresses to author their own stories expanded the sentimental narrative of the precious pearl to include an ever-widening variety of social origins, dramatic genres and acting techniques as the nineteenth century progressed. Yet once the Alexandrine era came to a close in 1825, the Russian actress found herself briefly eclipsed by her male peer, as actors such as Pavel Mochalov, Vasilii Karatygin and Mikhail Shchepkin began to occupy centre stage in mid-century. Only with the rise of a new generation of ingénues in the last third of the nineteenth century did the cult of the Russian actress experience a revival that once again located her artistic legitimacy in an idealized amalgam of life and art. Typical of this master narrative was Mariia Savina's motto: 'The theatre is my life', Glikheriia Fedotova's reputation as a 'vestal virgin of the temple of art' and Mariia Ermolova's two titles, 'the great silent one' and 'the Madonna'.[61] At the same time that these Silver Age actresses based their artistic authenticity on a seamless continuity between life and art, hearkening back to the early nineteenth century, they introduced two important innovations into the narrative of the precious pearl. First, as the titles of 'vestal virgin' and 'Madonna' imply, Silver Age actresses exerted greater control over their bodies as

---

60. Liubov Nikulina-Kositskaia, 'Notes', trans. by Mary F. Zirin, in *Russia Through Women's Eyes: Autobiographies from Tsarist Russia*, ed. Toby W. Clyman and Judith Vowles (New Haven: Yale University Press, 1996), pp. 124–25. For the original Russian of Nikulina-Kositskaia's memoirs, see 'Zapiski L. N. Nikulinoi-Kositskoi, artistki Imperatorskikh Moskovskikh teatrov', *Russkaia starina*, 21 (January 1878), 65–80; (February 1878), 281–304 and (March 1878), 609–24.
61. Schuler, *Women in Russian Theatre*, pp. 53, 72, 77.

both aesthetic and sexual objects than their Golden Age predecessors, thereby sublimating even more deeply the erotic and emotional energy they expressed on stage. Second, the Russian actress's increased control over the public display of her own body came with a newfound power to write her own story, not merely in historical hindsight, but as it unfolded. If Zhemchugova and Semenova were the subjects of a master plot composed by male patrons and spectators, while Asenkova, Karatygina and Nikulina-Kositskaia could only author their careers in retrospect, then Silver Age actresses rewrote and adapted the sentimental narrative of the early nineteenth-century to suit their own talents, repertoires and styles at the very height of their fame.

Perhaps the most vivid example of the Silver Age actress's ability to carry on the sentimental narrative of the precious pearl at the very same time that she tailored it to her own needs comes in the career of Vera Komissarzhevskaia.[62] Her carefully crafted persona of 'a fragile, suffering child of our times' earned Komissarzhevskaia scores of early twentieth-century fans, many of them women, whose devotion to the actress verged on the religious. Although she entered the theatre already in her twenties, Kommissarzhevkaia quickly identified her métier and concentrated on roles that embodied 'youth, degradation, and death'.[63] Following in the footsteps of other actress-entrepreneurs, such as Anna Brenko, Mariia Abramova, Elizaveta Goreva, Elizaveta Shabelskaia and Lidiia Iavorskaia, she opened her own theatre in St Petersburg in 1904, where many of the pre-revolutionary era's ground-breaking productions took place. Her iconic role, Nina Zarechnaia, the idealistic yet tragically fallen provincial actress in Chekhov's *The Seagull* (*Chaika*, 1895), was taken as an artistic rendering of Komissarzhevskaia herself. Unsurprisingly, the critic, Vasilii Rozanov, identified the most striking feature of Komissarzhevskaia's career as 'the overlap of role and reality, of living being and actress'.[64] Her premature death due to smallpox at the age of forty-six elevated this early twentieth-century incarnation of the precious pearl to the status of theatrical martyr,

---

62. For an overview of Komissarzhevskaia's career, see Schuler, *Women in Russian Theatre*, pp. 155–88. Victor Borovsky also provides a detailed biography, which preserves the zealous and almost religious veneration of Komissarzhevskaia's fans, in *A Triptych from the Russian Theatre: The Komissarzhevskys* (Iowa City: University of Iowa Press, 2001), pp. 72–231.
63. Schuler, *Women in Russian Theatre*, p. 164.
64. Schuler, *Women in Russian Theatre*, p. 164.

strengthening the perceived tie between Komissarzhevskaia and Nina Zarechnaia and inspiring a flock of young Russian women to embark on their own acting careers.[65]

Chekhov's character from *The Seagull* provides a fitting close to the story of the precious pearl of the nineteenth-century Russian theatre. As Nina Zarechnaia's famous monologue from Act Four of the play describes, the ability to be 'a genuine actress, [to act] with enjoyment, with rapture, [to become intoxicated] on the stage and [to feel] beautiful' arises only from tragic personal sacrifice, as well as the willingness to endure the unwanted attentions of male spectators.[66] Although Nina's social and artistic trajectory in the play – from emotionally authentic ingénue to provincial stock actress – is diametrically opposed to that of the female stars discussed above, her formula for successful acting relies on the same combination of art and life, of body and soul, first articulated for the early nineteenth-century Russian actress. In addition, Nina repeatedly confuses herself as actress with the taxidermied bird to which Chekhov's play owes its name, demonstrating the steep psychological price the actress must pay as she both tolerates the vulgar sexual advances of spectators and embodies the authentic suffering needed for a tear-jerking performance. Chekhov's fictional reconstruction of the narrative of the Russian actress points to the culturally constructed nature, as well as the surprising longevity, of the precious pearl of Russia's early nineteenth-century theatre.

---

65. For a discussion of what Schuler calls 'The Nina Zarechnaia Epidemic', see *Women in Russian Theatre*, pp. 19–40.
66. A. P. Chekhov, *Chaika*, in his *Polnoe sobranie sochinenii i pisem v tridtsati tomakh*, 30 vols, ed. by N. F. Bel'chikov (Moscow: Nauka, 1974–1983), XIII (1978), 3–60 (58).

8. 'How Women Should Write': Russian Women's Writing in the Nineteenth Century

Arja Rosenholm and Irina Savkina

The question of how to write about women in Russian literature of the nineteenth-century can be solved in various ways. We can add women writers into literary history, or we can try to write a separate women's history with the aim of identifying fields and genres where women's presence seems to be obvious, as did Barbara Heldt.[1] We can also look for the specificity, originality and independence of women's creativity and discuss women's writing within various models, which follow not the paradigm of struggle, but rather the 'model of connection and development', as suggested by Jehanne Gheith[2], or fall within the 'pattern of forgetfulness', as proposed by Catriona Kelly.[3] In our reading of women's literature we will bear in mind the 'double-voiced discourse'[4] of women in culture, and pay attention to the

---

1. Barbara Heldt, *Terrible Perfection: Women and Russian Literature* (Bloomington and Indianapolis: Indiana University Press, 1987).
2. Jehanne Gheith, 'Women of the 1830s and 1850s: Alternative Periodizations', in *A History of Women's Writing in Russia*, ed. by Adele Marie Barker and Jehanne M. Gheith (Cambridge: Cambridge University Press, 2002), p. 85.
3. Catriona Kelly, *A History of Russian Women's Writing 1820–1992* (Oxford: Clarendon Press, 1994), p. 9.
4. Elaine Showalter, 'Feminist Criticism in the Wilderness', in *The New Feminist Criticism*, ed. by Elaine Showalter (London: Virago Press, 1986), pp. 243–70.

means and ways by which women writers approach their cultural border existence and to how they negotiate their positions within the dominant patriarchal discourse and its ideological binaries. This short reflection on literary practices of Russian women writers in the nineteenth century seeks to depict and analyse strategies of women's creative 'nomadism', the ways of writing and finding one's own place within a strange cultural territory and to name some of the innovative approaches which helped women to write themselves for themselves and for the history of literature. We do not see the women authors as a homogenous group. Instead, we would like to pay attention to diversity of genre, different types of protagonists and the differences between ideas and themes and narrative strategies. We also recognize the differences among the authors' positions on literary creativity. If some tried to adopt and adapt literary imagery and topoi which were considered conventionally male, others created an alternative space for women in their own right within, but separate, from the male world. A third group chose a border existence, while a fourth spoke from the female margins which they recreated, renamed and revized into a space of innovative possibilities. Accordingly, it is our aim to trace women's literary history of the nineteenth century as a unity with differences.

When the Westernization of Russian culture began in the seventeenth century, women's writing was restricted to private correspondence, but in the following century women began to feature in the cultural landscape. 'Women in Russia, therefore, went in three generations from near-invisibility [...] to the greatest degree of political and public prominence their society could offer', writes Catriona Kelly,[5] commenting primarily on the lives and works of Catherine II and Ekaterina Dashkova.[6]

But an entirely new situation arose at the end of the century. The real foundation for women's participation in literature was the works and ideas of N. M. Karamzin, who used gender in his campaign for a new literary language and a new literature. As Iu. M. Lotman says: 'particular store was laid by women in this exercise. Ladies' taste was declared the supreme arbiter of literature, and the educator of future generations of enlightened Russians was declared to be the educated woman, familiar

---

5. Catriona Kelly, 'Sappho, Corinna, and Niobe: Genres and Personae in Russian Women's Writing, 1760–1820', in *A History of Women's Writing in Russia*, ed. by Adele Marie Barker and Jehanne M. Gheith (Cambridge: Cambridge University Press, 2002), pp. 38–39.
6. On women in eighteenth-century culture and literature see, for example, *Women and Gender in 18th-Century Russia*, ed. by Wendy Rosslyn (Aldershot: Ashgate, 2003).

with the heights of culture, and gracious within and without'.[7] A role in Karamzin's project was allotted to the woman writer, even if at first she wrote not in Russian but in French. As Lotman observes, for Karamzin the specific nature of women's writing had two manifestations: 'firstly this is pedagogical literature for children, and secondly the literature of feeling, devoted to love. Both, moreover, are distinguished by their intimacy – they are destined for the immediate audience. This is literature which arises from speech and from everyday life'.[8]

The feminization[9] of literature in Karamzin's time had a double aspect and contradictory outcome for women: on the one hand it legitimized femininity as publicly significant and creative; on the other hand it laid down strict limits for the creative representation of the female. Accepting the conditions proposed, women were to write according to defined rules, within a set thematic range and in appropriate language. Moreover, the 'inexperienced muses' were encouraged to be modest and unpretentious and therefore, most women writers prefaced their texts with excuses, figures of self-disparagement and protestations of lack of ambition,[10] which often derived from their immediate artistic and financial dependency on male patrons.

A complication in this situation was the role of sentimentalist feminization in the ideological conflict between the Karamzin and Shishkov schools. Feminization was associated with the former; the Shishkovites and (in a different manner) the supporters of serious ideologically-significant literature rejected the sensibility, sentimentality and the salon style which were associated with femininity. However, some women (Anna Bunina, Anna Volkova and Ekaterina Urusova) were accepted into the *Colloquium of Admirers of the Russian Word*, headed by Shishkov, though not into *Arzamas*, the grouping of literary innovators, with its principles of play and

---

7. Iu. M. Lotman, 'Russkaia literatura na frantsuzskom iazyke', in Iu. M. Lotman, *Izbrannye stat'i v trekh tomakh*, 3 vols (Tallinn: Aleksandra, 1992), II, 360.
8. Lotman, p. 60.
9. On feminization see Gitta Hammarberg, 'The Feminine Chronotope and Sentimentalist Canon Formation', in *Literature, Lives, and Legality in Catherine's Russia*, ed. by A. G. Cross and G. S. Smith (Nottingham: Astra, 1994), pp. 103–20; Judith Vowles, 'The "Feminization" of Russian Literature: Women, Language, and Literature in Eighteenth-Century Russia', in *Women Writers in Russian Literature*, ed. by Toby W. Clyman and Diana Greene, pp. 35–60.
10. Some similar examples from the works of Anna Naumova and Mariia Izvekova are discussed in, for example, Frank Göpfert, *Dichterinnen und Schriftstellerinnen in Russland von der Mitte des 18 bis zum Beginn des 20. Jahrhunderts: Eine Problemskizze* (München: Verlag Otto Sagner, 1992), pp. 46–51.

dilettantism, even though the sphere of dilettantism and wit, including linguistic play, was also often associated with women.[11]

Thus, at the very beginning of the nineteenth century we see the situation which was to reproduce itself over and over again during the century (and indeed later): the patriarchal cultural canon reconstructs and reorganizes itself. The male ideologists controlling these processes use conceptions of femininity and the practices of women's writing to construct their own theories and for the purpose of their own ideological battles, but all this has nothing to do directly with real women;[12] for women writers, and their life and literary practices, it creates the boundaries within which they are to exist and write. Some of them submit to the patriarchal dictat,[13] but others attempt to find the means to speak in their own language in the situation of linguistic and generic constraint, to exist where, in Lacan's expression, woman does not exist.

A typical example is the work of Anna Bunina (1774–1829), the first woman who can be called a professional poet with a public reputation.[14] Studies of her poetry speak of ambivalence[15] or the splitting and the splintering[16] of her personal and creative identity. Bunina did not support Karamzinist feminization and in her poems she attempted themes that

---

11. Gitta Hammarberg, 'Flirting with Words: Domestic Albums, 1770–1840', in *Russia-Women-Culture*, ed. by Helena Goscilo and Beth Holmgren (Bloomington-Indianapolis: Indiana University Press, 1996), pp. 297–320; Gitta Hammarberg, 'Women, Wit, and Wordplay: Bouts-rimés and the Subversive Feminization of Culture in Salons and Albums', in *Vieldeutiges Nicht-Zu-Ende-Sprechen. Thesen und Momentaufnahmen aus der Geschichte russischer Dichterinnen*, ed. by Arja Rosenholm and Frank Göpfert (Fichtenwalde: F. K. Göpfert, 2002) (FrauenLiteraturGeschichte. Band 16), pp. 61–78.
12. As Kelly correctly observes, the people on whom a woman was dependent in real life – father, husband, patron – were rarely reminscent of the ideal sensible hero of the sentimental tale (Catriona Kelly, 'Sappho, Corinna, and Niobe: Genres and Personae in Russian Women's Writing, 1760–1820', pp. 47–48.
13. See Yael Harussi, 'Women's Social Roles as Depicted by Women Writers in Early Nineteenth-Century Russian Fiction', in *Issues in Russian Literature before 1917. Selected Papers of the Third World Congress for Soviet and East European Studies*, ed. by J. Douglas Clayton (Columbus, Ohio: Slavica, 1989), pp. 35–48.
14. See Wendy Rosslyn, *Anna Bunina (1774–1829) and the Origins of Women's Poetry in Russia* (Lewiston, Queenston, Lampeter: Edwin Mellen Press, 1997).
15. Wendy Rosslyn, 'Conflicts over Gender and Status in Early Nineteenth-century Russian literature: the Case of Anna Bunina and her Poem *Padenie Faetona*', in *Gender and Russian Literature: New Perspectives*, trans. and ed. by Rosalind Marsh (Cambridge: Cambridge University Press, 1996), pp. 55–74.
16. Gerda Achinger, 'Das gespaltene Ich – Äusserungen zur Problematik des weiblichen Schreibens bei Anna Petrovna Bunina', in *Frauenbilder und Weiblichkeitsentwürfe in der russischen Frauenprosa*, ed. by Christina Parnell (Frankfurt am Main: Peter Lang, 1996), pp. 43–61.

were considered profoundly masculine (war, politics and philosophy) and did not limit herself to the recommended repertoire of love and sensibility. On the other hand, the theme of women's writing was personally important to her, as can be seen, for example, in the allegories 'The Peking Stadium' ('Pekinskoe ristalishche') and 'The Fall of Phaethon' ('Padenie Faetona'). In her poem 'A Conversation between Me and Women' ('Razgovor mezhdu mnoi i zhenshchinami'), the lyric heroine answers with bitter irony the bewildered question why she does not sing of women: because it is only possible to be a poet in the male literary world by playing by the rules of the stronger sex. The principled 'unfemininity' of her poetry is a free choice and a tactical decision in the situation of lack of creative freedom which Bunina well recognized. In the dilemma which offered itself – to be a woman or a poet[17] – Bunina chooses the latter, but this decision does not save her from inner disjunction, nor from condescending and sometimes mocking judgments on her poetic talent by male colleagues and critics, for whom she was still, to quote Wendy Rosslyn, 'an ambiguous figure'.[18]

The dual, double place of the female poet turned out to be a traumatic space for Bunina and most of her younger sisters. At the beginning of the nineteenth century the literary salon was the more 'natural', real and symbolic place where the legitimization of woman as a creative being, turned out to be possible.

Literary salons, the vogue for which came to Russia from France,[19] were primarily associated with *urbanité*. The skill of *urbanité* was principally acquired

---

17. A similar route was taken by Elizaveta Kul'man (1808–25). Key to her work was the reinterpretation of myth. As Judith Vowles writes, 'Her poetry thus belongs to a tradition of women's revisionary writing that rewrites and invents myths as a way of establishing female legitimacy and authority'. 'The Inexperienced Muse: Russian Women and Poetry in the First Half of the Nineteenth Century', in *A History of Women's Writing in Russia*, ed. by Adele Marie Barker and Jehanne M. Gheith (Cambridge: Cambridge University Press, 2002), p. 70. Another path was to agree to be not a poet but a poetess.See Diana Greene, 'Praskov'ia Bakunina and the Poetess's Dilemma' in *Russkie pisatel'nitsy i literaturnyi protsess v kontse XVIII -pervoi treti XX vv.*, comp. by M. Fainshtein (Wilhelmshorst: F. K. Göpfert, 1995), pp. 43–57.
18. Rosslyn, 'Conflicts over Gender and Status', p. 62.
19. On literary salons and the role of women within them see, for example, M. Aronson and S. A. Reiser, *Literaturnye kruzhki i salony* (Leningrad: Priboi, 1929); V. E. Vatsuro, *Iz istorii literaturnogo byta pushkinskoi pory* (Moscow: Kniga, 1989); *Literaturnye salony i kruzhki, pervaia polovina XIX veka*, ed. N. L. Brodskii (Moscow: Agraf, 2001); Lina Bernstein, 'Women on the Verge of a New Language: Russian Salon Hostesses in the First Half of the Nineteenth Century', in *Russia-Women-Culture*, pp. 209–224; I. Kontorovich, '"Samyi nezhnyi zvuk Moskvy": salon Zenaidy Volkonskoi', *Novoe literaturnoe obozrenie*, 20 (1996), 178–219.

through participation in lively and entertaining social conversation, the organization and maintenance of which, was thought to be women's business and skill.[20] Salons were associated with women's speech and narrative and were usually neutral territory, a space where people of different allegiances, ideas and literary parties met. The hostess was the guarantor of tolerance (and to some degree egalitarianism), the arbiter of taste, the 'legislator' and a culturally significant figure. As a rule, she was not only the organizer of conversation and a listener, but also a writer, who could 'publish', that is, offer her own works for reading and discussion.[21] In this sense the salon was a place of joint cultural activity for men and women, where women even had some advantage. However, it is important to recall that the conventions of social etiquette were in operation; the obligatory compliments showered on the 'authoresses' often had nothing in common with real discussion of texts and took them out of the sphere of serious literary life, into the sphere of ladies' dilettantism. Women who took up literature and were associated with salon culture (Zinaida Volkonskaia, Aleksandra Smirnova-Rosset, Evdokiia Rostopchina and to some degree Karolina Pavlova) existed in the sphere of 'artistic everyday life' (to use Iu. N. Tynianov's term)[22] and met with notable difficulties when they tried to demonstrate their right to engage in literary craft outside the drawing room on the professional literary stage. If they accepted the rules of the game and agreed to the conventions of feminization, which set the boundaries for women's self-expression, they gained the reputation of a 'salon or ballroom poetess',[23] like, for example, Evdokiia Rostopchina (1811–58).[24]

---

20. For example, the memoirist B. N. Chicherin never tires of mentioning the ability of salon hostesses to conduct 'lively, slightly mocking, brilliant conversation, full of playfulness and subtle irony'; 'unfailingly fluent lively and merry conversation, with a hint of the most overt and ingenuous coquettishness'. 'Vospominaniia', in *Russkoe obshchestvo 40–50-kh godov XIX v.*, ed. by S. L. Chernov (Moscow: MGU, 1991), p. 70.
21. Moreover, as Judith Vowles observes, publications associated with salons, 'almanacs, elegant literary collections modeled on Karamzin's *Aonidy*, offered a middle ground between private circulation and commercial publication: they were a favored place to make a debut' ('The Inexperienced Muse', p. 65).
22. Iu. N. Tynianov, 'Literaturnyi fakt', in his *Poetika. Istoriia literatury. Kino* (Moscow: Nauka, 1977), p. 264.
23. See Diana Greene, 'Nineteenth-Century Women Poets: Critical Reception vs Self-Definition', in *Women Writers in Russian Literature*, pp. 103–04.
24. Rostopchina was accorded literary fame in the 30s. Later, after 1846, her poetic fame faded and the new generation of critics (Chernyshevskii and Dobroliubov) wrote of her scornfully. Rostopchina wrote long poems, verse drama, stories and novels, but her most popular works (in the view both of contemporaries and later readers) were her lyrics. On Rostopchina see, for example, M. Sh. Fainshtein, *Pisatel'nitsy pushkinskoi pory: istoriko-literaturnye ocherki* (Leningrad: Nauka, 1989), pp. 83–104.

Key themes for Rostopchina's lyrics were those associated with society life: the masquerade and the ball. The exceptionally rich and metaphorically weighty motif of the masquerade was used in two ways in the romantic context. On the one hand, it was associated with the motifs of pretence, deception, mimesis and concealment: individuals act out what the mask they have assumed depicts. But on the other hand, the mask can be understood as a means for liberation. The mask does not conceal, but, on the contrary, protects the authentic I, it hides all the social roles and statuses inscribed on to the face and body and when wearing the mask it is possible to be authentically oneself. Both can be found in Rostopchina, in 'Putting on an Albanian Costume' ('Nadevaia albanskii kostium'), 'Why I Love Masquerades' ('Zachem ia liubliu maskarady') and other poems. There is always a gap between mask, costume and face, a space for play, in which it is possible to create one's own 'elusive', 'performative' identity. In Rostopchina's work the mask acquires not only standard romantic connotations, but also gender connotations,[25] as do the motifs of society, ball and dancing. The society drawing-room and the ballroom are, for Rostopchina, not only the territory of pretence, deception and worldliness, but her own positive space, characterized by positive epithets: merry, colourful, luxurious, festive, joyful and intoxicating. It is a place where women are allowed to speak and in describing it she can talk about themes which are branded taboo by the dominant discourse.

Poetry in general is a dangerous experiment and a dangerous occupation for women: Rostopchina agrees with these judgements by contemporary critics.[26] In her poem 'How Women Should Write' ('Kak dolzhny pisat' zhenshchiny'), she calls on women not to depict their feelings openly, but to shroud them with a veil of reticence and 'decency', not to display them to general view, to society. But repressed sensual experience can be illuminated indirectly, through the depiction of the ball, the dance and music. Here she can talk about the taboo experience of the body, about women's bodily pleasure, preserving the erotic connotations associated with the motif of

---

25. On masquerade and femininity see Ursula Chowanec, Ursula Phillips and Marja Rytkönen, 'Introduction', in *Masquerade and Femininity: Essays on Russian and Polish Women Writers*, ed. by Ursula Chowanec, Ursula Phillips and Marja Rytkönen (Cambridge: Cambridge Scholars Publishing, 2008), pp. 3–8.
26. On the critical reception of women's writing at this time see Irina Savkina '"Poeziia – opasnyi dar dlia devy"', in Irina Savkina, *Provintsialki russkoi literatury (zhenskaia proza 30–40-kh godov XIX veka)* (Wilhelmshorst: F. K. Göpfert, 1998), pp. 23–50.

dance in the culture of the time,[27] but reducing the theme of crime and punishment. Although the poetess entitles her key poem on this theme 'Temptation' ('Iskushenie'), it talks not about sin, but about joy, happiness, ecstasy and the bodily pleasure resulting from sensual experience of smell, taste and touch. Uncontrolled female pleasure is conveyed by the rhythmic pattern of the verse: in this pulsating flow of speech, the music, sound, and rhythm[28] (the semiotic in Kristeva's term),[29] are almost more important than the sense (the symbolic), which for contemporary feminist critics (Hélène Cixous)[30] is the sign of specifically female language, the female manner of writing. Contemporaries saw the source of this feminine element of Rostopchina's style as salon chatter, the tradition of brilliant, lively, flowing social conversation, and this (not only the theme of the poetry) was the reason for calling Rostopchina a 'salon poetess'.

Rostopchina, as Judith Vowles notes, sought the path to female creative self-realization within the separate, specifically female sphere, but did not consider it limited.[31] Her position met with various responses, approving and scornful, from male critics and with polemics from her female 'work colleagues'. Vowles writes of her sharp dispute[32] with the poet Elizaveta Shakhova (1821–99), who had chosen the path of intense religious mysticism and accused Rostopchina of shallowness and frivolity, in turn receiving reproaches of coldness and indifference from the latter.[33] Another polemical female response to Rostopchina's position, in Vowles' view, was the poetry of Iuliia Zhadovskaia (1824–83), where the image of the lyrical heroine (a modest provincial young woman) and the style (simple and 'natural') contrasted to the aristocratic Rostopchina's lyrics with their salon luxuriance and brilliance.[34] But Rostopchina's chief female opponent in

---

27. See Stephanie Sandler, 'Pleasure, Danger, and the Dance: Nineteenth-Century Russian Variations', in *Russia-Women-Culture*, pp. 247–72.
28. Some poems by Rostopchina, written at various times, are called 'Verses for Music' ('Stikhi dlia muzyki').
29. Julia Kristeva, *La révolution du langage poétique: l'avant-garde à la fin du XIXe siècle. Lautréamont et Mallarmé* (Paris: Seuil, 1974).
30. Hélène Cixous, 'The Laugh of the Medusa', in *Feminisms: An Anthology of Literary Theory and Criticism*, ed. by Robyn R. Warhol and Diane Price Herndl (New Brunswick, New Jersey: Rutgers University Press, 1977), pp. 345–62.
31. Vowles, 'The Inexperienced Muse', p. 74.
32. Vowles, 'The Inexperienced Muse', pp. 77–78.
33. See Rostopchina's poems 'To the Indifferent One' ('Ravnodushnoi', 1830) and Shakhova's reply, 'The Woman and the Ball' ('Zhenshchina i bal', 1840) and 'To Women Poets' ('K zhenshchinam-poetam', 1845).
34. Vowles, 'The Inexperienced Muse', pp. 78–79.

the view of both contemporaries and posterity was undoubtedly Karolina Pavlova (1807–93).

Pavlova has several texts addressed to Rostopchina, which are constructed on the device of contrast: 'We Are Contemporaries, Countess' ('My sovremenniki, grafinia'), 'To Countess Rostopchina' ('Grafine Rostopchinoi'), and 'Three Souls' ('Tri dushi').[35] Pavlova contrasts herself, with her Slavophilism, modesty, independence, sedentariness, domesticity and professionalism, to Rostopchina, the cosmopolitan Petersburger, follower of George Sand, aristocrat, the beauty showered with compliments, the free artist and the dilettante. Some of the self-characterizations mentioned are incorrect, or would be overturned by Pavlova's later life, when she decided on a public quarrel with her husband and a divorce, left Russia and lived in Germany. But the point of the argument was not biographical contrasts or similarities, but different understandings of the nature and role of the woman poet, emphasized by Pavlova. She considers Rostopchina's position to be treachery, betrayal of the artistic gift. In 'Three Souls', Pavlova writes of the woman poet who turned the 'sacred gift' into a 'noisy rattle' and chose 'humdrum banality', 'everyday dullness' and 'noisy high society' for the sake of compliments, pleasure and enjoyment. To Rostopchina's 'noisy rattle', Pavlova opposes her 'mute' muse, her 'sad verse' and her understanding of poetry as 'sacred craft'.[36]

The poetic dialogue described here has key significance for understanding the history of women's writing; Rostopchina and Pavlova chose different means of writing in the patriarchal world. Rostopchina accepts the rules of the game and remains within the sphere legitimized as feminine, but she destroys it from within or, to be more precise, she re-writes and remakes what is permitted by patriarchal discourse in her own way, she makes her own statements 'in italics', to use Nancy K. Miller's expression.[37] The female italics in Rostopchina's case are mainly intonation; Rostopchina's female language and the feminine element are associated with melody, music, rhythm and sound (in this sense Pavlova's mention of the 'noisy rattle' is very germane). Pavlova, however, chooses the path of resistance to feminization, the path of stubborn and, as she constantly emphasizes,

---

35. In this poem Rostopchina is not mentioned by name. However, the poem displays the very type of woman author as Rostopchina, who is explicitly addressed in former poems.
36. 'You who live on in the destitute heart' ('Ty, utselevshii v serdtse nishchem').
37. Nancy K. Miller, *Subject to Change: Reading Feminist Writing* (New York: Columbia University Press, 1988), p. 29.

hopeless struggle for woman's right to write 'unfemininely', to write as she feels like writing, about whatever, not looking over her shoulder at the recommendations and admonitions of the male censor. Acquisition of voice is achieved through overcoming the torments of muteness. The themes of muteness, wordlessness, silence and inexpressibility are key for Pavlova and are obviously associated, not only with the romantic tradition, but also with the struggle for women's right to speak.

Both strategies of women's writing are significant and productive, but recognition of this became possible only with a gender-oriented reading of the poetic epistles of the authors named. Amongst their contemporaries, Rostopchina had the reputation of being disreputable and Pavlova of being masculine.[38] However, these differences were unimportant for other patriarchal critics, who were concerned not with the real works of real women poets, but with existing *a priori* ideas about women's writing. This is why M. E. Saltykov-Shchedrin calls Pavlova's lyrics the work of a moth or siskin[39] and why V. Pereverzev accuses Pavlova of having seen and heard nothing apart from salon society and empty society conversation and of having depicted only this 'trivial little world' without 'introspection or self-analysis'.[40]

However, any attentive and fair-minded reader cannot fail to see that introspection and self-analysis are the main elements in Pavlova's lyrics. Hers is poetry which tells of stubborn resistance to fate and the banality of life, of the hidden life of a soul which goes from one 'hopeless hope' to another; it is a poetic history of losses, useless delusions and loneliness and at the same time a testimony to the triumph of will and the desire to move forward. These are lyrics which are full of reflection and merciless self-knowledge; they are tense and emotional, but absolutely unsentimental, even when the theme is love. It is not surprising that she was sometimes called 'male' (at times with admiration, at times with scorn). However, Pavlova's lyric heroine (not hero!) is neither masculinized nor sexless: she is always a woman, and a woman poet. In Pavlova's poetry the issues of

---

38. Diana Greene, 'Nineteenth-Century Women Poets: Critical Reception vs. Self-Definition', pp. 95–109. This tradition of contrasting and opposing Pavlova and Rastopchina continued also later. See, for example, V. F. Khodasevich's articles written in the early twentieth-century: 'Grafinia Rostopchina: ee zhizn' i lirika, *Russkaia mysl'* (1915), XI, part II, 35–53 and 'Odna iz zabytykh', *Novaia zhizn': Al'manakh* (1916), 3, 195–98.
39. M. E. Saltykov-Shchedrin, 'Stikhotvoreniia K. Pavlovoi', in his *Literaturnaia kritika* (Moscow: Sovremennik, 1982), pp. 134–39.
40. V. Pereverzev, 'Salonnaia poetessa', *Sovremennyi mir* (1915), 12, 185–88.

existential loneliness and the poet's failure to be understood, which are common to humanity in general and to the romantics, have an evident gender aspect. Pavlova's key motif of the path turns out to be particularly tragic, because the path is an element of women's fate: women pass from the paradise of innocent dreams, either straight to the 'banal life under lock and key' of social decency, or to the sufferings and disillusionments of the unrealized soul, which 'remembers itself as if it were another'.[41] This emotional concealment is intensified by women's muteness. The motif of muteness is associated both with the woman poet and with woman as such, whose soul is unable to speak, has not been taught to speak and cannot express itself.

The themes named here are combined in a very unusual text by Pavlova, the story 'A Double Life' ('Dvoinaia zhizn'', 1844–47), the prose part of which tells the 'usual story' of a young woman from high society; the poetic fragments describe the nocturnal life of her soul and tell us that Cecilia is a gifted poet, although no-one (least of all she, herself) suspects it. In her half-waking dreams the 'mute' heroine meets with a 'severe genius',[42] acquires speech and receives the potential to tell her own story in the first person, but the story finishes precisely at this moment, as Catriona Kelly remarks.[43] Even so, Cecilia's drama is not swallowed up by silence: it is narrated by the author's sister-voice.

Severely critical of the female world and the accepted representations of femininity, Pavlova constantly discusses them and tries to assert the right to speech and to a real life for herself and all her 'mute' sisters. A similar theme and the discourse of sisterhood can be heard unexpectedly forcefully in the work of Nadezhda Durova, in her romantic stories and especially in her famous 'Journals of a Cavalry Maiden' ('Kavalerist-devitsa, proisshestvie v Rossii', 1836). Here we meet with a surprising paradox: Durova, who in life assumed a male name, wore male clothing and led a male way of life, writes all her texts with a female narrator and the so-called 'female theme' occupies a prime place. In Durova's *Journals* the questions of the place and situation of women in traditional patriarchal society are raised very openly and fearlessly, especially in the chapters about childhood where the

---

41. 'Da mnogo nas, tainstvennykh podrug' ('And many of us, mysterious women friends'), 'Liubliu ia vas, mladye devy' ('I love you, young maidens'), *Laterna magica*.
42. Here Pavlova solves one of the most 'insoluble' problems of women's writing: she adapts the exclusively masculine image of the poet-genius, and the situation of his love for his beloved Muse, with the aid of inversion of gender roles.
43. Kelly, *A History of Russian Women's Writing*, pp. 106–07.

central figures are mother and daughter, whose relationship is depicted unsentimentally and dramatically, in contrast to the sentimental idealizing tradition. In the *Journals*, the mother (and other women) is associated with surveillance and coercion. Dependency, stereotypicality, absence of choice, primordial inferiority and subjection to unceasing observation and control are marked, especially by the mother, as essential attributes of femininity. Within the bounds of the female world, the heroine sees only two alternatives: to submit to the destiny of the eternal slave and prisoner, or to become a monster in public opinion. But she finds a third path: in order to remain herself, she ceases being a woman and becomes a soldier. As she tells the unusual story of her life, Durova creates the legend of a woman who found freedom and the possibility for self-realization in spite of all stereotypes. Part of this self-realization is her autodocumentary text, written in the person of a woman.[44] It is also important that in spite of the eccentricity of her own choice, Durova does differentiate herself sharply from other women and frequently addresses her 'young peers' in the text, particularly when discussing women's lot and their lack of freedom.

Discussion of femininity and masculinity can be seen, as mentioned, in some romantic stories by Durova, such as 'The Game of Fate, or Illegal Love' ('Igra sud'by, ili Protivozakonnaia liubov''), which was originally published under the title 'Elena, the Beauty of the City of T.' ('Elena, T-skaia krasavitsa') in 1837, and others. However, the novel became the dominant literary genre in the 1830s and 1840s, and came under the particularly rigid control of patriarchal institutions (publishing, journalism, criticism and censorship). The exclusively masculine, romantic concept of the prophetic genius, together with the theory of social realism and the demands that literature be the teacher of life and participate in ideological battles, relegated the female *a priori* – as secondary, insignificant and private – to the margins of the literary process.[45] The female was usurped by male literature and existed, as Barbara Heldt says, in a state of

---

44. Heldt, in her *Terrible Perfection*, pp. 64–76 sees special potential for women's self-expression in autobiographical genres and in lyrics. Even if one agrees in part, it must be observed that such texts were not in practice published in the author's lifetime. Durova's memoirs were the rarest exception. On women's ego-texts see, for example, Catherine Viollet and Elena Grechanaia, 'Dnevnik v Rossii v kontse XVIII – nachale XIX v. kak avtobiograficheskaia praktika', in *Avtobiograficheskaia praktika v Rossii i vo Frantsii*, ed. by Catherine Viollet and Elena Grechanaia (Moscow: IMLI RAN, 2006), pp. 57–111; I. Savkina, *Razgovory s zerkalom i Zazerkal'em: avtodokumental'nye teksty v russkoi literature pervoi poloviny XIX veka* (Moscow: Novoe literaturnoe obozrenie, 2007), pp. 9–289.
45. See Kelly, *A History of Russian Women's Writing*, pp. 3, 24–26; I. Savkina, 'Mozhet li zhenshchina byt' romanticheskim poetom?', in *Vieldeutiges Nicht-Zu-Ende-Sprechen*, pp. 97–111.

under-description.⁴⁶ The idealized, infantilized, de-individualized female was part of a world view that had no place for real women and women writers.

However, in spite of the dictat of the canon, women were also able to destabilize it surreptitiously in their prose and to find or invent possibilities for self-expression. Their innovations were not associated with central ideas (as seen by critics), nor with conflicts between ideas, nor with the development of plot paradigms, but primarily with narrative practices and changes of emphasis in the depiction of major and minor characters. The women writers of the 1840s and 1850s problematized the concepts of periphery and centre, undermining the division between them, and created the conditions for the literary legitimization of the female and the female voice. In the first half of the nineteenth century, the chief prose genre for women was the story. Jehanne M. Gheith says that women usually wrote diagnostic texts, society tales and works focusing on the problems of women.⁴⁷ Catriona Kelly notes that the women writers of the 1830s and 1840s used the society tale, transformed it and also created a new type of story, which she calls the provincial tale, defined as 'a medium-to-full-length prose narrative set in the Russian countryside, and depicting a young female protagonist's struggles not to limit her life according to the accepted expectations for women from landowning families'.⁴⁸ Women writers used existing popular genres and invented their own variations on the story genre and thus aimed to reconstruct cultural space in such a way as to find a place in it for the female heroine and female writing.

In the first half of the nineteenth century the most prominent figures in women's prose were Mariia Zhukova and Elena Gan (1814–42).

Practically all studies of Gan's work⁴⁹ agree that her chief interest was the unusual woman, the feminized variant of the romantic exile.⁵⁰

---

46. Heldt, *Terrible Perfection*, p. 16.
47. See Jehanne M. Gheith, 'Women of the 1830s and 1850s: Alternative Periodizations' in *A History of Women's Writing in Russia*, p. 88.
48. Kelly, *A History of Russian Women's Writing*, p. 58.
49. Joe Andrew, 'Elena Gan and A Futile Gift', in Andrew, Joe *Narrative and Desire in Russian Literature, 1822–49. The Feminine and the Masculine* (London: Macmillan, 1993), pp. 85–138; Kelly, *A History of Russian Women's Writing*, pp. 109–118; Elisabeth Cheauré, 'Liebeswunsch und Kunstbegehren. Elena A. Gan und ihre Erzählung "Ideal"', in *Frauenbilder und Weiblichkeitsentwürfe in der russischen Frauenprosa*, pp. 93–110; Frank Göpfert, 'Elena Gan. An der Schwelle einer sozialkritischen Frauenliteratur', in *Dichterinnen und Schriftstellerinnen*, pp. 103–06; Yael Harussi, 'Hinweis auf Elena Gan (1814–1841)', *Zeitschrift für Slavische Philologie*, 42 (1981), no. 2, 242–60; Marit Bjerkeng Nielsen, 'The Concept of Love and the Conflict of the Individual versus Society in Elena Gan's "Sud sveta"', *Scando-Slavica* (1978), 24, 125–38.
50. On the romantic exile as the literary prototype of Gan's heroines see Kelly, *A History of Russian Women's Writing*, p.112.

The extraordinary female protagonist is created in various ways: by using exotic material;[51] by taking traditional motifs in the depiction of women to extremes (the mania for self-sacrifice in 'Theophania Abbiadjio' ('Teofaniia Abbiadzhio', 1840), or in 'The Numbered Box' ('Numerovannaia lozha', 1842); or by depicting a strong heroine who experiences romantic alienation, a conflict with her surroundings, like Ol'ga in 'The Ideal' ('Ideal', 1840), or Zenaida in 'Society's Judgment' ('Sud sveta', 1840). The histories of these heroines are similar in many ways: childhood paradise, mother's early death, persecution by the crowd which makes accusations of excessive intellect and pride, self-sacrifice for a male other, and unfulfilled hopes for family happiness. Both texts conclude with the heroine's first-person narrative about herself, the leitmotif of which is the feeling of unrealized personality and rejection of ordinary life in favour of spiritual endeavour. The sharp conflict between woman and the world around her and the critical depiction of male characters, have allowed some researchers to call Gan 'the Russian George Sand', but the ideas at which her rebellious protagonists arrive have very little in common with women's emancipation or gender inversion, the assimilation of male roles. Gan's heroines are not satisfied with either male or female roles, only with angelic ones, signifying a total ban on sexuality.[52] However, whilst they refuse to tie themselves to the adult, sexual, male world and retreat into the nunnery of spiritual innocence, Gan's heroines still feel the imperative to create and write. The central themes of Gan's last unfinished work, 'A Futile Gift' ('Naprasnyi dar', 1842),[53] are the nature of female talent and the possibilities for women's creative self-realization. Here she distinguishes creativity[54] from authorship. The heroine of the story, Aniuta, is a female romantic poet (a soothsayer), who brings her gift to fruition and is happy so long as she lives by the laws of inexpressible, wordless, poetic revelation. However, the attempt to go public, the moment of contact with the real world and

---

51. *Utballa* (*Utballa*, 1837), *Divine Judgment* (*Sud bozhii*, 1840).
52. On this see Kelly, *A History of Russian Women's Writing*, p. 117 and Andrew, *Narrative and Desire in Russian Literature*, p. 131.
53. A detailed analysis of the story can be found in Joe Andrew, 'A Futile Gift: Elena Andreevna Gan and Writing', in *Gender Restructuring in Russian Studies*, ed. by Marianne Liljeström, Eila Mäntysaari, and Arja Rosenholm (Tampere: University of Tampere Press, 1993), pp. 1–14, and also Savkina, *Provintsialki russkoi literatury*, pp. 146–55.
54. Drawing here not on the romantic conceptions of the poet-prophet, but on the conceptions of the Jena romantics, which were assimilated in Russia and which viewed the feminine, the female, as creative. See Kelly, *A History of Russian Women's Writing*, p. 34 and N. Ia. Berkovskii, *Romantizm v Germanii* (Leningrad: Khudozhestvennaia literatura, 1973).

the reader, turns out to be extremely dangerous or even impossible for a woman – to adopt a rational, professional relation to creativity (within the male world of competition and conflict) is perceived as betrayal of her gift. With her typical romantic maximalism, Gan takes the problem to extremes and makes it visible and significant. In this sense, Catriona Kelly thinks, 'as a writer who eschewed compromise, she was suitably inspiring in the absolutist conditions of Russian culture'.[55]

Unlike Gan, her contemporary Mariia Zhukova (1805–55) was considered by contemporary and later critics to be a standard, mediocre writer with no special virtues or innovations. Only the "squint-eyed" view (Sigrid Weigel's term)[56] on her work by feminist critics helped to reveal the important innovatory potential of her prose, connected with the range of the (female) protagonists she depicts and the nature of the narrative.

Zhukova's prose, starting with her first work in her first cycle, 'Evenings by the River Karpovka' ('Vechera na Karpovke', 1837–38), gives a voice to those female types that had remained on the periphery of plot in contemporary literature, the silent extras and semi-comic figures: the plain Jane, the old maid, the provincial, the hanger-on, the kept woman and the old woman.[57] The main thing which interests her is the woman who does not usually become a literary heroine, the ordinary woman and her fate, which includes not only relationships with men, but also perhaps no-less-complex and often dramatic relationships with other women. Like Durova, Zhukova depicts conflictive mother-daughter relationships, complex simultaneously loving and competitive relationships between sisters and relationships between female friends.[58]

Zhukova's narrative practices are especially interesting. Beginning with 'Evenings by the River Karpovka', she presents rich contradictions and a tension between narrated stories and the framing plot, a frame which, in Joe Andrew's view, allows us to speak of the polyphony of a text that

---

55. Kelly, *A History of Russian Women's Writing*, p. 118.
56. Sigrid Weigel, 'Der schielende Blick: Thesen zur Geschichte weiblicher Schreibpraxis', in *Die verborgene Frau: Sechs Beiträge zu einer feministischen Literaturwissenschaft*, ed. by Ingrid Stephan and Sigrid Weigel (Berlin: Argument-Sonderband AS, 1988), pp. 83–137.
57. On the image of the benevolent matriarch see Joe Andrew, 'The Benevolent Matriarch in Elena Gan and Mar'ja Zhukova', in *Women and Russian Culture: Projections and Self-Perceptions*, ed. by Rosalind Marsh (New York-Oxford: Berghahn, 1998), pp 60–77 and on the controlling old woman, aunt, old maid and hanger-on see Savkina, *Provintsialki russkoi literatury*, pp. 195–202.
58. 'Naden'ka' ('Naden'ka); 'Two Sisters' ('Dve sestry'); 'An Episode from the Life of a Country Lady' ('Epizod iz zhizni derevenskoi damy'), 'Two Weddings' ('Dve svad'by').

problematizes ideas about authorship and gender: '[...] by using male narrators, whose view she does not necessarily share, she was able not only to create a truly polyphonic work, but also to problematize and interrogate the very notions of authorship and gender, as well as the interconnections between these two concepts'.[59] Hilde Hoogenboom uses the term pastiche[60] to denote this tension and sees in it a means for expressing female 'protest against traditional plots for women's lives'.[61] Hoogenboom considers that the numerous digressions (which so irritated the critic Belinskii) are a street demonstration of a literary kind: the looseness and incompleteness are a kind of protest against the social order. The idea expressed by the narrative of the fluidity, incompleteness and unpredictability of life is, in Hoogenboom's view, very important for Zhukova. Hoogenboom points out the special functions of the motifs of nature and the provinces in her work: 'In Zhukova's aesthetics, a country walk best evokes the large, relatively flat expanse of real lived life, the standard by which she measured narrative in realist fiction [...] This kind of progression actively resists the eventfulness of literary plot, which in some way revolves around a beginning, a middle, and an end. In her most subtle critique of the society tale, Zhukova uses a narrative strategy that subverts a linear narrative and closure'.[62]

The openness and unstructuredness which almost all Zhukova's commentators note (with or without approval) is connected with the fact that Zhukova orients her narrative strategies to oral narrative or chatter. In the late texts the narrator is often a female chatterbox or a provincial gossip. This narrative technique presents a female view of things and unites the public with the personal, the private, insisting on its value.

What is important here is the discourse of the provinces and also the special position of the female narrator, who is situated inside the outside (she is an insider who is simultaneously an outsider) and has a somewhat confused and distorted perspective. The narrator and Zhukova's heroines describe provincial space as marginal, but they do not escape[63] to the

---

59. Joe Andrew, 'Telling Tales. Zhukova as a Metaliterary Author', in *Vieldeutiges Nicht-Zu-Ende-Sprechen*, p. 122. Andrew calls this narrative situation 'narrutopia', using Isenberg's term.
60. Hilde Hoogenboom, 'The Society Tale as Pastiche: Maria Zhukova's Heroines Move to the Country', in *The Society Tale in Russian Literature From Odoevskii to Tolstoi*, ed. by Neil Cornwell (Amsterdam-Atlanta: Rodopi, 1998), pp. 85–97.
61. Hoogenboom, p. 92.
62. Hoogenboom, p. 91.
63. Cf. Kelly's ideas about the escape plot as an obligatory element of the provincial tale

centre or contest marginalization, rather they try to turn the latter into building blocks for the construction of their own identity, try to rehabilitate and reconstruct what the dominant cultural discourse sees as non-being, nonexistence. In a sense they repudiate the values of oppositional and hierarchical thinking and create new possibilities for Russian literature.[64]

The period 1830–50 was the time when women stepped into the literary arena, when women's writing and women writers were professionalized: in their lyrics, autodocumentary genres and prose, they try to find strategies and methods for representing the female in literary discourse, despite the patriarchal tradition that absolutely dominated criticism. And in this sense Aleksandra Zrazhevskaia (1805–67) is a complete exception, since she could be called the first critic of a pro-feminist persuasion in Russian literary history. Her essay 'The Menagerie' ('Zverinets', 1842), consists of letters to Varvara and Praskov'ia Bakunina. The first letter contains a short autobiographical sketch, a sort of reduced novel about the formation of a woman writer and in the second section, Zrazhevskaia polemises vigorously with patriarchal prejudices about the unnaturalness of women taking up literature and its dangers for them. She notes that women's inability to compete in the sciences and arts is associated with lack of education and the limited and false societal understanding of the nature and role of women. Zrazhevskaia describes the concrete means by which critics hold women writers back and counters with a short but favourable review of the women's writing of her time, naming Avdot'ia Glinka, Elizaveta Kul'man, Olimpiada Shishkina, Elena Gan, Mariia Zhukova, Nadezhda Durova, Elizaveta Kologrivova, Aleksandra Ishimova, Karolina Pavlova, Evdokiia Rostopchina and Zinaida Volkonskaia, offering a practically exhaustive list of the women writers of the 1830s and 1840s. In another article she suggests that women writers 'cease to act separately' and 'gather all together' to publish their own journal.[65] Here the woman question is articulated in part, which takes us to a new and different page in the history of Russian women's writing.

When Evdokiia Rostopchina stated regretfully that the 1850s, 'our chaotic and repugnant time', as she called it, were 'not in favour of poetry, and particularly not of women's poetry',[66] she was saying something

---

(*A History of Russian Women's Writing*, pp. 59–78).
64. Similar narrative strategies and themes can be seen in the stories of Sof'ia Zakrevskaia (1796?–1865?) and Anastasiia Marchenko (1830–1880?).
65. Aleksandra Zrazhevskaia, 'Zverinets', *Maiak* (1842), I, chapter 1, 1–18.
66. Evdokiia P. Rostopchina, *Talisman. Izbrannaia lirika. Neliudimka, drama. Dokumenty, pis'ma,*

essential about the shifting of aesthetic paradigms and the crucial effect it had on women's writing in the middle of the century. Rostopchina experienced the transition of values in her own literary career when she became the object of mockery in the pages of literary journals, such as *The Contemporary (Sovremennik)*, and among radical critics, such as Nekrasov, Dobroliubov and Chernyshevskii. For them, Rostopchina represented the social and gendered Otherness that the new members of the *raznochinets* intelligentsia associated with the decadent morality of the aristocratic past. For the emerging intelligentsia, who were to challenge the philosophical and aesthetic values of their romantic predecessors, an aristocratic woman writer was a cultural relic, self-deluded and unable to signify symbolic authority. As already pointed out, the literary discourse of the emancipatory 1860s was quite different from the earlier sentimental-romantics discourses that had openly presented gender difference. While the latter presented a complementary rhetoric, which, nevertheless, invited women writers to participate in generic literary innovations such as novels and diaries, the emancipatory Realism of the 1860s had its own contradictions: there was a tendency to absorb the difference, which did not favour women writers, since women were expected to write 'as well as men'.

The turbulent years of the great reforms – social, cultural and political transformations challenging the backwardness of Russian society, including the emancipation of the serfs in 1861 – promoted women to participation in higher education, individual liberation and equal cultural opportunities. The prominence of the 'woman question' as prime mover for the emancipation movement is evident.[67] However, in the 'awakening'[68] of women into a new consciousness, as the woman question was symbolically defined in the discourses of the 'thick journals', men and women were placed quite asymmetrically: women – still mainly from the upper classes – longing for cultural activities were to be re-educated, while male agents were the new teachers, as so well imagined in Chernyshevskii's novel, *What Is to Be Done? (Chto delat'?* 1863).

Expectations notwithstanding, the woman question did not have an entirely positive influence on women writers. Although its discourse encouraged

---

vospominaniia. (Moscow: Moskovskii rabochii, 1987), p. 289.
67. Richard Stites, *The Women's Liberation Movement in Russia: Feminism, Nihilism, and Bolshevism, 1860–1930*. (Princeton: Princeton University Press, 1978), p. 30.
68. *Rassvet, Zhurnal nauk, iskusstv i literatury dlia vzroslykh devits* (1859), no. 1.

women to go public and to appeal to the egalitarian programme to meet their educational needs, the educated woman was, nevertheless, unable to redress the balance of the asymmetric cultural and aesthetic tradition of woman as deviant, as the historical and aesthetic backward Other. The new egalitarian concept did not allow a woman writer to seek refuge in her difference when it came to the conventions of genres, themes, or narrative strategies. It demanded great courage to claim cultural difference in that 'egalitarian' time. And when Rostopchina did so, she became an object of malicious laughter that turned into misogynistic irony aimed at women's so-called 'original way of thinking', that is, not 'with the head' but 'with the heart'.[69]

Women involved in the teacher dyad were in an ambiguous situation. Dependent on the main values of the social transition, the new cultural type, the educated woman (the *kursistka* and *nigilistka*) was formed on the fragile basis of the rationalistic concepts of the master discourse. The 'new woman' seemed to be emerging as a derivative of utilitarian reason, as an adjunct of the rationalistic and egalitarian principles of the neo-enlightenment, according to which every human being, including women, had the promise of developing into a reasoning subject through (self) education. However, while aiming at new egalitarian knowledge, the new woman had to distance herself from the negative connotations of feminine backwardness embodied in the old ridiculed figures of the boarding-school girl (*institutka*) and the caricatured aristocratic *salonnière*. They represented the Other as the feminine difference which was marginalized outside the new 'learned woman', who now had to absorb the romantic erroneous delusions into the new ideal of rational perfectibility.

Women writers were also in an ambiguous situation: to be raised from cultural inferiority on to the stage of historical consciousness meant that they risked becoming disconnected from their cultural potential and from their female predecessors. We should be aware that the egalitarian woman question did not automatically provide new literary opportunities for women in the second third of the century. All too often, the sheer volume of (male) egalitarian rhetoric on the woman question drowned out women's voices and their literary imagination, which was denigrated as 'backward', 'too narrow', 'subjective', 'melodramatic' and lacking social relevance.[70] The disconnection between the woman question (the discourse of male critics shaping ideally liberated feminine images) and the issues of women's fiction,

---

69. N. N., 'Stikhotvoreniia grafini Rostopchinoi', *Otechestvennye zapiski* (1856), vol. 109, no. 12, 77–85, see especially pp. 81, 82, 85. See also Rosenholm, *Gendering Awakening*, pp. 361ff.
70. Rosenholm, *Gendering Awakening*, pp. 342ff.

with the way women wrote about them, resulted in frequent accusations that women writers were either not progressive or had nothing to say about the women's movement.[71] Neither the 'idea of the equality of all people without distinction' which was 'the magnet which drew so many young idealistic women into the "nihilist" camp',[72] nor the radical movement of the 1870s and 1880s, which offered many socially – and culturally – displaced women the fascination of the new 'family',[73] expected women to produce any autonomous aesthetic activities as a sign of their liberation.

The dilemma for many women writing in mid-century was that, on the one hand, they used fiction for discussing women's situation, doing so in large part through the topics and genre conventions common to their female predecessors of the 1830s; but on the other hand they experienced pressure to deny the female influence of women's prose, which was often held up as an example of bad writing.[74] This ambiguity, this being between different literary traditions, they absorbed into their writings. The egalitarian rhetoric, stressing social activity for the sake of the 'common cause', could have caused, as Catriona Kelly suggested when speaking of women writers of the 1860s, 'hostility towards imaginative writing and to ambivalent narrative stance amongst those committed to women's emancipation'.[75] We can find some confirmation for this thesis in the diaries and autobiographical writings of the women of the 1860s in their yearning for education in scientific knowledge; for example, in the aesthetically and historically significant memoirs of Elizaveta Nikolaevna Vodovozova (1844–1923) *At the Dawn of Life* (*Na zare zhizni*, 1911).[76] And yet, although we agree that the period was controversial for women's writing, there is still no doubt, as Jehanne Gheith has stated, that 'the second third of the nineteenth century was crucial in the development of Russian women's writing'.[77]

---

71. See, for example, N. Shelgunov on V. Krestovskii in Nikolai Shelgunov, 'Zhenskoe bezdushie (Po povodu sochinenii V. Krestovskogo-psevdonim)', *Delo* (1870), vol. 9, no. 11, pp. 1–34.
72. Stites, *The Women's Liberation Movement in Russia*, p. 100.
73. Barbara A. Engel, *Mothers and Daughters: Women of the Intelligentsia in Nineteenth-Century Russia* (Cambridge: Cambridge University Press, 1986), pp. 199–203.
74. For example, N. G. Chernyshevskii, *Sobranie sochinenii v piati tomakh* (Moscow Izd: Pravda, 1974), V, 205; see also Chernyshevskii on Karolina Pavlova, or Chernyshevskii on Tur, in N. G. Chernyshevskii, 'Tri pory zhizni. Roman Evgenii Tur. Tri Chasti., M. 1854', in his *Polnoe sobranie sochinenii v 10 tomakh*, 10 vols (St Petersburg: Izd. M. N. Chernyshevskogo, 1906), I, 115–23, 121–23, 115, 122.
75. Kelly, *A History of Russian Women's Writing*, p. 78.
76. E. N. Vodovozova, *Na zare zhizni*, 2 vols (Moscow: Khudozhestvennaia literatura, 1987), II, 82.
77. Gheith in *A History of Women's Writing in Russia*, ed. by Adele Marie Barker and Jehanne

There was a large number of women writers in the middle of the century. The first prose works of many of them came out in 1848 and 1849, when the fact that women's writings were not considered part of the realism of the 'social' worked in their favour: it was easier to get such writing published in a time of particularly restrictive censorship,[78] as Gheith sees the controversial 1850s. A contemporary critic, N. Sokolovskii, confirms this, noting in 1860 that 'one only has to follow our literary development of the most recent period to find out that there is an abundance of literary works that belong to women writers. One only has to scan any issue of *The Russian Herald* (*Russkii vestnik*) of the last two or three years to become convinced of my words'.[79] However, the radical advocates of the new Realism, such as Shelgunov and Chernyshevskii, who read and evaluated such popular women authors as, for example, Evgeniia Tur (1815–92), or Nadezhda Khvoshchinskaia, as if they were in the tradition of the male pen, failed to see them as writing on the 'burning questions' of the time. Women did, in fact, participate in the discussion of the woman question. They asked the question in an unexpected way, not in the utopian manner, but in a manner close to their everyday life, which meant they were not perceived as being 'progressive'. Jane Costlow has stated though, that 'the variety of their narratives as well as the diversity of their talents and strengths is apparent in their own efforts to name the "Woman Question"'.[80]

Ambivalence is a common position women writers share, despite their differences. We can speak of a frontier existence,[81] or writing from the middle ground,[82] from where they negotiate controversial norms and gender expectations, a place between extreme aesthetic and ideological positions, which they avoid or reject. The border existence relates both to aesthetic identities and cultural-historical locations; women writers, for example, seldom took the lead in aesthetic schools or political groupings and seldom participated openly in disputes between literary circles, which were the domain of the male authorities.[83]

M. Gheith, p. 85.
78. Jehanne M. Gheith, *Finding the Middle Ground. Krestovskii, Tur and the Power of Ambivalence in Nineteenth-Century Russian Women's Prose* (Evanston, Illinois: Northwestern University Press, 2004), p. 157.
79. N. Sokolovskii, 'Nasha zhenskaia literatura poslednego perioda', in *Svetoch* (1860), XII, 1–42 (1).
80. Jane Costlow, 'Love, Work, and the Woman Question in Mid-Nineteenth-Century Women's Writing', in *Women Writers in Russian Literature*, ed. by Toby W. Clyman and Diana Greene, pp. 61–75 (63).
81. Rosenholm, *Gendering Awakening*, pp. 338, 339, 341, 368.
82. Gheith, *Finding the Middle Ground*, p. 187.
83. A. M. Skabichevskii, a literary critic, stated in 1886, speaking of Krestovskii, that she 'stayed outside all existing movements of literary circles and parties of her time, [that]

Another common feature of women's Realist prose is the fact that women writers quite clearly chose female figures as their main characters and studied the world from a female viewpoint and in the family setting. Hardly any woman writers would not have discussed the awakening of the new woman. Here, too, is an ambiguity common to many realistic works of such popular, though different, writers as Khvoshchinskaia, Avdot'ia Panaeva, Tur, Nadezhda Zhadovskaia or Marko Vovchok. Although their heroines were not provided with the aura of the 'strong woman',[84] it is the female characters and their depiction that contribute to the evolution of the types and characters of realistic prose. Women's heroines are not just ready-made representations of utopian concepts, but diverse, complex, individual characters. They can also be interpreted positively as being as contradictory as life itself, as the contemporary prose-writer and critic Mariia Konstantinovna Tsebrikova (1835–1917) remarked, reviewing Khvoshchinskaia's heroines.[85]

Nadezhda Dmitrievna Khvoshchinskaia (1822–89),[86] one of the most important writers of the nineteenth century, was known for her many pseudonyms and wrote prose mainly under the name of V. Krestovskii. Her collected work published in six volumes[87] includes poetry, novels, stories, sketches, drama, art and literary criticism and translations. Her main characters are women – defenceless daughters, old maids, fallen women – victims of the social system and its hierarchy, which offered only limited options for women trying to escape arranged marriages and searching for alternative solutions. Like many other women writers of her time, she draws on the provincial environment which gives women's literature its specific tone. Like her sisters, Sof'ia Dmitrievna Khvoshchinskaia (Iv. Vesenev, 1824–65)

---

she lived thoroughly through her heart': in his *Istoriia noveishei russkoi literatury 1848–1890* (St Petersburg: tipografiia gazety 'Novosti', 1891), p. 237. Nikolai Kotliarevskii, another critic from the late nineteenth century, recognized that the literary activities of all these ladies [*dam*, A. R. and I. S.] [Zhukova, Gan, Khvoshchinskaia, Janish, Rostopchina, Korsini, Kokhanovskaia, and Tur] were not united by any universal programmes': in his 'Ocherki iz istorii obshchestvennogo nastroeniia shestidesiatykh godov', *Vestnik Evropy* (1914), vol. 2, pp. 225–52 (241).

84. Vera Sandomirsky Dunham, 'The Strong Woman Motif', in *The Transformation of Russian Society*, ed. by Cyril E. Black (Cambridge, Mass.: Harvard University Press, 1960), pp. 459–83.
85. Mariia Tsebrikova, 'V pamiat' V. Krestovskogo-psevdonima', *Novosti i birzhevaia gazeta*, 1889, no. 177, 2.
86. She was one of the three sisters, all writers of prose. On Sof'ia D. and P. D. Khvoshchinskaia see, for example, *Dictionary of Russian Women Writers*, ed. by Marina Ledkovsky, Charlotte Rosenthal, Mary Zirin (Westport et al.: Greenwood, 1994), pp. 289–91.
87. *Polnoe sobranie sochinenii V. Krestovskogo*, 6 vols (St Petersburg: A. A. Kaspari, 1912–13).

and Praskoviia Dmitrievna Khvoshchinskaia (1828–1916), she examines the impoverished gentry by focusing on the despotic and hierarchical relationships within the patriarchal family. In novels and novellas such as *Anna Mikhailovna, Who Actually Ended Up Satisfied?* (*Kto zh ostalsia dovolen?*, 1853), *Free Time* (*Svobodnoe vremia*, 1856), *Stagnant Water* (*Stoiachaia voda*, 1861) and *A Domestic Matter* (*Domashnee delo*, 1863), she describes conflicts between parents and children, which are reflections of the era and critiques of serfdom. Nadezhda Khvoshinskaia gives voice to the women of the provinces and holds a unique position in the development of Realist literature by her reworking of the narratives of the dispossessed and downtrodden.

Her pioneering novel, *The Boarding-School Girl* (*Pansionerka*, 1861),[88] which is central to the realistic representation of nineteenth-century literary heroines, focuses on process whilst presenting the Russia of the pre-reform 1850s. Her realist middle-ground position suggests – according to Gheith – that there are diverse historical, often invisible, layers of moral ideals in the memory of society and the individual, which should not be forgotten since they correspond to hopes and aims, to be tested later in more stable times.[89] Khvoshchinskaia is interested not in stasis or result but in process and struggle. Her focus is on growth, embedded in detailed depictions of the social setting and of the psychologically authentic inner world of the characters. Lelen'ka, the boarding-school girl, represents the educated woman whose voice echoes the thrilling promises of education and independent labour for the new woman. Lelen'ka's empowerment derives from her rejection of self-denial, of marriage and family as the only preserves for women. Instead, the story is of a woman's quest to be herself and to dream for herself. Lelen'ka refuses marriage and escapes to St Petersburg to become an artist and translator. What makes the novel significant, however, is not only the independence Lela vehemently manifests, but also the skilled narrative strategy. The omniscient narrator follows Lelen'ka's growth from the inner perspective and empathetically records the development of her mind and body. Her development is described with psychological realism and records self-doubt, conflicts, reversals and despair. However, in the last 'emancipatory' chapter, which covers a mere

---

88. N. D. Khvoshchinskaia (V. Krestovskii-psevdonim), 'Pansionerka', in N. D. Khvoshchinskaia (V. Krestovskii-psevdonim), *Povesti i rasskazy* (Moscow: Moskovskii rabochii, 1984), pp. 62–158; see the reading in Rosenholm, *Gendering Awakening*, pp. 446–99 and Joe Andrew, *Narrative, Space and Gender in Russian Fiction 1846–1903* (Amsterdam: Rodopi, 2007), pp. 105–30.
89. Gheith, *Finding the Middle Ground*, p. 159.

couple of hours, after seven chapters showing several years, the narrator ceases to comment on Lelen'ka's innermost feelings and withdraws. We now listen to the dialogue between the former teacher Veretitsyn and his female pupil, the Lelen'ka who has outgrown him. Empowered by will-power and work, Lelen'ka takes the role of the teacher. The disparity between the psychological and ideological narrative voices in the text is achieved by an aesthetic strategy which tunes into a historical dilemma. By this the author appears to claim that true emancipation for the new woman cannot be achieved without conflict between love and labour. The ending is left open and the choices made by the new woman reveal a dilemma which points to the limited liberties allowed by society, especially for women. The new woman's options of being free or lonely show the writer's skilful art and ideological realism: the 'unwholeness' of narrative and heroine implicitly criticizes ready-made and utopian concepts of emancipation, which did not take account of women's real-life circumstances and the unresolved struggle between emotion and willpower. Moreover, the openness and the narrator's silence respect Lelen'ka's convictions. Dialogue gives autonomy to the character; the narrator does not swallow her up; Lelen'ka does not dissolve in the other's power to give meaning, but has her own voice. Thanks to this narrative method, the new heroine is allowed to rescue her own story and thus she is spared the destiny of numerous literary ladies who vanish into the hero's story, as Joe Andrew has pointed out.[90]

Lelen'ka was exemplary for many, but another feature common to other women's works is that the woman question was not only about law and education. Mary Zirin comments on Chernyshevskii's *What is To Be Done?*: 'Women saw no such easy happy endings for their heroines'.[91] The domestic sphere and the family relationships, which are at the centre of women's prose throughout the century, reveal at the micro-level the hierarchical injustices deeply rooted in autocratic society. The texts are diagnostic in Gheith's term, 'showing the evils of Russian society – specifically, the difficulties of women's position – without suggesting a realisable resolution of them'.[92] Diagnostic prose includes the motifs of, for example, injustice, family and marriage, women's education, social prejudices,

---

90. Joe Andrew, '"The Lady Vanishes". A Feminist Reading of Turgenev', *Irish Slavonic Studies*, 1987, 8, 87–98.
91. Mary Zirin, 'Women's Prose Fiction in the Age of Realism', in *Women Writers in Russian Literature*, pp. 77–94 (87).
92. Gheith, in *A History of Women's Wriing in Russia*, ed. by Adele Marie Barker and Jehanne M. Gheith, p. 94.

the prominence of ethical commitments and moral norms in women's socialization and female self-sacrifice. An innovative sphere includes the reworking of female images to bring in whole communities of women missing from men's narratives. A third common element is the voice of Cassandra which women writers often use when they communicate with reality to express scepticism rather than Utopianism.

Critique of social injustice is one of the most common motifs in women's writing. Many women writers challenge social and other hierarchies and anticipate social transformations, as in such novels and novellas as *Sasha* (1858), *Three Fates* (*Tri doli,* 1861), *The Plaything* (*Igrushechk*a, 1858) and *A Living Soul* (*Zhivaia dusha*, 1868) by Marko Vochok (Mariia Aleksandrovna Markovich, née Vilinskaia, 1833–1907). Her prose resonates with the debate on serfdom and brings the folk voice and rhetoric into literature, especially the Ukrainian oral tradition, as well as provincial nobility and the escape plot. She introduces the peasant woman in the new role of proud narrator who tells of the iniquities in her life and speaks not only of suffering but also of love and hope; 'laughter, song and love itself – qualities which Vovchok always celebrates',[93] aid the downtrodden to bear the humiliations of life and subvert the power of the privileged.

Injustice is often linked with women's critique of the limited knowledge of the world provided for them by fiction and the perception that the romantic world is incompatible with real life. However, while women's formal education was limited, knowledge, in the form of a construct arising from special female life conditions, often devalued by the (male) public, could have the potential to undermine social and gender hierarchies and expectations. In the story 'The Touchstone' ('Kamen' pretknoveniia', 1862),[94] the prose-writer and memoirist Ol'ga N. (Sof'ia Vladimirovna Engel'gardt, 1828–94) points both to knowledge based on female experience and to the importance of reading novels as a means of communicating women's knowledge to other women, in order to build alliances, however virtual. This communication occurs between a young Russian widow and the French woman writer, George Sand, whose novel becomes a sign and a medium for the criticism of Westernizers' and Slavophiles' ideologies for their condescension to women.

---

93. Jane Costlow, 'Vovchok, Marko', in *Dictionary of Russian Women Writers*, ed. by Marina Ledkovsky, Charlotte Rosenthal, Mary Zirin, p. 732.
94. Mary Zirin, 'Engel'gardt, Sof'ia Vladimirovna', in *Dictionary of Russian Women Writers*, ed. by Marina Ledkovsky, Charlotte Rosenthal, Mary Zirin, pp. 172–74.

The most innovative element in women's novels from the middle of the century is the revision of women characters. Female characters refuse to be only 'silent bearers of ideology'[95] and begin to speak. To allow women to speak presupposes that they are given roles as narrators, as main characters and that they appear as actors in a cultural and historical context; they speak in domestic spheres, and with other women. Among the foremost prose-writers who rewrite women characters and give voices to women in their domestic lives are Evgeniia Tur (Elizaveta Vasil'evna Salias de Turnemir, 1815–92), Nadezhda Stepanovna Sokhanskaia and Iuliia Valerianovna Zhadovskaia (1824–83), who wrote from the 1850s to the 1870s.

Evgeniia Tur's literary texts were accused of being 'women's prose', lacking any contribution to society. However, her prose can be re-interpreted as highly social and re-valued as aesthetically innovative if we broaden the definition of social action. This approach assumes a clear reallocation of the point of view from hero to heroine and focus on her historically significant world of family and marriage as the locus of action. Both in her fictional works and large body of criticism, Tur examines families and marriages and their social implications with radicalism, especially when women, as in her novels, find a more fulfilling life, peace and harmony outside the conventional family. This happens in 'The Niece' ('Plemiannitsa', 1851) and 'Antonina' ('Antonina', 1851), which is what motivates Gheith to speak of the anti-marriage plot as a characteristic of Tur's stories.[96] By refusing (unhappy) marriage as the only way of life, women challenge autocratic society, since the social, economic and moral norms which structure relationships between genders and generations in the family correspond with those in society. By presenting society from the woman's point of view and examining women's experience in and outside marriage, Tur emphasizes women as social agents.

Gheith has shown in her analysis of Tur's prose works that she rewrites central elements of Realist nineteenth-century narratives by 'supplementing'.[97] On the one hand, the writer accepts the basic premises; on the other, the focus is relocated from the alienated hero (such as Turgenev's) to the heroine, who is empowered by participation

---

95. Mary Jacobus, 'The Difference of View', in *The Feminist Reader. Essays in Gender and the Politics of Literary Criticism* ed. by Catherine Belsey and Jane Moore (Basingstoke: Macmillan, 1989), pp. 49–62 (50).
96. Gheith, *Finding the Middle Ground*, p. 147.
97. Gheith, *Finding the Middle Ground*, p. 131.

in domestic female communities and, even more, by her communication with female family members. Gheith's analysis of *Antonina* shows that, for Tur, communication is an aesthetic and ethical concept. She tells the story of one woman as many (daughter, governess and mother), whose story will live on in the communication with other female destinies told in other stories, here by Antonina's stepdaughter. Gheith uses the term 'aesthetics of communication',[98] an ethical paradigm that resists alienation, death and cynicism and defends emotional commitment and the intimate dialogue that is so vivid and spontaneous in the everyday life of women-centred relationships.

The emphasis on communication and women-centred dialogue figures frequently in women's texts, so much so that we can say that communality and empathy mediated by dialogue[99] between women is significant in women's texts throughout the century. Bearing in mind Khvoshchinskaia's view[100] that it is rather the need to 'relate everything', the 'talkativeness', which is at the heart of women's Realism, and not the final word, we arrive again at the idea of communication as a mode for women's aesthetics. To give women their distinctive voice requires a female community which can provide a nurturing lap for empathy and support in the struggle for women's own voice.

A fine example from mid-century is the society tale, 'A Conversation After Dinner' ('Posle obeda v gost'iakh', 1858), by Nadezhda Stepanovna Sokhanskaia (Kokhanovskaia, 1823–84). Again we have a situation where one woman tells her life story to another. The narrator, a provincial upper-class woman, tells how she was married off by her mother to a man she hardly knew, and disliked, but in the end found peace with him, the marriage and herself. The plot can be read either as the forced/unhappy marriage plot, or as the heroine's growth and spiritual triumph through 'narrative death and resurrection'.[101] And yet what makes Sokhanskaia's story so challenging and captivating is the idea that only by telling her story, and by telling it to another woman, can the heroine restructure her experiences and give them new, positive meanings. The process of telling is at the very centre of the plot. We listen to women chatting in a corner,

---

98. Gheith, *Finding the Middle Ground*, p. 137.
99. Rosenholm, *Gendering Awakening*, pp. 403–04.
100. V. Porechnikov, 'Provintsial'nye pis'ma o nashei literature', in *Otechestvennye zapiski* (1862), 5, 24–52 (38).
101. Andrew, *Narrative, Space and Gender in Russian Fiction*, pp. 65, 74.

getting easily and almost immediately into mutual understanding and emotional commitment. The woman-centred dialogue is an alternative space for women in their own right, finding themselves within, but separate from the male world. This women-centredness is empowering. Women telling their life stories make sense of, and valorize their experiences, as has been suggested by Joe Andrew, 'against the background of the hostile, official (male) world of the government official in whose house they sit, two women sit together, *and create space and meaning for themselves, their own gynocentric "universum"'*.[102] Here we can also find a subversive element, analogous to Tur's 'supplementation'. We are told about a conventional 'tragedy' of a woman forced into an unhappy marriage, but who at the end is reconciled to her situation. The dialogue, with its connection to living language, on the other hand, points to the concept of story-telling amongst women and at the same time the significance of story-writing itself. Language, communication, conversation and story-telling bring women together, establish bonds between them and help women to create alternative spaces within the main male narrative and gendered culture.

Due to the radicals' resistance to female speech, one can assume that male critics felt uncomfortable whilst listening to women, whose Realism they criticized for its predilection for detail. Female critics and women writers saw it differently, like Khvoshchinskaia, who states that women's novels are interesting for their 'facts' and for 'being full of the small details of women's everyday life; details told by women are worthy of being trusted, since in the details you feel the truth'.[103] Details are given significance in women's Realism in general, not least by Khvoshchinskaia, who, 'like others, viewed as a fundamental challenge for Realist writing the relation between details and an idea or ideal'.[104] Details stand for the whole, as also do incidental events occurring throughout and explaining the whole: wallpaper, furniture, clothing, plants and animals and silent witnesses seem to know more than the protagonists' closest relatives. The innermost experiences of the characters are often encoded by a characteristic epithet, a physical detail, or a manner of speech. We get to know the characters through their surroundings, which point to their subjective worlds and emotional experiences; the object perceived becomes the subject, an

---

102. Andrew, *Narrative, Space and Gender in Russian Fiction*, p. 76. Italics original.
103. Porechnikov, p. 51.
104. Hilde Hoogenboom, '"Ia rab deistvitel'nosti". Nadezhda Khvoshchinskaia, Realism, and the Detail', in *Vieldeutiges Nicht-zu-Ende-Sprechen*, pp. 129–48 (129).

operation that shatters the boundary between art and life. Another feature of women's literary method is the inseparability of life and art.

The insistence on life's details – and the denial of separation and distance in favour of communities and communication – gives women's Realism its specific tone: narratives are told in a literary intonation which calls for empathy, but which also provides women's Realist voice with the tone of Cassandra; Mariia Tsebrikova hears women's prose opposing the easy solutions of the emancipation.[105] While praising the female speech in her review of a woman's text, Khvoshchinskaia stresses women's ability not only to speak the truth, but also to talk with empathy.[106] The truth, however, is bitter, as the writer says.[107] The statement indicates the reciprocal permeability of life and art by appealing to the authenticity of women's inner intonation. The bitter experience does not vanish into the text's spiritual 'idea', but goes on nomadizing in the narrating, in the pathos of tears and in barely suppressed anger.

A good example is the long novel, *Women's Lot* (*Zhenskaia dolia*, 1862) by Avdot'ia Iakovlevna Panaeva (1819/1820–93), author of *The Tal'nikov Family* (*Semeistvo Tal'nikovykh*, 1848),[108] 'one of the first fictionalized accounts of childhood in Russian literature',[109] and of several novels written in collaboration with N. A. Nekrasov. She was also author of the famous *Memoirs* (*Vospominaniia*, 1889) which reflects her unique private and professional involvement with one of the century's literary and political centres, the radical journal *The Contemporary*. The novel is in many ways representative of women's Realist literature and repeats many of the themes and aesthetic strategies of women's 'diagnostic'[110] literature; it focuses on various difficulties of women's situation in society, especially the moral and emotional challenges, but does not present any one particular solution. Its aims are didactic in that it calls for social improvement and change

---

105. N. D. Khvoshchinskaia's non-Utopian tone motivates Tsebrikova to recall the mythic Cassandra-figure, the female prophet and a stranger in the androcentric world, see Mariia Tsebrikova, 'Khudozhnik-psikholog (Romany i povesti V. Krestovskogo-psevdonima)' in *Obrazovanie* (1900), I, 17–34 (18) and (1900), 2, 37–54. See also Rosenholm, *Gendering Awakening*, p. 367.
106. Porechnikov, p. 38.
107. Porechnikov, p. 38.
108. The novel was, however, banned for 'undermining morality and parental authority', see Ruth Sobel, 'Avdot'ia Panaeva (1819–1893)', in *Russian Women Writers*, ed. by Christine D. Tomei, 2 vols (New York and London: Garland Publishing, 1999), I, 300.
109. Sobel, p. 300.
110. See Gheith, in *A History of Women's Writing in Russia*, ed. by Adele Marie Barker and Jehanne M. Gheith, p. 94.

in women's lives, including educational, economic and family reforms. While openly discussing the woman question and supporting it, the novel points out that legal reforms are insufficient without moral transformation: 'And don't expect anything for now from the emancipation of women!',[111] the (male) narrator warns women expecting liberation as a result of emancipation discourse. The development depends on men: 'So long as men do not grow morally, women's emancipation is totally impossible'.[112] Panaeva's scepticism may have an autobiographical basis, since she was the object of gossip on account of her unconventional marital relationships, but it also anticipates the critique of the equality discourse, which was made by feminist writers at the end of the century. Whilst Panaeva says that women should not trust in talk of liberation, she emphasizes the importance of women's own talk. Through 'true talk' women can be united, grow conscious of their common lot and create a community which can reflect their common oppression. Her voice is hopeful, though not without disharmony, as it expresses much scepticism and suspicion. A woman writer's answer to the woman question is far more realistic than that of her male utopian contemporaries, since she deals with the practical consequences of theoretical discussions, pointing out that women who are encouraged to awake into emancipation will also risk being judged 'shameless'.[113]

The 1870s and 1880s are notable not only because of the increased number of women writers, but also because of their diverse thematic, ideological and aesthetical orientations. Different generations of writers participated in the literary process simultaneously:[114] some writers from the 1860s, such as Khvoshchinskaia, were still writing, alongside young authors starting their careers in the 1880s. There are several reasons for the increased number of women writers. Thanks to secondary and higher education,[115] more women had the opportunity to participate in the literary process whilst urbanization and industrialization brought changes in women's social status. Above all, this affected the landed gentry, whose unmarried daughters were obliged to work to support themselves. By the turn of the century the majority

---

111. N. Stanitskii, 'Zhenskaia dolia', *Sovremennik* (1862), XCII, 3, 4–176; 4, 503–61; 5, 207–50.
112. Stanitskii (1862), 3, p. 51.
113. Gheith in *A History of Women's Writing in Russia*, ed. by Adele Marie Barker and Jehanne M. Gheith, p. 93.
114. See Frank Göpfert, *Dichterinnen und Schrifstellerinnen*, p. 138.
115. See, for example, Christine Johanson, *Women's Struggle for Higher Education in Russia, 1855–1900* (Montreal: McGill-Queen's University Press, 1987).

of women writers came from urban families or humble backgrounds, as had Valentina Dmitrieva and Elizaveta Militsyna (1869–1930). Apart from various areas of society still closed to women, art, literature and journalism offered educated women professional opportunities. Many women writers began their careers as journalists, amongst them Anastasiia Verbitskaia (1861–1928), Varvara Tsekhovskaia ('Ol'nem, O.N'., 1872–1941), the poet and dramatist Nadezhda Aleksandrovna Lokhvitskaia (Teffi, 1869/70–1905) and Liubov' Iakovlevna Gurevich (1866–1940), publisher and co-editor of the journal *Northern Herald* (*Severnyi vestnik*, 1885–98). The founding of journals addressed to women (*Zhenskoe delo*, 1899–1900, *Zhenskii vestnik*, 1904–16 and *Zhurnal dlia zhenshchin*, 1914–26) and the rise of mass publishing by the turn of the century helped women to popularize their prose in 'thick journals' and turned their sensational novels into bestsellers.[116]

Of the historical factors which increased women's literary activity and supported their artistic self-confidence, we should mention the fruitful inter-relationship, from the 1880s until 1917,[117] between the women's movement and various modernist movements, with their positive, if somewhat ambivalent influence. *Fin-de-siècle* aesthetics and philosophical movements defending individual and unconventional decisions in life, together with feminist ideas by the turn of the century, emphasized women's right to express themselves. Conflicts that the new woman experienced, and which she narrated in literature, were related to her devotion to a socio-political cause and to the struggle with emotional insecurities linked with taboo female sexuality. The linkage between the women's movement and the philosophical and aesthetic programmes that emerged with the advent of Modernism in the 1890s, the Silver Age, was complex and had great impact on women's lives. With Rosalind Marsh,[118] we argue that many women writers contributed to the women's movement through their fiction, translations, criticism and journalism, as well as through the new role-models they created, as did Sof'ia Vasil'evna Kovalevskaia (1850–91) for example, through her career as a mathematician and a writer of the popular semi-autobiographical novella, *The Nihilist Girl* (*Nigilistka*, 1892),

---

116. See Rosalind Marsh, 'Realist Prose Writers, 1881–1929', in *A History of Women's Writing in Russia*, ed. by Adele Marie Barker and Jehanne M. Gheith, pp. 175–206 (179); Jeffrey Brooks, *When Russia Learned to Read. Literacy and Popular Literature, 1861–1917* (Princeton: Princeton University Press, 1988), pp. 153–65.
117. See Linda H. Edmondson, *Feminism in Russia 1900–1917* (London: Heinemann Educational Books, 1984).
118. Marsh, 'Realist Prose Writers, 1881–1929', p. 178.

or Mariia Konstantinovna Bashkirtseva (1858–84), an artist famous for her *Journal* (1887), who became the inspirational embodiment of all 'those Russian men and women who rebelled against pragmatic collectivist ideals and exalted impressionism and the autonomy of art'[119] at the end of the nineteenth-century Realist age.

Unlike women writers of the 1860s with their ascetic spirit, while devoting their intellectual passions to a common socio-political cause, women writers at the turn of the century were attracted by artistic and literary creativity as a cause worthy of individual devotion. Women's self-confidence as literary subjects grew strongly, thanks to the encouraging legacy of female predecessors, both Western European and Russian. Women were also conscious of a number of contemporary female media professionals, editors, journalists and publishers, offering their support. Female writing was legitimized by a gender culture which preferred individualism and difference; women used the crisis discourse implicit in new theoretical, aesthetic and socio-political concepts to depict the new world and the new woman from a female perspective, analogous to that of their Western-European female colleagues, by the turn of the century.[120] Simultaneously, however, women had to resist the essentialist notions of the complementary gender ideology embedded in the Symbolist movement. The growth and ambiguity of the modern 'crisis', which seemed to support women's literary and artistic creativity at the turn of the century, reminds us of an analogous situation at the beginning of the century. Then, too, Russian women entered the literary arena, as writers and readers, by contributing to the differentiation of cultural and literary blocs – during the transformation of classicism into sentimental and, later, romantic paradigms. At both points we see the disintegration of old, social and symbolic agreements and of former canons. The analogy motivates us to ask whether it is this crisis discourse, the shift towards to the anti-rational, which reveals the disintegration of old, social and symbolic agreements of former canons, and whether it was this collapse which helped women to take part in the historical drama for the move on to the literary stage. Is it the moment of transformation which accepts the female as *one* of the differences and women's writing as an innovative force?

---

119. Anna Tavis, 'Marie Bashkirtseva (1860–1884)', in *Russian Women Writers*, ed. by Christine D. Tomei, pp. 221–31 (227).
120. As pointed out by Elaine Showalter, *A Literature of Their Own* (London: Virago, 1977), p. 160.

As in earlier women's literary history, it was women's aesthetic flexibility that made their literature elastic and topical enough to answer to the requirements of the new times. Women authors reacted to the new times with different literary genres, both as Realist writers condensing in their popular novels the 'signs of the times' and as Modernist authors focusing on metaphysical questions in the poetry and prose of the Silver Age from its decadent beginnings to High Symbolism.

Despite the differences in the socio-cultural situation of women writers by the turn of the century, compared to the period of the development of Realism between the 1830s and 1880s, there are certain themes, images and narrative forms that persist. The genres women preferred throughout these decades are the short story and the novella, which was serialized in 'thick journals'. The backbone of the Realist tradition was still the escape plot.[121] There was also a clear emphasis on socio-political themes. Women writers took up the 'accursed questions' with a commitment which showed political awareness, but also the limits of political activities in Russia, as in Tat'iana Shchepkina-Kupernik's *Her First Ball* (*Pervyi bal*, 1907), in which the heroine commits a terrorist act by shooting her dancing partner, a representative of reactionary power.

Women Realist writers at the turn of century were concerned with growing industrialization and urbanization; they depict the changing situation of peasant and working-class life with broadly-based ethnographic empiricism.[122] By the turn of the century, the disruptive growth of cities and industrialization, and the rapid intensification of social and cultural differences, as well as of political conflicts, had brought a new readership which included the nascent middle class and the mass audience in need of a new kind of reading and of authors skilled to create it. It was the new prose fiction of various women authors which appealed to the new readers.

One of the most talented and popular realists of the period was Valentina Iovovna Dmitrieva (1859–1947). Her work belongs to the transformation period; she wrote, on the one hand, in the tradition of nineteenth-century Realism, putting art to the service of the people, but on the other hand, took up all the major questions of the time: concerns of town and country, the peasant question, the social circumstances of urban workers and the intelligentsia.

---

121. Kelly, *A History of Russian Women's Writing*, p. 135.
122. Kelly, *A History of Russian Women's Writing*, p. 142; on ethnographics, see Catriona Kelly, 'Life at the Margins: Women, Culture and narodnost' 1890–1920', in *Gender Restructuring in Russian Studies*, pp. 139–54.

These topics she often approached with the perspective of a woman, not only oppressed within the patriarchal family, but also endowed with 'optimism reflect[ing] the life-affirming quality that characterizes most of her work',[123] like the heroines of *Khves'ka the Orderly* (*Bol'nichnyi storozh Khves'ka*, 1900) and *Akhmetka's Wife* (*Akhmetkina zhena*, 1881). Dmitrieva should be revalued for her large body of work, her thorough knowledge of, and intensive focus on, rural and urban working life, as an author whose Realist inspiration reached far into the Soviet period and not least for her anti-sentimental narrative view of peasant life, which should be noted when we rewrite the traditions of village prose. Of special interest are the detailed images of peasant life that the author knew through working as a teacher, village doctor and radical activist in rural villages. Her novellas and stories, like *Clouds* (*Tuchki*, 1904), *Heave-ho!* (*Maina-vira*, 1900) and *The Bees are Buzzing* (*Pchely zhuzhzhat*, 1906), deal with peasant life with deep understanding and empathy for the heavy burden of men, women and children, like the ten-year-old peasant boy Dimka slaving in the glass factory (*Dimka*, 1900). Dmitrieva's contribution to the Realist depiction of rural life testifies to innovative power; in authentic, non-standard language and with detailed knowledge, she shows women not only as victims, but as independent figures resisting social prejudices with courage and humour, as does Spirinodikha, the soldier's wife in *Akhmetka's Wife*, who has to take care of two husbands after the first, presumed dead, returns home. Dmitrieva's famous memoirs, *Round the Villages* (*Po derevniam*, 1896), deal with peasant life during a diphtheria epidemic and portray, in a fine and sensitive manner, the feelings of an intellectual woman who works in the villages as a doctor and tries to cope with the prejudices and cultural hostility of peasant and working-class society.

What is persistent in women's Realist literature throughout the century is that the criticism of society is made through depictions of women's lives. The great theme, in very different stories of the turn of the century, is that of happiness as imagined by the new woman.[124] This is also manifested in a number of story titles. Female happiness is the particular topic explored by Lidiia Ivanovna Veselitskaia (V. Mikulich, 1857–1936). In her humorous trilogy about Mimi ('Mimi the Bride' ('Mimochka – nevesta', 1883), 'Mimi

---

123. Mildred Davies, 'Valentina Dmitrieva (1859–1947)', in *Russian Women Writers*, ed. by Christine D. Tomei, II, 625–48 (631).
124. Irina Kazakova, 'Problema schast'ia v proizvedeniiakh russkikh pisatel'nits rubezha vekov', in *Vestnik proekta 'novye vozmozhnosti dlia zhenshchin'. Zhenshchina i kul'tura.* (Moscow: ITs NZhF, 1997), no. 9, 40–45 (40).

at the Spa' ('Mimochka na vodakh', 1891) and 'Mimi Poisoned Herself' ('Mimochka otravilas'', 1893), the author shows the 'commonest story of an upper-class woman', one of the Mimis and her *maman*. Mimi's story of boredom and dependence is, as it were, the latest link in the chain of frustrated heroines beginning with those of Bunina, Gan and Rostopchina. Why is Mimi not happy? She could dance, draw and play the piano quite well, but her soul was not ready for life. The author points out critically that the woman question is not only an economic, but also a moral question, in the sense that women should learn to take care of themselves and dare to make their own decisions. Marriage is not the only option any more, as the contemporary woman critic, E. Koltonovskaia wrote in her essay on Ol'ga Shapir's novella, *They Didn't Believe Her* (*Ne poverili*, 1904): 'Women of the bourgeois class understood that their salvation was in work'.[125]

The new moral and cultural values were now embodied by new women, who no longer only expressed the '*desire* for a profession in the abstract',[126] but were shown in their actual professional lives, where, though exploited and victimized, they were responsible for their actions. This is the topic of many stories, such as 'A Peasant Woman's Tears' ('Bab'i slezy', 1898), or 'Holiday' ('Otdykh', 1896), another strong story by Ekaterina Pavlovna Letkova (1856–1937), or 'Daughter of the People' ('Doch' naroda', 1904) by Anastas'iia Romanovna Krandievskaia (1865–1938), where the working-class girl goes her own independent way, notwithstanding the patronizing expectations of her two upper-class benefactresses. The traditional escape plot is now transferred to the working-class context and the new heroine's active stance is motivated by her professional commitment.[127] The new heroine is a cook's daughter who is becoming a teacher, as in Khvoshchinskaia's novella, *The Schoolmistress* (*Uchitel'nitsa*, 1880); and in Ol'ga Shapir's novella, *Avdot'ia's Daughters* (*Avdot'iny dochki*, 1898), Sasha becomes a midwife.

The work of Ol'ga Andreevna Shapir (1850–1916) awaits re-evaluation in the contexts of the history of Russian political movements and the history of Russian literature. Shapir, with more than thirty years of literary activity as a prose-writer and publicist and as an activist of the first wave of the women's movement,[128] was connected with liberal and revolutionary

---

125. E. Koltonovskaia in Kazakova, p. 41.
126. Kelly, *A History of Russian Women's Writing*, p. 143.
127. See Kelly, *A History of Russian Women's Writing*, p. 143.
128. Irina Jukina, 'Pobornitsa zhenskoi svobody', *Preobrazhenie* (1997), 5, 95 and Irina Jukina,

circles and reflected on political debates in many of her writings, such as her novel, *In The Stormy Years* (*V burnye gody*, 1906). She was also deeply involved in the European women's movement and the gender question became the main focus of her literary activities. We would like to point out that her role was, as Kelly has put it, 'in some ways the most "typical"',[129] but also one that gave a unique evaluation of the 'new woman' between historical periods, as Olekhova has pointed out.[130]

In her prose, Shapir develops the themes of female slavery (*rabstvo*), self-definition and the new woman. In her first period (1879–87), she explores female slavery in the novel, *A High Price to Pay: A Family Story* (*Dorogoi tsenoi: iz semeinoi prozy*, 1882), in which a heroine gives herself up totally to the needs of others, rejecting her own career and professional ambitions. An exemplary novel of female slavery is *Funeral Feast* (*Pominki*, 1886), which shows what remains after such a self-abnegating life: after her death, the life of Aunt Katia is barely recalled and her devotion to others is not appreciated by her descendants, indeed quite the opposite. The depiction of female self-abnegation reveals Shapir as a radical cultural critic: she rejects the sacred significance of female self-abnegation asserted by religious ideology. In the period 1879–1904, Shapir accomplishes a gendered inversion whereby, like other contemporary women writers, she replaces male characters with women whose desires and deeds now organize the plot. Shapir creates female characters who, in the 1870s and 1880s, still have to fight the same battles as the heroines from the beginning of the century, but then grow into independent 'new women', as envisioned by the socialist feminist Aleksandra Kollontai in her political essays and fiction written at the beginning of the twentieth century. As did many of her women contemporaries, Shapir explores the modern conditions of the 'new woman and contributes to the genre development of the Russian woman's novel'.[131] She combines the Realist traditions of her female predecessors, didactic and schematic plot lines with sharp and sensitive focus on society's new class hierarchies in order

---

'Zabytaia feministka Ol'ga Shapir', in *Vestnik proekta 'Novye vozmozhnosti dlia zhenshchin'*, pp. 21–39.
129. Kelly, *A History of Russian Women's Writing*, p. 181.
130. Irina P. Olekhova, *Belletristika O. A. Shapir: osobennosti problematiki i poetiki. Avtoreferat na soiskanie uchenoi stepeni kanditata fil. nauk* (Tver': Tverskoi gosudarstvennyi universitet, 2005).
131. Tatjana Antalovsky, *Der russische Frauenroman 1890–1917. Exemplarische Untersuchungen* (München: Slavistische Beiträge, Bd. 213, 1987).

to combine class and gender perspectives. It is the working-class woman whose life and setting the author vividly depicts in detail, and who, the author believes, is ready to take up the challenges of the modern world. The new woman is shown in contrast to an 'old' woman, like Eva in *One Woman of Many* (*Odna iz mnogikh*, 1897), or like Lidiia and Rita from the novel *Antipodes* (*Antipody*, 1880), both being figures of transformation but with different kinds of life strategies. Common to the new heroines is challenge to the tragic image – 'All or Nothing'[132] – of the woman in Russian literature.

The new woman reappears in the later work, such as the novels *Mirages* (*Mirazhi*, 1889) and *In The Stormy Years*. In the latter, Shapir shows three models for women which were possible in the 1870s-1880s, symbolized by three sisters: one embodies the female self-abnegation of a revolutionary, the second devotes herself to the medical profession and the third takes part in the 'stormy years' as an adventurous game. Shapir broadens the woman question, not only emphasizing work, but also the aim for equality in difference;[133] the new woman strives for independence in life and love. The author makes her new heroine reject the culture of 'slavish'[134] self-abnegation (*smirenie*) and self-victimization, the highly idealized values cultivated by Russian philosophical and aesthetic discourse as essential markers of a Russian woman.[135] In 1896–1904, the new woman is formed in such novels as *She Returned* (*Vernulas'*, 1892) and *Avdot'ia's Daughters* and the story 'Dunechka' ('Dunechka', 1904), where the main motif, the path, emphasizes the heroine's departure for a new foreign world. Shapir shows the difficult psychological obstacles that the new woman has to overcome. The author encourages the heroines to make their own decisions, however painful. The heroines are fatherless and mothers play an important role, not so much as educators, but rather as allies. Shapir recalls the literary tradition of her female predecessors, while simultaneously adopting the new possibilities given to women writers within the expanded ideological differentiation of Realism and within the feminist movement.

On this basis she realizes the aesthetics of difference. Shapir's gender awareness allows her to recognize the double standard of Russian literary critics who praise the male pen as the norm and devalue women's literature as second-rate. For Shapir the aim was to speak 'on behalf of women', not

---

132. Quoted by Jukina, in *Vestnik proekta 'novye vozmozhnosti dlia zhenshchin*, p. 27.
133. Jukina, 'Zabytaia feministka Ol'ga Shapir', p. 35.
134. Jukina, 'Zabytaia feministka Ol'ga Shapir', pp. 25–26.
135. See Oleg Riabov, *"Matushka-Rus'"* (Moscow: Ladomir, 2001), pp. 69–71.

to 'imitate the masculine pen'.[136] Not so much equality, as the equal value of gender difference, was Shapir's principal aim, which made her one of the most interesting and important feminist writers of the late nineteenth century.

A genre able to react to the social and cultural ambitions of the new broad reading public, to popular culture, as well as to the challenges and opportunities for writers in the new market-driven publishing world, was the sensational novel. The definition of the genre used by scholars[137] identifies its earlier Western European model and emphasizes its popularity, the material success of its authors, its woman-centred topics and characters and the female readers and writers. The women's sensational novel developed in the first decade of the twentieth century and became a best-seller which appealed above all to women, of all classes. It was a product of new aesthetic preferences, new kinds of fantasies and new forms of distribution by literary and commercial institutions.

Amongst the best-selling women novelists of the early twentieth century were Nadezhda Aleksandrovna Lappo-Danilevskaia (1874–1951),[138] Evdokiia Apollonovna Nagrodskaia (1866–1930), with her novels *The Wrath of Dionysus* (*Gnev Dionisa*, 1910) and *The Bronze Door* (*Bronzovaia dver'*, 1911), and Lidiia Alekseevna Charskaia (1875–1937), the celebrated children's writer.[139] The most famous was the playwright, prose-writer and publisher, Anastasiia Alekseevna Verbitskaia (1861–1928), with her massive romance novels. Verbitskaia's blockbusters were enormously popular among middlebrow readers, the target of highbrow attacks and were later rejected from the Soviet canon as pornographic and decadent. They are part of Russian and women's literary history, from the 1880s to the 1920s, and reach out to contemporary popular literature, merging literary and commercial impulses. With numerous editions of her works, Verbitskaia achieved a commercial success unparalleled in her time; this was later on achieved for other women too, as their publisher presented motifs and relationships

---

136. Irina Kazakova, 'Shapir, Ol'ga Andreevna', in *Dictionary of Russian Women Writers*, ed. by Marina Ledkovsky, Charlotte Rosenthal, Mary Zirin, pp. 577–80 (579).
137. See, for example, Marsh, 'Realist Prose Writers, 1881–1929', pp. 194–96 and Kelly, *A History of Russian Women's Writing*, pp. 149–52.
138. Her popular novels include, *The Minister's Wife* (*Zhena ministra*, 1912), *Princess Mara* (*Kniazhnia Mara*, 1914), *A Russian Gentleman* (*Russkii barin*, 1914) and *The Duty of Life* (*Dolg zhizni*, 1917).
139. Ruth Zernova and Evgeniia Putilova, 'Charskaia, Lidiia Alekseevna', in *Dictionary of Russian Women Writers*, ed. by Marina Ledkovsky, Charlotte Rosenthal, Mary Zirin, pp. 120–23.

that were repeated and varied by women prose-writers over the next three decades.[140]

Verbitskaia combines art and entertainment in a successful and appealing way, which invites readers to participate in the current, decadent lifestyle of self-gratification and sexual pleasures. The novels combine art, love, politics, personal freedom, philosophical and cultural trends and social and national types, attitudes and lifestyles, into a 'kind of cultural department store',[141] urging readers to 'shop for everything from Isadora Duncan to Nietzsche, Social Darwinism, anti-Semitism and Kraft-Ebbing's sexual theories as an explanation of mental disease'.[142] This 'digestible package, a consuming read',[143] coupled with 'an active social consciousness, a willingness to write for the market and a desire to popularize the messages worked out in "high" cultural forms for the rapidly growing "middlebrow" audience',[144] characterize her best-sellers, *The Spirit of the Time* (*Dukh vremeni*, 1906), *The Keys to Happiness* (*Kliuchi schast'ia*, 1908–1913) and the trilogy *Yoke of Love* (*Igo liubvi*, 1914). All her novels cross boundaries of gender and class. She emphasizes women's right to sexual desire 'not constrained by guilt',[145] making these novels innovative and radical. An example is the new heroine Mania El'tsova in *The Keys to Happiness*, an unconventional and liberated woman whose stormy life is recounted through various sexual entanglements and international artistic success. The significance of Verbitskaia's literature lies in her willingness to show independent-thinking women from various classes challenging social expectations, even if paying a price in personal happiness. Verbitskaia's novel transcends its own time:[146] she explores themes still relevant to women and her work invites the reader to see parallels between her *fin-de-siècle* pot-boilers and today's popular fiction where women writers again play a central role, introducing

---

140. Charlotte Rosenthal, 'Achievement and Obscurity: Women's Prose in the Silver Age', in *Women Writers in Russian* Literature, ed. by Toby W. Clyman and Diana Green, pp. 149–70 (153).
141. Laura Engelstein, *The Key to Happiness: Sex and the Search for Modernity in Fin-de-Siecle Russia* (Princeton: Princeton University Press, 1992), p. 404.
142. Natasha Kolchevska, 'Anastasiia Verbitskaia (1861–1928)', in *Russian Women Writers*, I, 605–24 (609).
143. Beth Holmgren, Helena Goscilo, 'Introduction. Who Was Anastasya Verbitskaya?', in Anastasya Verbitskaya, *Keys to Happiness*, trans. and ed. by Beth Holmgren and Helena Goscilo (Bloomington and Indianapolis: Indiana University Press, 1999), pp. xi-xxix (xiii).
144. Kolchevska, 'Anastasiia Verbitskaia (1861–1928)', p. 609.
145. Kelly, *A History of Russian Women's Writing*, p. 151.
146. Rosalind Marsh, 'Anastasiia Verbitskaia Reconsidered', in *Gender and Russian Literature*, pp. 184–205, p. 199.

readers to, and educating them about, new market-led lifestyles, depicting women's sexual and emotional differences from men, and as did Verbitskaia, introducing the new woman and reforming her sexual, emotional and intellectual capacity. Without doubt the appearance of women writers in the field of mass literature and their popularity among the readers can be seen as an innovative break. On the other hand, however, while women did write bestsellers, they wrote popular literature, which was not highly appreciated by the old elite. Women still wrote at the margins, i.e. in the field of popular culture, which was still young and uncanonized within Russian literature. From the point of view of the critics they still remained second-rank writers: here we also recognize the double standard which would take place in Russian Modernism and Symbolism as well: on the one hand, women authors enjoyed success among the readers and actively took part in the literary process, on the other hand, their literary work was not valued by established critical opinion.

Just as the first appearance of women on the literary stage in the early nineteenth century was a collective action, no less distinguished, strong and original was the literary performance of women authors at the end of the century. Charlotte Rosenthal perceives the richness of women's voices during that period: 'the Silver Age period was more a Golden Age for women writers, especially for female lyric poets'.[147] Apart from poetry, she also refers to the new 'women's novel' as a new genre and draws the conclusion, which has received general assent, that 'the modernist movement proved to be especially beneficial to women'.[148] Catriona Kelly, defining the years 1880–1917 as a distinguished period in women's literary history, also suggests that 'this era saw women prose writers develop a multi-faceted and powerful critical-realist tradition, but that it also saw an increase in the power and dynamism of a contradictory, anti-realist, tradition'.[149] It is quite easy to trace the different traditions of the period: the Realist narrative practised in 'thick journals', the sensational novel and Symbolist and post-Symbolist writing, mostly poetry, published in art journals and literary almanacs.

---

147. Charlotte Rosenthal, 'The Silver Age: A Highpoint for Women?', in *Women and Society in Russia and the Soviet Union*, ed. by Linda Edmondson (Cambridge: Cambridge University Press, 1992), pp. 32–47 (32).
148. Rosenthal, 'The SilverAge: A Highpoint for Women?' p. 32.
149. Kelly, *A History of Russian Women's Writing*, p. 13.

The Golden Age of Modernist women writers and the diversification of women's writing were linked to the discourse of crisis, which targeted the understanding of gender and femininity; this discourse emphasized disruption and the shaking foundations of Realism and Positivism, which would fracture in several directions, theoretical, political and aesthetic. In the spirit of the Nietzschean Superman, intellectuals were looking for the philosophical, 'other-than the rational subject'.[150] Women writers benefited from this concept of the unique personality to legitimate their literary activity and subject identities as artist and author.[151] Simultaneously, however, they had to resist the expectations that women were not creators, but rather objects of art. The Modernist period was thus highly contradictory for women's literary ambitions.

Femininity was given a central role in literary-philosophical discourses, both in popular and elite thinking. Especially for the Russian Symbolists, the feminine was essential to the aesthetic concept based on the utopian unity of dual forces beyond the real and the ideal realms. Femininity was endowed with the utopian and mythical powers of a mediator between the cosmic and earthly worlds, quite like the religio-mystical Eternal Femininity of Solov'ev's philosophical concept of the Divine Sophia which, together with Otto Weininger's ideas of gendered creativity in his *Geschlecht und Charakter* (1903), influenced the Symbolists' aesthetic aspirations.

However, as the critical research on Symbolism has shown,[152] the fact that gender was discovered as a layer of the human subject and that femininity had a firm place in modernist and Symbolist discourse did not mean that women were accepted as creative equals to men. The feminine category was perceived as the Other, a mirror, a reflection for the male creator's construction: it covered the unconscious forces of creativity, was comprehended as the 'other' to the masculine category in the complementary models of modernism, like androgyny. In Symbolist aesthetics the feminine was the material of art. Women writers, not accepted as purveyors of signs, functioned as signs for the male creator in need of a Muse and this became the main function for women in the social and the aesthetic world divided by gender roles and dominated by Symbolist men.[153]

---

150. Rosi Braidotti, *Patterns of Dissonance* (Cambridge: Cambridge University Press, 1991), p. 10.
151. Alla Gracheva, 'Russkoe nitssheanstvo i zhenskii roman nachala XX veka', in *Gender Restructuring in Russian Studies*, pp. 87–98.
152. Jenifer Presto, 'Women in Russian Symbolism: Beyond the Algebra of Love', in *A History of Women's Writing in Russia*, pp. 134–52; Kirsti Ekonen, *Tvorets, sub''ekt, zhenshchina: Strategii zhenskogo pis'ma v russkom simvolizme* (Moscow: Novoe literaturnoe obozrenie, 2011); see also Kelly, *A History of Russian Women's Writing*, pp. 161–72.
153. Presto, pp. 134–35; Ekonen, pp. 61–103.

Many women writers took up Decadent crisis discourse in order to reflect upon, and to clarify, what the mystic feminine meant for themselves. They expressed discomfort with the stereotype of reduction to a sign for the male interpreter and the function granted to women by Symbolist theory. They tested and varied representations of the Eternal Feminine and developed strategies of inversion accomplished by mimicry and deconstruction of dual gender hierarchies. Women writers reacted differently to expectations of them as women and poets. Their poetic and cultural strategies often remained ambiguous, like the practices of mimicry and subversion, which approached each other when women played out the function of the mystical Muse or the *femme fatale*. This is what, for example, Liudmila Vil'kina (1873–1920) did in her poetry. In her sonnet collection, *My Garden* (*Moi sad*, 1906), her aim is to identify feminine creative subjectivity. As Kirsti Ekonen has argued, she does this in ways similar to those identified decades later by Western feminist theoreticians such as Luce Irigaray,[154] by aspiring to language which is woman-centred, even within a male-centred world. Vil'kina tried to find her own womanly voice, but ended by saying farewell to the 'strange and dead words' of the Symbolist 'house of language'.[155] She turned towards a new kind of not-yet-existing language, embedded in the bonding between historical Russian women authors, such as Pavlova, and mythological female figures, such as Antigone. The strategy of turning towards something not yet in existence can be interpreted as unproductive, leaving *My Garden* as Vil'kina's sole published book, alienated outside the Symbolist context. Her voice was, however, original and innovative, premature in its form. Such was also that of many other highly talented and independent women writers of the modernist period, as Poliksena Sergeevna Solov'eva (1867–1924), Nina Ivanovna Petrovskaia (1884–1928)[156] and Lidia Zinov'eva-Annibal. Even if forgotten by high literature, their

---

154. Ekonen, pp. 195–235.
155. Ekonen, pp. 231, 234.
156. In her story, 'The Unheard-of Woman' ('Nebyvalaia', 1912), Poliksena Solov'eva depicts the relationship between a male philosopher and the muse, showing the muse as a product of male 'creative genius', without any empirical presence. Nina Petrovskaia, conventionally interpreted by literary history scholars as the very symbol of Decadence, rejects in her collection of stories *Sanctus amor* (1908) the mystification and metaphorifization of womanhood, revealing herself in her own works as anti-decadent, see Ekonen, pp. 236–61 and pp. 262–96; Nancy L. Cooper, 'Secret Truths and Unheard-of Women; Poliksena Solov'eva's Fiction as Commentary on Vladimir Solov'ev's Theory of Love', *Russian Review*, 56 (1997), 178–91.

voices are embedded in the heritage taken over by Russian women writers now, at the end of the twentieth century, which is again another period involved with crisis discourse and post-modern poetics' challenging role with its innovative woman-centred *écriture feminine*.

Modernist aesthetic movements demonstrate the double positioning of women writers and the split in their psycho-cultural identity which can easily be recognized throughout the nineteenth century: women writers were both in and outside the androcentric sphere of culture and women's writing, whether located at the margins of the system in a kind of alternative space, or integrated into the system and subject to its rules, was always dependent of the male canon. Its specific character was in relation to what was allowed to male writers, either as an overvaluation of, or as a rejection of, the male canon.[157] This becomes obvious in relation to the Symbolist movement. Women were given the right to join the cultural context, but in writing they had to cut themselves out of the concept of male interpretation of femininity, and go their own ways, stressful and lonely, without associating with any literary circle, a characteristic feature of Russian women's literary history during the nineteenth century. Crisis discourse, which sought to replace the exhausted canons, emphasizing difference, was the space which women adopted to their advantage for their aim at self-assertion by aesthetic performance. Esteemed forms of aesthetic activity were replaced by re-valued forms of creative communication, such as the salons which re-emerged as the space for women to combine public and private, pre-aesthetic and the high poetic of Symbolic aesthetics.

Zinaida Nikolaevna Gippius (1869–1945) was not only a famous *salonnière* in Petersburg and Paris, but a central figure in Symbolism, who influenced other women poets in several ways. She was a brilliant and innovative poet, a prose-writer, a productive critic and one of the few women canonized by high literature.[158] Her strong, masculine narrator's voice is heard above all in her poetry whose topics are often more spiritual, although they do not avoid the corporeal either. Gippius is exemplary in showing us that whatever aesthetic strategy and ideological position women writers of the Modernist period took up, they were forced to deal with femininity. She also discussed the female creator's subjectivity as a theoretical question in her essay,

---

157. Renate Lachmann, 'Thesen zu einer weiblichen Aesthetik', in *Weiblichkeit oder Feminismus*, edited by Claudia Opitz (Konstanz: Weingarten, 1984), pp. 181–94 (182).
158. Ekonen, pp. 153–94.

'The Beast-God' ('Zverebog', 1908), which deals with the double standards in the cultural sphere for men and women and criticizes femininity for its polarized essence, as a beast in the empirical world and as god, a feminine principle.[159] Femininity in its Symbolist contexts is the topic of many of her poems.[160] However, Gippius does not grant female creativity any positive qualities, even though she sees a special role for it in its utopian mode – as a metaphor for the new people in the stadium when the polarized relation between the sexes is overcome.[161] Like other women writers within the Symbolist context, Gippius also aimed to exceed dualist binaries. The strategy of androgyny, displaying herself as an extraordinary individual merging feminine and masculine categories, led her, however, into a dilemma: she was both inside and outside, an active stranger in the Symbolist circles where she saw women's experiences differing from those of men, though herself as a creative exception amongst women.[162] She adopted the canonical male voice for her poetry, as the active and creative agent (the spirit), while marking the feminine as the voice for passive contemplation (the soul).[163] She also irritated the public by creating contradictory images of the self, both in her art and her life, that made her virtually unreadable within the established gender binaries of Symbolist dualism.[164]

Finally, the gendered dilemma of the Symbolist movement is made obvious by the literary career of Lidia Dmitrievna Zinov'eva-Annibal (1866–1907), the Diotima of Russian Symbolism. Her biography has two versions: the first shows her as part of the life-creation (*zhiznetvorchestvo*) practicing within high Symbolist circles (along with her famous husband and the leading ideologist, Viacheslav Ivanov), where she is the embodiment of the Symbolist image of woman as the ideal Muse and passive object of worship; the second version shows her finding her own independent voice while writing herself out of Symbolist aesthetics.[165] The latter development is marked by a number of original works, including her play, *The Singing Ass* (*Pevuchii osel*, 1907), the short story 'Thirty-three Abominations' ('Tridtsat' tri uroda', 1907) and a collection of semi-autobiographical

---

159. Ekonen, pp. 158, 160, 174.
160. Ekonen analyses, for example, the poems 'Ona 1', 'Ona 2', 'Zhenskost'' and 'Vechnozhenstvennoe'.
161. Ekonen pp. 187–88.
162. Ekonen, p. 160.
163. Kelly, *A History of Russian Women's Writing*, p. 169.
164. Presto, p. 144.
165. Ekonen, p. 148–49.

short stories, *The Tragic Menagerie* (*Tragicheskii zverinets*, 1907). Already in *The Singing Ass,* Zinov'eva-Annibal responds to Symbolist ideas with 'ironic satire and subversion rather than [...] supportive echo', as Pamela Davidson has shown.[166] In 'Thirty-three Abominations', she shows that the construction of a female author-subject on the basis of the metaphors offered by Symbolist aesthetics was impossible and the gender discourse of the Symbolists became an object of parody. The story, which is based on the diary of the female narrator, tells the love story of two women actresses. The setting is the apartment of one of the women, and they never leave it, except at the end; in the catastrophic culmination, Vera sacrifices her love and the narrator to pose in front of thirty-three painters, who produce thirty-three abominations, but cannot reproduce the original. Vera commits suicide and the female narrator becomes a mistress of one of the male painters. The story is, obviously, metaliterary, taking place in the world of art and dealing with central categories of Symbolist aesthetics, such as mirrors and masks; it uses mimicry as the main strategy, in order to subvert the object of its parody, Symbolist aesthetics.[167] In the context of Symbolism, parodying mimicry shows that life cannot be turned into art, yet that art has an influence on life, like the thirty-three abominations which did change the women's lives.[168]

If 'Thirty-three Abominations' is the work of transformation showing the uselessness of Symbolist mythology for female creativity, *The Tragic Menagerie* is the key work, original and expressive, endowed with deep identity as well as with desire for an autonomous and female-centred world beyond isolation within male-centred cultural institutions. The work demonstrates the author's way of finding her own language while freeing herself from alien roles and the pressure of masculine inversion. The stories narrate the journey of a girl's self-discovery as an inner drama, where emotions and experiences are perceived in sensory contact with nature, animals and one's own body. It is this positive mythology of the 'green world'[169] that enables the author to name and to give shape to her creative existence beyond dualities and binaries. According to Costlow, 'as an account of the author's own genesis, *The Tragic Menagerie* imagines verbal creativity

---

166. Pamela Davidson, 'Lidiia Zinov'eva-Annibal's *The Singing Ass:* a Woman's View on Men and Eros', in *Gender and Russian Literature*, pp. 155–83 (163).
167. Ekonen, p. 305.
168. Ekonen, pp. 315, 318.
169. Annis Pratt, *Archetypal Patterns in Women's Fiction* (Bloomington: Indiana University Press, 1981).

grounded in a profound, often anarchic connection to Nature. A woman of profound imagination finds liberation not only from the constraints of scholarly institution and the "stone prison" of the city, but from words of authority that do not name her experience'.[170] Zinov'eva-Annibal's works emphasize that just as there is an inter-relationship between life and art, there is also a relationship between creativity, art and the natural world, where the human is embedded within. The dilemmas of human embeddedness in nature, as part of meadows, forests, seas and the animal world, as well as in our own animal nature, imply a more broadly painted view of the world and the future: with its implicit ecological visions the author 'suggest[s] that the destruction of nature is also a destruction of ourselves'.[171] In her critical voice protesting against the inequities between nature and culture, Zinov'eva-Annibal constitutes an important nodal point; her work reminds readers of the important role played by nature in nineteenth-century women's writing and speaks to future women writers who react to the environmentally and spiritually ravaged world of the post-Soviet period. With many other women writers from the turn of the century and the Silver Age, Zinov'eva-Annibal sank into oblivion for two generations of Russian readers; many abandoned fiction, and took to other literary activities, as editors, translators and reviewers, or went over to children's literature, as did Krestovskaia, Letkova, Shchepkina-Kupernik, Militsyna, Gurevich, Dmitrieva and Verbitskaia.

There were a number of writers of the twentieth century who were to take up the heritage of earlier generations and give shape to a new and original voice in Russian literature. Amongst them were such innovative authors as Sofiia Iakovlevna Parnok (1885–1933), Adelaida Kazimirovna Gertsyk (1874–1925) and Elizaveta Iurievna Kuzmina-Karavaeva (1891–1945), as well as the already well-known and great creators of Russian poetry, Marina Tsvetaeva and Anna Akhmatova. Throughout the nineteenth century, Russian women poets and prose-writers were engaged in the challenge trying to work out 'how women should write'. In literature-centred Russian culture, literature was always endowed with special ideological obligations that were, as a consequence of the high status of literature, submitted to rigorous control. The terms pointing to women and women's

---

170. Jane Costlow, 'The Gallop, the Wolf, the Caress: Eros and Nature in the Tragic Menagerie' *Russian Review,* 56.2 (1997), 192–08 (206).
171. Jane Costlow, 'Introduction', in Lydia Zinovieva-Annibal, *The Tragic Menagerie,* trans. by Jane Costlow (Evanston, Illinois: Northwestern University Press, 1999), pp. xi-xxi, p. xx.

practices of writing were used by the dominant patriarchal discourse in the cultural and ideological struggles: in the debates between 'archaists' and 'reformers' at the beginning of the nineteenth century, in the discourse on social emancipation and the 'woman question', in philosophical concepts of Russian Symbolism, and so on. The use of these gendered terms reveals that real women and the practices of their writing were set aside and ignored, displaced into Otherness, as an outcome of a structural marginalization and colonization of women's literature. Nevertheless, as we hope to have shown, women of the nineteenth century did not only accept the challenge and learn to answer the male questions, but they learned to formulate their own questions and topics. They broke out of the silence, adopted various genres, topics and narrative strategies. They learned to communicate while writing and they created a tradition, which was not – or to a very small extent – noticed by contemporary male critics. Meanwhile, we know that the history of Russian women's writing is not only a history of 'facts', neither is the silence, nor invisibility a proof of women's non-existence in literary history. Feminist literary criticism has succeeded in its task to narrate, and accordingly, to create a tradition of Russian women's literature of the nineteenth century to be passed on to successive generations.

9. Between Law and Morality: Violence against Women in Nineteenth-Century Russia

Marianna G. Muravyeva

One winter's day in 1883, the people of Chuguevo witnessed a woman harnessed to a cart, running alongside the horse to the cheerful jeering of her husband and father-in-law who were driving. The woman was badly beaten and soon lost consciousness. Later, when the case went to the local court, the villagers would learn that these two men had brought her back home, continued beating her and, finally, gang-raped her.[1] This story, reported by one of the central Russian newspapers, *Moskovskie vedomosti*, represents all the hardships Russian peasant women were experiencing in the nineteenth century. They could be punished by their husbands for the slightest disobedience, they could be regularly abused by their husbands' family members, and they could be raped by their fathers-in-law with the participation of their husbands. Yet, it was extremely difficult for these women to find justice.

In the nineteenth century, educated Russians paid quite a lot of attention to the situation of peasant women and asked uneasy questions about why and how the things described above could happen in their progressive and enlightened age. In the wake of the 'woman question', intellectuals,

---

I would like to express my deep gratitude to Christina Worobec for her helpful and excellent suggestions for improvement of this chapter.

1. 'Iz Chugueva soobshchaiut…', *Moskovskie vedomosti*, 29 March 1883, no. 88, 3.

statesmen, scholars and lawyers, while examining the legal and social status of women in Russian society, portrayed a horrifying picture of violence against women, employed by men to keep their wives and daughters in absolute subjection. Historians such as Serafim Shashkov, Il'ia Orshanskii, Aleksandr Savel'ev, Aleksandr Zagorovskii, Iakov Kantorovich and many others believed that the enormous scale of abuse was due to the low status of Russian women and patriarchal attitudes towards the family.[2] They also invoked a popular discourse of barbarity, stating that their low cultural standing prompted Russian men to beat, rape and torment their wives and daughters; they also suggest that, with the slow coming of civilization to Russia after Peter I's reforms in the early eighteenth century, at least the educated elite started to treat women as equals.[3] These ideas were further developed and supported by Soviet historiography that had its own ideological agenda for portraying the decay of the tsarist regime and the inevitability of revolution and popular uprisings against injustice and exploitation. The unenviable situation of women became one of the central illustrations of the despotism and tyranny penetrating Russian society at all levels from the common family to royalty.[4] But lately post-Soviet Russian historiography, with the help of Western colleagues, has been trying to argue that Russian women of all classes were not so unequal to men, that their status was much higher than we used to think, and that their position within the family was respected, although not without certain reservations.[5]

---

2. Serafim Shashkov, *Istoricheskie sud'by zhenshchiny, detoubiistvo i prostitutsiia* (St Petersburg: N. A. Shigin, 1871); Serafim Shashkov, *Istoriia russkoi zhenshchiny* (St Petersburg: Novoe vremia, 1879); Il'ia Zagorovskii, *Issledovaniia po russkomu pravu, obychnomu i brachnomu* (St Petersburg: A. E. Landau, 1879); Aleksandr Zagorovskii, *O razvode po russkomu pravu* (Khar'kov: M. F. Zil'berberg, 1884); Iakov Kantorovich, *Zhenshchina v prave* (St Petersburg: Ia. Kantorovich, 1895).
3. D. Bobrov, 'Po povodu bab'ikh stonov', *Iuridicheskii vestnik*, 10 (1885), 318–22; [A.] Vereshchagin, 'O bab'ikh stonah', *Iuridicheskii vestnik*, 4 (1885), 750–61; Ia. A. Ludmer, 'Bab'i stony: iz zametok mirovogo sud'i', *Iuridicheskii vestnik*, 11 (1884), 446–67; 12, 658–79; N. D[emert], 'Ugolovnoe proizvodstvo po supruzheskim delam', *Otechestvennye zapiski*, 12 (1872), 326–40; N. Demert, 'Nashi obshchestvennye dela', *Otechestvennye zapiski*, 12 (1872), 80–110. See this discussion in the context of abolishing corporal punishment for women: Abby M. Schrader, *Languages of the Lash. Corporal Punishment and Identity in Imperial Russia* (DeKalb, IL.: Northern Illinois University Press, 2002), pp. 161–68.
4. T. A. Bernshtam, *Molodezh v obriadovoi zhizni russkoi obshchiny XIX – nachala XX veka* (Leningrad: Nauka, 1988); M. M. Gromyko, *Mir russkoi derevni* (Moscow: Molodaia gvardiia, 1991); S. S. Kriukova, *Russkaia krestianskaia sem'ia vo vtoroi polovine XIX v.* (Moscow: IAE RAN, 1994); A. A. Minenko, *Zhivaia starina: Budni i prazdniki sibirskoi derevni v XVII –pervoi polovine XIX veka* (Novosibirsk: Nauka, 1989).
5. See, for example: V. A. Veremenko, 'Supruzheskie otnosheniia v dvorianskikh sem'iakh Rossii vo vtoroi polovine XIX–nachale XX veka: etapy evolutsii', in *Sotsial'naia istoriia:*

This trend comes mostly from research on the seventeenth and eighteenth centuries and creates an uneasy discrepancy with the nineteenth century. The main question here is why relatively powerful and well-protected Russian women suddenly turned into the powerless and abused chattels of their families?[6] What happened in the first half of the nineteenth century that demoted Russian women to the lowest level ever? Why did protection from rape, allegedly high in the seventeenth century, suddenly cease in the nineteenth century and leave women alone to prove their right to bodily integrity? This essay tries to suggest some answers by focusing on two important identifiers of gender inequality: sexual and domestic violence.

Public Violence against Women: Rape

It is difficult to provide a cohesive scholarship of rape in Russia: the social history of rape still needs to be written.[7] However, some historians of Slavic women have studied rape in the context of sexuality and patriarchy, using original court cases. Eve Levin, Nancy Shields Kollmann and Dan Kaiser came to the conclusion that Russian women in the seventeenth century, even prostitutes and those with a poor reputation, enjoyed solid protection.[8] The Military Code of 1716 explicitly stated that prostitutes could be raped, and thus needed equal protection.[9] This section will focus on the legal attitude to rape and other forms of sexual violence to highlight the ways sexual violence was constructed in relation to the male anxieties about false accusations and emerging bourgeois femininity. We will further see how these attitudes made it to the court room and whether women of all classes enjoyed the same proclaimed protection of their 'honour'.

Ezhegodnik, ed. by Natal'ia L. Pushkareva (Moscow: Aleteiia, 2008), pp. 47–66; Michelle L. Marrese, *A Woman's Kingdom: Noblewomen and the Control of Property in Russia, 1700–1861* (Ithaca and London: Cornell University Press, 2002).

6. M. Marrese, 'Gender and Legal Order in Imperial Russia', in *The Cambridge History of Russia*, ed. by Dominic Lieven, 3 vols (Cambridge: Cambridge University Press, 2006), II, 335–39; Daniel Kaiser, '"He Said, She Said": Rape and Gender Discourse in Early Modern Russia', *Kritika: Explorations in Russia and Eurasian History*, 3 (2002), 197–216.
7. For a discussion of the 'blank spot', in the historiography, see Marianna Muravyeva, 'Metodologicheskie problemy sovremennoi istoriografii seksual'nogo nasiliia na Zapade i v Rossii', *Gendernye issledovaniia*, 13 (2005), 171–89.
8. Daniel Kaiser, '"He Said, She Said"...'; Eve Levin, *Sex and Society in the World of the Orthodox Slavs, 900–1700* (Ithaca: Cornell University Press, 1989), pp. 212–46; Nancy Shields Kollmann, *By Honor Bound. State and Society in Early Modern Russia* (Ithaca: Cornell University Press, 1999), pp. 72–82.
9. 'Artikul Voinskii', in *Zakonodatel'stvo perioda stanovleniia absolutizma*, ed. by A. G. Man'kov (Moscow: Iuridicheskaia literatura, 1986), art. 167 commentary, p. 359.

There are more or less cohesive criminal statistics for the period between 1834 and 1899[10] which indicate that rape constituted only around 1–2% of all crimes reported in the Russian Empire, with a sharp rise in the 1880s to 3.5%. These numbers suggest a high underreporting of crimes. Only 8% of those accused of rape received sentences. The reporting of the crime was uneven in different parts of the Empire: there were higher numbers of reported rapes coming from Southern Russia (the Simferopol', Kherson and Ekaterinoslav regions) and from the Perm' region.[11]

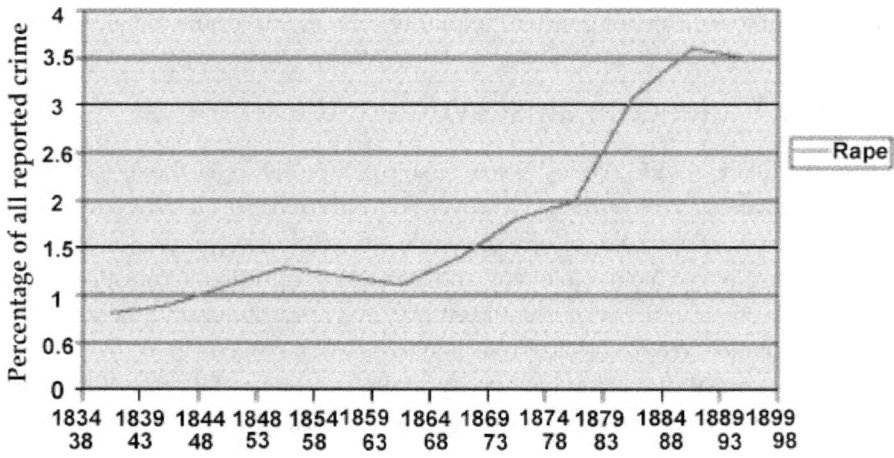

Fig. 6   The dynamics of rape, 1834-1899.

Criminal statistics provide only a glimpse into the true situation and illuminate the state's attitude to crime reporting and conviction practices. The leading numbers among reported crimes usually belong to property crimes (40 per cent of all crimes reported) and injuries together with homicide (30 per cent).[12] It is obvious from the given data that sexual violence was not considered a priority in terms of seeking justice; although

---

10. Russia did not have annual crime returns until 1834 when the Ministry of Justice started the systematic collection of criminal data. For the crime returns see [E. N. Tarnovskii], *Itogi ugolovnoi statistiki za 20 let (1874–1894)* (St Petersburg: Tipografiia Pravitel'stvuiushchego Senata, 1899); E. N. Tarnovskii, 'Dvizhenie prestupnosti v Rossiiskoi imperii za 1899–1908', *Zhurnal ministerstva iustitsii*, 9 (1909), 52–99; *Otchet ministerstva iustitsii* (St Petersburg: Ministerstvo iustitsii, 1834–1868).
11. [E. N. Tarnovskii], *Itogi ugolovnoi statistiki za 20 let*, pp. 131–32, 286–87.
12. [E. N. Tarnovskii], *Itogi ugolovnoi statistiki za 20 let*, pp. 131–32, 286–87. On priorities in crime reporting see Stephen P. Frank, *Crime, Cultural Conflict, and Justice in Rural Russia, 1856–1914* (Berkeley: University of California Press, 1999), pp. 3–5, 145–47.

that does not mean it was not regarded as important on the community level and prosecuted in an extra-judicial way.[13]

The treatment of sexual offences in pre-nineteenth-century Russian law[14] was closely tied up with the mid seventeenth-century redefinition of the Church's and state's jurisdictions over sexual offences, when the state took control of rape offences from the Church. Up until the 1830s, Russian courts recognized both state and canon law as valid sources for their rulings. The 1653 version of the *Kormchaia* – the Russian Code of Orthodox law that had Byzantine origins – and acts and ordinances issued by the Holy Synod (created in 1721 as the supreme ecclesiastical authority in the country), the Law Code of 1649 (*Sobornoe Ulozhenie*), the Military Penal Code (1716), the Naval Code (1720) and various acts and ordinances issued by the monarch and state institutions (such as the Senate) were all valid sources of law which Russian courts applied in practice. However, in the area of illicit sexuality it was the Church that provided the legal and ideological framework and primarily prosecuted sex offences in the seventeenth century with the exclusion of rape, which the state prosecuted according to the Law Code of 1649 and Newly Promulgated articles of 1669.[15] The understanding of rape differed between traditional canon law (embodied in the *Kormchaia*) and state law. Thus, according to canon law, rape could only be committed upon a virgin (in the form of violent defloration or *raptus*) or a married woman (in case of abduction or imprisonment by enemy forces during the war). The *Kormchaia* uses only the term *rastlenie* (defloration) to mark sexual assault.[16]

The state's much broader legal term for rape in the seventeenth century – *bludnoe nasil'stvo* – contained everything needed for

---

13. On extra-judicial ways of punishing sexual offences see Stephen P. Frank, *Crime, Cultural Conflict, and Justice in Rural Russia, 1856–1914*, p. 165; Natalia Pushkareva, 'Pozoriashchie nakazaniia dlia zhenshchin v Rossii XIX – nachala XX v.', *Etnograficheskoe obozreniie*, 5 (2009), 120–34.
14. On the legal treatment of sex crimes and sexual violence in pre-nineteenth-century Russia see Marianna Muravyeva, 'Relations sexuelles, fornication et inceste spirituel entre kimovia (campari) dans la culture traditionelle russe', in *Baptiser. Pratique sacramentelle, pratique sociale (XVIe-Xxe siecles)*, ed. by Guido Alfani, Philippe Castagnetti and Vincent Gourdon (Saint Etienne: Publications de l'Universite de Saint-Etienne, 2009), pp. 281–90; Marianna Muravyeva, 'Forms and Methods of Violence Against Women in Eighteenth-Century Russia: Law Against Morality', *Study Group on Eighteenth-Century Russia Newsletter*, 36 (2008), 15–19.
15. 'Sobornoe Ulozhenie 1649 goda', in *Akty zemskikh soborov*, ed. by A. G. Man'kov (Moscow: Iuridicheskaia literatura, 1985), pp. 97, 249; *Polnoe sobranie zakonov Rossiiskoi Imperii* [PSZ] (St Petersburg, 1830), 45 vols, I, no. 441, art. 102, 796.
16. *Kniga glagolemaia Kormchaia* (Moscow: pri Patriarchem dvore, 1653), pp. 19, 44 rev., 104 rev., 140, 181 rev., 232 rev., 273 rev., 386 rev. See Eve Levine's account of religious sources: Eve Levin, *Sex and Society*, pp. 27–35, 220–21.

understanding the act: violation (*nasil'stvo*) of the person's sexual sphere (*blud*). The Law Code of 1649 never mentioned the status of a woman as a marker for legitimate protection, and courts accordingly prosecuted sexual assault committed against any woman, even if she was found not to be a virgin.[17] Virginity was not even directly connected with the notion of 'honour' at the time.[18] Even the Church accepted this idea as, according to Patriarch Adrian's *Instruction to the Churchwardens* of 1697, an unmarried woman who got pregnant as a result of rape and managed to prove it was entitled to a *beschest'e* (dishonour) charge in the form of monetary compensation from the perpetrator.[19] She did not have to prove she had been a virgin prior to the assault.

Eighteenth-century Russian law continued the tradition of classifying rape as a violent crime against a person's security while treating all other sex offences (fornication, adultery, prostitution) as crimes against morality, a practice that was ultimately confirmed by Catherine II's *Instruction* (*Nakaz*) of 1768. Rape belonged to 'crimes against the citizens' security' together with arson and, more specifically, to 'crimes against the right of a citizen to the voluntary disposal of his body', the formula used in the contemporary criminal code (chapter 18).[20] Three crimes were mentioned as violating the security of citizens: kidnapping, *raptus* and rape. All those crimes, in two instances including women, were by nature violent. All women, chaste and unchaste, could be raped, and the rapist was to be punished by death for a complete act and 'at the consideration of a judge' for an attempted rape.[21] All other sex offences belonged to the category of those against 'morality'.

---

17. Both Dan Kaiser and Eve Levin show that various categories of women sought and found justice upon rape charges; many of them were not married, some had ill-reputation, others were prostitutes: Daniel Kaiser, '"He Said, She Said"'; Eve Levin, *Sex and Society*, pp. 212–46.
18. On the concept of honour in Early Modern Russia see Nancy Shields Kollmann, *By Honor Bound. State and Society in Early Modern Russia*, pp. 31–63.
19. *Polnoe Sobranie Zakonov Rossiiskoi Imperii*, 1st series, 45 vols (St Petersburg: v tipografii II otdelenia Sobstvennoi E. I. V. Kantseliarii, 1830), III, 1612, 418. Hereafter *PSZ*
20. The *Nakaz* suggested four groups of crimes: against faith and law, against morality, against peace and against the security of citizens. However, Catherine specifically pointed out that kidnapping and rape violated the citizen's security and all the rest referred to crimes against morality (article 77): Catherine II, 'Nakaz', in *Imperatritsa Ekaterina II, O velichii Rossii* (Moscow: Eksmo, 2003), pp. 78–79.
21. Aleksei Artem'ev, *Kratkoe nachertanie rimskikh i rossiiskikh prav, s pokazaniem kupno oboikh, ravnomerno, kak i chinopolozheniia onykh istorii* (Moscow: pri Imperatorskom Universitete, 1777), pp. 104–09.

Petr Guliaev (1793-after 1833), one of leading criminologists at the time, even considered rape to be a violent crime (*nasil'stvovanie*) that could be committed against both women and men.[22]

By the 1830s, when the first synthesized Code of Laws of the Russian Empire (*Svod zakonov Rossiiskoi Imperii*) was released, Russian legal thought treated various sexual offences according to the object of infringement, thus distinguishing violent crimes from non-violent but nevertheless sinful and depraved sexuality. However, the tradition was quickly broken with M. M. Speranskii's return to office in the late 1820s to finish compiling the *Svod zakonov*. Speranskii's revized *Svod zakonov* (1833) placed all sex offences together, making sex the central focus of these crimes and bringing back the religious attitude to rape as illicit sexual misconduct. Laura Engelstein has reasonably noted that secular standards were finally applied to sexual offences during the criminal code reform of the 1890s. This defined the arena of crime as the field of personal interaction, and was concerned with both the criminal's motivation and the victim's fate, and therefore revized the traditional patterns of hierarchy embedded in religious terms.[23]

Volume 15 of the Code of Laws of 1833, entitled Code of Criminal Laws (*Svod zakonov ugolovnykh*), became the new criminal code. Its selectivity and emphasis on certain aspects of the old laws resulted in major changes in how the state was to prosecute rape. Initially the Code of Criminal Laws divided all sexual offences into three groups: violating social rights by indecent behaviour, offences against family rights, and unlawful satisfaction of carnal passions. It is important to note which offences were considered to be against social and family rights and which ones constituted 'unlawful satisfaction'. The first group included all types of indecent behaviour of officials, both of noble and non-noble status: lechery, drunkenness, indecent behaviour (*zazornaia zhizn'*), gambling, imprudence and unruly public conduct (articles 422–30).[24] Offences against family rights included polygamy[25] and adultery (articles 661–65). Incest, fornication (together with producing illegitimate children), seduction,

---

22. Petr Guliaev, *Rossiiskoe ugolovnoe pravo* (Moscow: P. Kuznetsov, 1826), pp. 157–59.
23. Laura Engelstein, 'Gender and the Juridical Subject: Prostitution and Rape in Nineteenth-Century Russian Criminal Codes', *Journal of Modern History*, 60.3 (1988), 458–95 (459).
24. *Svod Zakonov Rossiiskoi Imperii*, 15 vols (St Petersburg: tipografiia II otdelenia Sobstvennoi E. I. V. kantseliarii, 1833), XV, 207–13. Hereafter: SZ.
25. In the Russian canonical tradition the crime was always called polygamy instead of bigamy, as it was suggested that a person might have more than two spouses at the same time.

infanticide, rape, sodomy and bestiality composed the 'unlawful satisfaction of carnal passions' (articles 666–78). The Code of Criminal Laws summed up the previous laws based on the relevant articles of the Law Code of 1649 and the Military Code of 1716.

The articles from the Law Code of 1649 included: rape by military men employed by the state, to be punished by death (VII, article 30); and breaking and entering for the purpose of raping or abducting the mistress of the house – both by those who broke in and for any of the victim's slaves who assisted in the offence or who failed to protect her – to be punished by death (XXII, article 16). Supplemented by articles 167 and 168 from the Military Code of 1716 (rape: death penalty; and kidnapping and rape: penal labour for life/death penalty),[26] these legal norms created the basis for the 1833 Code of Criminal laws. All types of sexual assault – rape of a married woman or a widow, violating a virgin or a minor – were summed up in article 675 with the same punishment (deprivation of rank and estate rights, flogging and penal labour). The procedural norm, derived from the comment for article 167 of the Military Code of 1716, insisted that violence must be real, the cry for help must be heard, bruises and other material evidence must be found on both victim and perpetrator, and the report must be filed before the end of the day.[27] Finally, the judges had to assess the degree of the woman's resistance to prove that resistance was genuine. The criminal lawyers of the time continued discussing whether rape was possible if an adult woman put up genuine resistance because of the assumption that if the resistance was genuine and serious then a man would hardly be able to rape her without inducing an unconscious state.[28] The rape of a non-virgin adult woman was missing from this law, suggesting that those who could not justify the loss of their virginity by marriage or widowhood could not be raped, because the law now protected the chastity of a woman (according to the Christian attitude to female chastity and the interpretation of rape in the *Kormchaia*).

---

26. 'Artikul Voinskii', pp. 358–60.
27. Art. 822 of 1833 Code of Criminal Laws was modified in the edition of 1842 (art. 789).
28. One of the leading lawyers at the time, Aleksandr Lokhvitskii, clearly states that rape is defined through the degree of resistance, which should be serious and permanent. As Lokhvitskii explains, women cannot give in without any resistance because female dignity requires them to have some, so to draw the line between a false resistance to maintain dignity and actual resistance to prevent rape, a genuine resistance is needed: Aleksandr V. Lokhvitskii, *Kurs russkogo ugolovnogo prava* (St Petersburg: Skoropechatnia Shredera, 1871), p. 581.

Russian lawyers never treated this edition of the Code of Criminal Laws favourably. It was harshly critiqued for its inconsistency and obsolete legal norms even while it was introduced. The faults of the Code of Criminal Laws, especially in its general part, resulted in immediate revisions and in 1836 the systematic revision process was ordered, which, after the death of Speranskii in 1839, passed under the control of count Bludov, whose surname ironically comes from the root word *blud*, meaning [illicit] sex. The writers of the draft created a code that was logically structured, and had milder punishments systematically applied according to the division of the crimes and according to the degree of their gravity. However, they managed to continue treating rape as a sex crime according to the 1833 Code of Criminal Laws. So they divided crimes according to their object: against state and public order and against private persons and property. Then the three groups of sex offences of the 1833 Code of Criminal Laws now were redistributed as crimes against public morals (in section VIII, 'Crimes against Public Order and Discipline'), crimes against the honour and chastity of women (part of chapter VI on crimes against honour in section X, 'Crimes against Life, Health, Freedom and Honour of Private Persons') and crimes against family rights (separate section XI). This structure was maintained in the final document which was released in 1845 with the title *Penal Code* (*Ulozhenie o Nakazaniiakh Ugolovnykh i Ispravitel'nykh*). This code replaced the Code of Criminal Laws and became volume 15 of the Code of Laws of the Russian Empire. Even this version was not final as, by the 1860s, when Alexander II's Great Reforms got underway, the *Penal Code* had to be adapted to the new situation and was once again revized. The version published in 1866, together with the Regulations of Criminal Proceedings (*Ustav ugolovnogo sudoproizvodstva*) finally created volume XV, which was used during the rest of the nineteenth and in the early twentieth centuries. However, the changes were mostly done in part of punishments (removing and substituting corporal punishment) but did not affect the material law.

According to the final version of 1866, molesting a female under the age of fourteen (articles 1523–24), rape of a woman (article 1525), *raptus* (articles 1529–30) and seduction (articles 1531–32) all fell under 'Crimes against the honour and chastity of women' (as part of chapter VI on crimes against honour in section X, 'Crimes against the Life, Health, Freedom and Honour of Private Persons'). Section X protected the most important 'goods' of a private person: life, health, freedom and honour. Female chastity (*tselomudrie*) was categorized as part of a person's 'honour', and the specific notions of female honour and chastity seem to be central to the legal understanding of rape in the nineteenth century. The composers of the Penal Code seem to suggest that the major offence here is a sort of insult to a woman's honour. The lexicographer Vladimir Dal' defined honour as the inner moral dignity of a person, prowess, honesty, nobility of soul and clear conscience.[29]

Other offences in this chapter include personal insults (including physical acts) and defamation and dissemination of offensive writings, pictures and rumours. The emphasis on a woman's honour seems to be consistent with the long tradition of the criminal prosecution of *beschest'e* (dishonour). The lawmakers here, however, departed from the old Russian legal notion of dishonour of a woman, which might have (and often did) include the loss of chastity and/or virginity, but was never solely reserved for these situations. Rather, a dishonour charge in seventeenth-century state law merely supplemented the charge of rape in order for the victim to be entitled to the monetary compensation in the same way as other assaults or injuries.[30] Post-reform lawyers pointed out this discrepancy between the new and old legal understandings of honour and suggested additional clarifications.[31] This change in the object of rape clearly pointed out the place of women in society:

---

29. V. Dal', *Tolkovyi slovar' zhivogo velikorusskogo iazyka* (Moscow: Obshchestvo liubitelei rossiiskoi slovestnosti, 1863–66), http://slovardalya.ru/description/chest/43009 [Last accessed 16 June 2011].
30. On the charge of *beschest'e* see N. Lange, 'O nakazaniiakh i vzyskaniiakh za bezchest'e po drevnemu russkomu pravu', *Zhurnal Ministerstva Narodnogo Prosveshcheniia*, 6 (1859), 161–224. Nancy Shields Kollmann lists rape as among the most 'dishonouring acts' in seventeenth-century Muscovy. She also states, 'As a rule, laws distinguished between dishonour (*beschest'e*) and physical injury (*uvech'e*) and did not consider most assaults as dishonouring. But certain types of physical assault were deemed humiliating, particularly those related to sexual infractions and reputation'. Nancy Shields Kollmann, *By Honour Bound. State and Society in Early Modern Russia*, p. 43. However, the same court data suggest that the sole charge of *beschest'e* did not mean sexual assault. There must have been a charge in 'bludnoe nasil'stvo' that explicitly meant rape and this one could be supplemented by the charge of *beschest'e*. On the other hand, the charge of *beschest'e* often included defamation and slander, especially sexual slander (for example, calling a woman a whore). See the collection of cases used by Levine (as well as by Kollmann): Eve Levin, *Sex and Society*, pp. 222–25. There should be an understanding of the difference between the social and legal concepts of honour and dishonour in seventeenth-century Russia. While the social concept was very much in tune with European concepts of female honour as based on chastity (*tselomudrie*) and virginity, the legal concept of dishonour was rather directed at protecting social status and its attributes, among which chastity was not the primary identifier.
31. Aleksandr V. Lokhvitskii, *Kurs russkogo ugolovnogo prava*, pp. 580–81; L. S. Belogrits-Korliarevskii, *Uchebnik russkogo ugolovnogo prava* (Kiev: F. A. Ioganson, 1903), pp. 522–26. The notion of honour disappears in the 1903 Criminal Code (which was never enacted in this part), as the notion of *liubodeianie* (literally: making love) emerges and rape goes into the chapter specifically devoted to sex crimes and called 'indecency'. See N. Tagantsev, *Ugolovnoe ulozhenie 22 marta 1903 goda* (St Petersburg: N. Tagantsev, 1904), pp. 697–718.

it was not their person which was to be protected but rather their honour, so supposedly those women who did not have any honour (or chastity) could not be subject to rape. This understanding of rape was consistent with the German tradition derived from *Constitutio Criminalis Carolina* of 1532, in which it was clearly stated that a whore (unchaste woman) could not be raped.[32]

The actual crime of rape, as defined by the new *Penal Code*, included intercourse between a man and a woman against the woman's will. In its turn intercourse consisted of penetration by a penis (not any other object) into the vagina (not anally or orally). The famous Grigor'ev and Mikirtumov cases confirmed this concept. The penetration of the girl's vagina by a finger so that she lost her virginity (Grigor'ev, 1869) was classified as an injury but not as rape, presumably because non-penial penetration could not result in a pregnancy.[33] Anal penetration (Mikirtumov, 1869) was considered unnatural and so subject to articles 995 and 996 on sodomy, although the Russian word for sodomy (*muzhelozhstvo*) suggested that only men participated in the act. For the sexual abuse of minors (under the age of fourteen) the *Penal Code* uses the term 'molestation' (*rastlenie*) and, for women older than fourteen, 'rape'. These two terms express the difference between exploiting the ignorance and innocence of the victim and using force and violence to commit the crime. It was not required for a minor under the age of fourteen to resist or to prove she had resisted because she was supposed to be innocent and ignorant of her sexuality and could not understand the meaning of sexual advances. From this point of view, the sexual abuse of a minor was classified as more serious than the rape of an adult woman. An adult woman had to prove that she had properly resisted the assault although that resistance did not have to be sustained throughout the act.[34] She had to express her refusal loudly and clearly; if she was non-consenting but silent, the man's actions could not be defined as rape.[35]

---

32. *Constitutio Criminalis Carolina*, art. 119. Publication in: *Die Peinliche Gerichtsordnung Kaiser Karls V.: Constitutio Criminalis Carolina*, ed. by J. Kohler and W. Scheel (Berlin: n.p., 1900). On the German legal attitudes to rape see Maren Lorenz, '"Da der anfängliche Schmerz in Liebeshitze übergehen kann": Das Delikt der "Nothzucht" im gerichtsmedizinischen Diskurs des 18. Jahrhunderts', *Österreichische Zeitschrift für Geschichtswissenschaft*, 5 (1994), 328–57; Sabine H. Smith, *Sexual Violence in German Culture: Rereading and Rewriting the Tradition* (Frankfurt/Main: Lang, 1998), pp. 35–50.
33. D. V. Lutkov, *Sbornik svedenii, raziasniaiushchikh primenenie na praktike Ulozheniia o nakazaniiakh* (Moscow: T. Ris, 1872), pp. 233–35.
34. The Gaidukov case (1870): G. Trakhtenberg, *Ukazatel' po iuridicheskim voprosam, razreshennym ugolovnym kassatsionnym i obshchim sobraniem kassatsionnykh departamentov senata* (St Petersburg: Ministerstvo iustitsii, 1874), p. 225.
35. The Rozhnov case (1870): G. Trakhtenberg, *Ukazatel'*, p. 228.

The punishment for rape varied between deprivation of social status and penal labour in a fortress for 10–12 years (for the rape of a minor) or in a factory for 4–8 years (for the rape of an adult women). If rape resulted in the death of the woman, the punishment was the same as for rape of a minor (article 1527). *Raptus* (kidnapping with the purpose of rape) was punished in the same way as any other kidnapping (which was defined as the abduction of a person with the purpose to receive ransom or other benefits), but if the kidnapper gave up willingly then imprisonment for 2–4 months followed. In any case, the burden of proof was on the complainant, that is, on the raped woman: she had to prove she resisted and did not consent.

Seduction, another offence against female honour and chastity, consisted of deception with the promise to marry (articles 1531–32). This article was intended for virgin women older than fourteen but still not of full age (which was twenty-one, according to the civil law) who remained under guardianship. If a guardian, or a teacher, or another person entrusted with her care, seduced her without using force (under the pretence of love and promise of marriage, for example) and had intercourse with her (the code uses the word 'dishonoured'), then he was prosecuted. Seduction by breach of trust suggested quite a harsh punishment (deprivation of social status and exile to Siberia or placement in a military company of prisoners for correction purposes (*arestantskie roty*). Thus, seduction became a type of a substitute for molestation, as it was understood that a woman over fourteen years old could not be as innocent as a girl under fourteen. The lawmakers, connecting this age with puberty and the biology of a woman, suggested that she might already understand advances of a sexual character. But the main asset here was virginity, so if a woman was not a virgin, the article did not apply, as she could not be dishonoured (she did not have the honour to be a virgin).[36] Aggravating circumstances (for example, if a woman was married, kidnapped, injured, mutilated, unconscious or her life threatened; or if the offence was committed by her guardian, teacher or servant) raised the degree of punishment. In other words, an unmarried woman who was not a virgin and showed no signs of injuries, but was conscious during the act of rape hardly stood a chance of winning a rape charge in court. The seduction charge reinforced the differential protection of women derived from the 1833 Code of Criminal Laws.

---

36. The Bakanov case (1872): G. Trakhtenberg, *Ukazatel'*, p. 491.

The new 1866 law protected only certain categories of women who fell under rigid gender categories and possessed 'honour', which was understood as either preserving their chastity (supposedly guaranteed by marriage or widowhood status) or virginity (guaranteed by physical integrity or certain age – fourteen or below). However, all these offences could be prosecuted only upon the complaint of the victim herself or her parents (guardians) or her husband, i.e., a private prosecution as stated in the note to article 1532. The Senate (the supreme appeal court) explained that even if this complaint was unofficial – made orally to the public or police officials – it must be prosecuted.[37] Private prosecution, in the opinion of the lawmakers, protected the honour of the woman and she (or the parents of the girl or the husband of the raped or kidnapped woman) had a right to choose to conceal the insult if she or they were not ready to go public.

Only men were defined by law as potential rapists (women were denied the possibility of committing rape and could only be an accomplice to the crime), so it was only men who were convicted of the crime. Among those sentenced to penal labour in Siberia between 1835 and 1846, rapists represented 2 per cent of the total convict population distributed among the following age groups: 11–15 (1.6%); 16–20 (11.7%); 21–30 (44%); 31–40 (18.2%); 41–50 (15.1%); 51–60 (7.8%); and over 60 (1.6%). The social status of rape convicts was as follows: noblemen (4%); clergy (2%); urban population (0.5%); state peasants (43%); private peasants (25%); and military (25.5%). Geographically, the majority of convicts came from Perm' (29%), Khar'kov (15%), Poltava (13%) and Kherson (10%).[38] So the typical rapist according to this data was a peasant or military male between 21 and 40 years old who was a resident of either Perm' or Southern Russia. The same pattern was still in place between 1874 and 1898, although peasant males tended to be younger, in the 17–30 age group.[39]

The procedural difficulties in proving rape are quite visible from the number of acquittals in rape cases. On average around 35 per cent of those accused were acquitted, which also included the verdict 'left in suspicion'[40].

---

37. *Polnoe sobranie zakonov Rossiskoi Imperii*, 2nd series, 55 vols (St Petersburg: v tipografii II otdelenia Sobstvennoi E. I. V. Kantseliarii 1839–84), II, no. 39776.
38. E. N. Anuchin, *Issledovaniia o protsente soslannykh v Sibir' v period 1827–1846 godov* (St Petersburg: Maikov, 1873), pp. 41, 66–67, 165.
39. See Stephen P. Frank, *Crime, Cultural Conflict and Justice in Rural Russia, 1856–1914*, p. 164.
40. [E. N. Tarnovskii], *Itogi ugolovnoi statistiki za 20 let (1874–94)*, pp. 131–32, 286–87; E. N. Tarnovskii, 'Dvizhenie prestupnosti v Rossiiskoi imperii za 1899–1908', pp. 52–99; *Otchet ministerstva iustitsii*.

For the man to have been sentenced the case had to be cast iron: having a victim with an unstained reputation (preferably a virgin girl), of the same social background, bruises on both victim and attacker, witnesses who clearly saw the act of rape and were ready to testify to that effect, and, of course, a confession.

Although the majority of men convicted and accused were of the lower classes, noblemen still had a visible presence in rape cases. Noblemen were convicted primarily for raping or molesting noblewomen or for cruelty towards their peasants, including raping serf women. But again, it was difficult for many of the victims to prove that rape had occurred. The typical case is that of Nikita Vulf who raped Mariia Il'ina, a young woman of noble origin, in 1859. Il'ina (who was nineteen years old) insisted that Vulf had raped her. She was examined by police doctors, evidence of resistance was found on her body, and her story was corroborated by witnesses' statements. However, the court, while acknowledging the fact of her defloration, questioned Mariia's degree of resistance as there was no evidence on the accused (no bruises, his dress was intact) and her cry for help was not taken seriously by the (male) servants. Vulf was left under 'serious suspicion of rape', which put him under police surveillance rather than in prison.[41]

It was rare for the rape of a woman of lower status by a nobleman to come to trial. To obtain a conviction was even more complicated. In the 1847 case, a young actress had to die as a result of a rape committed by a young prince in order for the police to investigate it. Avdot'ia Arshinina had been practically sold by her father for 10,000 rubles. She was so badly abused that she ended up in the hospital and died within a fortnight. The post mortem revealed such severe injuries to her genitals that it was very clear that rape had happened. The prince had been under police surveillance since 1846 for a similar crime. Avdot'ia was a virgin. And yet the Senate viewed the act as fornication (consensual sexual relations) and the injuries inflicted as accidental. The punishment involved the nobleman's military rank being demoted to that of an ordinary soldier, yet he did not lose his noble privileges, title, or social status.[42]

Victimized not only by their lower status but also by their gender, women of the lower classes constantly had to prove their right to legal protection

---

41. Aleksandr Liubavskii, *Russkie ugolovnye protsessy*, 4 vols (St Petersburg: Obshchestvennaia Pol'za, 1866), II, 226–36. Hereafter: *RUP*.
42. *RUP*, II, 193–222.

through a positive assessment of their reputations. The assessment of reputation was an integral part of an investigation's total search (*poval'nyi obysk*) and the court had to take such an assessment as evidence of the plaintiff's credibility. In 1861 Agnessa Dmitrieva, a liberated serf, accused Lieutenant Nadratovskii of rape, but the accusation was dismissed by the police because she was not a virgin, 'had long been known to have sexual relations with other men', had syphilis, and her bruises were not blue enough. In that same case another woman, Kovrigina, daughter of a townsman, accused Nadratovskii of attempted rape. To save her honour she had jumped out of the window and broken her arms and legs; the police and court were more favourably disposed to her as she had a solid reputation – she was hardworking, modest, religious, a virgin, and did not drink beer with Nadratovskii in the local inn. However, the auditor-general dismissed Kovrigina's accusations because, in his opinion, there was no proof of attempted rape (her dress was not torn and the accused did not have any signs of her resistance on him). Finally, Nadratovskii's actions were categorized as inflicting injuries and seduction, so he was sentenced to be excluded from army service and to pay Kovrigina compensation (instead of deprivation of rank and penal labour in Siberia).[43]

Dmitrieva's accusations in this case were never considered even as corroborative evidence for Kovrigina's claims. Both women were of low social status and could not put their cases on further appeal. Nor could they hire a good solicitor to represent them in court and argue upon the admissibility of the evidence in court. The judge did not identify their needs and did not sympathize with them as a result of their gender and social inferiority. Only in the case of equal social status could the sentence be just according to the law. The reputations of the victim and her family played a key role in getting an accusation taken seriously by the courts. In the case of 1852, the serf Prokopii Antipov accused his owner's brother of raping his fifteen-year-old daughter. However, the accusation was dismissed because Natal'ia was accused of flirtatious and immodest behaviour whilst her mother (who originally initiated the complaint) had the reputation of being a restless and audacious woman.[44]

Sexual exploitation of serf women by their owners represented one ugly face of pre-reform Russian society. Despite the official legal prohibitions of such exploitation and constant attention by the authorities and legal

---

43. *RUP*, IV, 287–93.
44. *RUP*, II, 237–46.

bodies (primarily the Senate) to such cases, the rape of serf women by their masters continued to be a frequent instrument of patriarchal power. Abused women could hardly find any justice against their masters. The mass rape of serf women was classified as 'cruel treatment of peasants' and usually came to light during investigations into large-scale abuse.[45]

In 1855, a special investigation against the high-ranking official (*tainyi sovetnik*) A. Zhadovskii, aged forty, was ordered by the governor of the Orenburg region. Five peasant women complained that they had been raped by Zhadovskii, who was their owner. Other peasants confirmed that he had sold or married other women to serfs in other villages. Some peasants witnessed Zhadovskii practicing *jus primae noctis* in one of his villages. Zhadovskii rejected all the accusations, and some of the Senate judges supported him on the basis of procedural inconsistencies (the women did not report immediately and there was no material evidence, among other things). Finally, however, he was convicted and sentenced to penal labour in Siberia as well as deprived of rank.[46]

The exact nature of abuses such as those committed by Zhadovskii was difficult to prove, as a result of which the investigation could last a long time. Thus, in the 1857 case of landowner Viktor Strashinskii (aged seventy-two), who had systematically raped under-age and young women for more than forty years (in total eighty-six women complained), the charges were brought more than once, in 1832 and then in 1845, but dropped by the local judges. Again, the case was based on witness testimonies and the women were constantly intimidated by their owner, which resulted in their withdrawal of the charges each time. Strashinskii was finally left 'under suspicion of rape' but there was no further punishment according to the Penal Code.[47]

Peasants in pre-emancipation Russia were subject to their own jurisdiction at the village level, and for state peasants also at the *volost'* court level on the basis of customary law. *Volost'* courts were extended to all peasants in the post-emancipation period. In both periods, local peasant community meetings, composed of village elders and (male) heads of local households, played a crucial role in distributing justice among peasants. Customary law had its own set of punishments which

---

45. There is quite a good collection of government files full of these cases: RGIA (*Rossiiskii gosudarstvennyi istoricheskii arkhiv*), f. 1400, op. 1, d. 367.
46. *RUP*, II, 330–45.
47. *RUP*, II, 345–57.

were different from the state law and official criminal code.[48] Peasant court practice from various regions of Russia suggests that rape was prosecuted only in the most abominable cases such as gang rape and molestation of children. In the Tomsk region for the period 1836–61, the courts heard fifty cases of rape, mostly of gang rape (compared to seventy-nine cases of infanticide, 111 cases of bestiality, four cases of sodomy, and 496 cases of murder) and 155 cases of molestation of children. However, the proceedings show that most of those cases did not go to the *volost'* court but to the state court, and not necessarily upon the victim's request or in her favour. For example, in 1851, Avdot'ia Kuznetsova from Elunino (Barnaul district) was gang raped by her neighbours. On the following day the community meeting decided to punish the offenders with lashes and she was ready to end the case with twenty-five rubles in compensation, but the men were dissatisfied with the (high) amount and the case went to the state court.[49] The most common sentences for this crime in the *volost'* courts were corporal punishment and monetary compensation, which differed from punishments demanded by the official penal code. In 1884, two peasants from the Buzuluk district raped a young woman and were sentenced by the *volost'* court to pay ten rubles to her parents as compensation and to buy half a bucket of vodka for the judges,[50] which constituted a typical decision.

Women often relied on their families in seeking justice, but families failed to provide safe environments for them as abuse could and often did start at home. Charges of incest (mostly cases of fathers raping their daughters) amounted to half of the rape charges. The crime of incest was considered abominable and invoked a very harsh punishment, but to prove it and not to commit another criminal offence – defamation of parents – was a difficult and painful process. Agaf'ia Uskova was raped by her father in 1860 and became pregnant as a result, after which her father tied her up and flogged her with a knout so that she

---

48. See on *volost'* courts: Cathy A. Frierson, 'Rural Justice in Public Opinion: The Volost' Court Debate 1861–1912', *Slavonic and East European Review*, 64 (1986), 526–45; Cathy A. Frierson, '"I Must Always Answer to the Law…": Rules and Responses in the Reformed Volost' Court', *Slavonic and East European Review*, 75 (1997), 308–34; Gareth Popkins, *The Russian Peasant Volost Court and Customary Law 1861–1917* (Oxford: Oxford University Press, 1995); Gareth Popkins, 'Code versus Custom? Norms and Tactics in Peasant Volost Court Appeals, 1889–1917', *Russian Review*, 59 (2000), 408–24.
49. N. Kostrov, *Iuridicheskie obychai krestian-starozhilov Tomskoi gubernii* (Tomsk: Tomskaia gubernskaia tipografiia, 1876), pp. 68–76.
50. 'Obrazets krestianskogo suda', *Moskovskie vedomosti*, 21 March 1884, no. 80, 3.

miscarried. Her mother and her brothers were so scared of the head of their family that they could not protect her or report the abuse to the authorities. Five months later, her mother called all the neighbours to the cattle shed so they could witness her husband raping her daughter. However, the judges from the official investigation doubted that the delay of five months in reporting the crime was due to fear of reprisal experienced by Agaf'ia and her relatives. As a result, Agaf'ia was sentenced to confinement in a monastery, which meant hard labour and further humiliation, whilst her father was sentenced according to the criminal code.[51] This case was not out of the ordinary; in cases of incest women quite often received punishment together with their fathers or fathers-in-law as it was considered to be their fault.

In Russian villages and Cossack communities, a daughter-in-law often became a victim of rape by her father-in-law. The crime was so common that it received a special name: *snokhachestvo*. Sometimes it was committed with the silent agreement of the husband who did not and often could not protest against the patriarch of the family, his father.[52] In the nineteenth century, *snokhachestvo* came to the attention of the authorities mostly due to the work of ethnographers and specialists in customary law who described this custom and condemned it as 'barbarous' and 'uncivilized'. According to ethnographic data, *snokhachestvo* was most common in central Russia and among the Cossacks, and was reported only in cases where open and direct violence was involved.[53] At the same time *snokhachestvo* constituted a grave offence under the law, being one of the aggravated forms of incest. Punishable by confinement in a monastery for between six months and a year, *snokhachestvo* was regarded as an offence against the family union. If rape could be proven, then those guilty received a rape charge.[54] *Snokhachestvo* highlighted the problems patriarchal families were facing: women were victimized not only in the public sphere but also in the sanctity of their homes.

---

51. *RUP*, II, 222–26.
52. S. S. Shashkov, 'Istoriia russkoi zhenshchiny', in *A se grekhi zlye, smertnye...' Russkaia semeinaia i seksual'naia kul'tura glazami istorikov, etnografov, literatorov, fol'kloristov, pravovedov i bogoslovov XIX-nachala XX veka*, 3 vols ed. by Natal'ia L. Pushkareva and L. V. Bessmertnykh (Moscow: Ladomir, 2004), II, 543–44.
53. N. Kostrov, *Iuridicheskie obychai*, pp. 75–76.
54. *Ulozhenie o nakazaniiakh ugolovnykh i ispravitel'nykh* (St Petersburg: v tipografii Pravitel'stvuiushchego Senata, 1845), pp. 819–20 (articles 2088–89).

Disciplining Wives: Russian Women in Violent Households

The idea of correction and discipline in family relations was supported by both the Church and the State. Religious writings citing the Church fathers' rules, apostolic canons and the Bible, insisted on the right of the husband to teach and discipline his wife, children and other household members.[55] Russian secular law guarded the borders of patriarchy, introducing a special punishment for the wife who killed her husband. The Law Code of 1649 prescribed that she was to be buried alive (XXII, article 14). Thus, women who killed their husbands were to be punished much more severely than men, who could supposedly kill their wives unpremeditatedly, through 'correction' and 'disciplining'. In 1689 burying alive was replaced by beheading.[56]

It was in the jurisdiction of the Church to rule on family disagreements and watch over family order. The consistory courts tried spousal abuse cases both on separate charges and as a reason for divorce.[57] However, modern state law did pay attention to family law and spousal relations. Peter I was very concerned about forced marriages contracted by parents. He introduced the postulate of consent into family law as a way of conforming to the Christian ideas of marriage as a free union and a sacrament. The parties then were to express their consent clearly and show willingness to marry.[58] On the other hand, in Peter's Military Code (1716) the punishment for killing a wife as a result of heavy beating was milder than that for regular murder. The lawmaker classified such a death to be a result of unpremeditated actions and accordingly awarded the lesser (although non-specified) punishment. At the same time, the Holy Synod, following the Byzantine tradition, recognized conspiracy to murder a spouse to be a valid reason for divorce (1723).[59] This gave some legal background

---

55. See Eve Levin, *Sex and Society* pp. 337–43. Nancy S. Kollmann, *By Honor Bound. State and Society in Early Modern Russia*, pp. 75–77; Nancy S. Kollmann, 'The Extremes of Patriarchy: Spousal Abuse and Murder in Early Modern Russia', *Russian History*, 25 (1998), 133–40.
56. *PSZ*, III, 1335.
57. See M. K. Tsaturova, *Russkoe semeinoe pravo XVI-XVIII vekov* (Moscow: Iuridicheskaia literatura, 1991), pp. 36–45.
58. On the Russian Orthodox treatment of marriage and family law see: V. N. Nikol'skii, *Obzor glavneishikh postanovlenii Petra I v oblasti lichnogo semeinogo prava* (Iaroslavl': v Gub., Tip., 1857); Gregory L. Freeze, 'Bringing Order to the Russian Family: Marriage and Divorce in Imperial Russia, 1760–1860', *Journal of Modern History*, 62 (1990), 709–48.
59. *Polnoe sobranie rasporiazhenii i postanovlenii po vedomstvu pravoslavnogo ispovedaniia Rossiiskoi Imperii*, 1st series, 10 vols (St Petersburg: v Sinodal'noi tipografii, 1869–1911), II, no. 1044.

for divorce proceedings on the basis of heavy beating with aggravating circumstances, such as injuries and miscarriages.

In the second half of the eighteenth century, during the reforms of Catherine II, the Church itself suggested that the state courts investigate 'wife-beating and tormenting', but to no avail. However, the attitude of the law to wife-beating definitely changed. The Police Regulations of 1782 state: 'let a husband join his wife in love and concord, respect her, protect her and excuse her defects, comfort her in sickness and provide her with a living according to his state and capability' and 'let a wife love, respect and obey her husband, please him and show her attachment as a mistress of the house'.[60] This rule never mentions a husband's privilege 'to teach or discipline his wife'. The 1833 Code of Laws reproduced Catherine's law, stating that 'a husband is obliged to love his wife, live with her in concord, protect her, excuse her defects and comfort her in sickness. He is obliged to provide for her according to his state and capability'. The wife 'is obliged to obey her husband as he is the head of the family, should stay in love with him, in deep respect and absolute obedience, please him and confide in him as a mistress of the house'. Additionally she was obliged to obey her husband's orders but to combine it with duties towards her parents.[61]

It is quite clear that, while the obligations of the husband towards his wife essentially did not change, those of a wife were made more difficult, especially with regard to obedience and respect. The husband was explicitly named the 'head of the family', and this entitlement put him in the official position of power, which before was supported by didactic writings and assumptions, rather than by de facto law.

However, physical punishment did not become a part of his powers, and that again reflected the liberal attitudes of the day. Based on this thinking, the *Penal Code* of 1845 awarded the same punishment for the abuse of a wife by her husband as for the injuries inflicted on any other person two degrees higher (usually a variety of deprivation of rank and social status and penal labour, depending on the degree of inflicted harm). In addition, persons of Orthodox faith had to undergo a penance, a traditional punishment for wife-abusers.[62] Thus, spousal abuse was officially recognized to be a

---

60. *PSZ*, XXI, 15379, art. D.41: VIII–IX.
61. See Mikhail S. Usov, *Grazhdanskie zakony, zakliuchaiushchiesia v desiatom tome Svoda Zakonov Rossiiskoi Imperii izdaniia 1842 goda i deviatnadstati prilozheniiakh* (St Petersburg: izd. Akademii Nauk, 1856), p. 16 (articles 108–10).
62. *Ulozhenie o nakazaniiakh ugolovnykh i ispravitel'nykh*, art. 2075–76, pp. 813–14.

matter of the state jurisdiction and such cases were now tried in the state courts only. Marital abuse among peasants went to the attention of the *volost'* courts, and the punishment there could be very different from the official criminal code; based on the decision of the village elders, it often put women in a disadvantageous position.

Wife-beating was assumed to be quite widespread among peasants and workers in the nineteenth century. Almost all contemporary ethnographers and lawyers provided some data confirming the spread of marital violence. In the opinion of many observers, wife-beating was due to the ignorance and 'low morality' of peasant society in general[63] as well as to the assumption among peasants that the husband had a lawful right to punish his wife. Russian newspapers and magazines were full of stories of cruelties, atrocities, lethal injuries and the unlimited patience of Russian peasant women, who were suffering the hardships of domestic patriarchy. After emancipation, peasant women who suffered from domestic abuse had to report to the *volost'* courts, whose purpose was not to protect the victim but to pacify the community. Thus, the instructions for the judges prescribed: if a husband is proven guilty he is subject to imprisonment or corporal punishment; if a wife is found guilty of misconduct (that is, she committed the actions for which her husband beat her), she is sentenced to community work or 'bread and water' imprisonment with regular admonition to obey her husband. The *volost'* court practices reveal that often both spouses were punished: the husband for 'evil treatment' (*durnoe obrashchenie*) and the wife for taking action against him, as she clearly did not show enough patience. The typical response to a wife's complaint to a *volost'* court was making her ask her husband for forgiveness[64] or, if she refused, sentencing her to flogging (ten lashes).[65]

Cases of marital abuse, besides regular battering, often included harnessing a woman to a cart, or tying her up to a horse and riding around for several miles, or beating her with a horsewhip or a knout.[66] Justification for the 'punishment' varied, but basically included the wife's disobedience,

---

63. See, for example, Vereshchagin, 'O bab'ikh stonakh'; Ludmer, 'Bab'i stony'.
64. As in a case from Kostroma region: V., 'Iurisdiktsiia volostnykh sudei', *Kostromskie gubernskie vedomosti*, 9 December 1867, no. 48, 474.
65. 'Sud po obychnomu pravu… "Domostroia"', *Russkii kur'er*, 19 October 1879, no. 51, 4.
66. See, for example, 'Dva sluchaia iz semeinoi zhizni', *Nedelia*, 9 January 1877, 2, 51–54; 'Sudebnaia khronika', *Russkie vedomosti*, 20 August 1872, no. 182, 2; 'Korrespondent Syna otechestva soobshchaet…', *Russkie vedomosti*, 6 August 1878, no. 199, 2; 'Iz Khar'kova v Kievlianin pishut', *Moskovskie vedomosti*, 18 December 1880, no. 350, 4; N., 'Iz stanitsy Golodaevki', *Donskie oblastnye vedomosti*, 19 December 1879, no. 99, 2.

refusal to live with her spouse (usually involving escape to her parents or to another village), or adultery;[67] or more often, no justification was needed.[68] Many ethnographers of the time assumed that wife-abusers went unpunished because the peasants believed that husbands had absolute power over their wives. Indeed, when *volost'* courts punished women for their disobedience, the verdict often stated that is was necessary to 'convince her to have absolute obedience to her husband',[69] which was in perfect conformity with the civil law. However, *volost'* court practice shows that the cases where the abusive husband was punished outnumber the cases where the perpetrator went unpunished, which means that the notion of absolute power did not include the notion of physical abuse. This was because a husband who could not keep his violence under control was potentially dangerous for the community, as wife-beating had a close connection with other 'disorders' such as child-beating,[70] disobedience to parents, drunkenness and poor management of the household.[71] On occasion, though, the husband could be acquitted if the court decided that his wife had provoked him. In one case from the Moscow district, the court refused to accept a complaint from an abused wife (her husband had battered her and torn out a tuft of her hair) on the grounds of her rude and insolent behaviour towards him in court.[72] In general, the picture emerging from the *volost'* courts' proceedings was not favourable towards women: they might have been seen as victims, but the courts were mostly concerned with preventing men from committing more serious offences rather than with protecting women. The safety of women did not constitute their primary concern; it was the stability of the household that mattered.

In the period of serfdom, even landowners were concerned that their peasants battered their wives. One landowner, A. S. Zelenago, stated that only ten per cent of cases came to his attention because wives were scared to report cruelty even to their owner. Thus, one peasant harnessed his wife to a wooden plough because his horse was sick, while another

---

67. As in the case of Vasilii Kriukov, whose wife had an illegitimate child while he was in military service: 'Delo ob istiazanii', *Volzhsko-Kamskoe slovo*, 3 June 1882, no. 119, 3.
68. See 'Iz Solikamskogo uezda Permskoi gubernii…', *Russkie vedomosti*, 19 July 1878, no. 183, 2.
69. *Trudy komissii po preobrazovaniiu volostnykh sudov*, 8 vols (St Petersburg: n.p., 1873), II, 490, no. 12. Hereafter: *TKV*.
70. *TKV*, I, 443.
71. *TKV*, II, 72, no. 1; 138, no. 35; 275, no. 25; III, 72, no. 49; 236, no. 10; 263, no. 152; 264, no. 4; 389, no. 3, etc.
72. *TKV*, II, 151, no. 24. See also similar cases: V, 33; VI, 254, no. 46; 650, no. 19; VII, 472.

used to tie his wife up to the crossbeam in the house for regular whipping. This landowner decided not to send the husbands to court because the punishment was too mild, and punished them himself (with whipping, imprisonment, army recruitment etc.).[73] This is a rare mention of private prosecution for spousal abuse. The landowner may have wanted to be seen as a progressive person by taking justice into his own hands. However, his revelations instead demonstrated a degree of enlightened despotism and mistrust of state justice.

Not only peasant women suffered from domestic abuse. Russian noblewomen were probably less abused than serfs in the nineteenth century, but still became victims of spousal violence. In the eighteenth century, many prominent noble women were abused: Countess Saltykova (1721); the wife of a colonel, Mariia Poretskaia (1724); Princess Anna Solntseva-Zasekina (1729); the wife of a colonel, Anna Rzhevskaia (1730); Countess Lopukhina (1731); Countess Praskoviia Egupova-Cherkasskaia (1742); Countess Tat'iana Musina-Pushkina (1746); Countess Natal'ia Apraksina (1771)[74] and even Duchess Augusta of Württemberg, sister-in-law of the Grand Prince Paul (1786),[75] together with many others. The data from the St Petersburg Consistory court for 1780–1800 suggests that half of all complaints about domestic violence came from noblewomen.[76]

However, as mentioned above, official attitudes to spousal violence changed in the late eighteenth and early nineteenth centuries, with the emergence of new ideas about gender and new interpretations of despotism and power. In her recent book, Barbara Engel connects these changes with the exemption of the nobility from corporal punishment according to the Charter of Nobility of 1785, which brought the notion of illegitimate

---

73. A. S. Zelenago, 'O zhestokom obrashchenii krest'ian s ikh zhenami', *Sovremennik*, 10 (1857), 271–73.
74. *Rossiiskii gosudarstvennyi istoricheskii arkhiv* (RGIA), f. 796, op. 1, no. 99; op. 5, no. 454; op. 10, no. 30; op. 11, no. 332; op. 12, no. 353; op. 23, no. 959; op. 27, no. 278; *Tsentral'nyi gosudarstvennyi istoricheskii arkhiv Sankt-Peterburga* (TsGIA StP), f. 19, op. 1, no. 7916.
75. Prince Dolgorukov in his memoirs describes the scene when Duchess Augusta (1764–88) knelt in front of Catherine II after the play in the Hermitage Theatre and begged her to protect her from her husband, who beat her regularly. Catherine ordered the Duke to leave Russia, which he did in 1787, and then she excluded him from the Russian service (he was Lieutenant-General of the Russian army and Governor-General of Vyborg). Duke Frederick Wilhelm Carl (1754–1816) became the first King of Württemberg. See Ivan M. Dolgorukov, *Povest' o rozhdenii moem, proiskhozhdenii i vsei zhizni* (St Petersburg: Nauka, 2004), 2 vols, I, 138–39; A. V. Khrapovitskii, *Pamiatnye zapiski A. V. Khrapovitskago, stats-sekretaria Imperatritsy Ekateriny II* (Moscow: Soiuzteatr, 1990), p. 17.
76. Of the 60 complaints, 29 came from noblewomen: TsGIA StP, f. 19, op. 1.

cruelty that undermined the legitimacy of marital violence among noble elites.[77] The cult of domesticity promoted by official discourse contributed to the redefinition of femininity and masculinity among the nobles. Proper masculinity became associated with self-command policies, which prohibited the violation of a woman's body. The use of violence was now thought to be limited to the lower classes.[78] At the same time, Abby Schrader argues that, despite the enlightened attitude of Russian officials to domestic violence in the1860s, their desire to reinforce patriarchal relations and the dominant position occupied by male householders outweighed their concerns about spousal abuse. The implication here is that containing spousal abuse within the private sphere by turning a blind eye to it was preferable to criminalizing wife-beating and making it part of the public record.[79] As a result of these attitudes, domestic violence in noble families was carefully kept inside the family and rarely became visible.

In 1831, a noblewoman Anna Shchepkina complained to her brother that 'my husband gave me a black eye so that I could not leave the house for two weeks'. In another letter, dated a month later, she wrote: 'My husband only insults and beats me; he took our last one hundred rubles and spent those on drinking and brawling...'.[80] She explained his cruelty by way of his lewd way of life and his debauchery, using traditional explanations for such behaviour. In the case of the noblewoman Nadezhda Stakhovicheva, who complained to the Third Section of His Majesty's Chancellery of her husband's mistreatment in 1835, the husband's behaviour equated that of a man of the lower classes.[81] If a peasant's cruelty to his wife did not require explanation, the behaviour of a nobleman had to be explained through the acceptable discourses of deviancy.

The cases of noble spousal abuse came to light when they were found especially heinous. In the case from 1851 looking into the cruel treatment of peasants, Lieutenant Karptsov was also accused of 'evil treatment' of his wife. His father-in-law brought the charges, stating that Karptsov threatened her

---

77. Barbara A. Engel, *Breaking the Ties That Bound. The Politics of Marital Strife in Late Imperial Russia* (Ithaca and London: Cornell University Press, 2011), pp. 103–04; Susan Morrissey, *Suicide and the Body Politics in Imperial Russia* (New York: Cambridge University Press, 2006), pp. 134–35.
78. Barbara A. Engel, *Breaking the Ties That Bound*, pp. 104, 168–71.
79. Abby M. Schrader, *Languages of the Lash. Corporal Punishment and Identity in Imperial Russia*, pp. 164–68.
80. Cited in A. V. Belova, *"Chetyre vozrasta zhenshchiny": povsednevnaia zhizn' russkoi provintsial'noi dvorianki XVIII-serediny XIX veka* (St Petersburg: Aleteiia, 2010), p. 291.
81. Cited in Barbara A. Engel, *Breaking the Ties That Bound*, p. 104.

with his pistol if she would not give him half her estate. Further investigation revealed that Karptsov tortured his wife with hot water and fire, locked her up, and constantly threatened to kill her in front of the peasants.[82] Karptsov was sentenced to deprivation of rank and social status and ten years of penal labour. Not all judges, however, were sympathetic to victims of wife-beating. In the 1879 case, State Councillor Bykov was brought in front of the justice of the peace on the charge of domestic abuse. The justice, however, acquitted Bykov immediately because in his opinion such acts did not constitute anything illegal and were merely a misunderstanding between spouses.[83] The judge followed the Senate's decisions on similar cases (the Soimonov case, 1862) and was ready to prosecute only if the abuse took place in public (the Sokolovskii case, 1869).[84]

Uxorial murder was often a result of heavy battering or other forms of domestic violence. As mentioned, there was a special article for the murder of a husband (burying alive) in the early 1649 code, but no complementary article for the murder of a wife; but this does not mean that wife-murderers did not receive their punishment. Murder, including murder of a wife, was considered a very grave crime and was punished as such by the death penalty (usually beheading). The eighteenth century brought the eradication of differences in punishment for the murder of a wife and the murder of a husband. These cases were tried in the state court and were sometimes referred to the ecclesiastical court for the imposition of a penance in addition to the punishment (the galleys or death) applied by the secular courts. The *Penal Code* of 1845 equated the punishment for wife/husband killing to that for recidivist premeditated murder, that is, deprivation of all ranks and status, and permanent exile into penal labour in the mines. For those not exempted from corporal punishment (the peasantry), additional flogging and branding were prescribed.[85] Corporal punishment and branding were removed in the 1866 edition. However, in many cases husbands still justified their behaviour, claiming that it was not premeditated and that they had tried to discipline their wives for their debauchery and adultery.

---

82. *RUP*, II, 293–321.
83. *Golos*, 16 March 1879, no. 75, 2.
84. *Resheniia Ugolovnogo kassatsionnogo departamenta Pravitel'stvuiuschego Senata za 1869 god* (St Petersburg: tipografiia II oteleniia, 1869), no. 551; V. A. Veremenko, 'Semeinye nesoglasiia i razdel'noe zhitel'stvo suprugov: problema zakonodatel'nogo regulirovaniia v Rossii vo vtoroi polovine XIX – nachale XX veka', *Dialog so vremenem*, 18 (2007), 334–35.
85. *Ulozhenie o nakazaniiakh ugolovnykh i ispravitel'nykh*, pp. 741–42 (article 1922).

In the famous case of 1858, Iakov Kosakovskii, a peasant from Volyn' province, killed his wife with an axe, insisting that she was promiscuous, a heavy drinker and regularly provoked fights with him. He had used all the corrective tools, he said, to restrain his wife from such a life, but was unsuccessful. He did not intend to kill her, but only used an axe to threaten his disorderly wife, but 'in his agitated state' hit her on the head. The witnesses corroborated his words. The case went to the lower district court. The judges recognized unpremeditated murder on the grounds of 'his not being known to be of such a cruel character' and sentenced him to forty lashes and a penance. The Volyn' high district court did not agree with the lower court's decision and sentenced Kosakovskii to deprivation of the rights of his estate, seventy lashes given in public by an executioner, branding and exile to the mines for twelve years, followed by permanent settlement in Siberia. In turn, the governor of Volyn' did not agree with the higher court's decision. The case went to the Senate, which decided that, because Kosakovskii was of a 'peaceful and quiet character', he should be subject to a criminal penalty of a medium degree: deprived of his estate rights, given ten lashes and sent to Siberia for permanent settlement.[86] This case was notorious for validating the guilty party's behaviour and the victim's reputation. Because Kosakovskii had a 'quiet character' and his murdered wife was guilty of 'quarrelsome and disorderly conduct', the murder could somehow be justified in the eyes of the judges.

It is quite difficult to estimate how often battering ended up in murder, as there were no regular statistics. Several groups of data might give some idea of the situation. In 1835–46, 250 men (2.7 per cent of all men sentenced for murder) were sentenced to penal labour in the Siberian mines for wife-killing and 416 women (19 per cent of all women sentenced for murder) were given the same sentence for husband-killing, which meant that women were much more often sentenced for spouse-killing. The majority of female spouse-murderers belonged to the young age group (16–30) while male spouse-murderers were evenly spread over all age groups.[87] According to Stephen Frank's estimation for 1874–1913, spousal killings among peasants constituted 7 per cent of all murders; the majority of the convicted were

---

86. *RUP*, I, 126–33.
87. E. N. Anuchin, *Issledovaniia o protsente soslannykh v Sibir'*, pp. 30–31, 41. See also on female criminality in nineteenth-century Russia: Stephen L. Frank, 'Narratives within Numbers: Women, Crime and Juridical Statistics in Imperial Russia, 1834–1913', *Russian Review*, 55 (1996), 541–66.

men (62 per cent) who killed their wives. However, men constituted only 4.7 per cent of all male convicts while women accounted for 31 per cent of all female convicts, which shows the same statistical pattern.[88] Women were clearly treated more severely than men due to the different interpretation of their actions. By killing their husband they also rebelled against proper authority which might have more serious consequences in terms of judicial leniency. It was consistent with the official desire to reinforce patriarchy by all possible means and harsh sentences provided an excellent opportunity to deter other women from committing such an act.

Battering and injury were not the only abuses to be suffered by wives; there was also isolation and restraint of liberty, as well as denial of food and clothing. As Russian women moved to their husbands' homes after marriage, and marriage law did not support joint marital property, women did not have any right to claim the house. Separate marital property was advantageous to noble and rich women, but played a reverse negative role among the poorer strata of society. Peasant women could claim their dowry and marital support, but not the house or any other immovable property.[89] Moreover, the husband's earnings belonged to him rather than to the family, and women who took money or other things from the husband's property were prosecuted on theft charges. A case from the Perm' region (1884) is a typical example. A woman came to the local *volost'* court with the complaint that her husband had tried to batter her to death and then expelled her from the house, with nowhere to stay. Her husband claimed he did it because she stole fifteen kopecks from him to buy ferial oil to make some pancakes for her six children. The wife confessed to stealing from her husband, but the *volost'* court, taking into consideration the family's situation, ruled to punish the husband for domestic abuse and not providing for his family.[90]

In general, the *volost'* courts regularly ruled in the favour of wives in cases when they were denied marital support and expelled from the house. In another case from the Moscow district, a woman complained that her husband had expelled her, together with their eight-year-old son and her son from her first marriage and did not give them any money for their living expenses. The court ordered the husband

---

88. Stephen P. Frank, *Crime, Cultural Conflict, and Justice in Rural Russia, 1856–1914*, pp. 166–67 (table 5.2).
89. There is a considerable literature on property law; see W. G. Wagner, *Marriage, Property, and Law in Late Imperial Russia* (Oxford: Oxford University Press, 1984); M. L. Marrese, *A Woman's Kingdom*; S. V. Pachman, *Obychnoe grazhdanskoe pravo v Rossii* (Moscow: Zertsalo, 2003).
90. E. Nagibin, 'Na volostnom sude', *Permskie gubernskie vedomosti*, 6 March 1885, no. 19, 121.

to take them back or pay alimony.⁹¹ The courts mostly obliged husbands to give some marital support to their wives (one or two rubles per month or twenty-five per year) or a portion of property (such as a cowshed to stay in).⁹² The situation prompted women to migrate to other places or to go to the cities and join the army of urban workers or prostitutes.⁹³

Nineteenth-century lawyers unanimously agreed that there could not be rape in marriage. N. A. Nekliudov, an authoritative criminologist at the time, explained that rape was a crime against woman's chastity and honour, which could not happen in spousal relations, as sexual intercourse was sanctioned by the sanctity of marriage.⁹⁴ In other words, a husband had absolute control over his wife's body and any sexual violence was classified as domestic abuse.

The courts recognized sexual violence only in the form of incest and when a husband allowed other men to have sex with his wife. Ethnographical data for the nineteenth century from the Tomsk region (where allegedly the tradition of wife-selling or wife-exchange was widely practiced) suggests that husbands still ordered their wives to have sex with strangers in exchange for goods or money.⁹⁵ At one of the goldmines, for example, people witnessed a husband beat up his wife with a bridle because she refused to sleep with his friend who offered three rubles for that privilege. His actions were supported by the eldest members of the family: they insisted that a wife should always obey her husband's orders and contribute to the family's wealth in any way necessary.⁹⁶

Instances of selling wives for sex were already known in the seventeenth century and were not unique to Russia.⁹⁷ There were two regions where the tradition of wife-sale allegedly existed in the nineteenth century: Siberia

---

91. *TKV*, II, 444, no. 30.
92. *TKV*, I, 287, no. 10, 341, no. 5; II, 275, no. 26; IV, 64, no. 36; VI, 72, no. 88, 98, no. 5, 388.
93. See Barbara A. Engel, *Between the Fields and the City: Women, Work, and Family in Russia, 1861–1914* (Cambridge: Cambridge University Press, 1994), pp. 64–101, 166–98; Marianna Muravyeva, 'Gosudarstvennoe prizrenie prostitutsii v predrevolutsionnom Peterburge', *Nuzhda i poriadok: istoriia sotsial'noi raboty v Rossii, XX v.*, ed. by Pavel Romanov and Elena Smirnova-Iarskaia (Saratov: Nauchnaia kniga, 2005), pp. 158–204.
94. N. A. Nekliudov, *Rukovodstvo k osobennoi chasti russkogo ugolovnogo prava*, 2 vols (St Petersburg: Tipografiia P. P. Merkur'eva, 1876), I, 406–09. See also Aleksandr V. Lokhvitskii, *Kurs russkogo ugolovnogo prava*, pp. 580–81.
95. N. Kostrov, *Iuridicheskie obychai*, pp. 24–26.
96. N. Kostrov, *Iuridicheskie obychai*, pp. 26–27.
97. See on wife-selling in England: Bridget Hill, *Women, Work and Sexual Politics in Eighteenth-century England* (London: Routledge, 1994); E. P. Thompson, 'The Selling of Wives', in his *Customs in Common* (London: Merlin Press, 1991), pp. 404–66.

and Southern Russia. Women could be sold, lent or exchanged for something more valuable (such as an ox). There are many examples: in the Kherson region, two peasants agreed to wife-sale for five rubles and made an official contract;[98] another peasant from Vinnitsa sold his wife to train conductors for thirty rubles;[99] two military men sealed a contract of wife-sale for twenty rubles with an additional clause of reverse property charge[100] and a drunken peasant lent his wife for half a bucket of vodka (thirty-five kopecks).[101] A final example involves a peasant from Boguchar, who exchanged his wife for two oxen during a fair; she was then rescued by her adult son, who paid back the debt.[102] These episodes confirm that in certain regions women were viewed as property and husbands exploited not only their labour but also their sexuality. This type of sexual slavery indicated the lowest possible status a woman had in peasant society.

Conclusion

The picture of the abuse of Russian women emerging from this chapter is mostly negative and calls for obvious conclusions about the place of women in nineteenth-century society. Patriarchal families led by men (and sometimes women) used every accessible tool to discipline, control and subjugate women to the family and community needs, often to the harm of their own interests. Women responded by using all available strategies to cope with the violence and to resist it through judiciary and extra-legal activities. Many women fled. Some killed their husbands and fathers-in-law in self-defence. Yet many preferred to conform because their well-being and livelihood often depended on the male head of the household.

Barbara Engel noted that it is difficult to assess how the majority of peasant women regarded beatings, but she is convinced that those women who charged their husbands with domestic abuse were not typical by definition. Christine Worobec has argued that, for the most part, peasant wives tolerated beatings, while Beatrice Farnsworth laid out evidence suggesting that daughters-in-law among the peasantry resisted domestic

---

98. 'Prodazha zheny', *Novoe vremia*, 26 February (10 March) 1879, no. 1076, 3.
99. 'S. Stanislavchik, Vinnitskii uezd', *Russkie vedomosti*, 28 May 1884, no. 146, 2.
100. 'Kupchaia na chuzhuiu zhenu', *Stavropol'skie gubernskie vedomosti*, 9 October 1876, no. 41, 6.
101. 'Prodazha zheny', *Moskovskie vedomosti*, 10 April 1884, no. 98, 2.
102. 'V gazetu *Russkii kur'er* soobshchaiut iz Buguchara', *Golos*, 25 May 1880, no. 144, 4.

abuse.[103] There is a great temptation to suggest that women might tolerate beatings because the whole society experienced corporal punishment for various offences committed, but harsh beatings were often reserved for the crimes of rebellion and resistance. However, even the number of reported cases of domestic abuse strongly points to the conclusion that women did not tolerate domestic abuse, and that, while socialized into the ideas of obedience and submission to the male family head, they did not accept physical violence as a part of their low status. They had certain understandings of their 'rights' in exchange for their obedience.

Russian women were trapped in the conflict between progress as it was understood by male intellectuals and government authorities at the time, and their own needs and choices. The differential treatment of men and women could have resulted in greater attention to women's needs (such as protection from sexual violence or exemption from corporal punishment). Instead, it strengthened the inequality between genders, placing women in a position of obedience and subjugation to their husbands' and fathers' decisions. Women were not always able to receive justice, but this did not prevent them from trying.

In the nineteenth century women experienced a backlash in the protection from sexual and domestic violence which was connected to new attitudes towards femininity and masculinity. Associating normative sexual behaviour (chastity) with the notion of honour and moving to the protection of honour rather than staying with the protection of a person, excluded many women from the distribution of justice. Only those women who conformed to the prescribed standards of femininity could find justice. Domestic abuse, although it became a marker of 'low-class' behaviour, and was disapproved by official and public discourses, continued to serve as a means of control. Yet it became invisible and withdrawn into the sphere of intimate spousal relations among upper classes, making it extremely difficult for women to ask for legal protection. However, women continued to complain to courts; they submitted appeals despite discouraging examples of others who failed. Their determination to achieve justice calls for further research into the legal consciousness and legal culture of Russian women over a longer period.

---

103. Barbara A. Engel, *Between the Fields and the City*, pp. 25–26; Christine Worobec, *Peasant Russia: Family and Community in the Post-Emancipation Period* (Princeton: Princeton University Press, 1991), pp. 188–94; Beatrice Farnsworth, 'The Litigious Daughter-in-Law: Family Relations in Rural Russia in the Second Half of the Nineteenth Century', *Slavic Review*, 45 (1986), 49–64.

Index

abbesses 61, 62
Abramtsevo 10-11, 111
Académie Julian 108, 110
Academy of Arts, St Petersburg 9, 10, 91, 92-93, 94, 96-98, 101, 102, 103, 104, 106-07, 108-10, 113, 125
actress 3, 5-6, 12-14, 24, 123, 131, 137-50, 205, 222
  as 'precious pearl' of the Russian theatre 137-39, 148-152, 154-55, 156, 157-59
  as prostitute 13, 139, 155 *See also* prostitution
  as public woman 139-43
  in Silver Age Russia 137-39, 157-58
Adaevskaia, Ella (pseud. of Ella Shul'ts) 132-33
adultery 27, 29, 38, 214, 215, 222, 230, 233
Afanas'ev, Aleksandr N. 42
Agafonova, Zinaida 32-37, 40
Agreneva-Slavianskaia, Ol'ga 133
Akhmatova, Anna 3, 107, 106
alcohol 225
  trade in 51
  alcoholism 36, 54-55, 146, 237
Aleksandra Fedorovna 124
Aleksandrova-Kochetova, Aleksandra 131
Aleksandrova, Liubov' 28-31, 32, 40
Alexander I, Emperor 97, 138
Alexander II, Emperor 107, 127, 132, 217
ambivalence 155, 164, 180, 191
Andrew, Joe 3, 175-76, 184, 188
Anna Ioannovna, Empress 141
anonymity 9, 11, 42, 71, 72, 78, 80, 85, 87, 122
Antipov, Prokopii 223
apocryphal texts 49, 67-68, 75, 82

applied arts 9, 92-93, 94, 95, 101, 103, 110, 116
Apraksina, Natal'ia, Countess 231
architecture 92, 94, 95, 97, 104, 107-08, 111, 113
archives 5, 7, 12, 14, 17, 150
Arshinina, Avdot'ia 222
Artel khudozhnikov 102
Arzamas 14, 163 *See also Beseda*
Asenkova, Aleksandra 156, 158
Astakhova, Alla 49
Attwood, Lynne 3
Augusta of Württemberg, Princess (later Countess Maria Fedorovna) 94, 231
authenticity
  of peasant life 8, 43, 48, 50
  artistic 68, 69, 139, 145, 167, 183, 194
  of theatrical performance 144, 146, 147, 150, 154, 156, 15
  as created through suffering 146
  as indicated by tears 144, 155
autobiography 5, 7, 15, 73, 143, 156, 157, 172, 177, 180, 190-91, 204-05
avant-garde 93, 113, 114, 115-17

Bakst, Lev 107
Bakunina, A. M. 98
Bakunina, Praskov'ia 177
Balakirev, Milii 127-28
Balkan Peninsula 45
ballet 141-42
Ballets Russes 113
baptism 41, 48, 53
Barker, Adele 3
Bashkirtseva, Mariia 192
Batiushkov, Konstantin 15, 154
Bekhterev family 49
Belinskii, Vissarion 4, 5, 176

Beseda 14, 163
bestiality 216, 225
best-sellers 16, 198, 199
Bezborodko, Aleksandr 124
Bible, biblical 52, 65, 67, 68, 71, 75-76, 227
binary oppositions 44, 112
biography 29, 48, 127, 129, 143, 146, 147, 150, 151, 152, 169, 204
Blakesley, Rosalind 9-11, 119, 120, 125, 129
Bludov, Dmitri, Count 217
Bonnell, Victoria E. 4
Borodin, Aleksandr 127
Bowlt, John E. 115
brideprice 41
Briullov, Karl 105
Briusov, Valerii 16, 135
Briusova, Nadezhda 135
Brokgaus-Èfron *Encyclopedic Dictionary* 2
Bullock, Philip Ross 11-12, 17, 92, 98
Bunina, Anna 14-15, 163, 164-65, 195

Cameron, Charles 95
capitalism 21, 46, 50
Cassiday, Julie 5, 12-14, 17, 124, 131
Catherine II (Catherine the Great) 11, 94, 95, 97-98, 104, 121, 124, 141, 149, 162, 214, 228, 231
catholicism 45, 69
censorship 7, 15, 42, 132, 170, 172, 181
census of 1897 52
Chaikovskii, Petr 119, 122, 126-27, 130-31
charity 10, 23, 58
charms 7, 49, 121, 145
Chekhov, Anton 43
  The Seagull (Chaika) 14, 158-59 See also Zarechnaia, Nina
  'Tat'iana Repina' 131
Chernogriazh, parish of 57
Chernyshevskii, Nikolai 15, 166, 180-81,
  What is to be done? (Chto delat'?) 178, 184
Chester, Pamela 3
Chet'i-Minei 68, 73
childbirth 53, 151
Christ 8, 52, 53, 55, 57

christianity 8, 43, 44, 45, 49, 61, 63-90, 216, 227
class 20, 34, 47, 59, 102, 134, 193, 194
  and gender 6, 8, 11-12, 22, 23-24, 32, 47, 61, 62, 103, 123, 126, 141, 144
classicism 94, 102-03, 192
  neo-classicism 122 149
Clements, Barbara 2
clergy (Russian Orthodox) 4, 8, 54, 61, 65-66, 70, 72, 73, 76, 79, 82-87
clothing 50, 60, 155, 171, 188, 235
Clyman, Toby 3
Colloquium of Admirers of the Russian Word See Beseda
commercial culture 6, 19, 21, 198
confessions 47-48, 145, 222
conservatoires 102, 125-26, 127, 130-31, 132, 133, 135
constructivism 107, 112, 116, 117
consumer culture 21, 40, 61
consumerism 23, 43, 51
Contemporary, The (Sovremennik) 170, 178, 189, 190
Costlow, Jane 3, 181, 205
cottage articraft See *kustar* crafts
cultural studies 3, 44
culture See also literacy; peasants; women
  elite 5, 9, 11-13, 16, 20-22, 23, 25, 42-44, 104, 142, 155, 200, 201, 210
  Marian-centred 63-90
  material 45
  official 43
  oral 41-42, 48, 64, 176, 185
  peasant 41-62, 121
  popular 5, , 120, 198, 200
  print 47
  urban 6, 19-40, 59
  written 9, 21, 43

dacha 34-36
Dashkova, Ekaterina 121, 162
Dedilovskaia sloboda 56
defloration 213, 222
Della-Vos-Kardovskaia, Ol'ga 107
demonic possession 48
Diaghilev, Sergei 112
dishonour 214, 218, 22
divorce 27, 37, 39-40, 48, 169, 227-28

Dmitrieva, Agnessa 223
Dmitrieva, Valentina 15, 191, 193-94, 206
Dmitrov district 57
domestic sphere 9, 30, 55, 92, 113, 183-85, 186, 187, 232
 domesticity 23, 61, 169, 232
 social gatherings 4, 13, 122, 123, 141
 violence 211, 229, 231-38
Dostoevskii, Fedor 1 15, 16
Dovgaleva, Marfa 98
dowries 42, 50, 59-60, 235
Drawing School for Auditors, St Petersburg 99 (fig. 4) 101-02, 111
drunkenness *See* alcoholism
Durova, Nadezhda 171-73, 175, 177
dvoeverie (dual faith) 8, 44

Eakins, Thomas 107
Easter 51, 52, 57, 116
Ecole des Beaux-Arts, Paris 109
Ecole Nationale de Dessin pour les Jeunes Filles 101
economic history 47
education 5, 20-21, 52 *See also* peasants; women
Egupova-Cherkasskaia, Praskoviia 231
Ekaterininskii Institute, Moscow 124
Ekaterinoslav 212
Ekonen, Kirsti 202
Ekster, Aleksandra 113, 115
Elena Pavlovna, grand duchess 126, 132
elite 20, 23, 25, 155, 232 *See also* culture
Elizaveta Petrovna (Elizabeth), Empress 121, 141
Elunino (Barnaul district) 225
emancipation
 of peasants (1861) 7, 41-43, 46, 49, 62, 178, 224-25, 229
 of women 9, 86, 128, 134-35, 174, 180, 183-84, 189, 190, 207 *See also* woman questrion
Engel, Barbara 2, 5, 6-7, 17
Engel'gardt, Sof'ia *See* Ol'ga N.
Engelstein, Laura 215
England 21, 109, 120, 143, 236
enlightenment 121, 124, 135, 140, 162, 179, 209-10, 231, 232
Esipova, Anna 131

Eucharist 57, 87
Evangelical groups 52
Exposition Universelle, Paris (1900) 112

family 4, 8, 13, 17, 19, 21, 22, 26, 28, 30, 32, 34, 37, 40, 42, 46, 48, 50-56, 61, 65, 72, 84-85, 97, 108, 123, 124, 142, 150, 153, 173, 174, 180, 182-87, 190, 191, 194, 209, 210-11, 215-16, 223, 225-26, 227-38 *See also* Orthodox clerical views
fashion 23, 32, 34, 36, 59, 60, 94, 103
 industry 2
 literary 15-16, 139
feasts *See* saints; religious feasts
femininity 138-39, 140, 144, 145, 163-65, 161-207, 211, 232, 238-39
Figes, Orlando 1
fine arts 3, 6, 9-11, 91-117, 119-20, 125, 130, 134, 135
First Ladies' Art Circle 108
Fletcher, Giles 120
flogging 216, 225, 229, 232
folklore 41, 42, 43, 44, 48-49, 59 *See also* peasants
folklorists 42, 45-46, 48
folk songs 11
fornication *See* adultery
France, French 4, 9, 11, 31, 70, 71, 73, 109, 149, 154
 fine arts 91, 101, 104, 108-09 *See also* Collot, Marie-Anne; Vigée-Lebrun, Marie Louise Elisabeth
 literature 149, 165, 185
 music 69, 121, 129, 130
 theatre 138, 141, 143, 145, 152
Frank, Stephen P. 42, 234
Frierson, Cathy 42

Gagarin family 40
Gagarin, Ivan (prince) 153-54
Galiatovskii, Ioannikii 69
gambling 215
Gan, Elena 173-75, 177, 182, 195
gay and lesbian artists 16, 119
German, Saint 54
Germany, Germans 23, 69, 70, 94, 97, 169, 219
 fine arts 94, 104, 153
 theatre 138

Gheith, Jehanne 3, 161, 173, 180, 181, 183, 184, 186-87
Gilbert, Sandra 14
Gippius, Zinaida 3, 203
Glinka, Avdot'ia 72-73, 74, 76-77, 81, 82, 177
Glinka, Mikhail 127, 128, 129-30
Golubkina, Anna 107
Goncharova, Natal'ia 93, 113-16
Göpfert, Frank 3
Gorshkov, Boris 46
Goscilo, Helena 3, 114
Government School of Art for Females, England 109
Great Britain *See* England
Greene, Diana 3
Greer, Germaine 109
Grigor'ev's case 219
Gubaidulina, Sof'ia 136
Gubar, Susan 14
Guggenheim Museum, New York 115
Guliaev, Petr 215

Hagen-Schwarz, Julie 104-05
handicrafts 9, 11, 110-11, 112
Heldt, Barbara 3, 7, 15, 160, 172-73
heroines 1, 173, 174, 176, 182-84, 188, 194-95
Hilton, Alison 91, 93, 110
historians 42, 44, 47, 52, 93, 103, 136, 148, 150-51, 153, 210-11
 historiography 119, 129, 210-11
Hoch, Steven L. 41
Holmgren, Beth 3
Holy Sepulchre, Church of the 54, 58
honour 31, 64, 86, 211, 214, 217-18, 221, 223, 236, 238
Hoogenboom, Hilde 176
Hubbs, Joanna 44
Hunt, Lynn 4

Iakunchikova, Maria Fedorovna 112
Iakunchikova, Maria Vasil'evna 112, 114
Iaroslavl' 60
icons 45, 55, 56
Il'ina, Mariia 222
illegitimate children 215, 230
illness 48, 54-55, 145
Imperial Chancellery for Receipt of Petitions 27, 36, 39
Imperial Society for the Encouragement of the Arts 98, 101
incest 213, 215, 225, 226, 236
indecent behaviour 30, 36, 215
industrialisation 19-21, 32, 37, 111, 190, 193
industry 50, 101, 111 *See also* fashion
 agricultural 46
 cottage 46
 service 47
 tanning 50
infanticide 216, 223
Inquisition 43
interdisciplinarity 47, 62
Ioann of Kronshtadt 55
Iretskaia, Natal'ia 131
Iudina, Mariia 136
Ivanova-Raevskaia, Mariia 106
Jerusalem 54, 56-57, 58, 70, 77, 79
Jews 16, 71

Kadmina, Evlaliia 131-32
Kaiser, Daniel 211, 214
Kamenskii, Count S.M. 144, 146, 151
Kankrin, Egor 101
Kantorovich, Iakov 210
Karamzin, Nikolai 14, 146, 162-64, 166
 See also Arzamas; sentimentalism
Karatygina, Aleksandra 155, 156
Karptsov case 232-33
Kazan' 53-55
Kelly, Catriona 3, 15, 161, 162, 164, 171, 173, 175, 180, 196, 200
Kherson 212, 221
Khilkova, Ekaterina 99 (fig. 4), 102, 103, 104
Khvoshchinskaia, Nadezhda 7, 10, 15, 181, 182, 183, 187, 188-90, 195
Khvoshchinskaia, Sof'ia 10, 182
Kiaer, Christina 116
Kiev 56
Kiprenskii, Orest 98
Kiui, Tsezar' 127, 134
Kizenko, Nadieszda 47, 48
Kokhanovskaia, Nadezhda 182, 187
Kollmann 211, 218
Kollontai, Aleksandra 2
Komissarzhevskaia, Vera 5, 14, 137, 158
Kornetchuk, Elena 114

Kosakovskii case 234
Kovaleva, Praskov'ia (Zhemchugova) 11, 13, 58, 123, 139, 142, 143, 148-49, 150, 151-52, 153, 156-57, 158
Kovalevskaia, Sof'ia 191
Kovrigina case 223
Kramskoi, Ivan 102, 111
Kronshtadt 55
Kruglikova, Elizaveta 113
Kuprin, Aleksandr 131
Kurt, Mariia 10, 99
kustar crafts 110-111
Kuz'mina, serf-actress 144
Kuznetsova case 225

Labzina, Anna 7
Lanoux, Andrea 3
Lavrovskaia, Elizaveta 131
law 16-17, 42, 184, 209-38
  censorship 42
  marriage and 27, 32
  passports and 37
  property and 32, 37
  prostitution and 31
Leberecht, Karl 94
lechery 215
Ledkovsky, Marina 3
Lermontov, Mikhail 10
'Lettre à M. d'Alembert sur les spectacles' by Jean-Jacques Rousseau 139, 140, 143, 155 *See also* Rousseau, Jean-Jacques
Levin, Eve 2, 44, 211
life-creation (*zhiznetvorchestvo*) 14
Lineva, Evgeniia 133, 134, 135
literacy 7, 47, 124 *See also* culture; peasants; women
  lack of 47, 56
literary salons 12, 22-23, 121-23, 163, 165-66, 168, 171, 203 *See also salonnière*
Liuleva, E. 87
Lopukhina, Countess 231
lubok (popular print) 58
Lutheranism 45

magic 43, 48
  folk 7, 48-49
Makukhina, Natal'ia 104
male writers 15, 203

Mamontov, Savva 130, 132
Maria Fedorovna, Empress, 91, 94, 95 (fig. 2) 96 (fig. 3), 97, 100 (fig. 5)
Maria Nikolaevna, Grand Duchess 101
marianism 45, 63-90
Markovich, Mariia Aleksandrovna 185
marriage 5, 13, 27, 28-29, 33, 40, 41, 51, 56, 60-61, 72, 76, 85, 88, 94, 97, 121, 124-25, 143, 148, 182, 183, 184, 186, 188, 195, 216, 221, 227 *See also* law; Mary, mother of God; Orthodox clerical views
  choice and 29, 32, 37
Marsh, Rosalind 3, 191
Mary, mother of God 6, 8, 9, 44, 45, 55, 61, 63-90
  aprocrypha 68
  devotion and imagination 70
  icons of 45, 55, 64, 69, 81-82, 90
  intercession of 48, 55
  imitation of 71
  prayer to 53
  Jesus' ministry 79
  leadership roles 81
  life of 72, 75, 87, 89
  marriage and family life 78
  motherhood 80, 82
  as Our Lady of Kazan' 53
  veneration of 45
  virginity 88
  vocation of 77
  women's liberation 88
masquerade 167
masculinity 172, 232, 238
matchmaking 58, 61
McReynolds, Louise 24
Mekk, Nadezhda fon 126-27, 134
memoirs 4, 6-7, 12, 13, 14, 47, 129, 141-42, 143, 147, 156, 166, 172, 180, 185, 189, 194, 231
merchants 6, 20, 23, 26, 34, 51, 53, 59, 99, 102, 131
Mercy-Argenteau, Countess 134
Messenger of Fashion (*Vestnik mody*) 33
migration 46, 50
Mikirtumov case 219
Miliukova, Antonina 126, 127
Ministry of Education 105
miracles 45 *See also* Mary, mother of

God
  tales of 45, 48
misogyny 23, 179
Mlle. Georges *See* Weimer, Marguerite-Joséphine
monasteries 53, 55, 56, 57, 61, 72, 226
  Nikolopestush monastery 57
  Saints Mary and Martha women's monastery 62
  Seraphim-Diveevo Trinity women's monastery 54
  Sviato-Nikolaevskii monastery 54
Moscow 25, 32, 34, 36, 38-39, 56, 68
  province 57, 68
Moscow Art Theatre 108
Moscow School of Painting, Sculpture, and Architecture 106
Mount Athos 56, 57
Muravyeva, Marianna 16-17
Murom 54
Museum of Modern Art, New York 116
Musina-Pushkina, Tat'iana 231
Musorgskii, Modest 127-29, 130

Nadratovskii case 223
Nagrodskaia, Evdokiia 198
Nekliudov, N.A. 236
neo-classicism *See* classicism
Newmarch, Rosa 134
Nicholas I, Emperor 101, 104, 124
Nikulina-Kositskaia, Liubov' 156
Nissen-Saloman, Henriette 131
Nizhnii Novgorod 54
noblewomen 22, 34, 56, 58, 60, 93, 141, 153, 222, 231, 232 *See also salonnière*
Northern Herald (Severnyi vestnik) 191
Norton, Barbara 2
novel 1, 5, 7, 9, 10, 15, 22, 73, 124, 149, 161-207

Odessa 56
Odoevskii, Vladimir 125
Old Believers 32, 34, 43, 47, 52, 86
Old Church Slavonic 52, 53 *See also Beseda*
Olearius, Adam 120
Olenina d'Al'geim, Mariia 129, 134
Ol'ga N. (pseud. of Sof'ia Vladimirovna Engel'gardt) 185
opera 11, 121, 123, 128, 130-31, 132, 134-35, 137, 141, 142, 149
oral history 48
Orshanskii, Il'ia 210
Orsi, Robert 63
Orthodox clerical views
  gender 84
  marriage and family 85
  Mary and the feminist movement 86
  women's preaching and ordination 87
orthodoxy 8, 32, 34, 63-90
Osipov, N. I. 59
Ostroumova-Lebedeva, Anna 113
Other, the 179, 201

paganism 43, 44, 45
painting 10
Panaeva, Aleksandra 130
Panaeva, Avdot'ia 182, 189
Panina, Varia 132
Paraskeva, Saint 44, 45
patriarchy 26
Paul I, Emperor 94, 97, 231
Pavlova, Karolina 12, 16, 166, 169-71, 177, 180, 202
Pavlovsk 94-96
Pazdery 50-52, 54, 57
peasants 7, 20
  and folklorists 42
  as entrepreneurs 51, 53, 59
  as scribes 52
  correspondence among 49, 51, 52, 61
  education of 52
  geographical mobility of 47
  household structure of 51
  influence of urban culture upon 60
  migration of 46
  representations of 42
  scholars of 47
  social mobility of 50, 51, 53, 59, 61
  state 49
peasant women 6, 7, 8, 9, 13, 20, 24
  abuse of 42
  and childbirth 48, 51, 52, 53
  as correspondents 49, 53, 55, 58, 60
  as healers 49
  biographies of 48
  culture of 44
  identities of 45, 61
  literacy and education 36, 47, 49

migration of 46
piety of 49, 50, 55, 56, 57, 62
representations of 42, 43
research on 49
voices of 41, 47
peasant writers 16
Pennsylvania Academy of the Fine Arts 107
Peredvizhniki (*The Wanderers*) 109-10, 112
Perm' 52, 212
  province 54
  region 47
Peter I (Peter the Great), Emperor 98, 121, 210, 227
Petrovskoe 41
Petrov-Vodkin, Kuz'ma 107
philanthropy 2, 108, 128-29, 150
photography 9, 59, 60, 107, 132
pilgrimages 8, 50, 54-57
pilgrims 54, 56, 71
  professional 57
  women 8, 54-55, 57
Platonova, Iuliia 130
Plevitskaia, Nadezhda 132
poetry, poets 4, 5, 6, 12, 15, 58, 59, 73, 130, 135, 143, 164, 165, 193, 203
  women 7, 14, 15, 16, 107, 133, 151, 164-77, 182, 191, 201, 202-07
Polenova, Elena 111, 112
polygamy 215
'Poor Liza' ('Bednaia Liza') by Nikolai Karamzin 146
Popova, Liubov' 93, 113, 115-17
popular culture 5, 22, 43, 120, 198, 200
Poretskaia, Mariia 231
Poselianin, Evgenii 70, 78, 80
post-structuralism 42
prayers 49, 53, 55, 56, 57
prescriptive literature 21, 35
printmaking 113
Prokof'ev, Sergei 131
prostitution 13, 22, 31, 139-43, 155, 211, 214, 236 *See also* actress; law
Protevangelium of James 67-68
pseudonym 5, 15, 132
psychiatry 48
public 9, 22, 29, 35, 99, 131, 153, 154, 198
  debates 84, 87

narrator 4
reading groups 78
sphere 4, 9, 12, 13, 19, 21-23, 29, 37, 84, 87, 92, 123, 123, 150, 152, 155
and women 6, 35-36, 38, 86, 120, 158, 162, 164, 169, 172, 176, 178, 184, 202, 204 *See also* public woman
Purgol'd, Aleksandra (later Molas) 127, 129
Purgol'd, Nadezhda (later Rimskaia-Korsakova) 127, 128, 134, 135
Pushkareva, Natalia 3
Pushkin, Aleksandr 8-9, 10, 16, 142, 153

Raifa 54, 55
Ransel, David L. 42, 48
rape 17, 212 (fig. 6), 209-38
  snokhachestvo 226
raptus 213
realism 178, 181, 184, 188, 189, 193, 197, 201
  in painting 105
religion/religious 4, 26, 34, 47, 63-90 *See also* Christ; Christianity; Orthodoxy
  religious donations 54, 56-57, 61
  experience 7, 14
  feasts 53, 54, 68, 71, 73, 77, 89, 196 *See also* saints
  lives 45, 47, 48, 58
  scholars of 47
religious beliefs
  canonical 44, 48, 49, 50
  non-canonical 48
  pre-Christian 45
Renne, Elizaveta 104
Repin, Il'ia 107
reputation 29, 42
  women's 6, 13, 14, 21, 30, 31, 133, 157, 164, 166, 170, 211, 218, 222, 223, 234
Revolt of the Fourteen 109
revolution 5, 8, 15
  commercial 19
  Industrial 21
  of 1905 27, 37
  of 1917 (October) 15, 93-94, 133, 135, 195, 187
  pre- 2, 5, 8, 48, 70-71, 76, 93, 115, 116, 135, 158
Rimskii-Korsakov, Andrei 135
Robertson, Christina 100 (fig. 5), 104

Rock, Stella 41, 45
Rodchenko, Aleksandr 116, 117
Rodigina, Liubov' 49, 50, 53, 61, 62
Rodigin family 49, 55, 61
Rodin, Auguste 108
Rogers, Douglas 47
Romanov, Sergei Aleksandrovich, Grand Duke 62
Romanova, Alexandra Fedorovna, Empress 62
Romanova, Anis'ia 57
Romanova, Elizaveta Fedorovna, Grand Duchess 62
romantic 167, 170, 172, 174, 178, 192
Rosenholm, Arja 14-17, 119, 125, 145
Rosenthal, Charlotte 3, 200
Rosslyn, Wendy 3, 17, 142, 165
Rostopchina, Evdokiia 5, 13, 16, 166, 167, 168, 169, 170, 177, 179, 182, 195
Rothstein, Robert 59
Rousseau, Jean-Jacques 13, 139, 140, 143, 155
Royal Academy, London 109
Rozanova, Ol'ga 93, 107, 115
Ruane, Christine 3, 41
Rubinshtein, Anton 126, 127, 132
Russian Academy 9, 108
Russian Academy of Sciences (Moscow) 9, 120
Russian Herald, The See Russkii vestnik
Russian Music Society 125
Russian Orthodox Church 27, 45, 46 See also Orthodox clerical views; Orthodoxy
  ecclesiastical hierarchy of 43
Rossiiskii gosudarstvennyi istoricheskii arkhiv (RGIA) 98, 231
Russkii palomnik (The Russian Pilgrim) 55
Russkii vestnik (The Russian Herald) 181
Rzhevskaia, Anna 231

saints
  feast days of 54 See also religious feasts
  graves of 55
  intercession of 48, 55
  lives of 57
  relics of 54, 55
  representations of 45
  shrines of 54
  uncorrupted bodies of 43
  veneration of 43, 45
Sakharova, Elena 112
Salmond, Wendy 91, 110, 111, 133
salonnière 179, 203
salons See literary salons
Sandunov, Sila 124
Sandunova, Elizaveta (née Elizaveta Uranova) 123-24
Sarapul 50, 51, 52, 53, 59
Sarov 54
satan 53
Savel'ev, Aleksandr 210
Savkina, Irina 14-17, 119, 125, 145
schools 124, 163 See also literacy
  art 101
  gymnasium 52
  teacher preparation 52
  zemstvo 50, 65
Schrader, Abby 232
Schuler, Catherine 3, 138, 152
Schumann, Clara Wieck 129
Seagull, The (Chaika) See Chekhov, Anton
sectarians 43
seduction 215, 217, 220, 223 See also adultery
self-fashioning 21, 23, 26, 28, 33, 40
Semenova, Ekaterina 13, 139, 142, 143, 148, 156
Semenova, Lidiia 37-40
Semenova Tian-Shanskaia, Ol'ga 6, 42
sentimentalism 12, 122-25, 138, 143, 146-48, 150-59, 163, 164, 159, 170, 172, 178, 192, 194 See also Karamzin
  of actress's life story 148, 152, 153, 157
Serebriakova, Zinaida 112
serfdom, serfs 41, 46, 49, 58
serfowners 41, 58
Serov, Aleksandr 132
Serov, Valentin 107, 108
Serova, Valentina (née Bergman) 132
Severnyi vestnik See Northern Herald
sex, sexuality 3, 8, 21, 23-24, 28-29, 30-31, 37-38, 43, 59, 114, 117, 119, 138, 139, 142-43, 146, 148-59, 174, 191, 199-200 See also women; rape
sexual propriety 29, 31, 38, 39
Shanks, Emilia 109

Shapir, Ol'ga 15, 195, 196, 197, 198
Sharp, Jane 91, 113-14, 116
Shashkov, Serafim 210
Shchepkina-Kupernik, Tat'iana 193, 206
Shepherd, David 15
Sheremetev, Nikolai Petrovich, count 58, 152
Shestakova, Liudmila 129
Shevzov, Vera 8, 9, 17, 45, 47, 97
Shoemaker, Stephen 74, 88
Shostakovich, Dmitrii 119
Shternberg, Vasilii 105
Siberia 220-21, 223-24, 234, 236
  Western Siberia 49, 50
Silver Age 14, 16, 200, 206 See also actress
Simeon, Saint 54
Simferopol' 212
skomorokhi (ministrels) 120-21
slavophiles 14, 169, 185
Smith, Douglas 11
Smol'nyi Institute for Young Ladies of the Nobility 97, 124
Smyth, Ethel 122
Snessoreva, Sof'ia 73, 76, 79, 82
social history 47, 211
social mobility 21-22, 40 See also peasants
Society of Travelling Art Exhibits 109
sodomy 216, 219, 225
Soimonov case 233
Sokhanskaia, Nadezhda 7
Sokolovskii case 233
Solntseva-Zasekina, Anna 231
Solomenko embroidery workshops 111, 112
Solov'eva, Poliksena 202
Solov'ev, Nikolai 132, 201
Solovki 56
Somov, Konstantin 114
sorcery 48
Soviet era 2, 4, 7, 15, 17 See also Revolution
Sovremennik See Contemporary, The
Speranskii, M. M., 215, 217
Staël, Madame de 122, 123
Stasov, Vladimir 127, 128, 129, 134
Stasova, Nadezhda 128
State Russian Museum, St Petersburg 116
State Tret'iakov Gallery, Moscow 105, 116
statistics 17, 22, 212, 234-35
  government 41
Stefanova, Praskov'ia Vasil'evna 51, 57
Stepanova, Varvara 113, 115
St Petersburg Society for the Encouragement of Female Artistic and Craft Work 108
Stravinskii, Igor' 133
Stroganov School of Drawing 101
Sukharev Tower 58
Sukhovo-Kobylina, Sof'ia 103, 104
superstitions 43, 82
Sviiazhsk 54-55
Sylva, Carmen, Queen of Rumania 133
Symbolism 15-16, 192, 193, 200-07
Szymanowska, Maria 123

Talashkino 111
Tate Modern, London 116
taverns 47, 63
Teffi (pseud. of Lokhvitskaia, Nadezhda Aleksandrovna) 191
Tenisheva, Mariia 111, 129
theatre 10, 12-14, 137-60 See also actress; Moscow Arts Theatre
  as cultural institution 138, 143
  professional 140, 142
  serf 145, 148, 152
  state 12
Theological Academy (Moscow) 65, 72
'Thieving Magpie, The' ('Soroka-vorovka') by Aleksandr Herzen 146, 147
Timofeev, A. V. 58
  'Vybor zheny' ('Choosing a Wife') 58
Tiumen' 49, 51, 57
Tobolsk 55
Tomei, Christine 3
Tomsk 225
Toporkov, Andrei 49
Tosi, Alessandra 1, 17
'Toupée Artist, The' ('Tupeinyi khudozhnik') by Nikolai Leskov 147, 149
townspeople 25, 26, 123
  family practices of 26, 32

women 19-40
transportation 19, 46, 51, 55
Tsarskoe Selo 94
Tsebrikova, Mariia 182, 189
Tsvetaeva, Marina 3, 5, 12, 206
Tugendkhol'd, Iakov 114
Tula province 56
Tupitsyn, Margarita 116
Tura river 49
Tur', Evgeniia 180, 181, 182, 186, 188
Turgenev, Ivan 129, 130, 131

Udal'tsova, Nadezhda 115
United States of America 110
Uskova case 225-26
Uspenskii, Gleb 43
Ustvol'skaia, Galina 136

Veisberg, Iuliia 135
Verbitskaia, Anastasiia 191, 198, 199, 206
Verkhotur'e 54
Vestnik mody See Messenger of Fashion
Vial'tseva, Anatas'ia 24, 132
Viardot, Pauline 129, 131
Viatka province 49, 50
Viel'gorskii, Matvei and Mikhail 125
Vigée-Lebrun, Marie Louise Elisabeth 9, 11, 91, 92 (fig. 1), 93, 94, 104, 122
Vil'kina, Liudmila 202
Vinnitsa 237
violence 3, 16-17, 22, 38, 209-38 *See also* domestic sphere; rape
Viollier, François 95
virginity 43, 71, 77, 88, 157, 213-14, 216, 218-19, 220-223 *See also* Mary, mother of God
Virpsha Studio 59
Vishnevskaia, Galina 136
Vodovozova, Elizaveta 7, 180
Volkonskaia, Zinaida 123, 166, 177
volost' court 42, 224
Volyn' 234
Vorob'eva-Petrova, Anna 130
Voronezh 56
Vovchok 185
Vowles, Judith 3, 166, 168
vows
   religious 53, 54, 58
Vulf case 222

Warner, Elizabeth 46
watercolors 9, 92
Weimer, Marguerite-Joséphine (Mlle. Georges) 152
Western Europe 1, 2, 7, 11, 13, 15, 19, 20-22, 23, 32, 42, 44, 66, 68-69, 70, 94, 105, 111, 116, 121-22, 127, 133, 134, 135, 137, 138-43, 162, 192, 198, 202, 210
wet-nursing 34, 46
White Sea 56
Wigzell, Faith 3
woman question 6, 8, 15, 33, 177, 178, 179, 181, 184, 190, 195, 197, 207
woman theologian 9
women
   artists 3, 6, 11, 91-118 *See also* actress; fine arts
   education of 10, 20, 27, 52, 84, 92
   employment of 20, 23, 24
   honour and 29, 30
   literacy of 25
   musicians 3, 6, 11, 12, 119-36
   proper behaviour of 29, 35, 37, 40 *See also* family
   religious beliefs of 6, 45, 62, 63-90
   religious communities of 50, 61, 63-90 *See also* monasteries
   self-expression and 25, 40
   sexuality and 22, 23, 26, 29, 31, 38
   upper-class 6, 8, 11 *See also* noblewomen; *salonnière*
   urban 19-40
   writers 161-208
Womens' Polytechnical Courses 113
World of Art 112, 114
Worobec, Christine 2, 6, 7, 8, 237

Yablonskaya, Miuda 115, 117
Yokoyama, Olga T. 49, 57

Zabela-Vrubel', Nadezhda 130
Zadonsk 56
Zagorovskii, Aleksandr 210
Zarechnaia, Nina (character in Chekhov's *The Seagull*) 158, 159
Zelenago 230
zemstvo schools *See* schools
Zhadovskii 224
Zhemchugova, Praskov'ia *See* Kovaleva, Praskov'ia

Zhenskii vestnik 191
Zhenskoe delo 191
Zhernokov family 49, 50, 51, 61
Zhernokov, Aleksei Lavrovich 51, 52, 53, 60
Zhernokov, Andrei Iakimovich 51
Zhernokov, Ivan Lavrovich 59
Zhernokov, Lavr Andreevich 51, 52, 53, 54, 55, 57
Zhernokov, Vasilii Lavrovich 49, 51, 52, 53, 55, 56, 57, 58, 59, 60
Zhernokova, Elizaveta Dmitr'evna 49, 50, 51, 52, 53, 54, 55, 56, 57, 58, 59, 60, 61
Zhernokova, Evdokiia Prokop'evna 52
Zhernokova, Raisa Davidovna 60
Zhernokova, Tat'iana Grigor'evna 51
Zhernokova, Tat'iana Lavrovna 49, 50, 52, 53, 60
Zhikharev, Stepan 154
Zhukova, Mariia 173, 175, 176, 177, 182
Zhukova, Pelageia 98
Zhurnal dlia zhenshchin 191
Zinov'eva-Annibal, Lidia 202, 204, 205, 206
Zirin, Mary 3, 184
Zoshchenko, Mikhail 108
Zrazhevskaia, Aleksandra 177
Zvantseva, Elizaveta 107

This book does not end here...

At Open Book Publishers, we are changing the nature of the traditional academic book. The title you have just read will not be left on a library shelf, but will be accessed online by hundreds of readers each month across the globe. We make all our books free to read online so that students, researchers and members of the public who can't afford a printed edition can still have access to the same ideas as you.

Our digital publishing model also allows us to produce online supplementary material, including extra chapters, reviews, links and other digital resources. Find *Women in Nineteenth-Century Russia* on our website to access its online extras. Please check this page regularly for ongoing updates, and join the conversation by leaving your own comments:

http://www.openbookpublishers.com/product.php/98

If you enjoyed the book you have just read, and feel that research like this should be available to all readers, regardless of their income, please think about donating to us. Our company is run entirely by academics, and our publishing decisions are based on intellectual merit and public value rather than on commercial viability. We do not operate for profit and all donations, as with all other revenue we generate, will be used to finance new Open Access publications.

For further information about what we do, how to donate to OBP, additional digital material related to our titles or to order our books, please visit our website.

www.ingramcontent.com/pod-product-compliance
Lightning Source LLC
Chambersburg PA
CBHW071835230426
43671CB00012B/1967